"Do not let your fire go out, spark by irreplaceable spark. In the hopeless swamps of the not quite, the not yet, and the not at all, do not let the hero in your soul perish and leave only frustration for the life you deserved, but never have been able to reach. The world you desire can be won, it exists, it is real, it is possible, it is yours."
- Ayn Rand

The SAT Prep Black Book

"The Most Effective SAT Strategies Ever Published"

By Mike Barrett

Dedication

The *SAT Prep Black Book* would never have been possible without the help, support, and patience of my family, to whom, and for whom, I am eternally grateful. I would also like to thank the many partners, advisors, and friends without whom my career in test prep would not be possible, especially Mimi, Michele, Xiggi, Gerry, Bruce, Melody, and Chris.

Of course, I would also like to express my gratitude to the tens of thousands of high-school students all around the world who have trusted me with a part of their futures over the years. You have taught me more than I ever would have thought possible back when I was tutoring my brothers' friends in my parents' dining room after work.

Finally, I would like to thank the people at Amazon for allowing me and everyone else to share our work with the world through the most sophisticated publishing platform ever built.

This book is dedicated to all of you.

Free Video Demonstrations

If you'd like to see videos of some sample SAT solutions like the ones in this book, please visit http://www.SATprepVideos.com. A selection of free videos is available for readers of this book.

Table Of Contents

Read This First!

"Give me six hours to chop down a tree, and I will spend the first four hours sharpening the axe."
- Abraham Lincoln

The approach you're about to learn from the SAT Prep Black Book has helped many, many people score much higher on the SAT than they thought they could. I'm confident it can help you, too, if you make a sincere effort to implement what I'm going to teach you.

If you have any previous experience with SAT prep, you'll probably find that this book is different from the 'traditional' advice you'll get from most other sources. That traditional advice is mostly based on memorizing things like vocabulary lists, math formulas, and essay examples. And if you've tried that stuff, or if you know somebody who has, then you know it doesn't work very well for most people.

My approach is different because it's based on understanding the design of the test, which allows you to take the vocabulary and math you already know and turn them into a great score—even a perfect 2400, if you're diligent enough in your preparation.

I've designed this approach to be as easy to learn as possible. You'll need to read this book carefully and be thorough in applying what I teach you, but I think you'll find it much less time-consuming and much more productive than the traditional approach.

But that doesn't mean you'll get the full benefit of this book just from flipping through it!

If you want me to be on your team for the SAT, then you have to give us both a fighting chance. That means reading this book with an open mind, looking carefully at the many example solutions to get an idea of how the principles apply to real College Board questions, going to www.SATprepVideos.com to watch the free video demonstrations, and—above all—sticking with it when you run into difficulties. I've done my part to help you beat the test by laying bare exactly how the SAT works and exactly where it's vulnerable. Now it's up to you to read the battle plan and mount your attack.

Stick With It

I can guarantee you that you will encounter real test questions that *seem* to violate the rules and patterns I talk about in this book. This is a normal part of the process—everyone, including myself, occasionally runs into a question that seems to break the rules.

When this happens, *it's always because the test-taker has made a mistake.*

So it's crucial that we remember the design of the SAT can't change, no matter how much it might seem to have changed on a particular question. It will be tempting to think, "Oh, I guess this one math question requires me to know trig, even though Mike said that would never happen," or "Well, I guess this passage question requires me to think about symbolism, even though that's supposed to be impossible on the SAT." As soon as you go down that road—as soon as you stop playing by the rules of the test and start treating the SAT like something it's not—your score will suffer.

So don't do that :)

How To Read This Book

The Black Book is designed so that a person who didn't know anything about the SAT could read it straight through and learn everything he needed to know. I've organized it this way based on over a decade of experience working with tens of thousands of people through a variety of formats.

So if you don't know anything about the SAT, or if you've had a rough time using other SAT books and you want to clear your mind and start from scratch, the best thing to do is to read this book straight through, just as it's written.

If you don't have the time for that, or if you know that you only need help with a particular section or question type, then you're free to skip just to those sections, of course. But I would still recommend that you read the following chapters as well:

- Setting (The Right) Goals
- How To Train For The SAT—Mastering The Ideas In This Book
- Only Work With Questions From The College Board!
- The Importance Of Details: Avoiding "Careless Errors"
- Where To Find "Missing Points"
- Time Management

If you're reading this the night before the test, or if you only need a few general pointers, then you might choose just to read the sections on the hidden rules and patterns of each question type, or even just follow along with some of the sample solutions in each section to get the hang of things.

But this book doesn't just address the mechanics of answering each type of question on the SAT. It also covers issues relating to planning, performance, time management, perseverance, and the other mental aspects surrounding the SAT. I strongly advise you to read those as well.

Using The Blue Book

The "Blue Book" that goes along with this Black Book is the second edition of the College Board publication *The Official SAT Study Guide*. You need a copy of the Blue Book because it's the only printed source of real SAT questions, and real SAT questions are an essential part of SAT preparation. The SAT Prep Black Book that you're reading right now will teach you all the rules, patterns, and design principles of real SAT questions, and will show you hundreds of solutions for real SAT questions, but you'll only be able to practice these ideas if you have the Blue Book.

I strongly, strongly advise you to follow along with the Blue Book solutions in this book, because seeing the proper approach to the SAT in action against real questions is an indispensable part of your preparation, and will make things a lot clearer.

You can probably get a copy of the Blue Book from a library, but I recommend that you get a copy of your own from Amazon, which usually has the lowest prices. That way you can mark up the copy as you would mark up a test booklet, and you won't have two worry about looking at other people's notes in a used copy. At the time of this writing, a new copy of the book is selling for around $10 on Amazon. Here's a link where I keep a page with the best deals on the Blue Book: http://www.SATprepBlackBook.com/blue-book.

If you combine this Black Book with the College Board's Blue Book, you won't need any other resources to prepare for the SAT.

Using This Book To Prepare For The PSAT

With the changes that were made to the PSAT and SAT in 2004 and 2005, the two tests became much more similar than they were before. Every type of multiple-choice question that appears on one test now appears on the other as well. This makes it much easier for you to prepare for the PSAT and the SAT at the same time.

The only important difference between the PSAT and the SAT is that the PSAT does NOT include a handwritten essay portion like the SAT does.

The two tests also have different numbers of sections and different numbers of questions per section.

So, as a practical matter, the best way to prepare for the PSAT is simply to prepare for the SAT as you normally would—the PSAT might even seem a little easier in comparison, just because it has fewer questions overall. If you don't have much time before the PSAT and you haven't started preparing for the SAT yet, then you can leave out the essay portion of your SAT prep and only focus on the parts of the SAT that will appear on the PSAT.

Frequently Asked Questions

I thought it would be a good idea to start the book with a section of Frequently Asked Questions, since certain issues and feedback seem almost universal. So let's dive right in.

General Questions

How long will I need to practice?

There is no set amount of time that every student should plan to spend practicing. It varies heavily from person to person. Your goal should be to develop a deep understanding of the way the SAT works, not to log an arbitrary number of practice hours. For more on this, see the section called "Things To Think About For Scheduling" in the chapter called "How To Train For The SAT—Mastering The Ideas In This Book."

Where did you learn these strategies?

I didn't "learn" these strategies in the sense of having some book or tutor explain them to me. I developed them on my own based on my own reasoning and analysis of the test. Over the years, I have refined both the strategies themselves and the way that I teach them to students. For more on my background and the way it has informed my test-prep training, please see the relevant articles on my blog at www.TestingIsEasy.com.

What's the best way to start implementing your strategies?

The best way to get started is generally to learn the strategies in an abstract way first, and then to see several sample solutions that implement the strategies against real College Board questions. Finally, it's important to try to implement the strategies yourself, and to try to figure things out on your own as much as you can when you get stuck. For more ideas on specific drills and exercises, please see the "Drills And Exercises" section in the chapter called "How To Train For The SAT—Mastering The Ideas In This Book." For a selection of videos that demonstrate the ideas in this book, please visit www.SATprepVideos.com (those sample videos are free to readers of this book).

Do these strategies work on the ACT? What about on the SAT Subject Tests?

All well-designed standardized tests must follow certain rules and patterns when they create their test questions—otherwise the tests wouldn't be standardized. But those particular rules and patterns don't have to be the same for every standardized test. ACT questions have their own standardized design elements that are different from those of SAT questions but still fairly similar to them. The SAT Subject Tests have the added wrinkle of involving a bit more subject-matter knowledge in most cases.

So the short answer is that the *specific* strategies in this book are aimed at the SAT in particular. Some will work fairly well on other tests, and some won't. But the general idea of analyzing a standardized test in terms of rules and patterns can still be applied successfully against the ACT and the SAT Subject Tests.

What if I want to score a 2400? What if I only need to score a 1500 (or 1800, or 2000, or whatever)?

Contrary to popular belief, you don't need to use different strategies to reach different score levels, because the design of the SAT is constant. It would be more accurate to say that in order to score a 2400 you need to be roughly 99% accurate in your execution of the SAT strategies in this Black Book, while in order to score an 1800 you must be roughly 80% accurate, and in order to score a 1500 you must be a little less than 50% accurate, and so on.

So scoring higher isn't a question of learning separate strategies; it's a question of how accurate you are when applying a fixed set of strategies.

What if I can't get the strategies to work?

Most students experience difficulty with some of these strategies at some point in their preparation, even if the difficulty is only limited to a specific practice question.

This can be frustrating, of course, but it's actually a great opportunity to improve your understanding of the test, because the experience of figuring out how to overcome these temporary setbacks can be very instructive if we let it.

When a strategy doesn't seem to work against a particular question, the first thing to do is to make sure that the practice question is a real SAT question from the College Board. The next thing is to verify that you haven't misread the answer key—I can't tell you how many times a student has reported struggling with a question for a long time, only to realize that he had misread the answer key, and that the correct answer would have made sense the whole time.

Assuming that you're looking at a real College Board question, and assuming that you haven't misread the answer key, the next thing to consider is whether the strategy you're trying to apply is really relevant to the question. Sometimes people mistakenly try to apply a strategy for the Improving Sentences questions to an Identifying Sentence Errors question, for instance.

If you're pretty sure the strategy you're trying to apply really should work on a particular question, then the issue is probably that you've overlooked some key detail of the question, or that you've misunderstood a word or two somewhere in the question. At this point, it can be a very useful exercise to start over from square one and go back through the question word-by-word, taking nothing for granted and making a sincere effort to see the question with new eyes.

If you do this well, you'll probably be able to figure out where you went wrong and why the question works the way it does. If you make an effort to incorporate the lessons from this experience into your future preparation, then it can be tremendously beneficial to your performance on test day.

On the other hand, if you keep staring at the question and you still can't figure out what the issue is, then I would recommend that you move on to something else for a while—but do make sure you come back to the troubling question at some point and try to work it out, because the standardized nature of the SAT makes it very likely that any troubling strategic issues you run into during practice will reappear on test day, in one form or another.

Which practice books should I buy?

I designed this book so you would only need "the Black Book and the Blue Book"—just this book, and the College Board's *Official SAT Study Guide*, which you can get here: http://www.SATprepBlackBook.com/blue-book. You can also sometimes find copies in the school library or in a local library, but those might have other people's work in them already, so I don't recommend doing it that way.

I'm having a hard time visualizing some of your techniques. What can I do?

Visit www.SATprepVideos.com, where I've made some sample video solutions available for free to readers of this book, to help you visualize some things more clearly.

Reading Questions

Which vocabulary words should I memorize?

I would say that you shouldn't memorize any, at least not in the traditional sense of that idea. As I mention in the section on Sentence Completion questions, vocabulary isn't the main obstacle for most test-takers. The main obstacle for most test-takers is that they don't know how the questions work in the first place, and that they don't follow the test's rules and patterns closely. This is one of several reasons why so many people who memorize hundreds of so-called "SAT words" complain that it hasn't helped their scores. (See the section in this book on Sentence Completion questions for more on this.)

But it can be very useful to learn how the College Board uses words like "humor," "argument," "undermine," and so on. These kinds of words aren't on most people's minds when they talk about learning vocabulary for the SAT, because they don't typically appear as answer choices on Sentence Completion questions. Instead, these words tend to appear in Passage-Based Reading questions, and they can cause you to miss questions if you don't know the specific ways the College Board uses them. (For more on that, please see the chapter on Passage-Based Reading questions.)

I know you say that the answer to each question is always spelled out on the page, but I found a question where that's not the case. Now what?

I completely understand that there are some questions where the answer doesn't seem to be on the page somewhere, but I promise you that the issue is always—*always*—some error on the part of the test-taker, not on the part of the test. (This assumes that you're working with a real SAT question published by the College Board, of course. Fake questions from other companies don't have to follow any rules, and the strategies in this book—the strategies for the real SAT—do not typically apply to fake questions written by companies like Kaplan, Princeton Review, McGraw-Hill, and so on. That's why it's so important to have a copy of the Blue Book.)

So if you think you've found a real SAT question that doesn't follow the rules, you need to try to figure out where you've gone wrong. It may be that you haven't read some critical part of the text, or that you misread it, or that you misread an answer choice. It may be that some of the words on the page don't actually mean what you think they mean. It may be a combination of all of the above, or even something else. But, somewhere in there, you've made a mistake.

I know it can be frustrating to hunt back through the question and the text to find your mistake, but I strongly advise you to do it, especially if your goal is to score really high. The process of figuring out your mistake will help you understand the test much better and greatly improve your future performance. (For more on these ideas, see the chapters called "How To Train For The SAT—Mastering The Ideas In This Book," "The Nature Of Elite Scores," and "The Importance Of Details: Avoiding 'Careless Errors'.")

I like my answer to a question better than the College Board's answer. What should I do about that?

It's normal to feel like the College Board has done a bad job of deciding the correct answer to one of its own questions. But we have to work very hard to overcome that feeling. We need to understand that the SAT isn't really a test of reading ability; it's a standardized test with questions and answers that can be reliably predicted because they follow certain rules and patterns.

So your job isn't really to find the answer choice that seems most satisfactory to you. Your job is to ask yourself, "Which choice will the SAT reward, based on the rules it follows for these questions?"

What do I do for questions about tone and mood, or about the author's attitude?

Questions about tone and mood should be treated just like any other Passage-Based Reading question, even though they might seem like they require us to interpret the text. For more on these questions, please see the part of this book called "What About 'Tone, Mood, And Attitude' Questions?"

Math Questions

Which math formulas are most important for the SAT?

If I had to pick, I would say that the formulas related to triangles, rectangles, and circles seem to me like they come up most often, in addition to the rules about complementary and supplementary angles, transversals, and so on.

But that answer is kind of misleading, for two reasons:

1. All the geometry formulas you'll need for the SAT Math section are included in the beginning of each SAT Math section, so it's not like you'll need to memorize how to find the area of a circle or anything.
2. In general, the best approach to the SAT Math section is to resist the use of formulas wherever possible.

For more on the right way to approach SAT Math, please see the SAT Math section in this book.

Which type of calculator should I use?

In general, I would recommend that you use the calculator that makes you feel the most confident on test day. It's also important to remember that there's very little a calculator can do for you on the SAT, because the challenge with most SAT Math questions comes down to figuring out which basic math concepts are involved in the question, not doing some kind of complicated calculation. For more, see the section of this book that deals with SAT Math.

I found a question that requires trigonometry, and you said I would never need to use trig. What gives?

There are no questions on the SAT 1 that require the use of trig. If you think you've found a real SAT 1 question from the College Board that can only be solved by using the sine, cosine, or tangent functions from trig, then there is something in the question that you've overlooked or misunderstood. I would strongly advise you to keep analyzing the question until you can figure out a solution that wouldn't require you to know trig, because the experience of figuring that out can be one of the most productive and effective ways to improve your understanding performance on the SAT. See the section of this Black Book called "The Importance Of Details: Avoiding 'Careless Errors.'"

I tried to apply your strategy of answering questions based only on the similarities among the answer choices, and it didn't work. Why not?

That pattern can't be used to predict the correct answer to a question 100% of the time, as I explain in the section of this book that covers SAT Math. It's a strong general tendency, not an absolute rule. So instead of using these general answer choice patterns to answer questions outright, we want to see them primarily as indicators of the issues that need to be resolved when answering the question, and we want to be aware that the elements that appear most frequently in the answer choices are *very likely* to be the elements of the correct answer, but that there are no guarantees. When you consider the similarities and differences among a set of answer choices, the final determination as to the correct answer needs to be based primarily on your understanding of basic math and the design of the SAT. See the section on SAT Math for more on that, especially the sample solutions.

Writing Questions

I found a question where the right answer doesn't follow the rules of grammar. How can that be?

Remember that the College Board isn't necessarily following the grammar rules that you learned in school, or even the rules that native speakers follow when they speak. Instead, the College Board has its own set of grammar rules. While those rules largely overlap with the current grammar of American English, there are some points where they differ sharply. Remember that your goal on the Writing section isn't to make them sound good to you, but to figure out which answer choice the College Board will reward based on the rules and patterns it follows. For more on this, see the parts of this book that deal with the SAT Writing Multiple Choice questions.

What should I do if I can't think of good examples for the SAT Essay?

Remember that it's okay to use personal examples, and that you're not penalized for using examples that are factually inaccurate. In other words, you can make up any kind of example you feel like, and tailor it to the exact needs of your argument. For more on this, please see the section of this book that deals with the SAT Essay.

I found a question where the right answer wasn't the shortest answer. Now what?

The shortest answer to an Improving Sentences question will be the correct answer if it's grammatically acceptable to the College Board. If you've found a question where the shortest answer choice is not correct, then it must contain a grammatical flaw, at least in the eyes of the College Board—remember that "SAT grammar" isn't always the same as American English grammar. For more on the rules of "SAT grammar," see the part of this book that covers the SAT Writing Multiple Choice section, and the Appendix.

Setting (The Right) Goals

"The secret of all victory lies in the organization of the non-obvious."
- Marcus Aurelius

At some point, most of my tutoring clients ask me what I think is the highest possible score they can hope for on the SAT. Sometimes they frame it in terms of their previous scores—"If I already have a 1560, can I possibly bring that up to a 2100?"

The answer to this question is simple on the surface, but there are actually many other issues surrounding this question that you want to make sure you consider.

But let's start with the simple stuff first.

If you can read American English pretty well, and if you know the basic principles of arithmetic, geometry, and algebra, then there's no reason why you can't *eventually* make a 2400, or any other score you want, because every question on the SAT relies on your ability to read and understand American English and/or to use basic math principles.

Please read that carefully, especially the word "eventually." I'm absolutely not saying that a person whose highest score so far is a 1400 can just snap her fingers and make a 2400 overnight. What I'm saying is that the SAT is a test of basic skills, and if we have those basic skills then there's no reason, in theory, why we shouldn't be able to answer every question correctly.

Of course, raising an SAT score significantly is going to take some effort, in just about every case. Approaching the SAT in the right way isn't necessarily *difficult*, but it is definitely *different* from the way you would approach tests in high school or college. If you want to raise your score a lot, then you'll really have to try to and think like the test—which, again, is not a difficult thing to do, but will take some conscious effort on your part.

(By the way, if you don't read American English very well, check out the section of this Black Book on advice for non-native speakers of American English. And if you don't know the basic concepts of arithmetic, geometry, and algebra, then review the Math Toolbox, and/or consider getting a math tutor.)

Getting Better At The SAT

We should think of the SAT as a test that asks us to do basically the same things over and over again.

And over again.

And over again, again.

For this reason, once you have a handle on the concepts spelled out in this book, getting better at the SAT isn't a matter of *learning* anything further—it's a matter of *improving your accuracy* in the application of principles you already know.

So it's a bit like improving your free-throws in basketball, or practicing for a piano recital, or even getting better at a video game. It's more an exercise in improving your technical execution, and less an exercise in broadening your intellect.

(Of course, this metaphor doesn't hold up completely. There are some parts of the SAT—most notably the Math section and the Sentence Completion questions—in which you'll have to think a bit creatively. But the way we attack the test should always rely on the basic concepts and strategies described in this book. The simple fact remains that the difference between a 600 and an 800 on a given section always comes down to strategy, execution, and accuracy, and not to knowledge or intelligence.)

How To Set Goals

The most popular way to set an SAT goal is usually to target a particular score. That can work fine, of course, but it's not the way I like to do it.

Instead, I recommend that you target particular levels of accuracy in particular skillsets, and then let the scores rise on their own as a consequence of your improved abilities.

In other words, rather than say, "I want to try to get a 600 in Critical Reading on my next practice test," say something like, "I want to go an entire section without missing a single question in which I know the meanings of all the words." Then try to achieve that standard of execution (which, by the way, would lead to a score much higher than 600 for most test-takers). Or, in the Math section, set a goal like "I want to go an entire practice test without making a 'careless' mental error," or "I want to make sure I understand at least one wrong answer choice with each question that I answer," and so on.

If you set these kinds of task-based goals, rather than score-based goals, your improvement will generally be more meaningful and lasting, and it will come more quickly and easily.

But Wait—Is It Even Worth It?

Remember when I said that there were some complicating issues surrounding the idea of improving your score? A lot of that stuff has to do with the question of whether a higher score is even likely to help you significantly in your admissions campaign. (After all, we should never lose sight of the fact that the only reason to care about the SAT is that it can help improve your chances at your target schools.)

I made you a video presentation to help explain some of the factors involved in your SAT goal-setting. You can find it on the fan page for my company, Testing Is Easy: http://bit.ly/college-planning.

How To Train For The SAT—Mastering The Ideas In This Book

"Under duress, we do not rise to our expectations—we fall to the level of our training."
- Bruce Lee

After questions about the structure of the test itself, the most common question I get has to do with the right way to "study" for the SAT. People want to know what order they should tackle the different parts of the test in, what kind of schedule they should follow, whether they should take a practice test on the last day before the real test—all kinds of stuff.

The short answer to all of these questions is that there really is no single best way to tackle the material in this book, because no two students will have the same exact needs when it comes to prepping. Different people will have different strengths and weaknesses, different schedules, different target scores, different starting points, different attention spans, and so on. So I'm not going to tell you exactly how to manage your preparation schedule. Instead, I'm going to give you guidelines to follow and things to make sure you consider, and then it's going to be up to you to figure out how you piece those things together in a way that works best for you.

So we'll handle it in this order:

- general concepts to govern your preparation
- guidelines for the order in which you tackle different parts of the test
- ideas for drills and exercises
- general notes on scheduling

Let's get started.

The Recommended Progression

Most people measure their progress by the scores they make on practice tests, but I don't advise that, at least not in the beginning. I'd rather see you measure your progress in terms of your overall understanding of the test. This is a subjective measurement, to be sure, but it's actually a lot more reliable than practice test results, because those can be heavily influenced by luck and other external factors.

So your first goal is to get a general grasp of the mechanics of each part of the test. You do this by reading the relevant portion of this Black Book, following along with some or all of the sample solutions, and checking out the free videos at www.SATprepVideos.com until you feel like you can understand the reasoning behind most or all of the test.

After you have a grasp of the foundation of the test, your next goal is to understand the mistakes you make when you look at questions on your own (whether we're talking about practice tests, practice sections, or just individual test items—more on that below). In other words, at this stage your main goal isn't really to keep from making mistakes; it's simply to *understand* your mistakes *after you make them*. You want to figure out what the mistake was, of course, but you also want to figure out why it happened, and what you should have noticed in the question that would have kept you from making the mistake in the first place, or would have allowed you to catch it and correct it after it was made. This is why I spend so much time in this Black Book talking about each question as a system of concepts and relationships, and explaining the ways that right answers differ from wrong answers, and the relationships that typically exist among them. Those are the things you want to get in the habit of noticing when you look at an SAT question, because if those things seem to be in order then you've probably understood the question correctly.

Once you have a solid grasp of the reasons you're making mistakes and the things you could do to avoid them, your next goal is to actually eliminate those mistakes, either by avoiding them in the first place or by noticing them after they happen and then correcting them. This is where it really helps to be aware of the test's rules and patterns, particularly when it comes to answer choices. At this stage, your goal is to make sure that you never miss a question as a result of a mistake on your part—you want to get to a point where the only reason you ever miss a question is that it might involve a word, grammar principle, or math concept that you were unfamiliar with, and that you can't work around. In other words, your goal is to eliminate so-called "careless mistakes."

When you have essentially eliminated careless mistakes, you'll probably be at a point where your scores on practice tests are more than satisfactory. If not, you need to think carefully about what's causing you to miss the remaining questions, and how to fix those issues. But be careful here—too many people jump to the incorrect conclusion that a weakness in vocabulary is the reason they miss a reading question, or that an unknown math formula is the reason they miss a math question. Remember the lessons of this book: the SAT really isn't an advanced test when it comes to subject matter. Of course, there are definitely questions in which vocabulary plays a very large part, and it can sometimes be difficult or impossible to work around an unknown word, but there are many, many more questions in which vocabulary only seems to be an issue, and you could actually find a work-around if you thought about it. Similarly, there are many SAT Math questions that seem specialized and advanced to most students, but none of them actually are.

You may also have to think about timing issues at this stage in your progression, though most people who get to a point where they've eliminated "careless errors" find that timing is no longer a concern. If timing is still an issue, review the portion of this Black Book on time management, and remember that it isn't a matter of doing a lot of work very quickly—it's a matter of streamlining and reducing the amount of work that goes into answering each question in the first place.

The Order Of Attack

I pretty much always recommend that students start with the Critical Reading section, because it's typically the part of the test where it's easiest to start noticing how the SAT uses rules and patterns to make questions predictable and objective even when they might seem not to be. It's also a good introduction to the extreme importance of reading carefully and paying attention to details.

There are only two reasons I might recommend not starting with the Critical Reading section, really. One would be if you already had a perfect 800 on that section. The other reason would be if you really wanted to work on your Math score AND just didn't have enough time before your test date to start with Critical Reading. In all other situations, though, I'd start with the Critical Reading, even if that isn't the part of the test that bothers you most. It's the foundation for the rest of the test.

Once you feel like the Critical Reading section is starting to make sense, I would turn my attention to the Math section. As I will mention many times in this book, the Math section is all about basic concepts being combined and presented in strange ways, and our goal is to learn how to look at a Math question that seems impossible at first and figure out which basic concepts are involved, and then use them to answer the question. Because there's more variation in the surface appearance of Math questions than there is in the appearance of the questions from other sections, learning how to think about them properly often takes more time than it might take for other question types. So be aware of that when you're planning your approach to the test.

I would advise most test-takers to focus on improving the Writing Multiple Choice questions and the SAT Essay last (in either order). Of course, this assumes that your target schools will even care about those scores. If they don't, then there's probably no point in devoting your energy to them. You can find out if your target schools consider the Writing score by looking at their websites or contacting their admissions departments and asking directly.

Drills And Exercises

Most people get ready for the SAT or PSAT the same way they would get ready for a school test: they try to memorize stuff (vocabulary, formulas, essay examples, whatever), and then they do a lot of practice questions. After you've read the sections of this book that deal with the way SAT questions work, you'll understand why the memorization/repetition approach won't help you. The SAT isn't a test of advanced knowledge, so memorizing obscure definitions and math formulas won't do much. And it doesn't repeat test items exactly, so taking tons of practice tests with the idea that you'll see the exact same questions on test day is also a bad idea.

(This, by the way, is why you probably know so many people who work so hard on the SAT or PSAT and have so little to show for it. They're getting ready for the test as though it were a final exam in a Geometry class, and that's not what it is.)

Of course, that raises an important question: if you're not supposed to get ready for the SAT by memorizing stuff and doing a million practice questions, then what are you supposed to do instead?

You're supposed to try to *understand* the test instead. When you understand how the SAT works—really, truly understand it—you'll find that it's a very basic test, and that you really don't need to spend a hundred hours getting ready for it. (If you're going for a perfect 2400, you may need to spend a bit more time than the average person, but we'll talk about that later).

You come to understand the SAT by thinking about how the test is designed and why it's designed that way, so that you can eventually see it the same way the College Board sees it. And you get to that point by thinking about the things that we talk about in this book, and by making a conscious and intentional effort to apply them to a sufficient sample of real test questions.

This process may incidentally involve a little memorization—you'll want to remember what kinds of patterns and things to look for, for example. And it will also involve a certain amount of practice as you learn to apply these ideas against real test questions. But our ultimate goal is to see the SAT as a coherent, predictable system of rules and patterns that we understand, instead of having to say, "I've memorized thousands of words and done 30 practice tests, but my score just isn't improving."

Ultimately, you want to realize that the SAT tests the same underlying principles according to the same rules and patterns on every test, but that each individual SAT question will appear unique to people who don't know how the test works. And you want to be able to identify the ways that an individual question follows those rules and patterns, so that you can "decode" each question and mark the answer that the College Board will reward.

Now let's talk about some different options for getting to that point. Here are three of my favorite exercises. I've given them ridiculous names to help them stick in your head, and to emphasize that they're different from just mindlessly repeating practice questions over and over again.

1. The Semi-Structured Stare-And-Ponder

The Semi-Structured Stare-And-Ponder is a great way to begin to appreciate how the SAT is actually designed. You start out by learning the general idea of how a certain question type works by reading the relevant portions of this Black Book and looking at a good number of the sample solutions in here. Then you find a question of the same general type (Passage-Based Reading, Improving Sentences, whatever) in the Blue Book or some other College Board source.

And then you stare at the question.

And you ponder it.

You try to figure out how that question is doing the kinds of things that I talk about in this book. You think carefully about the wording, the answer choices, all that stuff. Ultimately, your goal is to understand the College Board's motivation for writing the question in that way—why the right answer is right, why the wrong answers are wrong, and why the College Board thinks the wrong answers would be appealing to different types of test-takers who might make different types of mistakes.

When you feel you've stared at a particular question and pondered it long enough, you move on to another one, and stare at it (and ponder it, too). You look for the same types of design elements and relationships, with the same ultimate goal of seeing the question through the College Board's eyes, and being able to explain every aspect of the question's design.

Then you move on to the next question. Or you eat a sandwich, or go for a walk or something—when staring and pondering in a semi-structured way gets boring, you stop. You come back to it later, when you're interested to see how much more of the SAT you can figure out. Ideally, the process is relaxed, with no real consideration of time. You're just letting the ideas rattle around in your head, and letting your brain get used to looking for them in real SAT questions. You don't get frustrated if you can't see how something works. You're just getting used to a new way of looking at test questions in a low-pressure setting.

Of course, when you actually take the test, you won't want to approach it in this way. That goes without saying. But that shouldn't stop you from pondering all the different aspects of the test in this kind of relaxed way as a part of your preparation, because the more you do this kind of thing, the more quickly you'll be able to analyze and diagnose real test questions in the future. Let things percolate a bit and you may be surprised what you start to notice in the future.

2. Practice-And-A-Postie

The word "postie" here is short for the phrase "post mortem," which in this case refers to the idea of analyzing a test or a practice session after the fact. I included the word "postie" in the name of this exercise because I really, really want to emphasize that if you don't make a serious analysis of your practice work after you finish it, then you're really wasting the time you spend practicing.

So basically you start out by doing practice parts of a test, or even entire practice tests. You can do these practice sections with or without time limits, as you see fit (of course, the actual SAT will have a time limit, so you'll probably want to practice with a time limit at some point, but it might not be beneficial in the beginning).

I wouldn't recommend that you use practice sections or practice tests until you've made some progress in understanding the rules and patterns of the individual SAT questions—otherwise, you'll just end up wasting lots of time and getting frustrated when you miss a lot of questions and don't understand why.

I also wouldn't recommend that you do practice tests or sections without doing a full post-mortem on them, in which you go through all the questions and try to understand why the College Board wrote each question the way it did, what you could have done to answer the question correctly as quickly and directly as possible, and what lessons you can learn from that question that might be applicable to future questions. This post-mortem step is absolutely critical if you want to make a serious improvement on the SAT, but it's something that most people completely ignore, or do only halfway.

Since the whole point of your practice sessions is to prepare you to do well on test day, the most important thing you can learn from any question is how to recognize its rules and patterns at work in future questions. In other words, as weird as it may sound, the actual answer to a particular practice question doesn't really matter that much; what matters is whether the question can teach us how to answer future questions on test day. So it's much better to miss a practice question and learn something from it than to get lucky on a practice question and not learn anything.

And if you don't really sit and think about the questions you've missed, you're going to keep missing similar questions in the future—maybe not questions that seem similar on the surface (there may not even be any that seem similar on the surface), but you'll definitely miss questions with similar fundamentals, and there will probably be a lot of them.

So please make sure you give some serious thought to your practice sections after you finish them. Otherwise, the time you spend doing them is basically wasted. (By the way, if you do a good job on your post-mortems you should find that you dramatically reduce the amount of practice that you need to reach your goal, so you save yourself a ton of time in the long run.)

3. The Shortcut Search

In this exercise, which can be part of a post-mortem or just an exercise on its own, you look at some real SAT questions for which you already know the answers. If you've already done the questions and graded them, then you'll know the answers from that; if you haven't, then just look at the answer key and mark them down beforehand anyway.

Our goal with this exercise is not to figure out the right answer to a question, but to figure out the fastest and easiest way to arrive at that answer with certainty. For a Passage-Based Reading Question, we want to figure out which phrases in the text support the correct answer, and we want to figure out how we could have arrived at those key phrases with a minimal amount of reading and frustration. For a Math question, we might think about ways to use diagrams or answer choices (if the question has some) to avoid using formulas in our solutions. And so on.

4. WWMIR?

This abbreviation stands for "What Would Make It Right?" In this drill, you go through each answer choice in a question and ask yourself what would have to change about the question or the test for that answer choice to be the correct one. If a Math question asks for the area of a rectangle and one wrong answer is the perimeter, then the answer to "WWMIR" is something like "if the College Board had asked for perimeter instead of area here." If the shortest answer choice in an Improving Sentences question isn't correct, then the answer to "WWMIR" might be something like "if this noun had been singular instead of plural, or if the word 'it' had been 'they.'" And so on. Forcing yourself to try to re-imagine the questions in ways that would make the wrong answers right will help reinforce your understanding of how right and wrong answers work for particular parts of the SAT.

Things To Think About For Scheduling

As I mentioned above, years of working with a wide variety of students have left me convinced that there is no single best schedule for every test-taker. In fact, I think it would be closer to the truth to say that no two test-takers would probably have the same optimal preparation schedule. So now that we've talked about general ideas to use in your preparation, let's talk about the things you'll need to think about when you schedule that preparation.

Do You Like To Get An Early Start, Or Are You An Adrenaline Junkie?

Imagine that you're in a history class, and the teacher announces a massive research assignment that will be due in 2 months. There are two general reactions to a situation like this: some people rush home and start working on it right away, and some people already know that they'll pull a couple of all-nighters right before it's due and knock it out like that. I find that the same general tendencies exist when it comes to test prep. If you'd get started on a 2-month project when the due date is still 2 months away, then you should probably start as early as possible on your test preparation. If you're more of a last-minute person, then you're probably more of a last-minute prepper, too. I've seen both approaches work out very well tons of times, as long as the test-taker was comfortable with the particular approach.

How Long Can You Stand To Stare At The Same Page?

Some people have longer attention spans than others, and some are just naturally more interested in the SAT than others. If you really can't coax more than 10 to 30 minutes of sustained attention to the test out of yourself, then you'll probably want to do shorter and more frequent bouts of preparation. On the other hand, if you're the kind of person who can easily spend 2 hours thinking about the SAT without wanting to scream, it may make more sense for you to do an hour or two each weekend and largely ignore the test during the week.

What Kind Of Score Increase Do You Need?

This one is probably obvious: the more points you need to score, the earlier you'll probably want to start prepping.

How Much Free Time Do You Have?

Again, fairly obvious: the less free time you have in your schedule, the earlier you need to start prepping in order to accommodate a particular amount of prep time. (But one potential wrinkle in this part of the discussion is the fact that the actual amount of prep time you need may be significantly more or significantly less than you'd expect at the outset.)

How Many Questions/Sections/Tests Do You Need To Do?

It may come as a surprise, but there is no magic number of practice questions that will guarantee you hit your target score. Based on my fairly wide experience, I would say that over 99% of people do need to do some kind of actual practice work with the ideas in this book—it's very rare that a person is able to implement the strategies on test day with full effectiveness after merely reading about them. So you will want to do some number of practice questions or sections. The operative question is how many.

And the issue is one of quality, not quantity. Most people will assume (very incorrectly) that if they simply do a certain number of questions they're guaranteed to improve. But that really isn't the case, because of the unique way in which standardized tests are designed. It's much more important to try to *understand* a representative sample of questions than it is to crank out a million repetitions simply for its own sake. If you can look at a single real SAT and really, thoroughly understand what the College Board is doing in that test, and why, and how you can use the strategies in this book to beat it, then you're ready.

Do You Even Need A Schedule?

Finally, I'd like to close by pointing out that a specific test-prep schedule might not even be ideal for you in the first place. In my experience, students are often very bad at predicting how long it will take them to master a particular skill on the SAT, because the SAT is so different from traditional tests. You may pick up the Reading very quickly and take longer to build good SAT Math skills, or the other way around, and there may not be any correlation between those lengths of time and your academic strengths. Or you might rapidly build up good test-taking instincts for all the question types, and then have a difficult time eliminating your "careless mistakes" and spend weeks perfecting that. You may be full of enthusiasm and excitement one week, and then suddenly find yourself with no time at all on the next week. And so on. An overly rigid schedule may prevent you from adapting to these kinds of situations, or to others.

My general "scheduling" advice, then, is simple. If I were you, I would try to start prepping as early as you can, even if that just means flipping absent-mindedly through this Black Book in the very beginning. The earlier you start, the more gradual the prep can be, and the more likely it is to stick. At the same time, I would recommend prepping in ways that you find mentally engaging, and taking breaks when it gets boring and counter-productive. After every practice section or full-length practice test, I would *strongly* recommend a serious and sincere post-mortem.

And that's basically it. Modify it and make it your own as you see fit.

Be Careful With Diagnostics, Even From The College Board

"All our knowledge has its origin in our perceptions."
- Leonardo da Vinci

A lot of test-takers try to assess their weaknesses with some kind of diagnostic test, whether from the College Board itself or from a tutor or test prep company. In fact, the score report you receive from the College Board after you take an official SAT or PSAT provides a breakdown of your supposed strengths and weaknesses based on the questions that you missed.

In my opinion, you want to be very careful when you consider this kind of feedback, because it overlooks the fact that there are many, many ways to miss any given SAT question, and they might not have anything to do with the College Board's idea of the question's type.

For instance, you might miss a reading question because you don't know some of the words in the question, or you might miss it because you misread the question, or because you were in a hurry and didn't have time to consider it carefully enough. You might miss a math question for any of the same reasons, or because you made a simple mistake in the arithmetic component of an algebra question, or because you keyed something into the calculator incorrectly. And so on. But diagnostic reports can't measure the reasons that you miss things—they can only try to classify each question and then assume that people who miss a question are bad at answering questions of that class.

For instance, the score report might show that you missed a question that it considers to be an algebra question, and recommend that you improve your algebra as a result. But it may turn out that you really missed the question because you accidentally multiplied 2 and -2 and got 4, which has nothing to do with algebra.

So I rarely pay any attention to such diagnostic reports, and I don't encourage my students to worry about them in most cases. The only limited exception I would make would be in an extreme case. For example, if you miss every single Sentence Completion question on a practice test and don't miss any other questions in the Critical Reading section, then there's a good chance that you need to work on your approach to Sentence Completion questions.

Outside of those kinds of situations, though, I would recommend that you pay more attention to your own feelings about where your weak areas are, as long as you're trying to diagnose those weaknesses honestly. For instance, it's tempting to look at an SAT Math question that involves circles and assume that you missed it because you're not good with circles, but, if you pay close attention to how you tried to answer the question, you may realize that you actually missed it because you ignored two of the answer choices and didn't notice that the diagram was drawn to scale. Either way, the experience of looking back over a question you missed and trying to figure out why the correct answer is correct, and how you might have arrived at that correct answer if you had looked at the question differently, is far more helpful than accepting a diagnostic report at face value.

Only Work With Questions From The College Board!

"One must learn by doing the thing."
- Sophocles

Three of the most important themes in this book, which you'll see reflected on almost every level of my SAT advice, are the following:

1. SAT questions are written according to specific rules and patterns, and
2. learning to beat the SAT is a matter of learning to identify those rules and patterns and exploit their inherent weaknesses systematically, because
3. most of the problems that most people have on the SAT are the result of poor test-taking skills, not of deficiencies in subject-matter knowledge.

I'll expand on these ideas in the rest of this book, but for right now I want to impress something upon you that is extremely, extremely important: It is absolutely critical that you practice with real SAT questions written by the actual College Board itself, and not with any other kind of practice test or practice questions.

Only the real questions written by the actual College Board are guaranteed to behave like the questions you'll see on test day. Questions written by other companies (Kaplan, Princeton Review, Barron's, or anybody else) are simply not guaranteed to behave like the real thing. In some cases, the differences are obvious, and, frankly, shocking. Some companies write fake practice SAT Writing questions in which the passive voice is the difference between a right answer and a wrong answer. Some fake SAT Math questions rely on math formulas the SAT doesn't allow itself to test. Many fake SAT Reading questions require literary analysis. And so on.

Fake practice questions that break the rules of the real test will encourage you to develop bad test-taking habits, and will keep you from being able to develop good habits. For our purposes, then, fake SAT questions written by any company except the College Board are garbage. They are useless. If you want to learn how to beat the SAT, you have to work with real SAT questions.

Real SAT questions from the actual College Board are pretty easy to acquire. You can find some on the College Board's website, but the most common source is the College Board's "Blue Book," *The Official SAT Study Guide*. I keep a page with the best deals on the Blue Book here: http://www.SATprepBlackBook.com/blue-book.

The second edition of the Blue Book has ten practice tests in it, which should be more than enough for anybody if you use them correctly. See the section of this book called "How To Train For The SAT" for more on that.

What About Harder Questions?

One of the most common objections to the idea of using real test questions is that some companies (most notably Barron's) are known for writing practice questions that are harder than real test questions—the argument is that working with more difficult questions will make the real test seem like a breeze.

Unfortunately, this approach is too clever for its own good, because it overlooks the nature of difficulty on a test like the SAT. If the "harder" practice questions from a third-party company were "hard" in the same way that "hard" SAT questions are "hard," then training with harder question might be a good idea. But those fake questions are harder in a way that makes them totally unlike real questions, so they're a waste of time.

When a third-party company writes fake questions to be hard, it does so by incorporating some of the skills that a high-school student would need to use in advanced classes: knowledge of advanced math concepts, subtle literary analysis, and so on. But these skills have no place whatsoever on the SAT, because the SAT limits itself to very basic ideas, and tries to fool you by asking you about basic things in weird ways.

So if you want to raise your SAT score, the skill you need to develop is the ability to look at strange questions, figure out whatever basic thing they actually want you to do, and then do it. That's what this Black Book teaches you to do. In fact, the more familiar you become with the SAT, the more you'll see that "hard" SAT questions aren't really any different from "easy" ones when you get right down to it. This is why it's pointless to use fake questions, even if they're supposed to be more challenging than real questions.

Whenever students ask whether they should use "harder" questions to get ready for the SAT, I always answer with this analogy: It's true that performing on the flying trapeze is harder than making an omelet, but getting better at the trapeze won't make your omelets any better, because the two things have nothing to do with each other. Just because something is harder doesn't mean it's helpful.

I really can't stress this enough: If you're serious about improving your performance, you need to practice with real SAT questions written by the College Board, because real test questions are what you'll see on test day. There are no exceptions to this.

(I frequently have students who try to ignore this particular aspect of my SAT-taking approach, and the results are always bad. Seriously. Trust me on this. Use real questions from the College Board. There's a reason I keep repeating this idea :))

A Word On Guessing: Don't.

"Remember not only to say the right thing in the right place, but, far more difficult still, to leave unsaid the wrong thing at the tempting moment."
- Benjamin Franklin

There's another thing I need to clear up before we even start talking about taking specific SAT questions.

If you've ever been given any advice at all about how to take the SAT, it probably included this little pearl:

"If you ever get stumped on a question, just try to eliminate one or two answers and then guess from the rest."

It's the single most popular test-taking strategy of all time. Your friends have heard it. Every test prep company uses it. Your guidance counselors might have told you about it. Even the College Board tells you to do it. And as it turns out, it's an absolutely awful piece of advice in almost every case. Let's take a closer look at it.

First Things First: Guessing Defined

Before we can talk about why guessing on the SAT is bad, we have to make sure we're talking about the same thing when we use the word *guessing*. When we talk about guessing, we're talking about marking an answer choice on a multiple-choice question without being certain that the answer choice is correct.

We're NOT necessarily talking about marking an answer choice when we don't know the meaning of every word in the question, when we don't know what a sentence says, when we're not sure of the grammar, when we don't know for certain how to do the math involved, or anything like that.

Can you see the difference? Natural test-takers encounter things they don't know or have never heard of every time they take the SAT. It's totally normal. In fact, in a lot of ways it's inevitable. But if you know the test (and you will know it if you've studied this manual), you can still choose the correct answer choice reliably EVEN THOUGH YOU DON'T KNOW EVERYTHING IN THE QUESTION. In this case, for our purposes, you are NOT guessing—guessing only happens when you're not sure the answer you're marking is right. For our purposes, guessing has nothing to do with whether you understand the question you're being asked, and everything to do with whether you're certain the answer you mark is correct.

It's very important that you understand this distinction before we continue the discussion; otherwise, you might think I'm telling you to give up whenever you come to a question you don't understand fully, which is absolutely NOT what I'm telling you to do.

Now that we've got that straightened out, let's talk about why people guess on the SAT in the first place.

The Argument For Guessing

The argument for guessing on the SAT relies on the way the test is designed. As you may know, you get a single raw point for every correct answer to a multiple-choice question on the SAT. You lose a fraction of a raw point for each wrong answer to a multiple-choice question. This fractional loss is set up so that if you guess randomly on every single question on the test, you should come out with a total score of 0 raw points.

How can that be? Well, for a five-answer multiple-choice question, you'll get a full raw point if you're correct and you'll lose a quarter of a raw point if you're wrong. So if you guess randomly, in any five questions with five answers each, you should expect to get one correct answer and four incorrect answers—which would come out to a net score of 0 raw points.

The argument for guessing tries to change those odds. According to the guessing theory, if you could remove one or two answer choices from each question, and then guess randomly from what you had left, you should expect to beat the test and get a few extra raw points. The thinking works like this: If you can remove two answer choices for each question, then you should only really be guessing from three answer choices on each five-answer question. If you guess from three answer choices, you should be right every third time (instead of only being right every fifth time, which is what you would expect if you didn't remove any answer choices at all). But you'll still only be penalized one-fourth of a raw point for being wrong. Over time, if you guess correctly every three tries and you're only penalized as though you were guessing correctly every fifth time, you should come out significantly ahead.

If you've done other SAT prep before, you've probably heard this argument before. You might even be nodding in agreement. It's simple probability, right?

Wrong.

This is an example of what you might call *"over-simplified"* probability. The argument for guessing on the SAT assumes at least two things that just aren't true in real life.

The Problem With Guessing

In order for the argument for guessing to be any good, two things would have to happen:

1. You have to eliminate only incorrect answer choices.

2. You have to guess randomly from the remaining answer choices.

Do you see why this is?

In the first place, if you eliminate the correct answer choice from the pool of possible answers you'll consider, then how likely are you to get the question right by picking the eliminated answer? You're not likely to at all. In fact, you can't do it. It's impossible to pick an answer choice that you've eliminated from the guessing.

As for the second assumption, if you don't guess randomly, then the entire argument about what "should" happen according to "probability" goes right out the window. There's no probability involved at all if you don't make a completely random guess. (Making a guess where you consider the validity of each answer choice isn't random. "Random" means you don't interfere at all. For example, flipping a penny in the air to see how many times it comes up heads is random; catching it every time before it lands and setting it down tails-up destroys the randomness by interfering with the process. That's essentially what you're doing if you consider whether the answer choices are any good or not.)

What Really Happens

Most of the people who employ the classic so-called "guessing" strategy are actually doing something very different from eliminating incorrect answers and then making a random, impartial guess. So what are they really doing, and why doesn't it work?

When people who follow the guessing strategy come to a question they can't answer, the first thing they usually do is look for an answer choice they like. Then they look to see if they can find one or two other answer choices to "eliminate." They get rid of those, and then pick the choice they decided they liked in the first place, and (wrongly) call that a random guess. And that's it—they've basically used a bad theory based on a bad argument to justify marking a wrong answer in the vast majority of cases. And, as a result, they lose raw points left and right. They'd be much better off just leaving those questions blank.

Why Guessing Fails On The SAT

There's a reason it's almost impossible to satisfy the two assumptions of the guessing strategy. The SAT is intentionally written so that incorrect answer choices seem like correct answer choices to people who don't know how to answer the questions. In other words, the very thing that keeps you from understanding a question in the first place is also the thing that will probably keep you from (1) eliminating only wrong answers, and (2) making an impartial guess from the remaining choices.

What does all this mean? On the SAT, in order to use the classical "guessing" strategy effectively, you basically have to be wrong about why you're wrong. Or, to put it another (equally silly) way, you have to be unlucky in a lucky way. Which is just as nonsensically difficult as it sounds like it is, which is why this 'strategy' doesn't help most people very much.

(Here's a coincidence that borders on conspiracy: as I previously noted, the College Board endorses the traditional guessing strategy described above. And the College Board is also the group that writes SAT questions so that incorrect answer choices look like correct ones—which makes good guessing almost impossible. Hmmmm . . .)

What You Should Do Instead

So if you don't use the guessing strategy, what should you do instead? Simple. When you come to a question and you can't figure out the answer, skip it. Don't think about it—just do it. Remember, the only real alternative is to put down a wrong answer and lose points.

It takes discipline to leave a question blank on an important test like the SAT. But you have to do it sometimes. If you really can't figure out the answer, there's no better choice than skipping the question.

I'll repeat this again to make sure it's crystal-clear: If you can't figure out an answer, skip the question. That's all.

Proof That Guessing Is Bad

If you're like most people, you probably don't believe me when I say that SAT guessing is a bad idea. You've probably been told by almost everyone you know that you should eliminate the incorrect answer choices and guess from the remaining choices whenever you get stumped on the SAT. And the argument in support of guessing seems fairly seductive and clever, to be sure—until you examine the two things it relies on, at which point the argument falls apart for most people.

How else can I support what I'm saying? There are two ways. The first way is by pointing out that high-scorers (99th percentile and above) pretty much never rely on the traditional guessing approach. Find some and ask them.

But the second way to prove that guessing is a bad idea is much better, and much more relevant to you as an individual. Just take a sample test from the College Board publication *The Official SAT Study Guide*, and make a note on your answer sheet every time you mark an answer you're not sure of. Then, when you add up your score, calculate it first with all the questions included, and then compare that result to the score you would have received if you had omitted the questions where you weren't sure of the answers. You will almost certainly find that your score is higher when you omit the questions you guessed on.

If this is NOT what you find, there are two possible reasons. It might be that you're one of the few people on Earth who actually guesses well using the classical strategy, in which case you should count yourself lucky and write a thank-you letter to the College Board. The more likely explanation is that you're still scoring lower than you want to, and you haven't spent enough time with the processes and strategies in this book for them to make a difference in your score—you haven't spent enough time to develop a real sense of certainty about when you're right and when you're guessing. As you'll see, the higher your score goes, the less guessing you'll find that you do. People simply don't guess their way into a top score on the SAT.

The Origins Of Traditional Guessing

So if the traditional guessing strategy is such a flawed idea, where did it come from? Good question. There are two probable explanations.

First, major test prep companies need a piece of fall-back advice they can give to their students, and this must seem like a pretty good one. With this one strategy, even a person who had learned nothing at all from an 8-week class could feel empowered to tackle any SAT question and stand a decent chance of improving his score. And since the major test prep companies write their own practice questions, they can construct those questions so that certain answer choices are obviously incorrect—which isn't how real SAT questions are written, but who'll ever notice?

Second, the College Board itself must have a stake in perpetuating the traditional guessing approach. It's been a part of their official advice for years now. But let's think for a moment—in 2004 and 2005, the College Board came under heavy fire for the SAT and made several large-scale changes to the old version of the test. They cut out whole question types, added an entire section, changed the essay instrument from the old SAT Writing II essay, and added new content to the Math section, among other things. They did these things mostly because some colleges and universities complained about the old test design and what it showed (or didn't show) about a student's abilities. Now, we can be pretty sure that if there had been a problem with students guessing their way to higher scores, the College Board would have addressed the situation during its latest major overhaul. They didn't. If the College Board knew about the guessing strategy, and if that strategy worked so well, why didn't they change the test to make it impossible? And while we're at it, why do they keep telling people to use it? I'll leave the answers up to you.

Conclusion

Guessing on the SAT is almost certainly a losing proposition for you. Test it out and see for yourself. The best thing to do when you come to a question you can't answer is to skip it. I know it's hard, but it sure beats losing points!

(For more on knowing when to skip an answer, see the article called "No Two Ways About It" in this manual.)

Remember that "guessing" only refers to the act of marking an answer when you're not sure that the answer is correct. On the SAT, there are ways to know your answer is correct even when you don't completely understand the question. Marking an answer choice in that situation isn't guessing—it's smart, natural test-taking!

The Importance Of Details: Avoiding "Careless Errors"

"You will make all kinds of mistakes; but as long as you are generous and true, and also fierce, you cannot hurt the world or even seriously distress her."
- Winston Churchill

As you go through the test-taking strategies in this Black Book, one thing will become very clear to you: at every turn, the SAT is obsessed with details in a way that high school and college courses typically are not.

The correct answer to an SAT Critical Reading question might rely on the subtle difference between the words "unique" and "rare." A 10-word answer choice in an SAT Writing question might be right or wrong because of a single comma. An SAT Math question involving algebra and fractions might have the reciprocal and the complement of the correct answer as two of the incorrect answers. And so on.

This means that doing extremely well on the SAT isn't just a question of knowing the proper strategies (though that's a big part of it, of course!). It's also a question of being almost fanatically obsessed with the tiniest details. In fact, I would say that in most cases the biggest difference between someone who scores a 650 on a section of the SAT and someone who scores an 800 is not that the 800-scorer is any smarter or any more knowledgeable, but that she is much more diligent about paying attention to details.

This strong orientation to detail is exactly the opposite of what most teachers in most high schools reward in their classes. Generally speaking, teachers are more interested in things like participation, an ability to defend your position, and a willingness to think of the big picture, especially in humanities classes. On the SAT, those things rarely come in handy. What matters on the SAT is your ability to execute relatively simple strategies over and over again on a variety of questions without missing small details that would normally go overlooked in a classroom discussion.

For this reason, the attitude that most test-takers typically have towards so-called "careless errors"—which is that they don't matter as long as you basically understand what the question was about—is very destructive and needs to be corrected.

On the SAT, "careless errors" must be taken very seriously. In fact, I would even say that most test-takers could improve their scores by at least 50 to 100 points per section—usually more—if they would just eliminate these kinds of errors completely. But most people don't take these small mistakes seriously, and they don't know a reliable way to separate right answers from wrong answers anyway. So they usually end up focusing more on stuff they can memorize, which is of very little value on the test.

Why Are Careless Errors So Easy To Make On The SAT?

As always, when we try to figure out why the SAT is the way it is, we have to remember why it exists in the first place. The only reason for the SAT's existence is that colleges and universities find the data from the test to be useful when they're evaluating applicants. The SAT data is useful because it's consistent, reliable, and capable of making exacting distinctions among millions of test-takers every year. This is only possible because the test questions are written according to specific rules and patterns that don't change, and because the test uses the multiple-choice format, which limits student responses and allows the grading to be objective (at least in the sense that every answer to a multiple-choice question is graded without the inherent subjectivity of an essay-grading process).

Here's the kicker: the multiple-choice format itself, and the SAT's rules and patterns specifically, would be useless for the purpose of making fine, meaningful distinctions among millions of test-takers every year unless they were very, very, detailed. In other words, the College Board has to be obsessed with details because otherwise its data would be useless.

So the questions on the SAT are extremely nit-picky.

How Can We Pay Attention To Details And Avoid Careless Mistakes?

In the parts of this book that deal with specific strategies for the different types of SAT questions, you'll notice that I always try to talk about each question as a system of ideas. Instead of just explaining how the right answer fits with the prompt, I also talk about the patterns we can see in the wrong answers, and about how the wrong answers relate to the right answer. I do this for a variety of reasons, but one of the biggest reasons is that being aware of the interplay of the parts of a given question is one of the best ways to check that your answer makes sense within a larger context, which gives us a much higher level of confidence in our decisions and a greater degree of certainty that we haven't made a mistake.

On the other hand, most of the time when people make a mistake on the test, it's because they haven't considered the question in its entirety. Instead, they catch a couple of phrases or concepts, make an unwarranted leap or a faulty calculation, see an answer choice that reflects their mistake, and move on without re-considering their decisions.

So please do us both a favor and take a lesson from the way I think carefully about parts of each question that most people might consider irrelevant. I do that for a reason: it's silly to give points away for careless mistakes on such an important test.

Certainty And The SAT

"One must verify or expel his doubts, and convert them into the certainty of Yes or No."
- Thomas Carlyle

I've spent more hours than I can count helping my students raise their SAT scores, and all of that time has made me realize that there is a serious problem blocking most SAT-takers from realizing their full potential.

It's not a problem that has to do with strategy, memorization, timing, focus, or anything like that. This problem is at the root of the very nature of the SAT itself. And if you don't come to terms with it, your score can only be mediocre at best.

The problem is that the SAT only gives you one correct answer choice for each question, and this correct answer choice is totally, definitively, incontrovertibly the correct answer—there are no arguments to be made against it (once we know the test's rules).

But a lot of students never realize this. In this book, I talk a lot about all the specific ways that the SAT is different from tests you take in high school. But I really want to pound this one difference into your head, because it will affect every single thing you do as you prepare for the test.

So I'm saying it again—read closely:

SAT Multiple-Choice questions always have ONE, and only ONE, correct answer. Furthermore, the issue of which answer choice is the correct one is absolutely beyond disagreement. As surely as 2 and 2 make 4, and not 5 or 3, every single SAT question can only be correctly answered in one way.

A Real-Life Example

Why is this such a big deal, you ask?

Imagine this common high school situation, which you've probably been through yourself. Your history teacher is going over the answers to a multiple-choice test with you. It's a test he wrote himself, and he wrote it just for your class. And as he's going through the test, he tells you that the answer to number 9 is choice (D). Half the class groans—they all marked (B). One of the students who marked (B) raises her hand and makes a convincing argument as to why she should get credit for marking (B). She explains that if you read the question a certain way, (B) and (D) are equally good answers. The teacher, who wants to be open-minded and fair, reconsiders the question, and decides that it's poorly written. In light of the student's argument, he can understand why (B) might have looked like the right answer. And, because he's fair, he announces that he'll give equal credit for both (B) and (D).

That sort of thing happens every day in high schools all across the country. It's the natural result of a system in which teachers have to write their own classes' exams, and don't have enough time to proof-read them or even test them out on sample classes in advance. Inevitably, some poorly written questions get past the teacher. The teacher corrects the problem later by giving credit as necessary, throwing questions out, or whatever.

What message does this send to students? Unfortunately, students come to believe that the answers to *all* tests are open for discussion and debate, that *all* questions are written by stressed-out teachers who work with specific students in mind, that *any* question is potentially flawed and open to interpretation.

Then, when these students take the SAT, things get crazy. They can never settle on anything, because they've been taught that the proper approach to a multiple-choice test is to look for any way at all to bend every answer until it's correct. They mark wrong answers left and right—usually they manage to eliminate one or two choices, and then the rest all seem equally correct, so they take a stab at each question and move on to the next.

As we know from our discussion on guessing, most of these students are wrong way more often than they think, and they lose a lot of points.

And the thing of it is, they never even realize what's holding them back.

Two Key Realizations

If you're going to do well on the SAT, you have to realize two things. First, you have to know that the SAT is a totally objective test, and that every single question has only one right answer. This is not like a test you take in high school. Those tests are written by one or two people, usually with very little review. The SAT, on the other hand, is written by teams of people. Before a question appears on the SAT, it's been reviewed by experts and tested on real test-takers. SAT questions are basically bullet-proof. No matter how much it might seem otherwise, every question on the SAT has only one good answer. You can't approach it like you approach a high school multiple-choice test, where anything goes and you'll get a chance to argue your point later on.

Once you come to accept that, the second thing you have to realize is that you—specifically YOU, the person reading this right now—can find the answer to every SAT question if you learn what to look for. You can. And with the right practice, you will.

So let's wrap this whole thing up nice and simple:

1. The only way to do really well on the SAT is to mark the correct answer to most of the questions on the test.

2. The only reliable way to mark the correct answer consistently is to be able to identify it consistently.

3. Before you can identify the correct answer consistently, you have to know and believe that there will always be one correct answer for every question—if you're open to the possibility that more than one answer will be correct, you won't be strict about eliminating answers by using the rules and patterns of the test.

4. Most students never realize this, and as a result they never maximize their performance. Instead, they treat the SAT like a regular high school test, which is a huge mistake for the reasons we just discussed.

Now that we've established this very important concept, we have to talk about something that comes up often in testing situations . . .

What Do You Do When It Looks Like There Might Be Two Right Answers To A Question?

Even though you know there can only be one answer to every SAT question, there will be times on the test when you think more than one answer might be correct. It happens to everybody. It happens to me, and it will happen to you. When it does happen, you must immediately recognize that you've done something wrong—you missed a key word in the question, you left off a minus sign, something like that.

There are two ways to fix this situation. One way is to cut your losses and go on to the next question, planning to return to the difficult question later on, when your head has cleared. This is what I usually do.

The second way is to keep working on the difficult question. Try and figure out what might be causing the confusion while the question is still fresh in your mind, and resolve the issue right then and there. I'm not such a big fan of this one because I tend to find that things are clearer to me when I return to a question after skipping it. But some people find that moving on without answering a question just means they have to familiarize themselves with it all over again when they come back, and they prefer to stay focused on a particular question until they either find the right answer or decide to give up on it for good.

To see which type of person you are, just do what comes naturally, and experiment a little bit with both approaches.

Conclusion

The main thing to remember, for every question, is that there is only one correct answer. If we read a question and we think we see more than one possible answer to a question, we're wrong. That's it—no discussion.

To become successful on the SAT, you MUST realize that every multiple-choice question on the SAT has exactly one correct answer, and you must train yourself to find the correct answer every time. This isn't a regular high school test. Don't treat it like one.

(I realize, of course, that every once in a while an SAT question is successfully protested. This happens with such rarity that it's best to proceed as though it never happened at all. The odds are overwhelmingly in favor every SAT question you ever see being totally objective and valid.)

Where To Find "Missing Points"

"Nothing is less productive than to make more efficient what should not be done at all."
- Peter Drucker

Most test-takers have some idea of a target score that will make them competitive for their target schools, or for certain scholarship programs, and those target scores are usually somewhere in the range of 1500 to 2250, depending on the student's goals and situation (of course, there are some people whose target scores might be higher or lower, as well).

Most people try to hit their target scores by improving in the areas where they're weakest, and that's certainly understandable. But I would recommend that you also consider working to improve the areas where you're *strongest* first, for 3 reasons:

1) People usually feel more comfortable working on their strong areas, so there's less stress.
2) The mistakes you're making in your strong areas are more likely to be things related to "careless errors," or things you can correct with minimal effort.
3) The closer you are to the top of the scoring scale, the bigger the impact of each new question that you answer correctly. In other words, if you're scoring around a 710 in the Math section, then answering one or two more questions correctly might increase your math score by 30 points or more. But if you're scoring around a 520, then answering another one or two questions correctly might only raise your score 10 points. This is the result of the norming process that the College Board uses to "curve" the test scores.

So if you find yourself short of your goal score, it might be a good idea to focus first on making your strong areas even stronger, rather than struggling to bring your weak areas up.

But What If I Need To Meet A Target Score Within A Single Section?

Some test-takers don't just need to reach a certain overall score; sometimes schools are looking for scores on individual sections to meet particular cutoffs. But you can still use the strategy of improving on your strong areas even in these situations, because every section has different question types, and most students are naturally more inclined to some questions types than to others. I would recommend focusing on your preferred question types until you're basically perfect at answering them before going on to question types that you don't like as much.

As an example, if you need to raise your Reading score by 50 points, you could choose to start by focusing either on Sentence Completion questions or on Passage-Based Reading questions. If you dislike the Sentence Completion questions, then it's probably going to be more productive for you to focus on perfecting the Passage questions. Even if you're missing an average of 7 Sentence Completion questions on each practice test but only 4 Passage questions, it's probably easier to address the 4 Passage questions before turning to the Sentence ones, because it's easier to make progress on the parts of the section you enjoy more. This could reduce (or even eliminate) the need to make progress on other parts of the section. If you need to improve your Math score, on the other hand, then you should decide whether it's easier for you to improve on the multiple-choice questions or the Student-Produced Response questions. If you need to raise your Writing score, then you should decide whether to focus on the Essay, or on a type of multiple-choice question. And so on.

Time Management

". . . to realize the unimportance of time is the gate of wisdom."
- Bertrand Russell

To judge from my experience with new clients, time management is an issue that seems to affect the majority of untrained test-takers. There are a lot of factors that contribute to problems with time management, such as reading speed and anxiety, but the biggest and most common factor is a serious misunderstanding of the test in the first place.

Let me explain what I mean.

If you were to answer every single SAT question in the fastest possible way, even with average reading speed, you'd spend no more than 30 seconds on any given question. (If that sounds crazy, it will make a lot more sense after you've read the parts of this Black Book that deal with specific question types.) Even if we only answered *half* the questions on a section in less than 30 seconds each, we'd still have a lot more time than most test-takers end up with.

So the biggest problem facing most test-takers with time-management issues is that they're doing the questions very inefficiently. There's a reason that people who score in the 99th percentile often have tons of extra time on every section, and the reason is NOT that those high-scorers are super-geniuses who process everything ten times faster than the rest of us. The reason is that those people are doing less work to answer each question because they know how to handle each question with minimal effort.

For example, they know that Passage-Based Reading questions never actually require us to read 80 lines of text to answer a single question. On Math questions, they know that applying formulas is usually unnecessary and slow. They know which types of phrases to avoid on the Writing section, and which ones to pick. And so on.

So if you feel like you're doing a ton of work on most of the SAT questions you run into and running out of time as a result, then the first thing you should do is take a look at the processes you're using to answer your questions and figure out how you can streamline it using the ideas in this book.

Of course, other factors can also affect time management. Let's take a look at some of them.

Reading Speed

Some test-takers are naturally slower at reading than others, but most people find they read fast enough for the SAT if they're approaching questions in the most efficient way. As a general rule of thumb, if you don't have problems with the speed of your reading in your classes in school, then you probably read fast enough to do very well on the SAT if you're using the right strategies.

For what it's worth, most of us can make some kind of improvement on our reading speed just by making a conscious effort to read faster. I know that might sound simplistic, but it's true. If you constantly remind yourself to read faster, you'll find yourself reading faster. It's a bit like walking—most of us could walk noticeably faster if we tried.

If you have a serious issue with reading speed that can be diagnosed by a professional, then it might be a good idea to try to petition the College Board for extra time when you take the test.

Nerves

A lot of people get nervous at the thought of taking the SAT, and some people freeze up when they're nervous. If this kind of thing is affecting your time management, there are two different ways to attack it. First, you can work on consciously channeling your nervousness into productive energy. Let it make you read more carefully, or drive you to consider a new angle on a question that's troubling you. Second, you can recognize that the root of your nervousness is probably a feeling of frustration or even powerlessness when it comes to the SAT—and the best way to beat that feeling is by learning how the test works so you can see that it's actually not scary at all. It's just weird, and detail-oriented.

Wasting Time On Tough Questions

Most people who run out of time on the SAT try to answer all the questions in a section in order. This is a huge mistake, since some questions will be easier for you than others, and since every question in a section counts for the same number of raw points as any other question in that section.

When you run into a question you can't answer quickly, you should skip it and move on to other questions that are easier for you. You can always come back to the harder questions later. There's no sense in staring at question 6 for a full three minutes when you haven't even looked at question 7; in those three minutes, you might have been able to answer 7, 8, and 9 correctly.

Personally, when I look at a new question I give myself about 10 seconds to figure out how to approach it. If I can't work out an approach in that time, I move on to the next question without thinking twice. (Just to be clear, I'm not saying that I *solve* every question in less than 10 seconds; I'm saying that I give myself about 10 seconds to see if I can come up with an approach that will *eventually* solve it.)

If I've looked at a question for a full 10 seconds and I still have no idea how to attack it, then I've probably misunderstood some part of it, and I should move on to another question that makes sense to me. I can always come back to the harder question after I've gone through the section and answered everything I can figure out.

Recap

While every student is unique, most time-management issues come down to some combination of the ideas I've mentioned in this brief section. But I really want to stress that the most widespread cause of difficulty for most students is that they're addressing the test in the wrong way, and doing far too much work to answer each question. The best thing you can do to improve your time management is to work on your *efficiency*, not your processing *speed*. If you focus on trying to understand and apply the ideas in this book, you'll probably find that your time management issues largely disappear on their own.

The "Big Secret" Of The SAT

"There are no secrets that time does not reveal."
- Jean Racine

Before we get into all the strategies and advice for specific areas of the test, I want to start out by sharing something very important with you: the "secret" of the SAT.

Here it is: The SAT frustrates so many test-takers because it asks about very basic things in very strange (but repetitive) ways. The simple reason so many people struggle with the test is that they're looking at it in completely the wrong way.

Let's examine why this is.

Imagine that you're the College Board, which is the company that makes and administers the SAT. Colleges use your test scores to help them figure out which applicants to admit, and they only trust your test because it consistently provides them with reliable measurements. So how do you go about making a test that can be given to millions of students a year and still compare them all in a meaningful way, despite the wide variations in their backgrounds and abilities?

You can't just make a super-difficult test, because that won't really provide useful information to the colleges who rely on you. For example, you can't just focus the math test on advanced ideas from calculus and statistics, because most of the test-takers have never taken those subjects—and, even if they had, the results from your test wouldn't really tell the colleges anything they couldn't already learn from students' transcripts. And you can't make a test that relies on arbitrary interpretation or argumentation, because then the test results wouldn't correlate to anything meaningful on a large scale, and colleges wouldn't be able to rely on the data from your test.

So, if you're the College Board, you need to design the SAT so that it avoids testing advanced concepts and so that it avoids arbitrary interpretation. Otherwise, your test will be useless for colleges, because colleges want to use a test that measures something meaningful about every applicant in the same way every time.

In other words, you have to come up with an objective test of basic ideas.

But then you have another problem: if you give a traditional objective test of basic ideas to millions of college-bound, motivated students, a lot of them are going to do really well on it—and then your results will be useless for a different reason, because there will be so many high scores that colleges won't be able to use the results in their admissions decisions.

So how do you solve this problem?

The College Board solves this problem by combining basic ideas in weird, but repetitive, ways. The result is that doing well on the SAT involves the ability to look at a new test question and then figure out how it follows the rules that all SAT questions of that type must follow. And that's what this book will teach you to do.

This is why there are so many people who do so well in advanced classes in high school but have a relatively hard time with the SAT: the SAT tests simpler stuff in a stranger way. It basically requires a totally different skill-set from high school or college. (You may be wondering why some students do well on both the SAT and school. These people are just good at both skill-sets. It's a bit like being good at both football and wrestling: there's enough of an overlap that some people are naturally good at both, but enough of a difference that many people struggle with one or the other. Or both.)

Now that you know the SAT's big secret, the rest of this book—and the SAT itself—will probably make a lot more sense to you. This book is basically a road map to all the weird things the SAT does. It will teach you how to navigate the SAT's bizarre design, and how to exploit the many weaknesses inherent in that design.

SAT Passage-Based Reading

"Education . . . has produced a vast population able to read but unable to distinguish what is worth reading."
- G. M. Trevelyan

Overview and Important Reminders for SAT Passage-Based Reading

Students often tell me that Passage-Based Reading questions are their least favorite questions on the SAT. A lot of people think these questions are too subjective to be part of a standardized test—they think that questions about an author's intentions can be answered in more than one way, so it's unfair to write multiple-choice tests about them.

Fortunately, this isn't the case. The answer to an SAT Passage-Based Reading question is every bit as clear and definite as the answer to an SAT Math question. In this section, I'll show you how natural test-takers identify those answers.

But first, I want to say that again, because it's really important. I'll put it in caps, too. And center it, even:

THE ANSWER TO A READING QUESTION IS ALWAYS AS CLEAR AND DEFINITE AND
OBJECTIVELY PREDICTABLE AS THE ANSWER TO A MATH QUESTION.

If the reading questions required arbitrary interpretation, the SAT and PSAT would produce meaningless results, because there would be no objective basis for rewarding one answer choice and punishing the others. If the results from the SAT were meaningless, then colleges would stop using them. (For more on the role of standardized tests in the admissions process and the implications of that role for us test-takers, check out the article on the purpose of standardized testing at my blog, www.TestingIsEasy.com.)

You see, the main problem with SAT reading is that it requires you to look at a passage in a way that's totally different from the approach you would use in an English class. In the typical English class, you're rewarded for coming up with as many interpretations of a passage as you possibly can; every single interpretation that doesn't directly contradict the reading is welcomed with open arms.

But that approach clearly won't work for a multiple-choice question with only one correct answer. So on the SAT, you have to read everything as literally as you possibly can, without adding any of your own interpretation at all. (We'll get into this in a lot more detail below.)

After taking my class, most of my students change their minds about Passage-Based Reading questions. Actually, they often end up thinking that the Passage-Based Reading questions are the easiest ones on the entire test, and I tend to agree with them.

The Big Secret Of SAT Passage-Based Reading

In order for the College Board to develop Passage-Based Reading questions that would function properly on a multiple-choice test, it had to overcome a pretty big problem: it needed a way to ask questions about literature that weren't subjective, so that each question would only have one legitimate, objective answer.

So the College Board had to find a way to eliminate interpretation from the process of answering questions about a text. That way, they could write questions that would ask students to talk about a text while still using the multiple choice format in a valid, meaningful way.

If you think about it, there's only way you can possibly talk about a text without interpreting it—and this one way of talking about a text is the big secret of the SAT Critical Reading section. It applies to both the Passage-Based Reading questions and the Sentence Completion questions, as we'll see later on.

The only way to talk about a text without interpreting it is *to restate it without changing the meaning*. (I put that in italics because it's really important.)

In other words, believe it or not, we'll find that the correct answer to every single question on the Critical Reading section of the SAT is spelled out somewhere on the page.

Yes, really.

(At this point, if you've ever taken the SAT before, or ever had any kind of traditional SAT preparation, you're probably shaking your head angrily and cursing me for lying to you about the test. But trust me on this: the correct answers to SAT Critical Reading questions always function by restating relevant ideas from the text, and the incorrect answers are always wrong because they fail to restate ideas from the text.)

This might sound a little ridiculous, but let's think about this from the College Board's standpoint:

1. The College Board needs the SAT to include multiple-choice questions about passages.

2. The College Board needs to avoid any ambiguity and interpretation in order for the SAT to fulfill its role as a legitimate, reliable standardized test. (See my blog article on the purpose of standardized tests for more on this, at www.TestingIsEasy.com)

3. The only way to discuss a text without interpreting it is to restate it.

All of this leads to one conclusion:

4. The College Board has designed the correct answer choices on the SAT Critical Reading section to restate the texts.

At this point, you might be wondering something very important: if it really is as simple as I say, how can it be that so many intelligent people take the test every year without ever noticing that the correct answer to each question says exactly the same thing as the text they're reading?

This is a very good question. There are five reasons why most test-takers never notice how Passage-Based Reading questions work, and you need to know them are so you can prevent them from affecting you negatively:

1. Most students aren't even looking for an answer choice to be stated directly in the text.

Most SAT-takers are used to analyzing everything they read the way an English teacher would want, so when they read the passages on the SAT they try to analyze them automatically. In other words, most test-takers wouldn't even notice if an answer choice restated the text, because it never occurs to them to look for that. This is just one more way in which most test-takers are their own worst enemies.

2. The College Board deliberately phrases questions to make you think you should use subjective interpretation to find the answer.

If you've ever seen any real College Board reading questions, you've definitely seen that they use words like "primarily," "probably," "suggests," and so on, like this: "The author's use of the word 'miscreant' in line 14 primarily suggests which of the following?" The College Board deliberately phrases questions in this way to mislead you and get you to interpret the text. They want you to think that two or three answer choices might all be equally reasonable. So we have to learn to ignore words like "primarily" and "suggests." That's right: we ignore those words completely. When I read a question like "In line 10, the author primarily suggests which of the following?" I treat that question as though it said, "Which of the following ideas appears directly in the text somewhere close to line 10?"

3. We sometimes have to be extremely particular about the exact meanings of words, both in the text and in the answer choice.

The College Board can get very picky about the specific meanings of words. As a result, test-takers often conclude, incorrectly, that more than one answer choice restates the passage. One classic example of this from a real SAT involved a text that mentioned dolphins sharing certain abilities with "very few animals"—one of the wrong answers said dolphins had "unique" talents. But the answer with "unique" was wrong, because the word "unique" doesn't just mean that something is rare: in the strictest sense of the word, "unique" means that something is literally "one-of-a-kind," and unlike anything else. In a school setting, if you used the word "unique" in a loose way to mean "rare," most teachers wouldn't notice or care. But on the SAT, the difference between "unique" and "rare" can be the difference between right and wrong. So if you want to make a perfect score on the Reading section, you'll have to learn to *attack* every single word that you read, and you'll have to make sure you're only considering *exactly* what the word means, instead of working from your generalized assumptions about what it might mean, or what you think it implies. The College Board splits hairs when it comes to these things, and if you want to score high you'll have to learn to split them too.

4. Test-takers are sometimes mistaken about what words mean.

No matter how strong your vocabulary is, there are some words that you use incorrectly. I promise you this—it happens to all of us. Sometimes the differences are subtle. For example, I once had a student who mistakenly thought that "shrewd" had a strong negative connotation. He correctly understood that it involved being clever and intelligent, but incorrectly thought that it indicated a certain type of calculating evil. For this reason, he didn't pick an answer choice with the word "shrewd" since he didn't see anything in the text that reflected a negative connotation, and he missed the question. On the other hand, sometimes the differences are huge, and a little embarrassing—I always thought the word "pied" meant something like "renowned" or "famous," because of the story of the Pied Piper. But it actually means that a person wears clothes made of patches and rags. Needless to say, I drew a complete blank when a test question mentioned the word "pied" and my understanding of that word didn't match with anything on the page. Don't think that memorizing vocabulary words will help correct these issues—for reasons I'll discuss later, memorizing vocab might even contribute to making more of them. Just know that it's something you might be confronted with at some point. If you're looking at a question and none of the answer choices seems to restate the passage, the bottom line is that you've made a mistake somewhere.

5. The College Board has a special rule that it sometimes invokes.

On the Critical Reading section of the SAT, the College Board will treat two ideas expressed in quick succession as though they are perfectly synonymous; if there is a negating word between those two ideas, the College Board will treat those ideas as though they are perfect antonyms. This probably doesn't make any sense right now, but we'll explore it in more detail later on. I just wanted to mention this issue now to make you aware of it. (By the way, this issue only comes up a few times at most on any given test, so it's not something you need to be tremendously concerned about.)

So those are the five major reasons that most test-takers never realize that the correct answers to Passage-Based Reading questions function by directly restating the relevant portion of the text. I'll list them again briefly, for review:

1. Test-takers aren't even looking for restatements in the first place.
2. The College Board deliberately misleads you by using subjective phrasing.
3. You have to be extremely particular about what words actually mean.
4. Sometimes your understanding of a word you think you know might be flawed.
5. The College Board treats two ideas as synonyms if they're stated one right after another.

Now that we've covered the Big Secret Of SAT Reading, which is that the correct answers to all SAT Reading questions must be spelled out on the page, you might be wondering what the wrong answers do.

Well, simply put, the wrong answers are the ones that don't restate the passage. And the ways that they fail to restate the passage are standardized, just like every other important detail of the test, so it can be very beneficial for us to know the various ways that wrong answers tend to relate back to the text on the SAT. Let's take a look at those in the next section.

What Do Wrong Answers Do?

We've already seen that the right answer to a Passage-Based Reading question on the SAT will restate the ideas from the relevant portion of the passage. But what will wrong answers do?

Broadly speaking, wrong answers are wrong because they fail to restate the relevant portion of the passage. But there are a handful of ways that the College Board creates these wrong answers—that is, there are certain specific ways in which wrong answers fail to restate the passage exactly. And it can be very helpful for us to know what those ways are.

For the purposes of illustration, we'll use a fake question and fake wrong answers. In other words, what you see below did NOT come from a real College Board source. It came from my head. But I constructed it in the same ways that the College Board constructs its wrong answers. And later on, I'll demonstrate my methods in action against real questions from the College Board's Blue Book (remember, you should only ever practice with real test questions from the College Board itself).

Okay, so let's pretend our fake sample question reads like this:

Example Question:

> **According to the citation, research suggests that Benjamin Franklin invented bifocals because**

And let's pretend that the relevant citation is this part of the text:

Example Citation:

> . . . Researchers have shown that Benjamin
> Franklin's sister was visually impaired, which
> might explain the amount of energy that Franklin
> invested in the invention of bifocals. . . .

(By the way, as far as I know, Benjamin Franklin's sister had nothing to do with the invention of bifocals. In fact, I don't even know if he had a sister at all. It's an example—just go with it.)

Here are some of the various wrong answer types we might see for this kind of question.

Wrong Answer Type 1: Extra Information

In this wrong answer we find some information that was mentioned in the citation, and some information that was never mentioned in the citation at all.

Example:

> his sister was having difficulty seeing the
> equipment that she used to run her dress shop.

In this example, the wrong answer adds information about the specific problems that the sister was having with her vision. The text never said that Franklin's sister was specifically having trouble seeing equipment in a dress shop—just that she was having trouble seeing in general.

Wrong Answer Type 2: Direct Contradiction

This type of wrong answer directly contradicts something in the citation.

Example:

> his sister's perfect vision served as an inspiration.

Here, the wrong answer choice contradicts the cited fact that the sister has poor vision.

Wrong Answer Type 3: Complete Irrelevance

This type of wrong answer has absolutely nothing to do with the cited text. These wrong answers can actually be very tempting to a lot of test-takers. People can't believe the SAT would offer them an answer choice that's obviously wrong, but that's exactly what the test does. Remember, too, that a lot of test-takers are interpreting the text as though it were a piece of literature in an English class, and most students are taught in school not to reject any interpretation completely. So the College Board exploits your natural tendency to give the benefit of the doubt to anything that doesn't directly contradict the text by providing some wrong answers that have nothing to do with the text whatsoever.

Example:

> he wanted to revolutionize the way society viewed
> glasses.

This wrong answer has nothing to do with anything mentioned in the citation. Once we know that the correct answer must be spelled out directly in the passage, it's usually pretty easy to eliminate these irrelevant choices from consideration—but for the majority of test-takers, who have no idea how the SAT works, these kinds of irrelevant answer choices can often be quite tempting.

Wrong Answer Type 4: Confused Concepts

This type of wrong answer uses a lot of the ideas mentioned in the citation, but messes up the relationships between them. The College Board includes these types of wrong answers because they want to trap people who remember major concepts from the passage but who don't bother to pay attention to the details—this is just one more example of the ways in which small details play a tremendously important role on the SAT.

Example:

his sister invested in a cure for his vision problems.

This made-up example mentions the ideas of the sister, the investing, the vision problems, and the idea that the bifocals would correct those problems, but it messes up the relationships among those ideas. Students who don't read carefully often fall for these types of wrong answers.

Wrong Answer Type 5: Factual Accuracy

Sometimes the College Board will throw in a wrong answer that might be factually accurate, but that isn't specifically reflected in the text. This type of wrong answer doesn't appear too often, but if you do a few practice tests you'll probably run into it at least once or twice.

Example:

he was tired of having to switch between different types of glasses.

Students who know why Franklin really invented bifocals, but who don't know how the SAT actually works, might be tempted by such a factually accurate statement.

Wrong Answer Type 6: Off By One Word

This might be one of the most dangerous and insidious wrong answer types when it comes to trapping test-takers who know how the test works. For this type of wrong answer, the College Board provides a phrase that mirrors the text exactly—except for one or two words. Even when test-takers know they have to find answer choices that restate the passage, they can still fall for these kinds of wrong answers if they're not in the habit of constantly attacking every single word they read.

Example:

his sister had a congenital vision problem.

In this wrong answer, the ideas of "sister" and "had a vision problem" directly restate the phrase "Franklin's sister was visually impaired" from the fake citation. But the word "congenital" isn't reflected at all in the citation, so this answer choice would be wrong if this were a real SAT question. Remember that you have to look for a textual justification for every concept in every answer choice.

Wrong Answer Type 7: Valid Interpretation

The College Board frequently creates wrong answers that would be valid, defensible interpretations of the text in a literature class. Students often fall for these types of wrong answers if they're still mistakenly approaching the test in a subjective, interpretive way, instead of in the correct, objective way.

Example:

> **Franklin loved his sister and wanted to make her
> life easier.**

In this imaginary example, the answer choice reflects the fact that the text mentions Franklin's sister's eye problems as a motivation for the invention. But the answer choice adds an interpretation when it speculates that Franklin was motivated by love and a desire to ease his sister's suffering. While that would certainly be a plausible interpretation of the passage, *any* kind of interpretation—whether plausible or not—will be a wrong answer. Since the text didn't mention Franklin loving his sister, we're not allowed to assume that he did.

Conclusion

These wrong-answer types, or combinations of them, will account for most of the wrong answers you'll encounter in SAT Passage-Based Reading questions. Basically, they all boil down to the idea that wrong answers provide information that differs from the information found in the relevant portion of the text, while the right answer for each question will restate concepts from the relevant portion of the text.

Now that we've explored the types of wrong answers we're likely to encounter on Passage-Based Reading questions, you're probably eager to see how we actually go about answering questions. But before we get into that stuff, there's just one more thing we have to talk about: how to read passages on the SAT.

How To Read Passages On The SAT

One of the most common issues people have with the Passage-Based Reading questions is the issue of actually reading the passage. Another popular question is how to take notes on the passages.

So let's talk about those things. My answers are pretty simple, really:

1) You can read the passage in any way you want, as long as it leaves you enough time to finish the section. You can even skip reading the passage if you want, and just refer back to portions of the text on a question-by-question basis.
2) You shouldn't take any kind of notes whatsoever on the passage.

Like most good SAT advice, those two tactics contradict most of what you may have heard from teachers, tutors, and prep books. So let's explore them a little. (If you haven't already read my previous remarks on what makes right answers right and wrong answers wrong on Passage-Based Reading questions, I would recommend you go back and do that before proceeding.)

When we talked about correct answer choices for these questions, we indicated that they restate elements of the relevant portion of the original text. This is necessary because the College Board needs to have an objective, legitimate reason to say that one choice is correct and the others are incorrect, and the only real way to do that is to have the correct answer be the only choice that restates the passage.

This means there are always specific words and phrases in the passage that correspond to the correct answer. It also means that, technically, *the only portion of the text you need to read for any question is the specific portion that contains the ideas restated in the correct answer.*

So, in theory, if it were somehow possible to know in advance which portions of the text were going to contain the key phrases restated in the correct answer, we could avoid reading the rest of the passage.

In other words, there is literally *no benefit whatsoever* in trying to get an overall impression of the passage, because there will never be a real SAT question in which the only way to find the correct answer is to make a general inference from the entire text. (To be sure, there are some students who try to draw inferences from the text and have some success, but it's not the most efficient approach, and it's never *necessary*. We can always find the answer for every question spelled out somewhere in the text.)

For this reason, it doesn't really matter which specific method you use to read the text. All that matters is that you can locate the relevant portion of the text so that you can figure out which answer choice restates it as quickly as possible without sacrificing accuracy.

In general, there are three ways to do this, and I recommend you play around with them to see what works best for you. Again, you can mix, match, or modify these approaches as you see fit, so long as you come up with a system that lets you find the relevant portion of the text quickly enough to allow you to complete the entire section within the time limit.

The first approach is the old standard of simply reading the passage before attempting the questions. This is by far the most widely used approach. It can definitely work, as long as you don't read too slowly to finish the section before time is called. One note, though—if you read the passage first, don't worry about trying to understand it as an organic whole. *Definitely* don't take notes on it, for reasons we'll get into in a moment. Just give it a thorough once-over. You're going to have to come back to specific parts of it later to verify which answer choices are correct anyway, so just read it once and move on to the questions.

The second-most popular approach is to skip reading the passage and just move straight to the questions. Then you start with the questions that have specific line citations. For each citation question, you go back to the relevant portion of the text, read that portion, and then consider the answer choices. When you've finished all the citation questions, you'll generally have a good idea of how the passage is structured. Then you move on to the questions with no citations. Many of those questions will mention key concepts that you'll recall from the citation questions, so you'll know where to go back in the passage and locate those portions of the text again. When a question has no citation and also doesn't refer to something that you've already read, you can simply skim the portions of the text that you haven't read yet to find the relevant key terms, and proceed accordingly.

And that brings us to the third type of approach, which involves lightly skimming the passage before approaching the questions, in order to construct a rough mental map of where different terms and concepts appear in the passage. I want to stress that, so I'll say it again: in this type of skimming, you're just moving your eyes through the text quickly, NOT trying to understand the text, but trying to get a rough idea of where various concepts appear in the text so you can use your 'roadmap' for later. This way, if a question lacks a citation, you can look at the concepts in the question and in the answer choices and recall those concepts from your skimming. This allows you to zero in on the relevant part of the text and then find your answers. Of course, you can always re-skim if you need to.

Again, it's important to be aware of these different approaches, and to play around with them during your practice sessions so you can figure out what works best for you. Different students will prefer different approaches based on their personalities and skills.

You may be wondering why I'm opposed to the idea of taking notes on the text. The reason is simple, actually: taking notes involves interpreting the text, and interpreting the text isn't helpful on the SAT. As we keep discussing, the correct answer to every single question is spelled out somewhere on the page, so there's no need for you to interpret what you're reading.

But, above all, don't lose sight of the fact that the answer to every real SAT Passage-Based Reading question will be spelled out somewhere on the page.

The General Process For Answering Passage-Based Reading Questions

Most Passage-Based Reading questions can be answered with a fairly simple process, which we'll discuss now. Later, I'll show you how to answer other types of questions that might seem a bit odd. (Actually, the process we'll use for *all* Passage-Based Reading questions is basically the same process with a few very minor, very occasional modifications, but I'll present them as unique scenarios because most students have already been taught to see them that way by other tutors or books.)

Don't worry if this process feels uncomfortable or strange when you first read it. In later sections, we'll go through a lot of Blue Book questions together, and you can see the process in action for yourself. You could also watch the videos at www.SATprepVideos.com to get a feel for the process.

For the moment, we're only going to talk about questions with line citations. Then we'll cover the modifications for questions without them.

1. Read or skim the passage if you want to.

There are a lot of ways to approach reading the actual passage, as we discussed in the earlier section. Pick whichever approach works for you, whether it's one of the ones I explained above or your own approach.

2. Read the question, noting the citation. Then read the citation.

If the citation is a line citation and the cited line picks up in the middle of a sentence, go back up to the beginning of that sentence and start there. (It may also help to read the sentence before or after the sentences in the citation, but this often isn't necessary.)

3. Find four wrong answers.

It's generally easiest to find wrong answers first. For one thing, there are four times as many of them; for another, it's usually easier to identify ways that answer choices differ from the text than it is to feel confident that a choice says exactly the same thing as the text. Expect to find that most (and very possibly all) of the wrong answers you find will fit into one of the types I talked about earlier.

If you end up not being able to eliminate 4 choices, then you're making some kind of mistake. It might be that you've misread the text or the question. It might be that your understanding of one of the words you read is slightly (or very) inaccurate. It's often the case that people who are left with 2 or 3 answer choices that seem to restate the text probably aren't being picky enough about sticking to *exactly* what each word means to ensure an accurate restatement.

If you end up eliminating all 5 answer choices from consideration, then, again, you've made some kind of mistake, but it might be a different kind of mistake. You may have been referring to the wrong part of the passage, for instance. You might also have misread or misunderstood one or more words.

4. Look at the remaining answer choice.

See if the remaining answer choice fits the right answer pattern (in other words, see if it restates concepts and relationships from the relevant portion of the text). If it does, that's great.

If you still can't identify one choice that clearly restates the passage and four choices that don't restate the passage, you'll need to consider the prospect of guessing. I would advise the vast majority of students NOT to guess on SAT Passage-Based Reading questions, for the reasons discussed in the article in this book called "A Word on Guessing: Don't."

And that's it, believe it or not—the process for Passage-Based Reading questions typically isn't as complex as the processes for other question types can be.

As I noted above, the simple process we just went through works on all line-citation questions exactly as described. In a broader sense, it works on all Passage-Based Reading questions. But let's look at some specific, small adjustments we might make if the question isn't exactly a classic line-citation question.

What About Questions Without Citations?

When a question has no citation, very little actually changes in our approach to it. The answer to the question is still going to be spelled out somewhere in the passage, but now it might be anywhere in the passage, rather than being localized to a few lines.

Let me say that again: even though there's no specific citation, the answer is still going to be spelled out *somewhere*. You should NOT try to answer a question like this by making a broad inference from the overall passage that isn't directly supported by actual phrases from the text.

The only challenging thing that separates a question like this from a question with a citation is that it can sometimes be harder to locate the part of the text with the answer.

If the text is very short, we can probably just go ahead and read the whole thing without too much difficulty. If the text is longer, I'd recommend saving any general questions for the end—in other words, I would skip around and do all the citation questions first, then come back and pick up the more general questions. I do this because answering the citation questions will typically cause me to go back through most of the text, and I'll often find that the answers to general, non-citation questions are right there in the citations for other questions. So I can save some time and energy by doing the citation questions first.

Even if answering the citation questions doesn't actually cause me to read the part of the text that contains the answer to a general question, I can still save a little time because I don't need to re-read or skim those areas of the text when I go back to find the answers.

Again, the critical thing to remember with general passage questions is that the answer is always clearly spelled out in black and white somewhere within the passage, even though the question lacks a citation. There is literally never a moment on a real SAT in which the only way to answer a question is to draw a general inference from the overall 'feeling' of the text. If there were any questions that required those kinds of inferences, the reliability of the SAT would disappear.

What About "Tone, Mood, And Attitude" Questions?

Sometimes the College Board asks you about the tone or the mood of a passage, or about the author's attitude, or about how the passage might best be characterized, and so on. Test-takers are usually very tempted to try to answer these kinds of questions in the same ways they would tend to answer them in a literature class: they usually just read the passage and make a subjective assessment of how it makes them feel, and then look for an answer choice that describes their subjective feelings.

But, as we have mentioned repeatedly, the SAT would not be a valid, reliable standardized test if it relied on subjectivity and inference.

So even for the "tone, mood, and attitude" questions, the correct answer is going to be spelled out somewhere in the text. For example, if the correct answer is that a particular quotation is "nostalgic," then the passage would need to say something like "Tom kept thinking about the happy days of his past, and longing for them to return," because that would reflect the definition of the term "nostalgic." If the correct answer is going to be something like "enthusiastic," then the text would need to say something like "Everybody was very excited for the project to begin, and couldn't wait to enjoy the results," because that's what "enthusiastic" means.

So when you answer these kinds of questions, you're still just going to be looking through the text very carefully to match phrases in the text with one of the answer choices—just like you do for all of the Passage-Based Reading questions, basically.

What About "Similar Situation" Questions?

Some questions ask you to choose the answer choice that describes a situation that is similar to a situation described in the text. These are the only Passage-Based Reading questions on the test that can really be said not to involve direct paraphrasing, in the strictest sense of that term, because the correct answer will typically mention concepts that aren't in the passage.

But these questions still shouldn't be too difficult to answer if you stick very, very closely to the concepts in the text, and find an answer choice that demonstrates the same *relationships* among the concepts it includes. So we're still going to be reading the text very carefully, and we're still going to be reading the answer choices very carefully, and we're still going to be looking for the answer choice that echoes the text.

For instance, imagine that the text says, "Steven was surprised to discover that Lauren had never learned to throw a baseball, since she was so athletic in general," and the question asks us to pick the answer choice that describes a similar situation. The correct answer might say something like "a woman is stunned when she finds out that her friend, who is a great musician, has never learned to play the piano." In this hypothetical scenario, both the text and the correct answer would describe someone being surprised to find out that another person has a lot of talent in a particular field but has never learned a particular skill within that field.

Don't worry too much about these types of questions. For one thing, reading closely and paying attention to relationships will make these questions pretty easy. For another thing, there aren't many questions like this on any given test, anyway.

What About "Except" Questions?

Some questions seem to take the normal question-answering process and turn it on its head, often by using the word "except." Such a question might say something like "all of the following are found in Passage 1 EXCEPT . . .".

For a question like this, we're still going to read the relevant portion of the text carefully, but now the correct answer is going to be the only choice that does NOT appear in the passage.

It's always important to make sure you read all five answer choices for every question (it helps you catch mistakes). But it's ESPECIALLY important on these "except" questions because students often accidentally forget about the "except" and just choose the first choice that *does* appear in the text, and get the question wrong. If you accidentally overlook the word "except" but still read all five answer choices, you have a better chance of noticing your mistake.

What About "Vocabulary In Context" Questions?

Some questions ask you how a word is used in the passage. They often read something like this: "In line 14, the word 'sad' most nearly means . . ."

For these questions, just like for all the others, we're ultimately looking for an answer choice that restates something from the passage—and not just one that restates the original word in the question, because usually all the choices will do that in one sense or another. Instead, we need a word that restates an idea from the surrounding text. In the imaginary question above, if the text said, "The dilapidated old warehouse was in a sad state by the time the inspector closed it for safety reasons," then the correct answer would be something like "worn out," because "worn out" means the same thing as "dilapidated" in this context. In this hypothetical scenario, a choice like "weepy" wouldn't be supported by the text, even though it can be a synonym for the word "sad" in other situations.

What About Humor, Metaphor, And Irony?

Sometimes an answer choice will mention the idea of humor, metaphor, or irony. In order to evaluate these kinds of answer choices along SAT lines, we have to know that the College Board uses these terms in very particular ways that don't really reflect their use in everyday speech.

When the College Board refers to part of a passage as "humorous," "comical," "funny," or anything else along those lines, we should understand that to mean that the text cannot be true in a literal sense. For instance, if the text says something like "when I found out we would have homework over the vacation I was the mayor of Angrytown," then the College Board might refer to that remark as humorous, because the speaker wasn't really made the mayor of a place called Angrytown just because he found out about a test. Whether a real person would actually laugh at something doesn't matter on the SAT; all that matters is whether the text describes something that couldn't literally happen.

"Metaphor" is another word that the College Board uses differently from most modern speakers. On the SAT, when a question or answer choice refers to a metaphor, it's referring to any non-literal use of a term. If a sentence in an SAT passage said, "she ran as fast as lightning," then the correct answer might describe this as a metaphor, since a person cannot literally run as fast as lightning.

When the College Board refers to something as "ironic," we should understand that the text describes some kind of contradiction. If the text said, "John was working in a butcher's shop even though he never ate meat," a correct answer choice on the SAT might describe this as irony, because the ideas of a butcher shop and an aversion to meat are somewhat contradictory. This isn't really a proper use of the term "irony" in real life, but if you keep this idea of contradiction in mind when encountering the word "irony" on the Passage-Based Reading questions, you should be fine.

As long as you keep those specialized meanings in your head and apply them when the test mentions the concepts of humor, metaphor, or irony, you should still find that the correct answers to those questions match up with the relevant text.

(By the way, if this all seems a little much right now, don't worry—we'll see plenty of examples of these ideas at work in real SAT questions from the College Board's Blue Book in just a bit.)

What About Paired Passages?

Sometimes the College Board asks you questions about two passages at once. These questions often ask how the author of one passage would respond to a statement from the other passage. When this happens, students often worry that they need to read an author's mind, which seems very subjective and unfair.

But we have to remember that every answer to a Passage-Based Reading question is spelled out somewhere in the text, and these questions are no exception, even if they seem to be asking you to guess how an author would feel.

To answer these kinds of questions, we have to find a point in the text where the author we're being asked about discusses something that appears in the other passage, and then choose an answer that reflects that author's opinion on the subject.

This might sound a little complicated, but it's actually not that bad. Let's use a fake example to demonstrate how it works for now, and then you can see some real examples a few pages from now when I go through some questions from the Blue Book.

Imagine that a question asks how the author of passage 1 would respond to the views of the author of passage 2 on the subject of education. Let's say that passage 2 contains this sentence: "Formal education is vastly overrated." Finally, let's imagine that passage 1 contains this sentence: "People who criticize formal education are usually the ones who need it most."

In this imaginary scenario, the correct answer might say that the author of passage 1 "believes that the author of Passage 2 would benefit from further education." Two reasons combine to make this the right answer. First, this answer choice restates passage 1's claim that people who criticize formal education are in need of formal education; second, passage 2 criticizes formal education when it says that formal education is overrated. In other words, the text of passage 2 shows that its author would be one of the very people that the author of passage 1 discusses in his own passage.

Conclusion

So far, we've talked about the general processes for answering a wide range of Passage-Based Reading questions on the SAT. Adhering to the approach I've described here will get you through the vast majority of real test questions that you'll ever see on the SAT.

But there are a few questions that will involve one or two further considerations that you'll also need to be aware of. Let's talk about them in the next section.

Special Cases: Parallelism And Demonstration

As I've explained, the College Board had to lay down some ground rules when it created the Passage-Based Reading questions in order to make them work as valid multiple-choice questions that could be administered on a large scale. One of those ground rules was the Big Secret of Passage-Based Reading that we've been discussing for several pages now: the idea that the correct answer to a Passage-Based Reading question will be the only answer that says the same thing as the relevant part of the text.

Two other ground rules are a bit more obscure, and the College Board only uses them a few times on an average test. The first of these rules has to do with something I call "parallelism," and it says that two ideas stated in succession can be treated as *exact synonyms* if a question asks about them, even though they aren't synonyms in real life. If two ideas are stated in quick succession and they have some kind of negating phrase between them, then we should treat those two ideas as *exact antonyms* for the purpose of the SAT, even though they wouldn't have to be antonyms in real life.

This particular idea is too bizarre for me to feel comfortable making up a fake example, so in this case I'll use an example from the College Board's *Official SAT Study Guide.* The example is on page 392, starting at the middle of line 41, where the sentence reads, "Shadowy imaginings do not usually hold up in the light of real experience." In that sentence, using the College Board's way of looking at these things, we should know that the phrase "shadowy imaginings" can be thought of as the antonym of the phrase "real experience," even though "shadowy" isn't an exact antonym of "real" and "imaginings" isn't an exact antonym of "experience" in everyday speech. When question 13 on that page asks about the phrase "shadowy imaginings," we're supposed to realize that it means something opposite to "real experience," and choose "unsubstantiated" (because "un" is a negating prefix and "substantiated" can mean "real").

If you think that sounds like a little technical and complicated, you're right, it does. But the questions involving this parallelism idea pretty much always end up being complicated like that—they're often the hardest questions for students to answer. Luckily, there aren't going to be that many of them on any one test.

The other ground rule I'd like to talk about is the idea of demonstration. Sometimes—not often, but sometimes—the College Board expects you to identify a correct answer because it technically describes something that the text demonstrates, rather than restating it. One example appears on page 479 of the same book, in question 17. That question asks about lines 4 through 8 of the text, and the correct answer to the question mentions "vivid imagery." This answer is correct because the citation includes this sentence: "Raindrops . . . bounced against sidewalks in glistening sparks, then disappeared like tiny ephemeral jewels." This sentence is a demonstration of imagery, not a collection of words that mean the same thing as the word "imagery." Again, the College Board rarely asks questions of this type, but it's important to be aware that it may occasionally do so.

The Passage-Based Reading Process In Action Against Real Questions

To prove that the SAT Passage-Based Reading process works against real SAT questions like the ones you'll see on test day, and to help you learn how to use that process on your own, we'll go through all the Passage-Based Reading questions for the first Critical Reading section of the first test in the second edition of the College Board's Blue Book, *The Official SAT Study Guide*. You'll need a copy of that book to follow along. (Really, you'll need a copy anyway, since it's the only printed source of real SAT test questions—all printed practice tests from third-party prep companies contain fake tests that might not follow the same rules as the real test.) You can find a good deal on it here: http://www.SATprepBlackBook.com/blue-book.

We'll do the Passage-Based Reading questions starting on page 391 of *The Official SAT Study Guide*, second edition, since page 391 is the beginning of the first Critical Reading section in the first practice test in that book. After we go through those questions, we'll go through the entire College Board book and do a selection of questions that students have traditionally found challenging from other sections in other practice tests.

(If you would like to see some video demonstrations of these ideas, go to www.SATprepVideos.com for a selection of demonstration videos that are free to readers of this book.)

Page 391, Question 6

This is bit of a doozy to start off with, but oh well :)

First, let's talk about why the wrong answers are wrong:

(A) is irrelevant to the passage. A lot of students will assume that making mistakes is automatically human, but the text never mentions anyone making a mistake or doing anything wrong, so this can't be the answer.

(B) is irrelevant because the text doesn't mention company—it never says whether other people are present with the speaker or not.

(C) is irrelevant. It's true that the descriptions of nature are in the past tense, but the statement "It felt good to be human" is also in the past tense. Within the context of the passage, then, the good feeling of being human is happening at the same time as the rest of the paragraph.

(D) is correct—we'll talk more about it below.

(E) doesn't work because the text never mentions simplicity, nor a lack of complication, nor any other phrase that could mean the same thing as the word "simplicity." It would be a common mistake for students to assume that the author thinks nature is simple, but on the SAT we must avoid these kinds of assumptions. We have to stick to the exact wording of the text, and the exact wording of the text never mentions any idea synonymous with the word "simplicity."

Now let's talk about why (D) is correct. The text mentions the "wondrous spectacle" of the "night sky." The "night sky" is a natural thing, and the phrase "wondrous spectacle" is an appreciative, positive way to describe something that must be a visually appealing scene (because "wondrous" is positive and a "spectacle" is a visual scene), so the "night sky['s]" "wondrous spectacle" is an example of "nature's beauty." That part is fairly straightforward. What might not be so obvious is why we can use those phrases from line 10 when the question asks us about line 12.

To figure this out, we need to remember the College Board's unstated policy on ideas that appear consecutively in the text. This text talks about horses wandering past the speaker; the horses never look up at the "wondrous spectacle" of "the night sky," but the speaker does. The next sentence says "it feels good to be human." In SAT-code, this means that "to be human" is to do the opposite of what the horses do, and the horses aren't looking up.

Thus, "to be human" and to notice "the wondrous spectacle" of "the night sky" must be the same thing in the College Board's way of thinking.

This is the first question we've looked at together, but right away it jumps into some of the harder ideas we'll encounter on the SAT, like the parallelism issue. In a practical sense, many students would have an easier time recognizing that the four wrong answers are wrong than they would in singling out the correct answer right away. That's fine. Just keep on working at it, and remember that most questions won't be this challenging.

Page 391, Question 7

For this question, we have to remember that the College Board considers something "metaphorical" when it can only be taken non-literally. So (B) is correct because of phrases like "river of clouds," which aren't literally possible. Now let's look at the wrong answers:

(A) is going to be tempting to a lot of students who mistakenly view the SAT Reading section as a test of literary interpretation.

(B) is correct.

(C) doesn't work because there is no actual analogy here.

(D) is no good. Flashback doesn't work because, while the text is in the past tense, its point of reference is also in the past tense. In other words, at the time that the author was actually standing on the Peak, he wasn't thinking about his past. (Note that this wrong answer requires a mistake similar to the one that would lead us to choose (C) in the previous question.)

(E) is a problem because irony doesn't work. The text doesn't describe a contradiction that someone is unaware of.

Page 391, Question 8

Here, the correct answer is (C) because the passage tells us how she's celebrated ("biographies, plays, novels, films") and also why ("her fascinating life and lineage . . . have turned her into an icon").

(A) doesn't work because we aren't told why she liked computers.

(B) doesn't work because there's no discussion of her character.

(C) is correct.

(D) doesn't work because the text doesn't mention the modern-day computer. It *does* mention "computer science" in general, and it does mention early computing devices from the 19th century, but it never specifically mentions a "modern-day" device.

(E) doesn't work because the text doesn't say anything about wanting other women to pursue similar careers. Many students who view this test as a normal school test might be tempted by this answer choice, because they would argue that it will probably encourage some women to enter the field of computing. But the text doesn't actually say anything to encourage that, so (E) is wrong. Remember that, on the SAT, everything must be spelled out.

Page 391, Question 9

For this, we need a statement that contradicts the passage, because we're asked to find a statement with which the author would disagree. (A) is right because the passage says the reason she is an "icon" has something to do with her "lineage," which is her "family history" by definition.

(B) is wrong because the author says King's design was the "first," which means it *was* original. A lot of students would probably choose this by accident because they might accidentally misread the word "disagree" in the question stem.

(C) is wrong because the author specifically says she has become an icon, which means that interest in her exists in popular culture. Again, remember that we're looking for an answer choice that specifically contradicts the text, because of the word "disagree" in the question stem.

(D) doesn't work because the text never says that she was not well known long after her work was complete.

(E) doesn't work because the text specifically says her life is "fascinating," and we need to find the answer choice that contradicts the passage because of the word "disagree" in the question.

Students miss this question all the time in practice—not because they don't understand the passage or the answer choices, but because they misread the question in the first place. Remember that answering questions correctly on the SAT will *always* require careful reading and attention to detail.

Page 392, Question 10

A lot of students miss this question because they don't read it carefully enough. The correct answer is (D), because the passage is about the relationship between Africans and African-Americans, and it says that the world "takes note" of it, which means it is "significant."

(A) doesn't work because the passage doesn't mention African Americans having an impact on African societies.

(B) doesn't work because the passage doesn't mention embracing American culture. It does say that people reached out to each other for "reassurance, reaffirmation, fraternity, and strength," but reaching out for those things is not the same idea as embracing someone else's culture.

(C) doesn't work because of the word "ambivalent."

(D) is correct.

(E) doesn't work because of the word "nations." The text talks about Africans and about African Americans, but Africa is a continent, not a "nation," and African-Americans are a demographic group within the United States, not a "nation." Remember that every word has to fit!

When students miss this question, they almost always choose (E), and with good reason: (E) only differs from the text by one word, "nation." In fact, I would bet that if you were discussing this passage with a college professor and you accidentally referred to the groups in the text as nations, she wouldn't stop to correct you. (E) would be a fine remark to make in most classroom settings, but it's completely wrong on the SAT because it doesn't exactly match the original text. Remember to pay attention to details when you work on the SAT!

Page 392, Question 11

This one is hard for a lot of students. The "message" is that "ties . . . must be maintained . . . if a people is to survive." When you tell someone that they must do something in order to survive, you are cautioning them. (B) is the right answer for this reason.

(A) doesn't work because there is no criticism here. This part of the text doesn't mention anyone or anything being bad.

(B) is correct.

(C) might be tempting if it does happen to strike a reader as "questionable" that a tree can't stand without its roots, but we always have to remember that the correct answer will restate a concept from the text; our own impressions and interpretations of the text don't matter.

(D) doesn't work because no phrase in the text indicates nostalgia, and the message itself isn't described as being a fond memory.

(E) doesn't work because the message is not "optimistic," since it does not express hope for the future.

Page 392, Question 12

This question asks about a really bizarre proverb that students are unlikely to understand in any kind of clear way. Remember that, for these questions and for every question, we have to put aside our own interpretations and find the answer in the text. The text specifically says that the proverb "conveys the . . . instinctive pull of one's heritage [and] curiosity in our origins." This goes with (C), an interest in personal history. Note that "inherent" from the answer choice matches "instinctive" from the text, just as "interest in their history" goes with "curiosity in our origins." The rest of the answer choices don't reflect what the text says the maxim conveys. Many of the wrong answers might seem like decent literary or sociological interpretations if we were discussing this text in a real class, which is one more reason why we have to remember to stick to the stated message of the text for every single question.

Page 392, Question 13

This question was previously discussed in the section on parallelism. Here, we have to remember to read the text very carefully. The text says that "shadowy imaginings" don't stand up to "real experience." So "shadowy imaginings" and "real experience" are opposites as far as the College Board is concerned, because they are mentioned in quick succession and have a negating phrase between them.

Once we realize that the test wants us to treat "real experience" as the opposite of "shadowy imaginings," we realize that "shadowy" must be the opposite of "real," as far as the SAT is concerned. Now we have to find a word in the answer choices that can mean the opposite of the word "real." The only possible option is "unsubstantiated," because "substantiated" can mean "real" and "un" is a negating prefix. So the correct answer is (E).

The four wrong answers here might all sound like decent interpretations of the word "shadowy" in a literary sense, which is why it's so important for us to remember that we have to find the correct answer stated plainly in the text itself.

In my opinion, this question is one of the hardest ones in the whole book when it comes to analyzing the text and the answer choices. Some test-takers get the question right just through lucky guessing, but the process of working out the correct answer with certainty requires a high degree of familiarity with the test and attention to detail.

Page 393, Question 14

For this one, the phrase "wondered if we hadn't been mistaken" goes with the ideas of "uncertainty" and "doubt" in (C) and (E). It does not go with "fear," "anger," or "regret" from the other choices. (Be careful here—a lot of people might want to say that "uncertainty" goes with "regret," but those two ideas aren't actually the same if we think carefully about them. "Uncertainty" indicates a state in which we aren't sure of something, but "regret" indicates a state in which we feel bad about something.)

Between the answers with "uncertainty" and "doubt," we would want to see that "despair" doesn't describe anything in the text. The text does say that Africa "left its mark" on the people being described, and that the world is forced to take note of Africans and African-Americans, which is a demonstration of the author's "pride." So (E) is correct.

Page 393, Question 15

Test-takers miss this one frequently because they think "personal anecdotes" is the answer, but the author never relays a *personal* story, so (D) is wrong. (B), on the other hand, is right, because the author repeatedly refers generally to all Africans and all African-Americans as though they were all the same.

(C) is another wrong answer that often attracts a lot of test-takers. The text does mention some things in the past tense, but it doesn't give specific historical facts like "in 1492 Columbus captained three ships bound West from Spain." Instead, we have only broad, figurative statements like "for centuries, we have gazed at one another across the transatlantic divide."

Page 394, Question 16

(C) is correct because the popular appeal is mentioned in the first paragraph of Passage 1, which calls the *Mona Lisa* the "world's most famous portrait," and because Passage 2 says that the passage is "famous" in line 44 and in other places, and talks about its "renown" in line 67.

Some test-takers incorrectly choose (D) because the first passage talks about how the *Mona Lisa* was the first painting to include many features that were later adopted in other paintings (lines 10 through 15), and the second passage talks about how the painting captured the attention of Clarke and Barolsky. But Clarke and Barolsky are not described as *artists* in the second passage, and the answer (D) refers specifically to the painting's influence on *artists*, not on critics and historians.

Page 394, Question 17

For questions like this one, students often get frustrated because they feel it's impossible to find something stated directly in the text when we're asked what the author of one passage would have said about the other. But remember that, even in these situations, the correct answer is stated directly somewhere.

The phenomena in Passage 1 are the giant crowds of people that turned out to see the painting, and in line 68 the author of Passage 2 says that "people, institutions, processes . . . have turned the *Mona Lisa* into the best-known painting in the world." (A) restates this exactly, and no other choice does.

(B) is an answer choice that a lot of students will be attracted to, because it sounds like a decent interpretation that you could defend in a classroom discussion. But it's wrong because the author of passage 2 doesn't say anything about the true importance of the painting.

Page 395, Question 18

(A) doesn't work because the passage never actually says that the painting is beautiful, or that the woman's appearance was normal. Many test-takers will like this wrong answer because they personally believe the painting is beautiful or that the woman herself was normal in appearance, but we always have to remember that we're looking for an answer choice that appears directly in the text, not for a choice that matches our own interpretation.

(B) doesn't work because the passage doesn't say anything about the portrait's monetary value.

(C) doesn't work because of "untimely demise."

(D) doesn't work because the text doesn't mention a lack of charisma.

(E) is correct because "ordinary status" goes with "nobody special," and "set the standard for painting" goes with "aesthetic significance."

Page 395, Question 19
The text says that Leonardo is describing the effect of the technique in the sentence that begins on line 23, so (B) is correct. None of the other choices is spelled out in the text anywhere.

Page 395, Question 20
Again, even though the question is asking what one author would say about another author's work, which seems like a fairly subjective question to ask, the correct answer must be stated directly in the text. Passage 2 mentions "features" that bring "instant recognition." The only feature mentioned in Passage 1 is the "famous smile" in the last line, so the correct answer is (A). Note that "famous" in passage 1 goes with "brings instant recognition" in passage 2.

Page 395, Question 21
While each of the answer choices could be a synonym for the word "position" in a particular context, the correct answer will be the only one that restates something from the passage itself. Let's trace the word "position" back through the text and see what happens.

The sentence that contains the word "position" equates that word with the pronoun "it" in the beginning of the sentence. The word "it" is referring back to the phrase "this idea" from the previous sentence. The phrase "this idea" is referring back to what the historians "argue" in line 38. So the word "position" is ultimately being equated with what people "argue" in line 38, which means the correct answer is that it's a "view." So (D) is correct here.

Some students incorrectly choose "policy," but a policy isn't the same thing as an opinion or view—a policy is a standard way of handling a particular situation, not a belief. As always, it's very critical to think about exactly what each word specifically means, so you don't end up choosing a wrong answer just because it's somewhat close to the text.

Page 395, Question 22
Both people say that the painting seems three-dimensional. Passage 1 mentions this in lines 22 and 23, while Barolsky mentions the creation of "depth." So (E) is the answer.

A lot of students get this one wrong, though.

(B) is a very popular wrong answer, because students often overlook the word "unduly." Nobody ever mentions whether the painting deserves its recognition, so that single word makes the entire answer choice wrong.

(C) is reflected in the first passage, but Barolsky never specifically mentions any influence on other artists, so (C) doesn't work.

(D) is close to something in passage 1, but it's not reflected in Barolsky's remark at all.

Page 395, Question 23
When we see unattributed quotation marks in a reading question, they are almost always serving to call the meaning of the quoted word into question. So (E) is the correct answer here.

Page 395, Question 24
(A) doesn't work because the first passage doesn't focus on the smile, and the second passage doesn't focus on mystery.

(B) is also totally irrelevant.

(C) is correct because the first passage mentions the original techniques that Leonardo used to create the illusion of depth, while the second passage talks about the reasons why the painting is so famous.

(D) is wrong because the first text doesn't speculate on the life of the subject. It only briefly mentions her probable identity. The second passage doesn't reject art history, either—in fact, the author considers himself to be "like most historians" in line 66.

(E) is wrong because, among other things, the second text doesn't debate the artistic merits of the painting. It does quote Barolsky's comment on Leonardo's technique, but it never offers an opposing viewpoint on that technique, so there is no debate.

A Selection of Challenging Questions

By now you should have a pretty strong idea of the proper application of the Passage-Based Reading strategies. Remember at all times that the critical element for all questions is to find the correct answer directly on the page, in black and white, with no inference or interpretation. Remember that it will often be necessary to read very carefully and make fine distinctions among the exact meanings of particular words in order to distinguish wrong answers from right answers.

Now that we've gone through a section of Passage-Based Reading questions, let's take a look at a sample of some of the more challenging questions from the College Board's Blue Book, the *Official SAT Study Guide*.

These questions are some of the ones that students have asked me about the most over the years. Like all Passage-Based Reading questions, they can be answered correctly and with total certainty if we read the text and the answer choices very carefully and follow the rules of the SAT. So it's not that these questions do anything differently from the questions that are less challenging; it's just that they are sometimes a bit more subtle about what they're doing.

(If you would like to see some video demonstrations of these ideas, go to www.SATprepVideos.com for a selection of demonstration videos that are free to readers of this book.)

As with other question explanations in this book, you'll need a copy of the College Board's Blue Book to follow along. Let's get started—and remember, these questions are generally among the ones that other students have struggled with most, so don't worry that every question on the test will be as challenging as these are.

I highly recommend that you follow along with these solutions as a way to continue to improve your understanding of Passage-Based Reading questions and how to answer them.

Page 403, Question 11

This is one of those questions that asks us how the author of one passage would respond to an idea from another passage. As always, we'll answer it by looking directly in the text.

The enthusiasm in the second passage is felt with regard to "the mechanization that he saw around him" in line 13. So we need to find something in the first passage that mentions an idea related to mechanization or enthusiasm.

Passage 1 talks about "the forces of industrialization and urbanization," which is essentially the same idea in this context as the "mechanization" referred to in the second passage. So let's take a look and see what the first passage has to say about the "industrialization and urbanization."

It says that Americans "protested the intrusion" of "industrialization and urbanization." In other words, they didn't like it—by definition, if you "protest" something, you must be against it. Passage 1 also says that Thoreau's book is "an illustration of the intensity" of that protest. Along the same lines, the earlier part of the text calls Thoreau the "epitome" of this anti-industrial protest. So Thoreau is the embodiment (the "epitome" and "illustration") of this protest.

Passage 2, though, said that Thoreau was sometimes "enthusiastic" about the mechanization.

This goes with choice (E), which says that Thoreau's enthusiasm was at odds with what people thought about his attitudes. Again, the first passage says that people see Thoreau as the epitome of an anti-industrial feeling, but the second passage says he was sometimes enthusiastic about it. So (E) is correct.

The other answer choices don't work for a variety of reasons. (B) is the direct contradiction of what passage 1 says. So is (C). (D) might be an interesting interpretation, but the text never says anything about Thoreau's feelings being shaped by his experiment.

Page 459, Question 10

To understand why (C) is the correct answer here, we need to know about a certain stylistic construction in English that many students are unaware of: in English, if we say that something is "as X as it is Y," we mean that it is *very* X and *very* Y, not just that it is equally X and Y.

For instance, if I said "that dog is as beautiful as he is smart," I don't just mean that the dog is equally beautiful and smart—I'm not saying that he's kind of rough-looking and also pretty stupid. I'm saying that he's extremely beautiful and also extremely smart. So this construction doesn't just indicate equality between two attributes; it also indicates an abundance of both attributes.

For this reason, when the text says something is "as widespread as it is wrong," it's emphasizing that the widespread-ness and the wrong-ness are both extreme. This is why the answer is (C). We might like to think of this as one of those "demonstration" kinds of questions I mentioned earlier, in which the specific structure of the relevant text indicates the answer. But, again, in order to get this, we have to be familiar with the "as X as it is Y" construction, and a lot of students just aren't.

But don't worry about this question too much. For one thing, if you ever happen to see another SAT question about a phrase in the "as X as it is Y" structure, you'll know what to do. But, more importantly, you're probably never going to see another real SAT question exactly like this. As I mentioned earlier, these "demonstration" questions are pretty rare.

The other choices don't work because nothing in the text indicates that the author is wistful, dismayed, ambivalent, or apologetic.

Page 462, Question 25

This difficult question combines two challenging elements. First, we have to realize that it's actually Lewis's remark that illustrates for us what Bobby is saying, because the two ideas are stated in succession and joined by the word "and" at the beginning of Lewis's quote (remember that the College Board treats two ideas stated in this way as though they were synonyms). Second, we have to realize that Lewis's remark can be considered humorous by the College Board because it can't be taken literally.

Lewis says that people who lie down until a feeling passes will be in the cemetery before they think about getting up. There are two ways to take this statement, and both are impossible: Either he means that people will be dead and buried in the cemetery and then think about getting up, or he means that they will lie down somewhere else and somehow be transported to the cemetery without getting up. Either interpretation is logically impossible, so the College Board can refer to this remark as a humorous one, meaning that the answer is (C).

On top of that, the phrase can be taken as a 'synonym' of Bobby's remark because Lewis begins his remark with the word "and."

This is one of the more challenging questions in the book, in my opinion. But, as always, we can still find a reliable answer if we stick to the rules of the test that were previously explained in this book, and read the text carefully.

Page 479, Question 17

This is one of the questions we mentioned in the discussion of "demonstration" questions. Here, the phrase "captured the dim silver glow of street lamps, bounced against sidewalks in glistening sparks, then disappeared like tiny ephemeral jewels" is a direct example of the "vivid imagery" mentioned in choice (B), because "imagery" means "visually descriptive language," and those phrases are visual descriptions. So (B) is correct.

Some students choose (C) incorrectly here—the wording of these phrases doesn't satisfy the College Board's requirement for "humorous" texts, because it doesn't describe something that can't be taken literally. It's possible for streetlights to have a "dim silver glow," and it's possible for raindrops to bounce and glisten, and it's possible for them to be *like* jewels—notice the text doesn't say raindrops *are* jewels, which would be impossible; it says they are "*like* jewels" (emphasis mine).

This question is just one more example of how important it is to read everything very carefully and to keep the unwritten rules of the SAT firmly in your mind when you work on these questions.

Page 521, Question 10

Students often miss this question because they don't catch the connection between the phrase "robust media profits" in line 15 and the phrase "economic well-being" in choice (E), which is the correct answer. If we say that something is "robust," we mean that it's strong, healthy, functional, et cetera. So if profits are robust, there is economic well-being.

(A) doesn't work because the idea of "core values" only appears in the first passage, but we were asked to find something that was only in the second passage. This is a classic type of wrong answer for a question that asks us to find something from one passage but not the other, and something you definitely have to look out for—simply misreading "passage 2" as "passage 1" or vice versa could lead you to believe that this choice was valid.

(B) doesn't work because both texts specifically mention Rosensteil.

(C) doesn't work because the second passage doesn't mention the history of journalism.

(D) doesn't work because sensationalism appears in both passages.

Page 523, Question 18

Like many challenging Passage-Based Reading question, this one is difficult because we have to read very carefully, not because we have to make any kind of inference or have very advanced vocabularies.

First, we need to look carefully to see what the text says "scientists originally thought." We see that what they originally thought was "that the purpose of yawning was to increase the amount of oxygen in the blood or to release some accumulated carbon dioxide."

The question asks us to find the answer choice that disproves what scientists originally thought, so we have to find the choice that disproves the idea that people yawn to increase oxygen in their blood or to release carbon dioxide.

(A) might look promising at first, because it mentions carbon dioxide and breathing rates, which appear together in the sentence that runs from lines 49 to 52.

(B) is irrelevant because it mentions sleep, and the text doesn't say that scientists originally thought yawning had anything to do with sleep. The text just says they thought it had to do with oxygen or carbon dioxide.

(C) would be *supporting* what scientists originally thought: they originally thought that yawning was a mechanism to increase the amount of oxygen in the blood, and this choice says exactly that. This is a classic example of a wrong answer that does exactly the opposite of what we were asked to do. The College Board includes these types of wrong answers because they know that some students will get sort of 'turned around' if they're asked to contradict something, and accidentally end up restating it.

(D) would tend to disprove what scientists thought. The text says that scientists thought people yawned because they needed to increase their blood oxygen; this choice points out that people don't yawn very much in places where the oxygen is low. If what the scientists originally thought were correct, we would expect people in low-oxygen environments to yawn a lot, so they would get more oxygen into their blood.

(E) would also support what scientists originally thought, just like (C). One of the things that scientists originally thought was that yawning was a way to release carbon dioxide, and this choice says people yawn more when their carbon dioxide levels are higher.

So on a first read-through, you might end up kind of liking both (A) and (D). Now it's time to scrutinize those two choices and see which one ends up working, and which one has a flaw. (A) talks about *breathing rates*, but the text only tells us what scientists thought about *yawning*. The idea of breathing faster is mentioned later in the paragraph, but not as part of what "scientists originally thought" in line 46. So now we have to ask ourselves whether a breathing rate is the same thing as a yawn. The answer is no, it isn't. While yawning might be related to breathing rates if we tried to force ourselves to see a connection between them, the fact remains that the text says scientists had a belief about the purpose of yawning, not a belief about how anything affected the breathing rate *per se*. So, after careful consideration, we see that (A) was never actually a direct fit with the text, while (D) talks about people in a low-oxygen environment not yawning a lot, which would contradict the idea that people yawn because they need more oxygen. So (D) is the correct answer.

Page 538, Question 7

This is one of the questions that students ask about more than any other. Most people who answer it incorrectly choose (E). The paragraph does describe the author's childhood artistic endeavors, and the author's desire to be a "Renaissance artist," but the text does not specifically say that it was the wish to be a Renaissance artist that led to a "devotion to visual arts." There are at least two major problems with this phrase.

First, the author indicates that he was drawing and painting before he began writing poems, and he seems to be equating writing poems with the desire to be a Renaissance artist, so that desire can't be the thing that "initiated a devotion to the visual arts," since he was already devoted to the visual arts before he had the desire to write poems.

Second, the phrase "visual arts" doesn't fit with the author's explanation of what it means to be a "Renaissance artist." The author says that being such an artist involves writing, painting, composing, and inventing; from that list, only painting is a "visual art." So the desire to be a Renaissance artist must involve more than the desire to devote oneself to the "visual arts."

(C) ends up being correct because of the parenthetical phrase "too seriously!" in the original text. We have to read really carefully here, and we have to be somewhat aware of the meanings of the words "naïve" and "grandiose" (or we have to be able to realize that the other four choices don't work). People often think "naïve" can only mean "inexperienced," but it can also mean something along the lines of "sincere" or "direct." This goes with the idea of being "serious." The word "grandiose" in this context indicates that someone has an exaggerated sense of his own abilities or importance, and the word "too" in the text before "seriously" indicates that the author considers his youthful commitment to have been excessive.

Finally, the word "ambition" from the answer choices goes with the part of the text that says the author "wanted to be a Renaissance artist." Remember that the College Board wants us to treat ideas stated in succession as though they were synonyms, so the author's statement about wanting to be an artist can be taken into consideration for this question.

It's subtle, but it's there: the phrase "too seriously!" matches with the words "naïve and grandiose," and the word "ambition" matches with the phrase "I wanted to be."

Remember, as always, that it's absolutely critical to pay attention to details in answer choices and in the relevant parts of the text!

Page 540, Question 12

This question often seems weird to students because they have a hard time seeing how a "monster" can be a "process." But we have to remember that answering these questions is always a matter of seeing exactly what's in the text, and the text here says that "everything . . . issues . . . from a benign monster called manufacture," which means the "benign monster" is the source of "everything." (The verb "to issue from" means "to come from" in this case.) So the text says that everything comes from this "benign monster," which is why (C) is right when it says we're talking about the process by which these goods come into existence.

Page 577, Question 9

This is one of the best questions in the entire Blue Book when it comes to demonstrating the various ways that the College Board can make an answer choice wrong even though it might sound like an intelligent analysis of the text.

The correct answer here is (C). The word "insights" goes with "penetrating intuition;" the word "character" goes with "female heart" ("heart" is meant in the sense of "core" or "essence," not in the anatomical sense); the phrase "in his everyday life" goes with "the real man." The text says that people who were drawn to him because of his insight into people's hearts were surprised that the real man was actually insensitive; the answer choice says that Balzac's knowledge of character wasn't present in his everyday life.

Now let's talk about a couple of the wrong answers, and what makes them wrong. Pay special attention here, because this question has some uniquely frustrating wrong answers.

(A) is basically the opposite of the text—the text says that female readers were drawn to him.

(B) is basically the opposite of an earlier part of the text. Line 2 says Balzac's fiction was "financially wise."

(C) is correct.

(D) is fairly close to the text, but doesn't repeat it exactly. The text says that people who knew "the real man" were "appalled to discover" how he was, and that seems pretty close to the answer choice's ideas of knowing him "personally" and not being able to "respect him." The problem here is the phrase "as an artist," which isn't reflected in the text. It might feel like a natural assumption to think that being appalled by someone in person would cause you to lose respect for the person as an artist, but we have to remember that the College Board is extremely nit-picky about these kinds of things. We can't make assumptions when we're looking for the answers; if it doesn't specifically mention how people felt about Balzac *as an artist*, then we can't choose (D).

(E) is probably the sneakiest choice of all. The text definitely says that people were "appalled to discover" how Balzac was, and this choice says that people expected Balzac to be a certain way. The main problem here is the word "unreasonable"—the text never indicates whether readers were *reasonable* when they expected Balzac to live up to the expectations they formed from reading his work. Remember that a difference of even one word from the text is enough to make an answer choice wrong.

Page 579, Question 15

This is yet another example of a question that is extremely, extremely nit-picky. Almost everyone who misses this question chooses (D), because the text says in line 41 that "only the male's initials" were eventually on the token. But here's the problem: the question asks about "the seventeenth century," but line 41 is talking about "the late eighteenth century." So (D) is restating an idea from the passage that applies to a timeframe different from the one the question asked about. The correct answer is (E), because the text says that "in the . . . seventeenth century, . . . tokens . . . carried the initials of the man's and woman's first names and the couple's surname." Later, it describes a seventeenth-century woman who "confidently joined in the family . . . business."

As always, it's critical to pay attention to every detail in every answer choice.

Page 580, Question 23

So-called "tone" questions like this are typically answered by finding a phrase in the text that reflects the definition of the correct answer choice. For instance, if (A) were the correct answer here, we'd have to see phrases in the passages like "those wonderful years of the past that will never return," because that would be an example of "affectionate nostalgia."

Here, we have a special case: neither text uses any kind of language that betrays any particular tone, so the answer is (B), because being "analytical" and "detached" essentially means that you write with no emotion at all.

Some people see words like "agitating" in line 91 and assume that the correct answer is either (C), which mentions "regret," or (D), which mentions "indignation." But there are several problems with this type of thinking, from an SAT standpoint. First of all, and perhaps most importantly, "agitating" for something is not precisely the same thing as feeling "regret" or "indignation." It's true that agitation, regret, and indignation are all negative emotions, but they're not the same as one another. Further, if we read line 91 carefully, we see that the author is not the one doing the agitating; instead, the author is referring to another person's agitation. The text itself can still maintain an analytical tone even though it's referring to someone else being agitated.

Page 588, Question 9

Students often miss this question because they don't know all the meanings of the word "authority." Most people think that the word refers to someone with some kind of official power over others, like a police officer; they might also think it refers to a recognized expert in a field. But the word "authority" can be used in general to refer to anyone who is the source of a quote, idea, influence, et cetera. So (E) basically says "quotes someone." That's why it's correct: the author of passage 1 quotes someone directly, while the author of passage 2 does not.

Page 589, Question 10

This question is a great example of how we sometimes have to trace concepts back through the text in order to figure out which answer choice is restating it accurately.

Almost everyone chooses (D) because the word "humorous" seems to fit nicely with "funny," "good joke," and "laughed" from the text. But the text also includes the idea of "mak[ing] matters worse," which seems a little odd if (D) is going to be correct, and might make us read a bit more carefully. Remember that the question is asking how Waverly felt about the advertisement, but the words "funny," "joke," and "laughed" are describing how the company at the table reacted to Waverly herself, which is a different thing. Furthermore, even if we accidentally like "humorous," we have a problem because the word "effective" isn't reflected anywhere in the text at all.

The correct answer is (A), because of the phrase "not sophisticated" in line 8. But, if you read carefully (and you should be reading carefully!), you'll notice that the question asks how *Waverly* characterizes the advertisement, but line 8 is a quote from *June's mother*. Why is that suddenly okay?

It's okay because the quote from June's mother comes directly after Waverly's quote, and it begins with the word "true," which indicates that June's mother is agreeing with whatever Waverly just said. So Waverly says what she says, and then the mom says, "true . . . June is not sophisticated." According to the rules of SAT Reading that we've discussed in this book, this means we can equate Waverly's remark with the idea that June is "not sophisticated."

That's why "unsophisticated and heavy-handed" is correct. "Unsophisticated" is a pretty clear restatement of "not sophisticated," and "heavy-handed" is basically a synonym for "unsophisticated" or for the idea of lacking "style."

Page 592, Question 20

This question is challenging for a variety of reasons. For one thing, it's one of those questions that ask us to think about an author's argument, which means the correct answer might technically involve concepts not explicitly stated in the text (for a refresher on those questions, see the article called "Special Cases: Parallelism And Demonstration" earlier in this book). For another thing, the question is basically a double-reversal, because it asks for the answer choice that "detracts least," which can be confusing for a lot of people.

But, as with any confusing SAT question, the key thing here is to remain calm, read very carefully, and pick our way through each phrase as we come to it.

Since the question asks for the choice that would detract the least from the argument, we should expect to find four wrong answers that all detract from the argument in some way, and one correct answer that does not detract at all. (Don't be put off by the word "least." Remember that the College Board deliberately attempts to mislead students by using these kinds of relative terms, but the SAT only has value if each question has exactly one correct answer, and the only way to achieve that is to avoid interpretation and deal in absolutes.)

Now we have to figure out what the argument is that the author is making in the cited lines. In those lines, the author makes a few related points. He says we have a "human need to wake by day and sleep by night." He says, "night is when we dream, and . . . reality is warped." He says, "we are accustomed to mastering our world by day," but at night we are "vulnerable as prey," so bats seem to "threaten" our "safety."

Now let's take a look at the answer choices. Remember, we're looking for the one answer choice that does NOT detract from the argument in the text.

(A) does detract, because the argument says that people wake by day and sleep by night, but this choice says that many people do the opposite.

(B) also detracts, because the argument says that things that hunt at night scare us, but this choice says that some things that hunt at night don't scare us.

(C) also detracts, because the argument says that the night is when we are prey, but this choice says that some dangerous things hunt during the day.

(D) also detracts, because the entire paragraph is full of references to how "we," as humans, dislike bats because they are active at night. This choice says that some humans think of bats positively.

(E) is the correct answer because it does NOT detract from the argument—in fact, it's not really relevant to the argument at all. The original argument does say something about "reality" being "warped" during "dreamtime," but it doesn't say anything about where dream imagery comes from. Since the argument doesn't make any claims about the source of dream imagery, this statement about the source of dream imagery can't contradict the argument.

Page 607, Question 13

I just wanted to touch on this question briefly because students who have used other preparation materials before are often put off by the word "scornful," which seems extreme to them. (There are some tutors and books that claim that extreme answer choices are never correct on the SAT.)

So I wanted to use this question to point out that we don't really need to worry about whether answer choices are extreme or not; all that matters is whether they restate ideas from the text. If the text is extreme (and this particular text is quite extreme), then correct answers that describe the text accurately will also have to be extreme. This is why it's okay for (B) to be correct here.

Page 607, Question 14

This question troubles a lot of students. Most of the people who miss it seem to choose (D), because line 49 of the text talks about "manipulators and manipulated, actors and imitators, simulants and simulated, stupefiers and stupefied." But the text never talks about "blurring the line" between those groups, so (D) doesn't work. Remember: every part of the answer choice has to be reflected in the original text!

(E) is right because of statements like "all these theories are rather unconvincing" in line 36.

Page 645, Question 7

Students often miss this question because of not reading the text and the answer choices carefully enough. Most people who miss the question either choose (A) or (B).

(A) is wrong for a couple of reasons, but the largest is probably the phrase "literary persona." The article talks about Wilson "speaking directly through his letters," but a "literary persona" would be a false personality deliberately adopted when writing a work of literature.

(B) doesn't work because the text doesn't actually mention whether Wilson was mature. It says he was direct, and that he wrote the same way at every stage of his life, but it doesn't actually say that when he was young he wrote with the maturity of an older man. For all we know from the text, it might be that even as an old man he wrote with the immaturity of a young man.

(E) ends up being correct because the passage says that the same kind of writing (speaking "directly" and "informal(ly) for the most part," et cetera) appears in letters Wilson wrote when he was "young, middle-aged, and old," which means his style was consistent.

Page 646, Question 10

This is another question that often tricks students who don't read carefully enough. Most people who miss the question choose (D), but (D) talks about "the discovery of the Andromeda galaxy," which isn't mentioned in the text at all. The idea of "Andromeda" is mentioned, but its discovery is not.

(B) ends up being correct because the text describes a now-extinct primate being alive, which is a "differen[ce]." (The footnote tells us that *Australopithecus* is extinct.) The word "dramatize" in this context basically means "illustrate" or "demonstrate." "Two million years ago" is exactly from the text.

Page 649, Question 23

This question stumps a lot of people. The important thing with these "attitude" questions is to remember that the answer must be spelled out in specific phrases within the text, so we have to look for those. We don't answer a question like this (or any other question) by just going with a rough idea of our impression of the text; we answer questions by finding choices that specifically restate the text.

Here, (E) is correct. Line 32 says that most people are "out of their depth" when considering real art; to be "out of your depth" means to be too unintelligent or inexperienced to deal with a new situation, so this is a "condescending" remark. Lines 4 and 5 say that "people in general" are not members of a "special class," but that the special class isn't necessarily "better;" this is a "tolerant" remark.

Let's take a look at what makes the wrong answers wrong:

(A) doesn't work because of "puzzled." The author never says that the majority of people puzzle him, or that he can't understand anything about them.

(B) doesn't work because the author never specifically says anything hostile about the majority of people, either. He never says that he wishes anything painful or devastating would happen to them, even though it's pretty clear that he doesn't have much respect for their intellectual abilities.

(C) doesn't work because the author never says anything to indicate that he respects the majority of people.

(D) doesn't work because the author never says that he doesn't care about the majority of people, which is what "indifferent" would require if it were going to be the correct answer to this question.

Page 674, Question 9

This question often seems challenging at first, but if we remember to follow the text carefully we can get through it. Most students, instead, try to answer it by interpreting the passage from a literary standpoint, which can only bring trouble.

The sentences about Clayton's complexion appear at the end of a paragraph about Clayton's behavior and appearance. That paragraph indicates that his sense of humor was a "counterpoint to his own beliefs," indicating that at least one aspect of his personality seems to contradict another aspect of it. This is why (A), which mentions his "complicated nature," is the correct answer.

The other choices can't be right, since the text doesn't mention him being erratic, complacent, loyal, or argumentative in the text surrounding the citation.

This question often causes students to give up on the idea of finding an answer spelled out on the page, so it's a very good example of how we must *always* insist on an objective answer, even when there doesn't seem to be one at first.

Page 707, Question 8

People often fail to read this question carefully enough, and get it wrong as a result.

Many people incorrectly choose (B), because the first passage mentions an "exclusive" "concern" with "classification," while the second passage mentions the ways certain scientific "possibilities" are "limit[ed]" (lines 18 and 19). But the problem with (B) is that the answer choice talks about the limits on "present-day science," while passage 1 talks about an exclusive concern that lasted "for the next hundred years" after Linnaeus's work, which happened in the 18th century according to line 1. So the first passage is talking about a limit that existed for 100 years after the 18th century, which means it wouldn't apply to "present-day science," since the present day is much more than 100 years after the 18th century.

(A) ends up being correct because the first author refers to Linnaeus's "enormous and essential contribution to natural history," while the second author mentions "the value of the tool [Linnaeus] gave natural science." (For this answer choice, it helps to realize that the terms "natural history" and "natural science" both refer to an area of study that is probably best known these days as "biology." In other words, "natural science" and "natural history" are synonyms, even if the words "science" and "history" aren't synonyms by themselves.)

Once again, the test gives us an excellent reminder of the importance of reading everything very carefully.

Page 708, Question 11

Here, as always, it will be very important to read the question, the answer choices, and the relevant text extremely carefully to make sure we don't fall for any traps.

The correct answer is (C) because the text describes how an actor would seem to die in one movie and then reappear alive, and transformed into someone new, in a later movie (lines 11 through 14). It then talks about movies being "illusions" in line 18 and their characters as "imaginary" in line 24, so (C) is correct.

Many people choose (E), which seems like a very similar choice, but we have to be careful to note the differences between (E) and (C). (E) says that the actual *plots* of the movies were implausible, but this doesn't reflect the original text if we read carefully. The original text describes somebody dying *in one movie* and then appearing alive and in a different costume *in another movie.* So we're not talking about a plot in which someone dies and is resurrected and transformed, which might be "implausible;" we're talking about one movie in which someone dies (which is plausible) and another movie where another character played by the same actor is an "Arab sheik" (which, again, is plausible). So the idea of a story with an implausible plot being told doesn't fit the text; the text says that people were upset to realize that the actual things on the screen couldn't be real, since people who died in one movie were alive in a later movie. It doesn't say that the individual plot of a particular movie itself was implausible.

By the way, while we're on the subject of this question, let's talk about the very fine difference between an "imaginary" "illusion" and something that is "implausible." If something is "implausible," it is difficult to imagine or believe. On the other hand, if something is "imaginary," then it's not real. It's possible that something could be imaginary while still being quite plausible: a short story about a child who draws on the sidewalk with chalk could be a work of fiction (and therefore imaginary) while still being very believable (and therefore plausible).

In most classroom situations, if you referred to an illusion as something "implausible," your teacher would probably have no problem with that; on the SAT, though, these kinds of subtle distinctions matter. The text describes things that didn't happen; it doesn't specifically describe the plot of any movie as "implausible."

Page 725, Question 11

This question often looks challenging to test-takers, but, if we stay calm and consider each choice carefully, remembering that we want to find an answer choice that's directly reflected in the text, we can work through it fairly easily.

(A) is wrong because the text doesn't specifically say anything about the particular spots where things are found, and it doesn't say anything about "social significance," even though it mentions "social structures" in line 9.

(B) works because the text specifically says "much less is known" about a civilization "because linguists have yet to decipher the . . . script found on recovered objects." In other words, it specifically says that the reason we don't know as much about the Indus civilization is that we don't understand its language, which means that understanding its language would help us know much more than we know right now. Note the similarities between "decipher" and "decode." So (B) is correct.

(C) doesn't work because the text doesn't specifically mention any such similarities. It does talk about social structures, and it does talk about old cultures, but it doesn't specifically say that structures of old cultures were all similar to one another.

(D) doesn't work for a variety of reasons. For one thing, there is a difference between "learn[ing] the language" and "decipher[ing] the script" of a language—we could learn to decipher written texts without actually knowing how to speak the language of that text. Another problem is the word "effective"—nothing in the text gives any specific indication of what would constitute "effective" archaeology.

(E) doesn't work because the text only mentions "Harappan script." It doesn't make any generalizations about other "ancient languages."

Page 727, Question 19

This is one of those questions in which the College Board gives credit for an answer choice involving the idea of humor, but most test-takers don't find anything humorous in the text.

(B) is correct because the phrase "wickedness incarnate" can't be meant literally—remember that the College Board will be okay with us calling things humorous (or, in this, calling something a "parody") when the text describes something that can't be taken literally. "Incarnate" literally means "made into flesh" (note the similarities of the roots in "incarnate" and "carnivore.") So the text would be saying that people on the Right think that "government regulations" are always "wickedness incarnate." (You may want to read lines 82 - 84 carefully to see what I'm talking about. The text says that some people are afraid of good news because it would mean that regulations can sometimes be "something other than wickedness incarnate." This means that their assumption is that all regulations are normally "wickedness incarnate.") The idea of "people with certain political leanings" from the answer choice matches with the phrase "the Right" in line 82: people on "the Right" tend to be conservatives.

(C) also talks about "humor," but the phrase "deep longing of the author" has no parallel in the text.

Page 763, Question 7

This is a question in which we're asked to find an answer choice with a scenario that parallels a scenario in the text. Strictly speaking, these kinds of questions can involve finding answer choices with concepts that aren't directly stated in the text, but the relationships among the concepts will still be exactly the same as what appears in the text.

In this question, we need to start by figuring out what "the problem presented in the passage" actually is. We see that it's "the difficulty . . . in narrating personal experience in one language when one has lived in another." This must be the "problem . . . in the passage," because "difficulty" in line 6 is the only word that matches up with "problem" from the question.

So we're looking for an example of somebody narrating in one language after living in another language.

(A) doesn't work because it doesn't even mention narrating things.

(B) doesn't work because it's talking about an assumption—like (A), it doesn't even mention narrating personal events.

(C) doesn't work for a few reasons; perhaps the easiest to spot is that it's not talking about multiple languages.

(D) is correct because it talks about somebody trying to "articulate" things in "English," even though he is "Russian." So we have the idea of multiple languages, and we have the idea of articulation to match the text's reference to narration.

(E) doesn't work because the answer choice doesn't indicate which languages the journalist might be working in; it also doesn't say which language(s) she would be writing in. Even if we assume she would write in Japanese for the Japanese audience and in English for the American audience, as many students do assume, that wouldn't parallel the text, because the text is talking about living in one language and then writing in another.

Page 764, Question 11

Here we have another great example of a question that test-takers often miss because they read it as though they were in a classroom discussion.

The correct answer is (E) because the cited text talks about women "exerting influence on political events" by doing the tasks mentioned in the question, and (E) says those tasks are "examples of political activities."

Many students incorrectly choose (A), (C), or (D), because these choices are fairly close to the text and would probably be decent interpretations of the text. But we have to remember not to interpret the text at all when we're working on the SAT. So (A) fails because the text doesn't specifically say whether those activities "altered the course" of anything. (C) is wrong because the text doesn't say that women were unable to do anything besides those activities. (D) is wrong because the text doesn't say whether those activities directly affected households or not.

Page 767, Question 21

This is another question in which we have to look carefully at the text and find the answer choice that parallels the situation described in the text. With a question like this, the key thing to do is to read really carefully, as always.

The phrase "essential lessons" in the text is referring to what "young animals may be learning" in the previous line, which is "the limits of their strength and how to control themselves among others." So we need an answer choice that reflects this.

(A) doesn't work because, among other things, it doesn't specifically indicate that the class is "young."

(B) is correct because it incorporates the idea of being "young" and the idea of being on a team, which would necessarily involve being around others.

(C) doesn't work because it doesn't specifically mention the idea of the child being around other children.

(D) doesn't work because it doesn't say that the bear is a "young animal."

(E) doesn't work because it doesn't mention the idea of the kitten being around other animals.

Page 783, Question 15

Students often miss this question, along with many others about these two passages, because they make assumptions about what the author means, instead of reading carefully.

The relevant text says that "both the . . . inner voice . . . and the . . . literary or stylistic voice are . . . sexed."

(A) is wrong because the text never mentions the idea of "stylistic problems" being created for the "writer."

(B) is wrong because the author never mentions a preference on the part of the reader. A lot of students mistakenly choose this answer because they think it would make sense that people would prefer a writer of their own gender, but the text never says anything about a preference.

(C) doesn't work because the text doesn't mention romantic love.

(D) is correct because it restates exactly what appears in the text. The text says that the "stylistic voice" is "sexed." The word "voice" can refer to a writer's specific way of expressing himself, so the phrase "stylistic voice" in the text means exactly the same thing as "use of language" in the answer choice. If something is "sexed," it means that it has typical characteristics of one gender, so saying that the "stylistic voice" is "sexed" is the same thing as saying that the "use of language" is "shape[d]" by "gender."

(E) is another commonly chosen wrong answer. It doesn't work because nothing in the text talks about a reader having difficulty expressing *his own* voice. The text talks about the fact that it's sometimes hard for the reader to imagine *the writer's* voice if the writer is of a different gender. Once more, we see how critical it is to read every detail of every answer choice, and to take nothing for granted!

Page 793, Question 11

Students often have a lot of questions about this passage. As always, those questions tend to arise from not reading carefully enough.

Here, we're asked to find an answer choice that reflects Mulcahy's mood or attitude at the time that he "smile[s]" in line 33. The rest of the sentence that mentions the smile says that Mulcahy feels "a kind of pity, mingled with contempt and dry amusement." So we want an answer choice that reflects those emotions.

Many people like (A), but (A) has problems that keep it from being correct. The original text doesn't say that Mulcahy feels pity for himself, but (A) mentions "self-pity." The original text also doesn't specifically say anything about being cynical or skeptical in those lines.

Some people also like (D), but the text doesn't specifically talk about "disappointment," even if it seems natural to assume that someone who has just been fired might be disappointed.

(E) ends up being correct because the phrase "condescending sympathy" goes with "a kind of pity," while "amused scorn" in the answer choice goes with "amusement" and "contempt" in the text.

Page 827, Question 13

People often miss this question because they don't stop to think about the specific meanings of the words "that" and "how," and about the difference between those meanings.

In this context, the word "that" indicates the existence of a particular fact; when the author says "I can show *that* Fido is alert," he means that he can demonstrate the truth of a particular fact, which is the fact that the dog is alert to something.

In this context, the word "how" indicates the specific way in which something is happening. When the author says he can't show "*how* [Fido is alert]," he's saying that he can't demonstrate the specific way in which Fido is alert.

If we put these ideas together, we see that the author is saying he can show the truth of the alertness, but not the way the alertness works.

When we realize that "awareness" and "alertness" are synonyms in this context, and when we realize that the phrase "the nature of" goes with the idea of "how" something happens, we see that (D) restates what the author says, so it's the correct answer.

People who get this wrong tend to choose all four of the wrong answers with more-or-less equal frequency, so let's take a look at them.

(A) doesn't work because the difference between "seeing" and "believing" is mentioned in lines 39 and 40, and it's not mentioned in connection with the difference between "*that*" and "*how*" that we're being asked about. This is a great example of how we have to read very carefully to make sure that we're choosing an answer choice that combines the right ideas from the text.

(B) doesn't work because the text doesn't mention how the cat perceives things.

(C) doesn't work because the text doesn't mention anything to do with the difference between a hypothesis and a speculation.

(E) might seem attractive at first, because the text does mention "falsifyingly literal representations" in line 44. But there's a problem here: the text doesn't say anything to match with the phrase "accurate representations" in this answer choice.

Page 828, Question 16

This question is yet another good example of how we have to read very carefully when we work on the SAT. It's also a good example of the way we have to be willing to treat consecutive statements as synonymous on the Passage-Based Reading questions. The first sentence of the essay talks about "two warring souls," and then line 6 talks about "the tension between race pride and identification with the nation as a whole." The idea of "tension" between two things in that second sentence goes with the idea of "warring" in the first sentence, so the two "souls" at "war" are "race pride" and "identification with the nation as a whole."

That's exactly what (C) refers to, which is why (C) is correct.

Again, it's important to read everything carefully, and to force ourselves to find the answer in the text. A lot of people just talk themselves into (B), (D), or (E) because they don't insist on finding an exact match in the text.

Page 846, Question 24

This question seems to be asking us to speculate about how something in one passage would be applied to another passage. In these types of questions, it's critical to remember that no speculation is actually called for. We'll find the correct answer directly in the text, as always.

In the final paragraph of passage 2, the author says, ". . . the shrillest critics are not necessarily the most authoritative." He adds that "the very shrillness of their cries . . . quickly exhausts their wind."

The majority of passage 1 is dedicated to a variety of criticisms.

The correct answer, then, is (E), which talks about how critics who are "loud" will have influences that are "short-lived." Notice how "loud" goes with "shrill" in the text, while "short-lived" goes with the idea of the critics being "quickly exhaust[ed]."

None of the other choices reflects anything that the author of passage 2 mentions in the last paragraph. That paragraph doesn't talk about constructive advice, conforming to public opinion, being widely read, or being taken seriously.

Page 856, Question 19

People who miss this question almost always do so because they give up on the idea of finding the answer directly in the text, and just talk themselves into something so they can move on. But the answer *is* in the text for this question, just like it is for every other Passage-Based Reading question on a real SAT.

In the second line of the italicized print at the beginning of the passage, we learn that the narrator is writing about "his grandmother, Susan Ward." In line 10, we learn about "the grandfather she [Susan Ward] was writing about."

So both the narrator and Susan Ward are writing about a grandparent, which makes (C) correct.

Let this question serve as a reminder of two things. First, it's important to remember that the answer is always spelled out in the text, no matter how much difficulty we might have in identifying that from time to time. Second, it's important to remember not to give up looking for the correct answer—if you decide that something is weird about this question and you just take your best guess, you've basically made a decision to give points away for no reason.

Page 901, Question 19

This question asks about an assumption, but, as always, we'll find the correct answer choice by reading the relevant text very carefully. The quote we were told to read says, "'Adaptation follows a different path in each person. The nervous system creates its own paths. You're the neurologist—you must see this all the time.'"

Note that the last sentence of the quote says, in black and white, that the reason the listener must know about the nervous system is that he sees it all the time, since he's a neurologist. The text isn't requiring us to know anything about neurology; we don't have to make any assumptions about what neurologists do or don't know. Instead, the quoted text specifically says that a neurologist "*must*" (emphasis mine) be familiar with how the nervous system adapts.

This fits with choice (C), which says "all neurologists are aware" of the "adaptability." Note how "adaptability" from the answer choice fits with "adaptation" in line 37. So (C) is correct.

Some students get hung up on the phrase "all neurologists," because the quote in the text is only directed at a single neurologist. But "all" is appropriate here, since we were asked to figure out which assumption underlies the quote: if it were possible for there to be any neurologists who didn't know about adaptation, then the statement "you *must* know *because you're a neurologist*" wouldn't make any sense. So the assumption must be that *all* neurologists know about it.

Some of the wrong answers incorrectly combine concepts that appear in the passage. (B), for instance, includes the idea of different paths, the idea of understanding, and the idea of neurologists, but it doesn't tie those ideas together in the same way the text does. We have to make sure we don't talk ourselves into this kind of answer!

Page 914, Question 23

This question gives a lot of students the impression that they need to interpret the text, since the passage is a work of fiction and the question is asking about a character's emotional state. But it's important for us to remember that literary interpretation is never the way to go on the SAT.

In line 45, we're told that the young clerk "was cut to the heart," and that he felt like Akakyevitch was saying "I am your brother."

So the correct answer here is (E), which says that the clerk feels "compassion." To understand why, it might help to know that the expression "to be cut to the heart" means something like "to be profoundly moved." Further, the word "compassion" literally means that we feel something with someone else.

In the text, the clerk watches Akakyevitch getting teased, and the clerk himself feels "cut to the heart." In other words, the clerk feels a deep emotion in response to watching Akakyevitch's suffering. This is what "compassion" means by definition.

Most of the other answer choices don't make any sense relative to the text—from a literary standpoint we might be able to explain a choice like "fear" by saying that the new clerk might have been afraid he would be harassed like Akakyevitch, but on the SAT that doesn't work, since the passage never mentions the new clerk being nervous or worried about being targeted.

Some people also like the choice "confusion," because the text says the clerk "thought . . . he heard other" "words." But the rest of the text in that sentence doesn't describe someone being confused or unsure of himself; it describes someone feeling an emotion in response to watching someone else be tormented. When the text says that the clerk thought he heard other words, then, it means that the clerk was so moved that he *felt* as though Akakyevitch were crying out "I am your brother." This is the only way to read the text that makes the rest of the sentence have any coherent meaning.

Page 922, Question 14

The College Board often asks us about the function of quotation marks in a passage. If quotation marks are used in an SAT passage without the quote being attributed to a specific source, then they are being used to show that the author doesn't completely agree with the way someone else would use a particular word. Think of these quotation marks like the "air-quotes" that people sometimes make with their fingers while they're speaking, to show that they're using a word or phrase in a way that they might not personally agree with.

In this case, the authors of both passages are showing that they don't agree with the common uses of the words "frees," "verbs," "nouns," "stealing," or "property" in the contexts in which they are used in these passages. So the correct answer is (D).

Remember that when the SAT asks about the usage of quotation marks for unattributed quotes, the correct answer will involve the idea that the author does not agree with the common usages of the phrases in quotes.

Page 963, Question 16

A lot of test-takers miss this question because they make the mistake of trying to analyze the text. But if we adopt the more passive, reactive approach of simply checking through the answer choices to see which one is supported by the text, we'll find the answer with much less difficulty.

(A) doesn't work because no actual "event" is being "dramatized" here. In other words, the joke isn't describing anything that actually happened—jokes, by their nature, are fictional.

(B) doesn't work because there is no particular point being argued *within or by the joke itself*. The essay as a whole is arguing a point, as all essays do, but the joke isn't arguing a point by itself. Since the question asked us about the role of the joke in the passage, and not about the role of the passage overall, (B) is wrong.

(C) is the correct answer because the text says, in line 33, that the joke "allows me to jump right into an idea . . ." The idea that the author can now "jump right into" after telling the joke is the "topic" being "introduc[ed]" in the answer choice.

(D) is wrong because the joke doesn't involve defining any terms.

(E) is wrong because of the word "misleading," among other things. It's true that the end of the joke does involve the word "assume," and it's true that cows aren't spherical, but the text itself never says that the assumption is "misleading." This is yet another example of how careful we have to be not to impose our own interpretation on the text; in order for this answer choice to be correct, the text would have to say directly that the assumption was false or misleading. Since it doesn't say that, (E) is wrong.

Page 976, Question 24

Of all the questions in the "Trabb's boy" passage, this is the one that students ask about the most often. Many of them get caught up in the phrase "pervasive comic strategy" in the question prompt, because they don't feel like they know what that phrase means. But we can actually work around that phrase by remembering that the correct answer must reflect something that appears directly in the text. So let's go through the answer choices and see what we have:

(A) can't work because the onlooking townspeople don't say anything in the entire passage.

(B) works because the author says his "position was a distinguished one" in line 9, which indicates that he had a sense of dignity, and because Trabb's boy is clearly engaging in what we might call "antics." So (B) is correct.

(C) is wrong because the author never says that he didn't understand anything.

(D) doesn't work because the text doesn't invoke fate to "rationalize human faults." The text does mention "fate" in the first paragraph, but there's no rationalization of anything. In other words, there is no attempt by the author to explain something away by relying on, or referring to, fate.

(E) doesn't work because the townspeople are ridiculing the author, not the boy. This is another example of how the College Board likes to create wrong answers that involve major concepts from the text but don't reflect the correct relationships among those concepts.

Page 985, Question 16

This is another question that asks us how the author of one passage might respond to something from another passage. As always, we'll find the answer spelled out directly in the text.

The academic historians in the first passage "have not given [Williamsburg] the significance it deserves," according to lines 8 and 9, and have "dismiss[ed] it" and seen it as "harmless but amusing."

But, starting in line 82, the author of passage 2 says that Williamsburg is a "crime against art and history" that is evidence of "an established element of popular culture" that "has also given a license to destroy."

Choice (E) is correct then. The phrase "fail to take seriously" in the answer choice goes with the phrases "dismiss" and "harmless but amusing" in passage 1. The phrase "damage done" in the answer choice goes with the idea of the "license to destroy" in passage 2. The phrase "cultural trend" in the answer choice goes with the phrase "established element of popular culture" in passage 2.

(A) is incorrect because the academics in passage 1 never say anything about how much history can be learned.

(B) is incorrect because the author of passage 2 also thinks the environments are an "established element of popular culture."

(C) doesn't work because the academics don't say anything about the necessity of simplifying history.

(D) doesn't work because the academics don't endorse anything.

Conclusion

Now that we've gone through a lot of these Passage-Based Reading questions, you're probably beginning to be able to find the correct answers pretty reliably. Your abilities will improve with practice, especially when you have to figure out questions that seem challenging at first. Hang in there, and keep the rules of the test in mind!

If you'd like to see a selection of free video solutions to help you keep improving, then check out www.SATprepVideos.com.

SAT Passage-Based Reading Quick Summary

This is a one-page summary of the major relevant concepts. Use it to evaluate your comprehension or jog your memory. For a more in-depth treatment of these ideas, see the rest of the section.

The Big Secret: The answer to every question comes directly from what's on the page. No interpretation whatsoever.

The rules for Passage-Based Reading on the SAT are simple; the only challenging thing is making sure you follow them all the time, no matter what. Here they are:

- Correct answers are always directly supported in the text.
- Don't overlook details. The difference between right and wrong is often just one word.
- Remember there is always exactly one right answer per question.

Here are the most common wrong-answer patterns you'll see:

- Answer choice contains statements that go beyond what is mentioned in the text.
- Answer choice mentions concepts from the text but confuses the relationship between them.
- Answer choice is completely irrelevant to the text.
- Answer choice says the opposite of what the text says.
- Answer choice would be a decent interpretation if you were in a literature class.

Here's the general Passage-Based Reading process:

1. Skim or read the passage (whichever you're more comfortable with). Or even skip it altogether.
2. Read the question and note any citation.
3. Read the relevant portion of the text (the citation if there is one, otherwise the part that has similar concepts to the question).
4. Find four wrong-answer choices (look for wrong-answer patterns).
5. Confirm remaining answer choice.
6. Mark the correct answer.
7. Save general passage questions for last.

Special notes:

Two consecutive statements in a passage should be treated like synonyms if the College Board asks about them. If they have a negating word like "not" or "never" between them, then they should be treated like antonyms.

The words "metaphor" and "humor" in an answer choice refer to a non-literal phrase in the passage.

The word "irony" refers to a contradiction.

If you think 2 or more answer choices are equally valid, then you're overlooking some small detail.

See the many example solutions in this Black Book for demonstrations of these principles.

SAT Sentence Completion

"Knowledge of things and knowledge of the words for them grow together."
- William Hazlitt

Overview and Important Reminders for SAT Sentence Completion

When talking about the Reading section of the SAT, most tutors and courses prefer to start with the Sentence Completion questions. This is because most people hold two incorrect beliefs about the SAT Critical Reading section:

1) They think that students will improve significantly if they simply memorize enough vocabulary words, and
2) they think that improvement on the Passage-Based Reading questions is impossible for most students, because they don't realize how those questions work.

But, as usual, we do things differently in the Black Book. You'll notice that I started with a discussion of Passage-Based Reading questions. There are also two reasons for this:

1) The central concept that we use in solving Passage-Based Reading questions, which is the idea that the correct answer must restate something directly in the passage, still applies to the Sentence Completion questions, and
2) many years of experience have taught me that most students have an easier time grasping that idea in the Passage-Based Reading questions than they do in the Sentence Completion questions.

There are two main types of Sentence Completion questions, and they're very similar to each other. The first type is the Single-Blank question, and the second is the Double-Blank question. The only difference between them is that the first type asks you to fill in one blank, and the second type asks you to fill in two blanks. You use basically the same process to answer either question type, but the two-blank questions sometimes allow room for a little more creativity on your part.

In this section, we'll go over the ways that natural test-takers find the answers to Sentence Completion questions, including an explanation of why memorizing vocabulary is generally not the best way to prepare.

More importantly, we'll talk about what you should actually do if you want to improve your performance on these questions.

5 Reasons Why Memorizing Vocabulary Is Not The Best Way To Go

Most students try to approach SAT Sentence Completion questions by memorizing hundreds, or even thousands, of vocabulary words. This is a terrible idea, left over from the days when the SAT had analogies and antonyms on it (it was a terrible idea even then, but it's an even worse idea now).

Even though there's a whole industry built around teaching SAT vocabulary to high school students, there are a lot of problems with the idea of cramming vocab in order to raise your SAT score. Let's take a look at some of them now.

The Questions Are Clearly Not Designed To Test Vocabulary Directly

Because most people never stop to think about the SAT from the College Board's standpoint, it never dawns on them that the Sentence Completion format is actually a really bad one if you're trying to evaluate somebody's vocabulary. If the College Board wanted to measure vocabulary knowledge in the most simple and direct way possible, it could have simply created a question format in which it would provide a single word as the prompt, and then five potential definitions as answer choices, and asked you to select the correct definition for the word in the prompt. That would be a much more direct test of your vocabulary knowledge. Instead, the Sentence Completion format gives you a variety of potential clues and connections to make, both within the sentence and among the answer choices.

Further, most students will find that they know all the necessary words to answer at least half of these questions, and possibly nearly all of them, without feeling like they're going outside of their comfort zone in terms of vocabulary. Why would the College Board include questions with these kinds of simple words if the goal were purely to test your vocabulary? For that matter, back when the College Board dropped the analogies from this part of the test in 2005, why did they change the name of this section from the "Verbal" section to the "Critical Reading" section? In my opinion, the most likely answer to all of these questions is that the College Board recognizes there's a lot more going on here than just vocabulary knowledge.

Now, don't get me wrong: I agree that, all things being equal, it would be more helpful on these questions to have a larger vocabulary than a smaller vocabulary. I also agree that there are sometimes questions (often the last question or two in a page of Sentence Completion questions) that would definitely be easier if you knew all the words in the answer choices.

But even recognizing the existence of the more vocabulary-intensive questions forces us to admit that the rest of the questions just aren't like that. And even in the more vocabulary-intensive questions, the more challenging words tend to involve multiple syllables, and they also tend to be derived from, or similar to, words from Latin, French, or Spanish, or even popular brand names. In other words, they're often (not always, but often) words that students have a fighting chance at figuring out.

If the College Board wanted to test vocabulary directly, it would use single-syllable words derived from sources that were less likely to be familiar to test-takers, like "dun" or "kith." The potential meanings of these kinds of words would be nearly impossible to figure out unless a student already knew them.

The Questions Aren't Standardized For Vocabulary

Despite what students seem to think, and despite what many test prep companies want you to believe, the SAT does not appear to be standardized for vocabulary.

In other words, we won't find the same set of challenging words being used over and over again on the Critical Reading part of the SAT. It's not as though there is a list of 200 words that the College Board consistently draws from when creating Sentence Completion questions. If there were, then it might be a good strategy just to invest our time in learning that list of words.

This is why the companies that sell you vocabulary lists must constantly update the lists they publish to reflect the words that have appeared on the most recent tests. If the College Board were sticking to a standardized list of vocabulary words, those commercial lists wouldn't need to be updated every year. But it doesn't, so they do.

Even the so-called "high-frequency" SAT lists demonstrate the lack of standardization on the test. Many companies sell a list of hundreds of "high-frequency" SAT words for students to memorize. If we accept the idea that there are 500 "high-frequency" words (which is already a little odd, since each test only has approximately 150 words that appear in answer choices for Sentence Completion questions, and a large portion of those words are pretty common words), how many "low-frequency" words would we expect? Another 500? One thousand? If we apply the Pareto principle we might expect that there could be another 2,000 potential "low-frequency" words.

Contrast this situation with the idea of preparing for the Math or Writing sections. Both of those sections are clearly standardized for a defined set of relevant principles that the test-taker is clearly supposed to know. On the Math section, students clearly need to know how to solve for a variable, the sum of the degree measurements in the angles of a triangle, and so on. On the Writing section, students need to know about subject-verb agreement, dangling modifiers, and other clearly defined principles of grammar and style. If you were to write books explaining all the math and writing concepts that were necessary for the Math and Writing section of the current version of the SAT, you would literally *never* need to update them (assuming you did a thorough job in the beginning) because the concepts that are tested in the Math and Writing section *literally never change*. That's the whole purpose of standardizing a test.

But the commercial vocabulary lists need constant updating, because the same words don't appear over and over again on each SAT. Can it be that the College Board, which did such a good job of standardizing its Math and Writing subject matter, just forgot how to standardize stuff when it created its so-called "vocabulary" test? Of course not. The much simpler explanation is that the Sentence Completion questions were never intended as a vocabulary test in the first place.

The Vast Majority Of Time Spent Memorizing Vocabulary Is Wasted On The SAT

We just discussed the idea that some test prep companies sell lists of so-called "high-frequency" words that appear on the SAT, which might imply the existence of as many as 2,500 challenging words in total that could appear on any particular SAT. Those are fairly large numbers.

They seem even larger when we think about how many challenging words a test-taker is even likely to encounter on any given test, and how many of those challenging words she actually needs to know in order to answer a question correctly.

But it's also important to remember that *most challenging words are irrelevant to the test*. In other words, for every Sentence Completion question on the SAT, it's actually possible to arrive at the correct answer knowing *only the correct answer choice*. In some two-blank questions (definitely not all, but some), it's possible to figure out the correct answer if we only know one of the ten words in the answer choices. It's sometimes possible to figure out a correct answer choice by eliminating other choices that we might be more familiar with, even if we don't actually know the meaning of the correct answer choice. And so on—we'll see many actual examples of this a little later in this book.

In my experience, after having worked with tens of thousands of students from a variety of educational backgrounds and through a variety of media and formats, I can say that, on average, most test-takers will encounter somewhere between 2 and 8 questions per test in which challenging vocabulary actually poses a serious obstacle.

So we'd be potentially talking about memorizing anywhere from hundreds to thousands of words in order to have a better chance—hopefully—of answering maybe a half-dozen questions or so on the actual day of the test. When we consider that there are so many easier, more reliable ways of improving performance on other areas of the test, it's a little ridiculous, in my opinion, to devote all that memorization effort to the hope that it *might* help us answer 6 more questions correctly.

And that reminds me—there's no guarantee that the words you memorize will actually be the words that trouble you on test day, because the test isn't standardized for vocabulary anyway.

Knowing The Words Doesn't Guarantee A Right Answer, And Not Knowing Them Doesn't Prevent One

More times than I could possibly count, I have seen people miss Sentence Completion questions even when they knew all of the necessary words. This tends to happen for two reasons: either the person didn't know how Sentence Completion questions on the SAT were designed, or the person didn't read the question carefully enough. (Remember: it's not by accident that the College Board calls the part of the test with the Sentence Completion questions the "Critical Reading" section.)

I have also seen students find clever ways to work around holes in their vocabulary, in order to find correct answers with certainty, even when they might not have known all (or any) of the words in the answer choices before answering the question. This can't be done in every case, of course, but it can be done much more often than most people think.

The prevalence of both types of scenarios (people missing questions when they know the words, and people getting questions right when they don't know all the words) strongly supports the idea that these questions are not primarily about vocabulary, and that memorizing definitions is generally a waste of time and energy, at least for the SAT.

It's Often Possible To Score Above 750 While Omitting 3 Or 4 Questions

A lot of people don't realize this, but the "curve" on the Critical Reading section is typically much more generous than the one on the Math section. Often, you can miss a question (sometimes even 2) and still have a "perfect" 800 on the section. In fact, if your goal is to be above a 750, your cushion might be a handful of questions. If you want to be in the 650+ range, you can often omit a dozen or so questions, assuming all of the answers you do mark are correct.

So it's not the case that you'll need to answer every single Sentence Completion question correctly in order to have any hope of an elite score on this section of the test.

Memorizing Definitions Is A Bad Way To Learn Vocabulary Anyhow

One of the dirty little secrets of the vocabulary business is that forced memorization doesn't usually help people learn vocabulary anyway—at least, not in an ideal way.

Time after time, I've had students remark to me that they know they memorized the definition of a particular word once, but they can no longer recall what it means. Sometimes, even when they do think they recall a word's definition, they're wrong—either because they're remembering incorrectly, or because the definition they memorized was incorrect or inexact in the first place.

This happens because our brains aren't designed to think of the words in our vocabularies as entries in a database, as things that can be memorized efficiently from flashcards. Think about the words that you feel comfortable with, and how you learned them. Nobody ever sat you down and taught you the word "table" with a flashcard. You learned the word "table" by living in and around people who used the word consistently and correctly, and you automatically picked up its meaning because that's what your brain was designed to do: extract the meaning of a particular word through repeated exposure in its correct context. Think about all the other words and phrases you've probably learned over the past few weeks or months: nicknames for celebrities, the names of popular dances, specialized techniques for playing an instrument or a video game, who knows what. In every case, I'm willing to bet that you learned these words without giving them much thought. You just picked them up because they were constantly around you, and because *you actually cared what they meant*.

Now contrast this with the plight of someone trying to memorize the definition of the word "ameliorate" off the back of a flashcard. The context is gone. The exposure is limited and artificial. And, more importantly, you have no real interest in it—if you really cared what the word "ameliorate" meant, you'd probably know it already. No real learning is going to happen in that situation.

I'm not saying you can't force yourself to remember a list of definitions and then recall those definitions when presented with the appropriate words. I'm not even saying that you can't do that with 5,000 words if you feel like it, or more. You totally can. People do it all the time.

I'm just saying that these feats of memorization aren't really the same thing as actually knowing how to use the words you're studying.

I've seen this kind of artificial memorization cause a lot of problems for a lot of people. Perhaps the most extreme example was a student who wrote in an essay that something happened "for the inaugural interval in 20 years," instead of writing "for the first time in 20 years," because he had memorized that "inaugural" meant "first," and that "interval" meant "time." More subtly, and more problematically, I've seen students answer Sentence Completion questions incorrectly because they had memorized an incorrect, misleading, or inadequate "definition" of a particular term.

Don't get me wrong here. I'm fully in favor of having the largest vocabulary possible when it comes to real life. But the value of forced memorization is negligible at best when it comes to building a powerful vocabulary. And a powerful vocabulary isn't as important on the SAT as most people think, anyway.

(By the way—not that you asked, but the way to develop an advanced vocabulary is to become genuinely interested in advanced stuff (politics, art, philosophy, history, whatever), so that you read about it and seek out other people who are also interested in it. If you do this for any period of time you'll quickly learn all sorts of new words and phrases, and you won't even notice it.) (Not that it'll probably help on the SAT, though.)

Okay . . . So Now What?

After our thorough discussion of some of the major reasons why memorizing vocabulary isn't the best way to go for most test-takers, you may be wondering how to approach Sentence Completion questions.

The answer is that you approach SAT Sentence Completion questions in much the same way that you would approach Passage-Based Reading questions: the correct answer to a Sentence Completion question will restate a concept from the sentence, just as the correct answer to a Passage-Based Reading question will restate a concept from the text.

So, if you happen to know what all the words in a particular Sentence Completion question mean, answering that question correctly is just a matter of reading carefully and paying attention to details.

But what if you don't know what all the words mean?

Every single test-taker is going to run into at least one question on test day that involves a word he doesn't know. Most of us will run into a handful of them. Some will run into even more. For these situations, we have backup strategies that can often (but not always) help us figure out how to answer the questions.

We'll talk about those back-up strategies in just a moment, but, before we do, I want to lay out the proper way to prioritize all this stuff, from a preparation standpoint.

Now that we know that the entire Critical Reading section on the SAT basically rewards us for choosing answers that restate things directly from the page in front of us, we should focus on making sure that we never miss a question in which we know the meanings of every relevant word. This is basically just a matter of reading carefully, remembering how the test works, and paying attention to details.

So the first order of business, and the most important concern from here on out, is this: *make sure you grab every possible point from the questions where you know all the relevant words!*

After you get to a point where you can correctly answer any SAT Critical Reading question you come across when vocabulary isn't a problem, your next priority should be to focus on improving Math and Writing as much as possible.

Finally, after you feel you've made all the progress you can make on the Math and Writing stuff, and after you've reached a point where you basically never miss a Critical Reading question when you know all the relevant words, then, and *only* then, would I say it's a good idea to devote serious consideration to the Sentence Completion questions with difficult words.

So let me reiterate that, because this is important and most people get it very, very wrong. My list of priorities would be the following:

1) Basically perfecting Passage-Based Reading and Sentence Completion questions in which vocabulary is not a significant issue.
2) Just about anything SAT-related that doesn't involve worrying about vocabulary (in other words, Math, Writing, et cetera).
3) Worrying about questions that involve difficult vocabulary words placed in positions that cannot be ignored or worked around.

In other words, the thing that many people consider to be the single most important SAT prep task—memorizing vocabulary words—is actually the thing that I would rank as the single least important in the grand scheme of the test. I place it dead last in my list of SAT priorities because the payoff is relatively small (or even nonexistent) for the amount of effort that it requires. I can't possibly over-emphasize how important it is to focus on perfecting the process of correctly answering the Critical Reading questions where you know the words before you start spending any time memorizing definitions that are unlikely to help you on test day anyway.

But What Do We Do About Words We Don't Know?

When my students hear me say that I don't recommend memorizing vocabulary as a strategy for the SAT, they're often quite surprised. Their surprise quickly turns to doubt, and sometimes even indignation. Sometimes they ask, "Well, if I'm not building my vocabulary, what am I supposed to do when I run into SAT words that I don't know?"

And this is when I have to break it to them that there will almost always be words you don't know on the Critical Reading part of the SAT . . . *no matter how many words you try to memorize beforehand.*

Remember what we said earlier:

• There are tons and tons of words the College Board can use.

• They seem to use new ones all the time.

• The lists people study only reflect the words that have appeared on past tests instead of accurately predicting words that will appear on future tests.

For all of these reasons, it's impossible to avoid that scary feeling of running into unknown words on the SAT.

On test day, you're going to run into words you don't know. It's going to happen, whether you memorize words or not. Count on it.

So we were going to need strategies for dealing with unknown words in Sentence Completion questions no matter what.

Since you'll need backup strategies for dealing with unknown words anyway, my recommendation is that you just get really, really good at those backup strategies. So we'll talk about those kinds of strategies in a little bit—but only if you promise me you understand that these strategies are the *least* important part of taking the SAT. Before you worry about this stuff, you should be worrying about picking up all the Critical Reading questions in which vocabulary is not an issue for you.

(You'll notice that I repeat this idea of de-prioritizing vocabulary a lot. There's a reason: I've tutored tons and tons of people, and many of them have deliberately ignored my advice about not trying to memorize vocab words for the SAT. They even seem to do well on their practice tests, because most of the words they memorized were taken from the available practice tests. Then they go take the test officially and run into a lot of words they don't know, and they have a hard time since they haven't worked on any backup strategies for that situation. Do not be like these people. Take me seriously when I say that memorizing vocabulary should be your last priority, not your first one.)

The Big Secret Of Sentence Completion Questions

The big secret of Sentence Completion questions is essentially identical to the big secret of the Passage-Based Reading questions: correct answer choices will restate ideas from the sentence.

In other words, we are not simply looking for words that make okay-sounding sentences when inserted in the blanks. On many questions, you will find more than one answer choice that makes a decent-sounding sentence. We want the only answer choice that specifically restates an idea from the sentence.

For some questions (often, but not always, the first ones in a set), the way that the correct answer restates a part of the sentence is pretty clear. The grammar of these kinds of sentences is straightforward, and the correct answer choices for these kinds of questions involve fairly normal words.

For other questions, the words in the question may be fairly easy words for most test-takers, but the grammar of the sentence may be so complicated that some test-takers lose track of its meaning and aren't sure which ideas should be restated in the blanks.

Finally, there are other questions where the words are very challenging, and you might not really have much of an idea what the sentence or the words mean when you read the question for the first time. (As I've said many times by now, these types of questions are the ones that make people feel like they should memorize a lot of vocabulary. But that isn't the best way to handle them. We'll get to that later.)

We said before that there are basically two kinds of Sentence Completion questions, from the College Board's standpoint: questions with one blank, and questions with two blanks. But it would also be true to say that, from a test-taker's standpoint, there's a more important way to divide up the Sentence Completion questions: there are questions where we know enough of the words to be sure which answer choice restates part of the sentence, and questions where we don't know enough words to be sure.

The General Process For Answering Sentence-Completion Questions When We Know Enough Of The Words To Be Certain

This fairly simple process will let you answer Sentence Completion questions with total accuracy as long as you follow it faithfully.

1. Read the sentence and the answer choices with an open mind.

Many SAT-prep tutors, authors, and courses recommend "pre-forming" your answer, but I don't like that advice. "Pre-forming" is exactly what it sounds like: you read the sentence without looking at the answer choices, decide what you think the answer should be on your own, and then look for that answer. The problem with this is that you might misread or misunderstand the sentence, and then talk yourself into a wrong answer. Instead, I prefer to read the sentence and the answer choices, and then think about both the sentence and the answer choices as part of a system. (To be clear, there's nothing inherently wrong with the pre-forming approach. If you could execute that approach flawlessly, you would answer every single question correctly. In my experience as a tutor, the problem with pre-forming is that it makes it more likely that test-takers will make mistakes, and less likely that they'll be able to catch those mistakes after they make them.) So read the sentence and the answer choices without trying to jump the gun.

2. Look for an answer choice that restates the key elements of the sentence.

Again, just like with the Passage-Based Reading questions, the whole key to the Sentence-Completion questions is to find an answer choice that restates an idea in the text. If you know enough of the words in the sentence and you know the meaning of the correct answer choice, this part should be fairly straightforward. (If you don't, then you're reading the wrong thing right now—this is the process for situations where you know the words. We'll talk about what to do when you don't know enough of the words later on.)

3. Make sure you're absolutely certain that the answer choice you like restates an idea from the sentence.

This is where most test-takers make mistakes. Remember, again, that this whole section of the SAT is all about restating ideas that are on the page. In order for the correct answer to be valid, it must mean *exactly* what the phrase from the sentence means. A lot of students aren't precise enough with this, though, and they end up losing points when they don't need to. As one example, I had a student who recently chose the word "elaborate" to restate the word "instructive." She explained that a lot of things that are instructive are also complicated, which is true; the problem is that the two words aren't synonyms, even if many things are both instructive and elaborate. It's possible to be instructive without being elaborate, and it's possible to be elaborate without being instructive, so "elaborate" was the wrong answer to restate "instructive." Note that this student absolutely knew the meanings of "elaborate" and "instructive," and still talked herself into a wrong answer anyway because she ignored the unwritten rules of the test when she should have known better. This is the kind of thing you have to keep yourself from doing if you want to score high. It's way more important than memorizing words—no matter how big your vocabulary is, you'll run into trouble if you don't force yourself to be very precise with the meanings of the words you know.

4. Re-read the sentence, substituting the answer choice you like for the blank (or blanks).

This is a very important part of the process, and one that a lot of people overlook. The correct answer must fit exactly into the sentence, in a way that is grammatically acceptable. If it sounds awkward, it's not right, and you've misread or misunderstood something somewhere along the way. If it's a two-blank question, the words in the answer choices for both blanks have to fit exactly. If one fits great but the other one doesn't, then the whole answer is wrong.

Conclusion

Like I said, the process is pretty straightforward if we really know enough of the words. Basically, as long as you read carefully and force yourself to be very precise when you think about what the words mean, you can't go wrong.

The real difficulty can arise when we don't know enough of the words to be sure of the correct answer right away. Let's talk about some strategies we may find helpful in those situations.

What Do We Do When We Don't Know Enough Of The Words?

If you've been reading the sections of this book in order (which I highly recommend, by the way—that's why I wrote them in this order . . .), then you've heard me say several times already that not knowing the words in a Sentence Completion question is not one of our primary concerns on the SAT. It's much more important to focus on answering questions correctly when we do know all the relevant words, for at least two reasons:

1. Questions where you don't know enough of the words to answer with confidence will probably be in the minority, and they don't count for any more points than any other question on the Critical Reading section.

2. People often miss questions even when vocabulary isn't an issue, so it's important to make sure you fix that problem before addressing questions where vocabulary is an issue.

Still, we want to take our best shot at every single question on the test, so it's important to have strategies in place for dealing with these challenging words, once you've perfected your approach to questions where the words aren't an issue.

Let me say one final thing before we get into these strategies: a certain amount of creative thinking is required to answer Sentence Completion questions with challenging words, at least in the sense that there's a lot of potential variation from one question to the next. Sometimes a challenging question has one blank, and sometimes it has two; sometimes you'll have no idea what any of the words mean, and sometimes you'll have a pretty good idea what most of them mean, and sometimes you'll know something between those two extremes; sometimes words you don't know won't really matter, and sometimes they will; sometimes it will be easier to get an idea of the meaning of an unknown word, and sometimes it will be very difficult, and sometimes it will be downright impossible. And so on.

So you have to go into these situations with a willingness to play around a little bit, and you'll probably need to spend a little more time with these questions than you would spend on questions where you know enough of the words to be certain of your answers. Keep that in mind.

The Most Important Strategy: Skip What You Don't Know And Come Back To It

When most test-takers run into Sentence Completion questions where vocabulary is an issue, they groan and stare at the question for a while, hoping something will come to them. This is a natural reaction, but it's the wrong one. The most important thing you can do in these moments is to skip the question once you realize that you won't be able to answer it quickly and with confidence.

I'm not saying you skip the question for good. I'm saying you skip it for the moment, and come back to it later. (Maybe you'll end up skipping it for good anyway, if you still can't figure it out on your second or third shot.)

The reason for this is pretty simple: Since every question on the Critical Reading section counts for exactly one raw point in the scoring process, there's no point at all in spending extra time on harder questions when there could be a lot of easier questions for you on the next page.

So remember: when you first open up the Critical Reading section and start in on the Sentence Completion questions, your goal is to complete all the questions you can answer with total confidence as quickly as you possibly can, and to skip all the questions that you can't answer with total confidence and save them for later, if you have time. There's no reason to struggle with a hard question when you could be answering easier questions somewhere else.

For the rest of our discussion of challenging Sentence Completion questions, I'm going to assume that you've followed this advice about skipping the question on the first time around and coming back to it later.

Now let's take a look at another important strategy:

We Only Care If A Word Could Be Right. We Don't Care About Its Exact Meaning.

When we're trying to answer a Sentence Completion question, we know that the correct answer choice will restate the relevant part of the sentence. It may not seem obvious at first, but knowing this gives us a subtle advantage when we run into challenging words. Unlike other test-takers, we don't necessarily worry about what the word actually means. Instead, we're only trying to figure out if the word seems like it *could possibly mean* what it would need to mean to be the right answer.

For instance, if we had a sentence like "Reginald was so (blank) that he kept jumping for joy," then we would know that the word in the blank would have to mean something along the lines of "extremely joyful." If one of the answer choices were "disconsolate," for example, we might be able to realize that "disconsolate" doesn't seem to have any features that would suggest that it's related to being joyful. In that case, we could be pretty sure that "disconsolate" was the wrong answer, even if we didn't know exactly what it actually meant. (Of course, that might not be enough on its own to tell us what the *right* answer actually is, but it can often be helpful.)

We'll see several more examples of this idea as we look at actual SAT questions in the coming pages.

Keep this in mind as you practice the rest of the strategies in this section, and as you take the test. You're not necessarily trying to figure out what a word actually means; you're just trying to figure out if it could possibly mean what it needs to mean in order to be the right answer.

Don't Be Afraid Of Different Forms Of A Familiar Word

Many times I've had students who are afraid to make small logical leaps when figuring out what words mean, often because they've been taught (incorrectly) that they shouldn't make those leaps.

As an example, I once had a student who knew the meaning of the word "therapy," but didn't feel like he knew the meaning of the word "therapist." I asked him if he knew what the suffix "-ist" meant, in words like "pianist" or "receptionist." He said he did. When I said, "So does it seem like a 'therapist' might be somebody who does something related to therapy, just as a 'pianist' does something related to pianos and a 'receptionist' does something related to receiving people?" He said, "I guess so. I mean, I thought of that, but I wasn't sure."

I'm telling you that you can go ahead and make those assumptions safely, no matter what your teachers may have told you in the past. If you know how a suffix works, and that suffix is attached to a word that looks like something else you know, then you can be fairly certain that the meaning of the word is essentially what it would seem to be based on its parts. There are occasional exceptions to this, of course, but remember that *we're not trying to figure out exactly what a word means.* We're just trying to figure out if it could possibly mean what it needs to mean in order to be the right answer to the question.

This leads me to a more general word-deciphering strategy:

Break Words Into Syllables And Attack From Right To Left

I have said, repeatedly, that the Sentence Completion questions on the SAT aren't purely about memorizing vocabulary. One of the major pieces of evidence supporting this conclusion is the fact that the College Board frequently uses "challenging" words that involve multiple syllables and/or have some connection to Latin, French, or Spanish words that many test-takers may be slightly familiar with. (Of course, there will be some challenging words on the SAT that don't have these characteristics, and this particular strategy may not be very useful on those words.)

So we want to get in the habit of breaking unknown words into their syllables, so we can try to get a better idea of how they're put together and whether they might be appropriate answers for our Sentence Completion questions.

When we break the words apart, we want to consider their components in the following order: first the suffixes, then the roots, and finally the prefixes. We want to go backwards, in a sense.

This might seem odd, but there's a good reason for it. The suffix (if there is one) is the most easily identifiable and reliable component of most words, and the prefix (if there is one) is usually the least reliable component of the word.

For thorough examples of how this idea works in the context of real SAT questions, you'll want to take a look at the sample solutions that appear a little later in this book. But for now, let's consider a few imaginary examples, just for practice.

Imagine that one of our answer choices includes the word "indefatigable." In this case, we might be able to break the word up and realize the following:

- the suffix seems to be "-able"

- the root seems to be something like "fatig"

- the prefix seems to be either "inde," or a combination of "in-" and "de-"

From here, we might be able to figure out that this word has something to do with the idea of whether something can have a certain action done to it, because of the suffix "-able." (Along similar lines, the word "forgettable" means something can be forgotten, and the word "understandable" means something can be understood.) The action in question seems to have something to do with the idea of "fatigue," or being tired. And the prefixes might indicate a double opposite, or they might not; it's hard to tell with these prefixes. "In-" sometimes indicates an opposite (as in "insincere") and sometimes indicates reinforcement (as in "intense"). "De-" sometimes indicates an opposite, but not always (the word "defend" is not the opposite of the word "fend," for instance). So we wouldn't know for sure what this word meant just from taking it apart, but we might be able to tell it has something to do with the idea of whether something can be fatigued, and that might be enough for us to figure out whether the word has anything to do with the sentence in the question.

As another example, imagine the word "relentless." We might identify the suffix "-less," which indicates the absence of something. The root would be either "relent" or "lent," with the possible prefix "re-." A student of Latin, French, or Spanish might recognize that the syllable "lent" could have something to do with the idea of being slow. The possible prefix "re-" might have something to do with the idea of repeating an action, or in some other way strengthening an idea. So we might eventually get the idea that the word "relentless" means something related to an absence of slowing or stopping—again, this doesn't fully spell out the meaning of the word on its own, but it could very well give us a strong idea of whether "relentless" might be appropriate for a particular question.

Let's try one more example, this time with the word "kindred." "Kindred" doesn't seem to have any kind of familiar suffix or root. We might look at this word and wonder if it's related to the word "kind," or the word "kindle." But neither of those seems promising, especially because they would involve something along the lines of "-red" as a suffix, and that wouldn't really make a lot of sense because we can't think of any other words where "-red" is a suffix. So if we ran into the word "kindred" in an answer choice and didn't already know what it meant, we would probably have little choice but to try to work around it and hope that we could figure some things out about some other words. As I said before, this strategy of taking words apart isn't always going to work, and we won't always be able to figure out a correct answer when we don't know some of the words in a question. Often we will, but sometimes we won't. That's just the way the test goes. Remember that it's still possible to score well in the 700+ range on the Critical Reading section even if you omit 6 or 7 of the Sentence Completion questions on the test.

And when you're taking words apart and trying to get an idea of what they might mean, consider the following strategy, as well.

Don't Forget Cultural References

Sometimes you can figure out roughly what a word means based on its similarity to a brand name, or even to words in popular novels, songs, or movies. Don't shy away from those connections, even if it might feel a little silly to use something from a Harry Potter novel to answer a question on the SAT.

When you try to use these references, remember that you're not trying to figure out what a word actually means; all you're trying to figure out is whether it's likely to be able to mean what it would need to mean to be the right answer.

For example, I had a student once who was working on a double-blank question in which she eliminated three of the answer choices, but was having a difficult time choosing between the last two, because she didn't feel like she knew any of the words in either choice. But she knew from the structure of the sentence that the word in the second blank needed to be a negative-sounding word, and she saw that one of the answer choices had the word "prudent" for that second blank.

While she didn't know the word "prudent" itself, she did recall that she had seen television commercials for a company called "Prudential." She reasoned, correctly, that a company wouldn't name itself something negative—nobody would call their company a name that meant "Horrible Company, Incorporated." She also knew that the suffix "-ial" didn't change the overall meaning of the word. So if "Prudential" was a positive-sounding word, then "prudent" probably wasn't a negative-sounding word . . . which meant it wasn't the right answer for the second blank in this particular question. She eliminated that answer choice and chose the remaining one, and got the question right.

Note that she still didn't actually know what the word "prudent" meant by the time she was done with the question. She only knew it didn't fit the sentence, which was all she needed to know. And this brings us to our next strategy.

Don't Feel Bias Towards A Word Just Because You Know It

I cannot tell you how many times a test-taker has told me he chose an answer for a Sentence Completion question simply because he knew what it meant.

Let me say, very clearly, that knowing the meaning of a word is ABSOLUTELY NOT a good enough reason for picking that word on a Sentence Completion question. The College Board is not obligated to make the correct answer be a word you know, so the fact that you know a word does not increase the likelihood that the word is the right answer.

In fact, I've seen it happen many times that a well-trained test-taker ends up choosing a correct answer to a question even though he doesn't know what it means, because he's been able to figure out that all the other answer choices don't work for one reason or another.

When you run into a situation where you know the meanings of some words but not all of them, you should start by considering the words you know and determining if they restate elements of the sentence. If they do, you're in luck—you must have the right answer. But if they don't restate part of the sentence, then you should simply eliminate them and set to work trying to figure something out about the remaining answer choices. That's all you can do in that situation, unfortunately. You shouldn't try to rationalize putting down a wrong answer just because you're comfortable with the word itself if it doesn't actually restate part of the sentence.

And here's one last important strategy I wanted to mention. You won't see it on the test too much, but it can make a real difference whenever it does come up.

Don't Rule Out A Word Based On Its Part Of Speech

Although I don't believe the College Board ever comes out and says so directly, all of the options for a particular blank will *always* be the same part of speech. They're either all nouns, or they're all verbs, or they're all adjectives, or whatever.

Many students are unaware of this rule, and they'll sometimes reject a correct answer because they think it can only be a noun when it needs to be a verb. But the College Board doesn't try to trick us in this way. When you're looking at an answer choice, don't worry about whether you're familiar with every possible part of speech the word might be. Instead, just think about what the word means, and whether that idea restates another idea in the sentence. Trust that the College Board isn't trying to mislead you by giving you a word that's the wrong part of speech.

The Sentence Completion Process in Action Against Real Questions

By this point, we've seen the process for answering questions when we know enough of the words to be sure we're right, and we've talked about some general strategies we can try to follow in situations where we don't know enough of the words right away to be certain that we're right.

Now it's time to take all of these abstract concepts and apply them to some concrete questions from the College Board's Blue Book, *The Official SAT Study Guide.* As I said earlier and will say again (often), the Blue Book is the only substantial printed source of real SAT questions that were actually written by the College Board, which means it is the only substantial source of questions that are guaranteed to follow all the same rules and patterns that the SAT will follow when you take it for real.

You can find the best deal on the Blue Book here: http://www.SATprepBlackBook.com/blue-book.

First, we'll do the Sentence Completion questions from page 390 in the second edition of the College Board's *Official SAT Study Guide*, since that's the first set of Sentence Completion questions from the first practice test in that book. Then, we'll go through a selection of questions from the Blue Book that students have traditionally had difficulty with, so that you can see the strategies in action in a variety of situations.

To show that we don't need to know all the words on the SAT, I'll proceed as though we don't know some of the words in various questions, when my experience with students would suggest that those words might not be widely known by most test-takers.

Page 390, Question 1

This is a single-blank question in which many students will be able to recognize that the word "foresight" restates the idea of "accurately predict[ing]" something. We can see that the word "predict" has the prefix "pre-" in it, which typically indicates something happening in advance of something else; we can also see that the word "foresight" has the prefix "fore-," which also indicates the idea of something being before something else. So (A) is correct.

Some students get nervous on this question because they aren't sure about the words "nostalgia" and "folly," but there's no need to worry about them if we're sure that "foresight" is correct. If you know that one answer choice restates the correct part of the sentence, then it doesn't matter what the other choices mean: the College Board will never create a question in which two answer choices accurately restate the relevant parts of the sentence.

Some students are also drawn to the word "despair," because it seems to them like a writer would probably be sad if his books weren't allowed to appear in his native country. But we have to remember that we're not just looking for an okay-sounding sentence; we specifically need a word that restates part of the existing sentence. "Despair" doesn't satisfy that criterion because the sentence doesn't actually say anything about being extremely sad or upset.

Page 390, Question 2

Here, we want a word that will mean the same thing as "simple and direct."

Many students will know the meanings of (A), (D), and (E), and will be able to tell that those words don't mean the same thing as "simple and direct."

But what about (B) and (C)?

(C) might seem like a word that could be broken up and analyzed. If we did that, we would probably conclude that "-atious" was the suffix (or compound suffix), and that the root was something like "ostent." But that probably doesn't help much—it's unlikely that we might be able to think of any word related to that.

(B) might offer more promise, actually. In this age of camera-phones and social media, many students are familiar with the idea of "candids," which are un-posed, un-planned photographs. This might be enough of a connection to let them realize that the word "candid" means "simple and direct"—in other words, it refers to something that has no pretense or staging about it.

If a student makes that connection, he should mark (B) and be confident of his choice. If not, and he's left with more than one or two choices seeming possible, this might be a good question to skip.

Many students miss this question because they choose either "intricate" or "fictional," even though the students who choose those answers often know what those words mean. While it might be possible in real life (I guess) for photographs to "provide an intricate reflection" or "provide a fictional reflection," neither "intricate" nor "fictional" actually restates an idea from the rest of the sentence, which means that those choices are incorrect on SAT Sentence Completion questions.

Notice, too, that we don't need to know what the phrase "bygone social milieu" means at the end of the sentence. Remember that it's possible for us to answer Sentence Completion questions with total confidence even if we don't know every single word involved in the question!

Page 390, Question 3

This is a single-blank questions that many, many test-takers will correctly choose to skip. This is a question with a fairly large share of challenging words, and the words that might be easier for test-takers to figure out are, unfortunately, not the correct answer.

We want a word that means "impulsive," and indicates a willingness to follow "sudden whims."

Many students will choose to begin by attacking (D) and (E). We can probably tell that (D) will mean something like "lacking passion," which isn't going to be the right answer here. (E) also seems like it doesn't have anything to do with the idea of being impulsive; it seems more related to words like "decoration" or "decorum."

We may also be able to tell that (C) is vaguely related to words like "eloquent" if we can realize that "-acious" is a compound suffix and the root is something like "loq." Maybe we figure that out, maybe we don't.

Even if we do figure out that "loquacious" isn't a restatement of the idea of being "impulsive," we're still stuck with the words "capricious" and "bombastic." "Capricious" will be a hard word to take apart—its root will seem to be something like "capric" or "capr," but most test-takers won't really know what to do with that root. "Bombastic," on the other hand, is probably easier to take apart—so much easier, in fact, that many test-takers will incorrectly choose it, just because they feel comfortable with the root "bomb."

Test-takers often like the idea of the root "bomb" restating the idea of something being "impulsive," because a bomb is a device for creating a destructive impulse of energy. But the rest of the sentence involves the idea of "sudden whims," and nothing in the idea of a "bomb" should strike us as inherently whimsical.

So if we can realize that "bombastic" doesn't go with the idea of "sudden whims," then we might be able to tell that "capricious" is the only choice we haven't been able to eliminate (assuming we can also work out that "loquacious" is unlikely to be correct). This could be enough for us to be able to see that (A) is correct.

Unfortunately, most test-takers who try to work out an answer here will choose "bombastic" because they ignore the idea of the "sudden whims." This is one more good example of how critical it is to pay attention to details on the SAT, and not to fall in love with an answer choice just because it kind of seems to work for part of a sentence but not all of it.

For most people, then, skipping this question will ultimately be the best option.

Page 390, Question 4

This is a classic example of a question that untrained test-takers miss all the time, even though they typically know all the necessary words to find the right answer. For most students who get this question wrong, the major issues will be the grammatical complexity of the sentence and the difficulty posed by the word "visceral."

The key thing here, as always, is to read very carefully, and to remember that all questions in the Critical Reading section of the SAT rely on the idea of restating concepts exactly.

The phrase "that is" in the last line of the sentence indicates that everything after the comma is a restatement of everything before the semicolon. In other words, if we call the first blank "X" and the second blank "Y," the fact that it was "visceral . . . rather than X" is the same thing as the fact that it was "not . . . rational [but] Y."

Let's keep that in mind as we work through this.

For most people, the easiest place to start will be with the second blank, because we can tell that the word in the second blank needs to be the opposite of the word "rational." The second word in choice (A), though, is a synonym for "rational," so it won't work. The second word in choice (B) is unrelated to the idea of being rational, so it won't work either. (C), on the other hand, offers an antonym of "rational" in its second blank, so it's okay; (D) works too. (E) offers another synonym of "rational," so it's out.

So we can tell that (C) and (D) are the only two choices that offer antonyms of the word "rational" for their second blanks. Now we have to figure out whether "intuitive" or "deliberate" is the right option for the first blank.

We can see that the first blank needs to be the opposite of the word "visceral," but a lot of test-takers won't know what the word "visceral" means. It might look like we're stuck . . . until we remember that the last part of the sentence is a restatement of the first part, as we discussed above.

So the word in the first blank isn't just the opposite of "visceral." *It must also be the same thing as "rational"!* We know that because the first half of the sentence says the decision was "visceral" instead of the word in the first blank, and then the rest of the sentence says the decision wasn't "rational." So "rational" and the word in the first blank must be synonyms, because of the College Board's unwritten rules about things in Sentence Completion questions restating each other.

We probably know that the word "intuitive" refers to something being a gut feeling, while the word "deliberate" refers to something that is carefully considered, or "rational." So, out of these two options, we want the word "deliberate" for the first blank. That makes (D) the right answer.

Remember that reading carefully and knowing the rules for these questions is more important than memorizing a lot of vocabulary words! Also remember that you can often work around difficult words, just like we could work around the word "visceral" in this question.

This kind of question is the sort of thing you want to focus on during your preparation and testing, rather than something like number 3 on the same page, because the technique that we use to reason through this question will be broadly applicable on all Sentence Completion questions, while the strange words in a question like 3 will probably never appear in positions that matter when you take the test for real.

Page 390, Question 5

This question is a great example of the type of thing that most test-takers will miss, even if they've memorized a ton of vocabulary, because the words in the answer choices are fairly obscure and the grammar of the sentence is more complex than usual.

But a well-trained test-taker can easily take this question apart and find the right answer in seconds.

The question talks about the idea of a "transformation" that results in the destruction of something. From years of experience with many, many students, I know that most people will have a difficult time with nearly all the words in these answer choices, with the possible exception of the words in choice (D). In fact, people often make the mistake of choosing (D) just because they know what those words mean, even though "innovation" is definitely a positive idea and the word in the second blank definitely needs to be negative (since it "destroyed" good things like "adaptability"). Let this question be one more reminder of the fact that you shouldn't pick a choice just because you know what the words mean—they have to mean the right things in the context of the question in order to be right!

But even if we don't know the rest of the words, we can probably take their suffixes apart. Notice that the sentence talks about something being done to these "business stratagems;" something about them is ultimately changed as the result of a "transformation." Now notice that some of the answer words in the answer choices sound like words that involve some kind of transformation process being applied.

For instance, (A) has the word "streamlined," which definitely sounds like it could be used to describe something that has been transformed by streamlining. (B) has "mitigated"—even if we don't know what that means, the "-ate" suffix there tells us this is probably an adjective made out of some kind of "mitigation" process. So that might seem like it could work, too.

But notice the second words for (A) and (B). (A) has the word "infighting," which doesn't really sound like any kind of transformative process. (B) has "jingoism," and even if we don't know what that word means, the suffix "-ism" usually indicates a set of beliefs, not a process.

Apart from (D), which can't be right because "innovation" is positive, there's only one answer choice that has two words in it that both sound like some kind of process: (C) has both "ossified" and "bureaucratization." "Ossified" sounds like some kind of transformative process because of the suffix "-ify," which we also find in words like "classify" or "pacify" or "rectify," all of which describe the idea of doing some action to something. "Bureaucratization" has that suffix "-ization," which also sounds like a kind of active, transforming process, like we see in the words "pasteurization," "ionization," and "immunization."

Believe it or not, we can be sure (C) is right if we simply realize that "innovation" doesn't work and that (C) is the only other choice with two words that could describe a transformation. We don't even need to know what those words mean.

Now, let me be very clear that this exact type of solution will not be possible on every single Sentence Completion question, for the reasons I described earlier in this section: the College Board uses a wide variety of sentence structures and a wide variety of words, so we have to be flexible in our solutions. Sometimes we'll look at a question with a lot of unknown words and there just won't be anything we can do. But sometimes we'll be able to work out the question mostly by reading carefully and paying attention to suffixes, and that's what happened here.

Conclusion

This might feel like a strange, unreliable way of answering SAT questions. If it seems that way to you, it means you're still thinking as a traditional, cramming-oriented test-taker. Just loosen up a little bit and try using these techniques in practice. After a few questions they'll begin to feel much more natural.

It will probably help to check out www.SATprepVideos.com, where a selection of free videos is available for readers of this book.

In order to help that process along, let's take a look throughout the rest of the College Board's book at some other test items that students have often had questions about.

A Selection of Challenging Questions

Now let's talk about some solutions for the SAT Sentence Completion questions that people typically have difficulties with. As always, you'll need a copy of the College Board's Blue Book to follow along.

I strongly advise you to follow along with these solutions as a way to continue to improve your performance on Sentence Completion questions.

Page 402, Question 6

This is a two-blank question that a lot of students miss because they don't bother to consider their answer in the context of the original sentence. Most people who miss this question choose (A), because the idea of "cheapen[ing]" something seems to fit nicely in the sentence for the first blank, and "affordable" definitely works for the second blank.

The problem, though, is that it doesn't make sense to say that the new method "cheapened" an "industry." A product might have been cheapened, but the industry as a whole can't technically be cheapened—the industry doesn't have a price that could be lowered, which is what "cheapening" would have to mean in this context.

If we go back to the original sentence and imagine saying it with the word "cheapened" in place of the first blank, we can probably feel right away that it's odd to talk about an "industry" being "cheapened." But, again, a lot of students don't catch this mistake because they don't take the time necessary to go back and fit the word back in the sentence to make sure it's correct.

So now let's look at the other choices, and see if we can find some words that could work in the first blank. Industries can be "transformed" or "revolutionized," and maybe even "stimulated." It sounds a little odd to talk about "provok[ing]" an industry, though.

Now let's consider the other words in choices (B), (C), and (E).

For (B), we might not know what "viable" means, so let's skip it for the moment.

(C) doesn't quite work. Even if we don't know "prohibitive," we probably know words like "prohibited" and "prohibition," so we can tell that "prohibitive" has to do with making something difficult or impossible. That doesn't go with the idea of things being "inexpensive" from the early part of the sentence.

(E) doesn't work either, for the same reason—nothing in the sentence talks about making it harder to access anything.

So now we can tell that (B) is correct, especially if we know what "viable" means, or if we can realize it might be related to words like "vive" in French or "viva" in Spanish, which have to do with living or surviving.

Let this question remind you that you always have to pay attention to small details on the SAT. People choose (A) all the time on this question because they don't check the details. For most people, missing this question isn't a matter of vocabulary—it's a matter of not following the rules of the test.

Page 402, Question 8

This is a question that many people will probably choose to skip. We want a word that means "disloyal," but most students will be very unfamiliar with every word in the answer choices except, perhaps, "tenacity," which isn't the right answer. These particular words will also be fairly hard to take apart in terms of roots and suffixes. It also doesn't help that the first four answer choices are all negative-sounding words, which makes it hard to eliminate any of them.

So, again, the best thing for most test-takers to do is to skip this question, unless you just happen to know the word "perfidy" for some reason and can tell that choice (C) is correct.

Why am I talking about this question, then?

This question is the kind of thing most people think about when they think about the Critical Reading section of the SAT: a question with difficult, obscure words, and very little context. But this question is actually pretty abnormal, if you compare it to the rest of the questions in the section. The only other question in the whole section that might have similarly difficult words with so little context is number 7, but the remaining 22 questions in the section are nothing like those two.

If you skip 7 and 8, but lock down the other questions on the section, including questions like 6, by paying attention to details with words you actually know—and if you maintain a similar pace on the other two Critical Reading sections—you'll have a score above 700.

So the reason I wanted to talk about this question is to reiterate that it's not the sort of thing you should be focusing on in your SAT preparation. There's much more useful stuff we can learn from questions like number 6 on the same page, and there are many opportunities on the Critical Reading section to answer more questions with less effort in the amount of time we might spend trying to answer this one.

Page 425, Question 5

Lots of test-takers incorrectly choose (D) here. Their reasoning is usually something like this: "Well, I can imagine that it might be possible for some luxurious fabric to be really thin and transparent, so I guess 'luxurious' is a good answer—plus, I know what it means."

But remember that we can't just pick an answer because we know what it means. We have to check and make sure it's appropriate to the sentence.

In this case, the word "luxurious" simply does not mean "basically transparent." It's true that *some* luxurious things might be transparent, and *some* transparent things might be luxurious, but the two terms are not identical. So (D) is wrong.

Now, what about the other choices?

Many test-takers can figure out that (C) probably has something to do with the idea of variation, and that it's irrelevant to the sentence.

We may also recognize that (E) is related to the word "anomaly," which is also not appropriate here.

(A) is a bit more of a reach for most people. If we can figure out that (A) is related to the idea of being able to touch or feel something, then we can tell that it must not be correct.

That would allow us to know that (B) must be right, since the other four answers are wrong. We could work this out even if we can't figure out anything about (B) on its own.

But if we can't figure out that (A) doesn't work, or if we don't recognize that (E) doesn't work, then we should probably skip this question.

No matter what, though, we shouldn't pick "luxurious." We know it's not the same as the word "transparent."

Page 458, Question 8

In this question, we want a word that relates to the idea of being "unpredictable" and "given to . . . shifting moods."

Many of the answer choices will be hard for a lot of test-takers to figure out, but let's give them a try.

(A) probably reminds us of the word "mercury," or possibly the planet of the same name. If you've ever studied the element mercury in school, you know that it behaves very oddly and is often an exception to a lot of chemical trends. But let's leave that aside for a moment.

(B) is a word you might recognize from warning labels on household cleaners, or on the sides of trucks on the highway. Neither context really involves something being unpredictable.

(C) is a word we can probably take apart. Its root seems to be related to the idea of being genuine, and the "dis-" and "in-" prefixes could possibly indicate a few different things (as we noted earlier, prefixes are often less reliable than other parts of a word). But the idea of being genuine probably also doesn't have much to do with the idea of being "unpredictable."

(D) looks like it would mean something along the lines of "unable to be placed" or "unable to be placated." But neither of those possibilities seems like it would mean the same thing as being "unpredictable" or "constantly shifting."

(E) is a tough word for a lot of people to recognize on paper, though many people say the root of this word out loud when they get sick. The root is "phlegm," pronounced "flem," as in the gunk that can coat your lungs when you're sick. If we can recognize the pronunciation from the spelling, we can probably also tell that nothing about the word "phlegm" specifically involves the idea of being predictable or not.

So if we can put all of that together, we can see that (A) might make sense, while the other answers don't. In that case, we go ahead and mark (A), and get the question right. But if we end up being stuck with a few answer choices feeling unresolved, then we leave the question blank—remember that we can omit a half-dozen Critical Reading questions on most test days and still score above a 700 on that section of the SAT.

Page 475, Question 3

As we've discussed, we're supposed to realize that, in SAT code, the first blank will mean the same thing as "brief," and that the second blank will mean "instructive."

Many people incorrectly choose (B) for this one because they realize that "concise" works great for the first blank without noticing that "elaborate" doesn't mean the same thing as "instructive" for the second blank.

It's true that there might be some things that are both "instructive" and "elaborate," but the two words are not synonymous—not all "instructive" things are "elaborate." Some are quite simple.

(D) is the correct option here because "succinct" is a synonym for "brief" and "enlightening" is a synonym for "instructive."

Let this question serve as one more reminder of the fact that it's very important to pay careful attention to every detail, especially on questions where you know what the words mean! I've talked to a lot of people who incorrectly chose (B) for this question, and every single one of them knew what "elaborate" and "instructive" meant, but let themselves pick (B) anyway. Don't do that.

Page 487, Question 5

This is a difficult question for a lot of test-takers, and many of them choose to answer it incorrectly rather than leave it blank.

From the structure of the sentence and our knowledge of the SAT's rules, we can tell that the word in the blank needs to restate the idea of being "preoccup[ied] with daily life in rural and agricultural settings."

Many people choose (B) because they know that the word "prolific" is something that can be applied to writers or other artists who produce a large volume of work. But that word doesn't fit here, because we're looking for a word to describe the actual *novels*, and novels can't produce large volumes of work. (On top of that, the sentence doesn't say anything about producing a lot of work anyway.)

(E) might also be attractive to people who don't pay close enough attention to detail, and for the same reason. It's true that metaphors are related to the idea of literature, but "metaphorical" doesn't mean the same thing as being interested in "rural and agricultural settings," which is what the right answer needs to mean.

The words in (A), (C), and (D) might be a little harder to deal with, though, and this is why I'd recommend that most test-takers skip this question and invest their energy in other questions, where it would be more likely to pay off. These 3 words will be hard to take apart, and most test-takers will be left guessing and probably losing points.

Of course, if we happen to know the word "bucolic," we'll know that (A) is correct. But most test-takers won't know that word—and, even if you do know it, the chances that it will be helpful on a future SAT question are practically zero.

(Many people who prep in the traditional way will see this question and decide they need to learn the words "bucolic," "lugubrious," and "sundry." But the odds are very small that you would ever see those words again in a position on the SAT that actually matters. If you want to learn those words to further your own education, that's a different story, of course. Just don't expect them to make a difference when you take the test for real.)

Page 487, Question 6
Unlike the previous question, this is one that most test-takers should invest their time and energy in, because it's a question we can probably answer correctly by reading carefully and relying on the meanings of words we know.

From reading the sentence carefully and remembering the rules of the SAT, we can tell that the word in the first blank needs to mean "foolish." The word in the second blank needs to mean something that a person could be "accuse[d]" of for applying "skewed data."

For the first blank, then, (A), (B), and (E) might all seem like good ideas. That means we need to figure out whether "remonstrance," "erudition," or "chicanery" might be the best option for the second blank, the thing that somebody would be accused of for applying skewed data.

If we know the meanings of those words, the answer is pretty clear. But let's assume that we don't, and attack the words to try to figure out what they might mean.

"Remonstrance" looks like it might have a meaning similar to "demonstration," since both words seem to have a prefix stuck on the root "monstr." (We might also wonder if the word is related to "monster," but, even if it is, it wouldn't have anything to do with applying skewed data.)

For "erudition," we might see a connection to the ides of "rudeness," or of something being "rudimentary." "Rudeness" does seem like something that a person could be accused of, so it might look tempting, but the sentence says that a person would be accused of rudeness *because he "appl[ied] skewed data,"* and that doesn't really work, unfortunately—the word "rude" applies to somebody who does something impolite, not to somebody who applies bad data.

That leaves us with "chicanery." This is a word that's probably pretty hard to take apart. But if we're reasonably confident that the other four answer choices don't work, and that the first half of this one definitely does work, then I'd go ahead and mark (E) and get the question right.

This, then, is an example of a question that looks pretty challenging at first but can probably ultimately be figured out by reading carefully and paying close attention to the rules of the test and to the *exact* meanings of words.

Page 520, Question 7
In this question, we can see that the word in the blank needs to refer to the idea of having "insights . . . beyond ordinary perception." Many test-takers incorrectly choose (B) for this question because the idea of being a stockbroker seems to be related to the idea of making a profit, but this is yet another example of how important it

is to read everything on the SAT very carefully: the word in the blank needs to restate the ideas at the end of the sentence, not the idea of being a stockbroker.

Most students will know the meaning of the word in (A), and will be able to tell that a "mentor" is not necessarily someone who has extra-sensory perception. The same goes for (C): most test-takers will know the word "counterfeit" and will realize that this choice has nothing to do with special insights. (E), as well, is another word that relates to something most test-takers will recognize—in this case, the word "propaganda," from history classes.

That leaves us with (D), a word we may have a hard time taking apart (students of French will realize that the word means "clear-seeing" in French, which certainly goes along with the idea of having extremely good perception, since sight is one way to perceive things). But, even if we can't take it apart, we know for sure that the other 4 choices don't work, and that means (D) must be right.

Page 520, Question 8

This is one more excellent example of the general uselessness of memorizing vocabulary words for the majority of Sentence Completion questions. The correct answer here is the word "discriminating," because the word "discriminating" originally referred to the idea that a person had very good taste and could separate good things from bad things in a way that the average person would not be able to do. (Of course, the more common use of the word "discriminating" today simply refers to the idea of treating people differently based on their race, gender, age, and so on—in that context, it's obviously not a positive thing.)

I would be willing to bet that most students who approach Sentence Completion questions as an exercise in vocabulary knowledge would not even bother to memorize the word "discriminating" if they saw it on a list because they would be sure they already knew what it meant. And they would probably end up missing this question as a result.

But if we approach the test correctly, thinking more about the words we know and about the rules of the test rather than simply looking to apply one of the 3,000 oversimplified definitions we might have learned from a flashcard, this question is probably answerable.

We can tell that (A) doesn't work because the sentence doesn't refer to the judges as being unknown or difficult to find, which is what "obscure" would mean.

(B) might be a bit more of a challenge for a lot of test-takers, though, because the root of "deferential" might sound an awful lot like the root of "differences" in the text, but there's a difference between "deferring " and "differing." To "defer" something is to put it off for later, while "differing" involves being different. Since the text doesn't talk about people putting anything off for later, "deferential" isn't going to be correct.

(D) is a word a lot of test-takers pick because it seems hard to take apart, and because they mistakenly assume that (C) must not be correct. But if we look more carefully, we may see that "sanctimonious" has something like "sanct" for a root, and we may realize that this is similar to the idea of "sanctuary," a word we might know from political or religious contexts. If we can work that out, we can realize that (D) isn't the right answer either.

(E) also doesn't work—if we don't know this word, we might be able to break it apart and realize the root is "lent," which has a relationship to the idea of being slow in French and Spanish. But nothing in the sentence is talking about anyone being slow or fast, so this is the wrong answer.

At this point, it would be good for a lot of test-takers to revisit the word "discriminating." We know that "discrimination" in the more common context involves focusing on differences between people; hopefully, given the fact that the rest of the words don't work, we can realize that, in the context of evaluating food, the idea of "discriminating" also involves focusing on differences, though of a different type. This makes (C) correct.

Page 549, Question 4

This is another example of a question in which most test-takers will try to make an ill-informed guess based on their gut feelings, and be wrong.

The key in this question is the phrase "diametrically opposite." The word "opposite" goes with the prefix "anti-" in choice (B), which is how we know that (B) is correct.

Many people will choose (D) or (E) because their prefixes seem to suggest the idea of two things, but the sentence doesn't just say that New Zealand and Spain are two different countries—its says they are opposites in some way.

Let me use this question as an opportunity to remind you that it's extremely important to pay careful attention to these kinds of small details! The people who score in the top 5 or 10 percent on the SAT are not, generally, people who memorize a ton of stuff; instead, they're people who pay careful attention to the important parts of each question, and who avoid making small mistakes.

Page 549, Question 6

This is another question in which paying careful attention to the rules of the test might let us figure out the correct answer even if we don't know all the words in the answer choices.

The sentence refers to a "sound" being made by a youth orchestra. Note that the word "cacophonous" has the root "phon" in it, which indicates a relationship to the idea of sound in a lot of other words (like "telephone," "phonics," and "homophone"). This connection alone might be enough for us to feel certain that (A) is the right answer.

If we want further proof, we should note that the sound causes the members of the orchestra to be "abashed." If we can tell that the word "abashed" is probably negative (it might help if we realize it could be related to "bashful"), then we know that the word in the first blank must be a negative word. That would make it impossible for (C) or (D) to be correct.

Some students won't feel comfortable choosing (A) purely on the strength of the relationship between the root "phon" in the answer choice and the word "sound" in the sentence. But this is the kind of connection we need to start looking out for on Sentence Completion questions, because in many cases it can allow us to realize that answers like (A) are correct even if we couldn't have defined the words in those answers on our own before seeing the question.

Page 576, Question 5

This question is one that people miss all the time, even though the people who miss it nearly always know the meanings of every word in the question. This makes it a great example of the types of mistakes people can make because they either don't know the rules of the SAT or don't pay careful attention to details.

Because of the College Board's unwritten rule about parallelism on the Critical Reading section (which we talked about in our discussion on Passage-Based Reading), we can tell that the first blank needs to go with the idea of "light" from earlier in the sentence, and the second blank needs to go with the idea of "insulation."

So when we pair the word in the first blank with the idea of "incoming sunlight," it needs to go with the idea of "offer[ing] . . . light" from the beginning of the sentence. The only choice that works for the first blank, then, is (C), because "admit[ting] incoming sunlight" would be a way to "offer . . . light."

Let's check out the word in the second blank for (C) to make sure we haven't made a mistake. We have to ask ourselves this question: is "contain[ing] heat radiated from the ground" the same thing as "offer [ing] . . . insulation" and "preventing warmth from escaping?" The answer is yes, so we're sure that (C) is right.

Page 576, Question 8

This question is one that some students manage to figure out, but that most students would be better off leaving blank. It's also a good example of the pitfalls of memorizing vocabulary as an approach to prepping for the SAT.

From the sentence, we can tell that we need a word that means "very sentimental." (We have to read carefully to figure that out: the sentence says the films are called X, but that they're not sentimental enough to deserve that. That means that X must be a word that indicates a lot of sentimentality.)

If we don't know what the word "sentimental" means, then it will be just about impossible to develop a good idea of the answer to this question, and we should definitely skip it.

If we do know the word "sentimental," then the next challenge is to attack the answer choices.

(A) is a word that most test-takers won't recognize at all.

(B) looks like it might have some relationship to the word "cursor," or to "curse," but neither of those possibilities would suggest that the word means something related to sentimentality, so this is probably not a correct answer.

(C) looks like it might be related to the word "prose," which we may recognize from literature class. While some prose is sentimental, it's certainly not true that all prose is sentimental, so "prosaic" is unlikely to mean "very sentimental."

(D) is a word that a lot of test-takers know. It's not related to the idea of being sentimental, so it's out.

(E) is a difficult word for a lot of people, but if we attack it we may see that it's probably related to words like "secret" or "sacred," neither of which is related to being sentimental.

So here's the situation: *if* we know what "sentimental" means, and *if* we're able to work out that choices (B), (C), (D), and (E) really don't seem like they mean "sentimental," then—*and only then*—we might go ahead and mark (A), and know that we're correct. But if we don't know "sentimental" or we can't quite figure out that the other four words don't fit—which is the situation I suspect most of us will be in—then this is definitely a question we should skip.

Remember, once more, that the Critical Reading section is fairly forgiving when it comes to these kinds of things. We can still make a perfect score on the Critical Reading section if we miss one question on most days, and omitting even a half-dozen questions will typically put us right around a 750 out of 800. So this type of question isn't the thing you should be preparing for unless you've already completely mastered every other part of the test; it's much more important to work on practicing your basic skills so you can make sure to answer every question correctly in which you know enough of the words.

Page 587, Question 4

This is a question in which the word we choose for one blank will determine what the other blank needs to mean. (There are always a few questions like this on each test. We haven't talked about them separately because they don't require any kind of special treatment or anything.)

This is also a question that a lot of people miss because they don't pay attention, even though they typically know the meanings of all the necessary words.

In this case, I'd probably start by looking at the options for the second blank, since the word in that blank needs to be something that someone can be "accused" of. We can probably tell that (A), (D), and (E) could work for the second blank, because they're negative-sounding words. So now we need to see which of those choices has a word for the first blank that fits with the second blank.

A lot of test-takers won't know the word "vacillated," so let's move on to (D). Does it make sense to say that a person "experimented" so much that he was accused of "inflexibility?" No, it really doesn't—being inflexible means not being open to new things. It has nothing to do with the idea of experimenting a lot.

(E) presents a similar problem, even though a lot of test-takers incorrectly choose it. This is a very good example of how important it is to keep the SAT's unwritten rules about restatement in mind. In real life, to say that a person "relied so frequently" on prevention that he was accused of "negligence" could almost make sense, especially if there were some context. For example, this sentence would make a lot of sense if it appeared in the middle of a paragraph that was claiming that doctors should know how to cure diseases instead of hoping to prevent them. But we have to remember that the SAT doesn't allow an answer choice to be correct just because it might result in an interesting sentence. On this part of the SAT, it's all about restating things, and *relying on disease-prevention is not specifically the same thing as being negligent.* So this is not the correct answer.

Once we figure that out, we can realize that (A) must be the correct answer. But, again, it all depends on being alert to the rules of the test, and realizing that (E) doesn't actually work. If we can be very precise when we think about the meanings of the words we know, then we can work out correct answers to a lot of questions that most test-takers will miss.

Page 587, Question 5

This is yet another example of a question that test-takers can often attack successfully even without knowing what all the words mean, provided they read carefully and follow the rules of the test.

First, let's start with a careful reading of the sentence itself. (This is always important, but it's especially worth mentioning in this sentence because this one is a bit more complicated than most of them will be.) We can tell that the word in the first blank needs to mean something like "depict[ing] both the strengths and weaknesses" and "avoiding . . . extremes." The word in the second blank needs to be the opposite of "indictment"—we know this because of the phrase "two extremes," which indicates that the next blank must be the opposite of "indictment" (otherwise there would be only one extreme, mentioned twice). If we're alert to the College Board's unwritten rules, we know that the second blank goes with the idea of "depict[ing] strengths," just as "indictment" must go with the idea of "depict[ing] . . . weaknesses."

So let's start with the first blank. Based on what we've just figured out, (A) might seem like a good option for the first blank initially, but there's a problem with it. If something is "polarized," then it involves the idea of two polar opposites or extremes, but the second half of the sentence talks about "avoiding . . . extremes." So if we read carefully, (A) actually doesn't work, even though (A) is the choice test-takers usually go with when they get the question wrong.

As always, it's important to think about *exactly* what words mean, and *exactly* what the text says.

(B) doesn't work either, because the idea of being imaginative has nothing to do with the idea of "depict[ing] strengths and weaknesses."

(C) has a word for the first blank that most test-takers won't recognize, so let's come back to it.

(D) doesn't work because it would only involve depicting strengths.

(E) might be another unknown word, but perhaps we can realize that the root "equi" probably indicates the idea of equality, which could be related to the idea of showing both the good and the bad.

So, after some careful reading and thinking, we can realize that (C) and (E) might work for the first blank. Now the issue is to figure out what could work for the second blank, out of "censure" and "eulogy."

"Censure" sounds a lot like "censor" and seems to have a similar meaning, so it's not a good match for the idea of "depict[ing] . . . the strengths."

"Eulogy" is a word that a lot of test-takers might recognize from funerals, and that connotation of death might seem like a negative thing at first. But let's think about it for a second: the eulogy at a funeral is always a positive speech, full of kind thoughts and funny stories. So a "eulogy" really could be a "depict[ion]" of "strengths," just as the sentence requires, and (E) must be the right answer.

Of course, we don't even have to realize that "eulogy" works if we can work out that "censure" doesn't, and that only (C) and (E) have acceptable options for the first blank.

But notice, again, that this entire thought process requires us to read carefully and to play by the test's rules. If we just throw in whatever sounds kind of good to us and don't pay attention to the details, we'll end up missing questions like this for no reason.

Page 605, Question 6

Students often miss this question because they don't pay enough attention to the details. (How many times have you heard me say that by now? The reason it keeps coming up is that the SAT does the same things over and over again, and if you want to beat the test you have to be trained to look for those things automatically.)

From the sentence, we can tell that the first blank needs to restate the idea of "automatically reject[ing]" things that "seem silly or superstitious." (We know this because the sentence says that scientists shouldn't do that, and then says being a scientist isn't a license for whatever goes in the first blank.) So let's start with that. "Experimentation" doesn't work for the first blank, and neither does "humility" or "rigidity," because none of those words describe the idea of rejecting things because you think they're silly. But "arrogance" and "smugness" work well for that idea. So let's take a look at the other words in (B) and (D).

(B) doesn't fit if we put it in the sentence, because we would be saying that "qualifications" don't "pursue prejudice" (the word "they" right before the second blank refers back to the word "qualifications"). A qualification can't pursue anything, though—only people or animals can choose to pursue something.

But some people also have a problem with (D), because it seems to them like "legitimate" should be an adjective, and the sentence is clearly calling for a verb in the second blank. We have to remember, though, that all of the options for a particular blank are always the same part of speech; in other words, if the second blank needs to be a verb, and all the other answer choices for that blank can be verbs, then it must be that "legitimate" can also be used as a verb. (By the way, the verb form of "legitimate" is pronounced "luh – jit – uh – MATE.")

So (D) can work, because the verb "legitimate" restates the idea of being a "license" for something.

Remember, once more, how important it is to know the rules of the SAT when answering Sentence Completion questions. The many people who miss this question don't do so because they don't know the words "pursue" and "legitimate." They miss this question because they don't pay attention to details on the SAT.

Page 644, Question 5

This is another question that students nearly always ask me about. Many test-takers would probably do best to skip this one, but there are some things here that we can figure out.

First, we know that the word in the first blank must mean "elaborately contrived." We also know that the word in the second blank must restate the idea of "master[ing]" something.

Now let's look at the answer choices.

Most people won't know anything about either word in (A), so we'll skip that for now.

For (B), people will often think that being "conscientious" might be kind of related to mastering something. But if we think about it very carefully, we can see there's a distinction there—while many masters are very conscientious in their devotion to their chosen fields, it's possible to master something without doing it conscientiously. People can master tying their shoes without conscientious study, for instance. It's also possible to be conscientious about something without mastering it. Further, the word "nefarious" has a negative feel to it (because of the prefix "ne-") that doesn't really reflect anything in the sentence. So this one is out.

For (C), the word "devious" doesn't really fit with the idea of something being "elaborate" from the text. It's true that some "strategies" can be "devious," but that still doesn't address the idea of being "elaborately contrived."

For (D), "onerous" probably seems like a difficult word to figure out, but in "slipshod" we can see the root "slip." Since the idea of slipping generally indicates that something is not working properly (like when a car's transmission "slips") or that something has happened by accident (like when someone lets a detail "slip" or when an athlete "slips" on the playing field), it seems unlikely that the word "slipshod" is appropriate to describe someone who "master[s]" something. So this one is probably out, too.

For (E), the word "predictable" doesn't restate the idea of something being "elaborate." So this one is out, too.

That leaves us with only (A). Even though most test-takers don't know what either word in (A) means, we can still probably figure out that something is wrong with the other 4 choices, and that (A) must be correct . . . *assuming we read carefully and respect the rules of the test.* Most people who miss this question will choose (B), because they ignore the negative connotation of "nefarious" and talk themselves into thinking that "conscientious" restates the idea of "master[ing]" something. Don't make those kinds of mistakes. Don't give points away for no reason.

Page 662, Question 8
In this question, the word in the first blank needs to restate the idea of being "openhanded." Many test-takers will probably be unfamiliar with that word, but that might not be enough to kill our chances on this question. We might also be able to tell that the two words in the blank should contradict each other, because the sentence says it's "difficult to reconcile" the two words, which means they must be antonyms according to the College Board's unwritten rules.

Now our job is to look for an answer choice with two antonyms in it. We can probably tell that the words in (A) aren't opposites, and we might also be able to tell that the words in (B) aren't, either. (C) is a choice that many test-takers will skip the first time through because they don't know what its words mean. The words in (D) are both synonyms. If we know the words in (E), we can tell they're kind of similar to each other but not actually synonyms. If we don't know them, then we should hold off on eliminating them.

At this point, then, if we can work out that (A), (B), (D), and (E) aren't right, then we can confidently mark (C), and be correct. Of course, that assumes that we're comfortable enough with the words "insolence" and "solicitousness" to be able to determine that (B) and (E) are wrong. If not, we may have to skip this question.

(There's one other possible approach we could take: we might be able to recognize that the root of "magnanimity" is "magna," which means "big" in Latin, and that the root of "pettiness" is "petty," which comes from the French word for "small." Realizing that could let us figure out that the words in (C) are opposites.)

Page 706, Question 5
Here, the first blank needs to be something with a negative connotation, because it reflects what the institute's opponents call it, and it also needs to restate something about the idea of nobility. The second blank needs to reflect the idea of something that nobility might have had.

(A) probably looks good for the first word, because "elitist" is a word with a negative connotation that could describe something related to nobility. (It's true that "elite" by itself is a positive word, but an "elitist" is someone who considers himself elite and will only deal with other elites—in other words, a snob.) We probably don't recognize the second word here (it's NOT "pre-requisites," which is how many people incorrectly read it). So (A) seems like it might be possible at this point. Let's move on and see our other options.

(B) might seem pretty good for the idea of "nobility" in the text, but this is yet another time when considering something very carefully becomes extremely important. The word "monarchical" technically refers to a form of government in which there is only one ruler. It's true that some monarchical systems also included a class of nobles, but not all do. This is a critical distinction in this case, because the sentence is talking about a group of people ("scholars") in an "institute." It's not talking about a single person with power over others, which is what the word "monarchical" would indicate. So (B) is wrong. To a lot of people, this analysis will sound like splitting hairs, but this is exactly the kind of thing we should be on the lookout for if we want to maximize our scores on the SAT. Picking up on these subtle attributes of words you already know (not memorizing hundreds of extra definitions!) is what will help push you to an exceptional score.

(C) seems to work for the second blank, but most test-takers won't know the first word. Let's hold on to this one as a possibility and keep going.

(D) doesn't work because of the second blank—nothing in the sentence mentions anyone or anything being afflicted.

(E) doesn't work because of the first blank. "Commend[ing]" something means praising it, and the opponents of an institute wouldn't praise it (at least, not on a Sentence Completion question on the SAT).

So in this hypothetical scenario, we're left liking the first word in (A) and the second word in (C). At this point I would recommend most people should skip the question, because I don't like to put down an answer unless I'm positive I'm right (see my remarks on guessing earlier in this book, if you haven't already).

If you feel confident, you may be able to figure out that "perquisites" sounds an awful lot like "perks," the word used to describe bonuses that a person might receive at work or through a rewards program. If you notice the relationship between those two words, then you can be sure (A) is right. On the other hand, you might be able to recall that "reproach" is a negative word, so calling something "irreproachable" is actually a compliment, which wouldn't work for the first blank, so (C) would have to be wrong.

But, again, for most test-takers this is probably going to be a good question to skip.

Page 734, Question 5

This question is one that test-takers often miss, even though they can usually figure it out if they think carefully about it.

At first, it might look like we need to know the meanings of the words "skepticism" and "nihilism," but we actually don't; in fact, we don't need to know the word "elucidate," either. What really matters here is the word "helps," which tells us that the ancient philosophy went along with the 19th-century philosophy in some way.

When we look at the answer choices, the only one that works is (E), for two reasons. The first reason is that the prefix "fore-" captures the possible relationship that ancient philosophers would have to the 19th-century: they came before it. The second reason is that the idea of "foreshadow[ing]" goes along with the idea of "help[ing]" that's in the sentence.

(A), which is what people typically choose when they miss this question, doesn't work because something from the ancient past can't actively "suppress" something that ended up happening thousands of years later.

Page 762, Question 4

The key issue in this sentence is the phrase "on the contrary," which tells us that the word in the second blank must be the opposite of "humanitarian." It also tells us that the word in the first blank will have to indicate that the Professor doesn't believe something.

Let's start with the second blank. (A) is really the only option that gives us a workable word for the second blank. A lot of test-takers mistakenly think (B) offers a good option for that second blank, but, as always, we have to think very carefully about what that word actually means. It's true that being "contemptible" is bad and that being a "humanitarian" is good, but the two words aren't antonyms, and on the SAT we need antonyms in a situation like this.

Just to be sure, of course, I would check the other half of (A). "Dubious" works because the Professor doesn't believe that the government is "humanitarian" (we know this because the Professor "insist[s]" something "on the contrary"). So we know that (A) is correct.

This is another good example of how being very careful with the meanings of words in the answer choices and in the sentence can help us zero in on correct answers.

Page 780, Question 8

In this sentence, the word in the second blank needs to go along with the idea of "fail[ing] to comprehend" something. That's probably the best place to start, so let's take a look at the answer choices.

(A) gives us a second word that most test-takers won't know, so let's come back to it.

(B) is a word we might be able to take apart if we don't know it. "Vocal" indicates a relationship to the voice, "equi" indicates something to do with equality, and "un-" is a negating prefix. So this word seems like it has to do with the idea of not having equal voices, or of not giving equal voice to multiple things, or something along those lines. But none of that seems to mean the same thing as not comprehending something, so (B) is out.

(C) can work for us if we're familiar with the use of "penetrate" to mean "understand." Even if we don't know that usage, though, we might still like this word for the structure of it. The combination of "-able" and "im-" means that this word is talking about the state of not being able to do something, which goes with the idea of "fail[ing]" in the original sentence.

(D) will tempt a lot of people with the word "exotic," because it kind of seems to go along with the idea of not understanding something. But the word "exotic" doesn't specifically mean that something can't be understood! This is one more example of how important it is to pay careful attention to the exact meanings of words.

(E) doesn't work, either. We're probably familiar with the idea of a cheese grater, or of a grate in the ground, and neither of those concepts seems relevant to the idea of failing to comprehend something.

At this point, then, (A) seems possible (since we don't know what the word in the second blank means), and (C) might seem good, at least in terms of its structure. Let's check out the other words in those two choices.

The first word in (A) presents a problem, because "accessible" indicates that something can be accessed easily, but the sentence is talking about people failing to understand something. "Accessible" indicates that something is easy to figure out, so it doesn't work for the first blank.

That leaves us, again, with (C). At this point we have clear ideas why (A), (B), (D), and (E) don't work, and we have (C) with two strange words, the second of which seems to be structured in a way that reflects the idea of failing to do something. At this point, we should go ahead and mark (C) with confidence, and get the question right.

Note, once more, that this entire type of analysis can only be successful because we're very careful to make sure we treat the word "exotic" correctly in choice (D). Most untrained test-takers will still consider it a possibility, but it's really not, because being "exotic" and being impossible to comprehend aren't the same idea.

Page 791, Question 6

Unlike the question we just talked about, which we could probably figure out through careful reading and reasoning, this question is very likely to be one that most test-takers end up skipping.

We can tell that the correct answer choice should mean "separat[e] the good from the bad," but the difficulty is that at least a couple of these words will probably be unknown to us, and the ones we're likely to know, such as (B) and (E), aren't correct.

There's very little we can do in a situation like this. If we know the word "winnow," then we can tell that (D) must be right. But most people don't know the word "winnow." And even if you memorize the words in these answer choices now, the chance is almost zero that they'll come up on the SAT in a way that matters when you take the test for real.

So most test-takers should skip this question.

I wanted to mention this question to use it as a counterpoint to the one we just talked about, in which we were probably able to figure out the right answer by reading carefully and thinking carefully. It's because of questions like this one, in which we're probably helpless and have to skip to the next thing, that it's so important to make sure we pick up questions that we can actually figure out.

Page 824, Question 5

For this sentence, we want a word that would describe someone who has come to expect something that they would never even have dreamed of once.

Most students miss this because they choose (E), but the sentence doesn't actually say anything about anyone feeling bitter, so (E) is wrong.

The other words are often challenging for students, but we may be able to work through them. We may recognize that (A) means something like "surprised," which doesn't work here because it doesn't capture the idea of something becoming common that was once uncommon—if something is common, it can't surprise you. (B) is a word we might know from everyday conversation, or from television or movies; if we do know it, we can tell it isn't correct, because it means something along the lines of "a little angry" or "upset." (C) is a word most of us would have to skip. (D) is related to words like "aware" and "beware," but neither of those has to do with things becoming common, either.

So we may be able to rule things out and realize that (C) is the only possibility, and the correct answer. Of course, as is often the case, being able to arrive at this correct answer with confidence is only possible if we pay strict attention to the meanings of words and the rules of the test. Many people will get sucked in by the word "embittered" and never stop to realize that the sentence doesn't talk about anyone being bitter.

Page 842, Question 5

This sentence is one that bears careful reading. A lot of people choose (A) incorrectly, because they realize that the ideas of "gradual[ness]" and "abruptness" are important to the question, but don't realize that the clues aren't "signaling" the "abruptness" itself. The clues are signaling that sleep is coming, but they're not signaling that the coming will be abrupt. Furthermore, (A) gets the relationship between the halves of the sentence backwards.

But let's back up a little bit. The words "actually" and "though" indicate that some contradictory ideas will be presented here. The phrase "for several minutes" near the end of the sentence indicates that the first half of the sentence will be talking about something happening in one instant (since the first half of the sentence contradicts the last half).

So let's take a look at our remaining choices for words in the first blank. (B) doesn't offer anything to do with the idea of the opposite of "several minutes." (C) gives us a word related to the idea of time, but it's still not actually relevant to the sentence—one more example of why it's so important to read carefully and think carefully. Being "temporar[y]" has nothing to do with whether something occurs quickly or spread out over several minutes. (D) doesn't work for the first blank, either. (E) does—in fact, it has the word "instant" right in the beginning of it.

So let's take a look at the other half of (E) to make sure we haven't made a mistake. "Onset" works nicely in the sentence, and restates the idea of when the "sleep actually occurs." So we can tell that (E) must be correct.

There's one more thing I'd like to point out about this question. You may recall that I said I was against "pre-forming" answers to Sentence Completion questions, even though the strategy is widely recommended in many other sources. In this particular question, though, I pointed out that we were probably looking for a word that would mean something like "in one instant," and then the correct answer ended up including the word "instantaneously." So it might seem like pre-forming worked out for me here. But I wasn't actually pre-forming an answer to this question, because part of the pre-forming strategy is that you decide what the correct answer should look like beforehand and then go through the choices and try to find a word that matches your preconceived notion. I didn't do that: I considered each answer choice on its own as I came to it, and it just happened coincidentally that the correct answer sounded similar to something I thought about when I was explaining what the question looked like to me.

It's not uncommon for something like this to happen, especially as you develop more familiarity with the test, but it's very important that you never actually get in the habit of *insisting* that an answer choice include a certain word beforehand. Sometimes we misread sentences, or sometimes there might be more than one part of a sentence that a blank could restate, or sometimes a blank might be restating a word in another blank in the same sentence, or who knows what. It's important to sit back and let the sentence come to you, rather than trying to force the sentence to say something that it doesn't actually say.

Page 853, Question 4

A lot of test-takers incorrectly choose "nondescript" for this question because the sentence describes people who "neither spoke nor smiled." But, as always, it's important to think carefully about what these words actually mean.

"Nondescript" means that something has no particular description, as we can probably tell from the word itself. But the sentence actually describes the auditors: it describes them by saying that they "neither spoke nor smiled." So (E) doesn't actually work.

Let's try the other words. (A) certainly doesn't work. (B) is a word that often describes auditors in general, because people who choose to become auditors are typically motivated by their ethics, but the sentence itself doesn't say anything about ethics, so (B) is wrong. (C) is related to the word "glacier," which might not seem to be related. And (D) definitely doesn't work, because you have to speak to "taunt" someone.

So now what?

Well, if we're pretty sure that all 5 answers are wrong, there's only one possible conclusion: we made a mistake somewhere. So let's go back over our assumptions and see if we can figure out what we did wrong.

(A) definitely means "friendly," since we can recognize "ami" right at the beginning of it, which means "friend" in French and is similar to "amigo" in Spanish or "amicus" in Latin.

(B) definitely refers to ethics, which isn't relevant here.

What about (C)? We might realize at this point that glaciers are very cold things, and that the attitude of the auditors could certainly be called cold. It's also imaginable that a glacier might be intimidating. Could it be that when the word "glacial" is applied to a person it means that the person is cold and imposing, like a glacier?

Sure, why not? Given the circumstances, "glacial" must be correct.

This especially makes sense when we consider that the other 4 words are all clearly wrong.

Sometimes we have to go back and revisit our assumptions. There's nothing wrong with that—it's just smart test-taking. As always, careful reading and careful thinking are much more powerful than memorizing vocabulary—the people who miss this question don't miss it because they don't know the word "nondescript," or because they don't know what a glacier is. They miss it because they aren't paying attention to details.

Page 853, Question 6

This is a question that many test-takers will probably end up skipping, because high school students often lack familiarity with financial terms and this question can quickly turn into a dead-end without that familiarity. Still, we might be able to work our way through it.

In this question, we need a word for the second blank that could indicate some kind of cash award coming in the form of a loan. We may be able to recognize that (A) and (C) offer workable options for the second word. But what about the first word?

If we think carefully, we may realize that a "rebate" can only be given after something has been bought—you've probably heard commercials for car dealerships where new buyers are promised a rebate. The sentence doesn't say anything about the museum buying anything, so (C) doesn't actually work.

But a lot of students may not trust the word "reprieve" in choice (A). A "reprieve" is a chance to be let out of doing something, let off the hook. That works here because the sentence talks about the museum being "on the verge of . . . collapse."

So if we can figure out that (C) doesn't quite work, and if we have the confidence to trust (A) even though it sounds odd to many test-takers, then we can pull out the correct answer here and mark (A). Otherwise, we're probably better off skipping this one.

Page 898, Question 7

Coincidentally enough, this is another question in which some awareness of financial terms would be helpful, and not all test-takers are likely to know all of the relevant jargon. Still, let's give it a shot.

The words "although" and "actually" indicate that the sentence is putting forward contradictory ideas. So the word in the first blank needs to indicate the opposite of the idea of being able to stay in business. Let's start there.

(A) gives us a word for the first blank that most test-takers won't know, so let's skip it for now.

(B) gives us a word that won't work here, as we can probably figure out. You may recall that earlier in the book I cited "prudent" as a word that we might be able to recognize from its similarity to "Prudential," a financial services company you might have seen advertised. From this association we can tell that "prudent" is a positive word—nobody would name their company "Stupid, Unreliable Financial Services." That means it doesn't work here.

(C) is a word that many students might not recognize. But we can recognize the prefix "auto-," which has to do with the idea of self-directed activity. Does that seem relevant here? Probably not. So this one is probably no good.

(D) definitely seems like a word that contradicts the idea of being able to stay in business.

(E) definitely doesn't work, because it's a positive adjective.

So that would leave us with (D) as a word that seems to work, (A) as a word we don't know, and (C) as another word we don't know that's unlikely to be correct. Now let's take a look at the other blank.

The word in the second blank needs to describe some kind of activity that could let a company stay in business even when it shouldn't be in business.

(A) definitely seems to work for that second blank, then.

(C) really doesn't offer us much for the second blank. Even if we don't know what "subordinate" means, we can probably recognize that "sub-" means something is underneath something else, and that really doesn't seem relevant here.

(D) doesn't work for the second blank. There's no way that "engaging in charitable activities," which would basically mean giving stuff away for free, would allow a company to stay in business if it were bankrupt.

So at this point we may be able to figure out that (A) must be correct, since it has a word for the second blank that definitely fits and a word for the first blank that we don't really know, and since all the other choices have flaws in them.

Page 909, Question 4

This is another example of a question in which the words in the blanks will rely on one another. In other words, if the first blank says something like "contradicted," then the second blank needs to say something like "growing;" if the first blank were something like "supported," though, then the second blank would need to be something like "shrinking."

So we'll really have to make sure that we pay attention to both blanks. (That's always important, of course, but it's extra important here to consider the words we choose not only in relation to the given part of the sentence, but also to one another.)

For (A), we might not know what the first word means, but the prefix "co-" or "cor-" probably suggests the idea of going along with something. The second word, though, would be going against the "warning" in the sentence, because "prospering" is the opposite of "declining." So this one seems not to work as an answer.

For (B), "confirmed" seems like it might be able to go in the first blank, but we might not know what "extant" means. So let's skip this for now.

For (C), we might not know "belied," but it could have something to do with the word "lied," which is related to falsehood. "Dwindling" is a synonym for "declining," though, so these two words also don't seem to fit together to complete the sentence.

For (D), it sounds a little odd to say that a "warning" was "diminished." Still, even if we accept that, the word "debilitated" goes along with the word "declining." So this choice doesn't hold together—as we said at the beginning of this discussion, if the first word is something negative, then the second word would have to be something positive.

For (E), we might not recognize the word "tempered" in this context. But "thriving" definitely seems relevant to the idea of a population "declining"—"thriving" is the exact opposite of "declining" in this context.

So we're left with (B) and (E) as possible choices at this point. Let's review them. (B) will be right if "extant" means something like "declining." (E) will be right if "tempered" means something like "called into question."

As it turns out, (E) is correct, but a lot of test-takers may not feel confident enough in deciding that, and they should skip this question if that's the case.

Page 960, Question 8

For this sentence, we probably want a word in the first blank that would indicate using something up completely, and a word for the second blank that will mean the opposite of that idea (because the sentence mentions "replac[ing]" one with the other.

Let's take a look at our options for the first blank. (B), (C), and (D) all have words for the first blank that we can probably recognize as valid options for the first blank. (A) and (E) don't work for the first blank.

Now let's take a look at the options for the second blank. Again, we're looking for a word that would describe a policy that will not "deplete" "natural resources" "forever."

"Dispersion" doesn't really work here, because the idea of "dispers[ing]" "natural resources" is nonsensical.

"Gathering" is a synonym of "harvesting." If "harvesting" might lead to "deplet[ion]," then so might "gathering."

"Husbandry" seems like an odd word to a lot of test-takers, most of whom are unfamiliar with the term. It clearly has some relationship to the word "husband," but is that enough to make it right?

Well, let's think about that, especially in light of the fact that all the other choices definitely seem to be wrong. Could it be that the root idea of the word "husband" might be something along the lines of "protector" or "guardian?" That seems possible—and, if it is possible, then "husbandry" in this case might refer to the idea of protecting resources so they aren't "deplete[d] . . . forever." Again, this seems especially coherent when we remember that we're probably pretty familiar with all the other words we've looked at, and we're sure they don't work. So "husbandry" is part of the right answer, and (D) must be right.

This is the kind of problem-solving that the Sentence Completion portion of the SAT rewards. We read carefully, we think carefully, and we work stuff out based on our fundamental knowledge of everyday words.

Page 982, Question 5

Here, the word "although" indicates that there's a contradiction between the ideas of the way Keller was treated as a "hero" and the way he was "in the political arena." We can also probably tell that the word in the first blank needs to be positive, since the sentence says he "achieved" it, and since a "hero" is a good thing to be. Finally, the word in the second blank needs to be negative, to go with the idea of something being "painful."

(A), (C), and (D) might seem like good choices for that first blank, then. Now, our job is to figure out which of those options could work for the second blank. (A) is unlikely to work, since the word "versatility" is positive. (C) is also no good, since "finesse" is positive (we can see the word "fine" right there in the beginning of it). (D), on the other hand, looks promising, since "ineptitude" is a negative-sounding word that indicates inability (notice its apparent difference from the positive word "apt").

Given all of this, it's probably pretty clear that (D) is correct. A lot of test-takers accidentally choose (A) or (C), though, because they decide they like the first half of the answer choice and then don't bother to consider the second half and see that it doesn't fit.

Conclusion

This section has discussed all the rules, patterns, and strategies for SAT Sentence Completion questions. We've learned a process to answer those questions, and we've used that process on some real SAT questions from the Blue Book, second edition of the College Board publication *The Official SAT Study Guide*.

The most important part of SAT Sentence Completion is that we don't give up just because we don't know a word—but we never guess, either! We rely on careful reading, careful thinking, and an awareness of the SAT's rules. When necessary, we attack words to figure out if they might be relevant to the concepts in a sentence. Finally, we remember that we can always skip a question if we can't figure out the answer with certainty.

Working with this section and your copy of *The Official SAT Study Guide* will help you get better and better at SAT Sentence Completion questions. Keep it up!

By now, you've seen that the SAT Passage-Based Reading questions aren't really about the kind of reading you do in high school, and that the SAT Sentence Completion questions aren't really about memorizing vocabulary. In fact, we're establishing a general theme that the SAT is pretty horrible at testing the things it claims to be testing.

You've also probably noticed by now that the general approach to each question is the same: we read very carefully, we think very carefully about words that we know the meanings of, we avoid any interpretation, and we skip questions we can't answer. If you practice using those simple principles and get very good at them, you'll have an amazing score on the SAT. That's truly all there is to it. Most of the people who fail to get an amazing score on the SAT either aren't aware of how the test actually works, or they don't get good enough at reading and thinking very carefully.

Video Demonstrations

If you'd like to see videos of some sample solutions like the ones in this Black Book, please visit www.SATprepVideos.com. A selection of free videos is available for readers of this book.

SAT Sentence Completion Quick Summary

This is a one-page summary of the major relevant concepts. Use it to evaluate your comprehension or jog your memory. For a more in-depth treatment of these ideas, see the rest of the section.

The Big Secret: Vocabulary doesn't matter as much as everybody thinks. Careful reading is much more important.

Remember to read carefully at all times.

The right answer will restate some other part of the sentence.

Focus on the questions where vocabulary isn't an issue first.

Don't choose a word just because you know what it means. Only choose it if you think it restates a part of the sentence.

There are a few special techniques that will help you better understand words you don't know:

- Think of any connotation the unknown word might have for you.
- Remove any suffixes the word may have, and see if it sounds more familiar.
- See if the suffix indicates anything about the word's possible meaning. For example, "-able" indicates that some action can be done to something. "-ism" indicates a philosophy. And so on.
- Consider any likely prefixes, and possible meanings of the word without them.
- Consider possible cognates from other languages, books, company names, etc.
- The goal isn't to figure out exactly what a word means. The goal is to figure out if the word might be related to the ideas in the sentence.

Rules for this part of the test include:

- The correct answer must restate some part of the sentence.
- The correct answer must make a natural-sounding English sentence.

Here's the general Sentence Completion process:

1. Read the sentence and answer choices with an open mind. Don't pre-form the answer.
2. Look for an answer choice that restates key elements of the sentence.
3. Use the special Sentence Completion techniques on any words with unknown meanings.
4. Make certain your choice restates key elements of the sentence.
5. Read the sentence with your answer choice in the blank (or blanks) to make sure it fits.
6. Mark your answer.
7. Skip the question if you run into too many unknown words and can't work around them with the techniques above. Make sure you answer all the questions correctly where you know enough of the words to do so. The most important thing is to avoid careless mistakes.

For demonstrations of these ideas, see the many sample solutions in this Black Book.

SAT Math

"The essence of mathematics is not to make simple things complicated, but to make complicated things simple."
- S. Gudder

Overview and Important Reminders for SAT Math

The Math questions on the SAT are a very mixed bag. The current version of the SAT features several different types of math; almost everything you could study in high school math is on there except calculus, trigonometry, and advanced statistics. On top of that, an individual question can be a combination of any of those areas, which often makes the questions hard to classify.

Some students cover all the basics of SAT Math before they reach high school, and some students take geometry as seniors and never even have classes in algebra. For the first type of student, SAT Math concepts are almost forgotten; for the second type of student, they are just barely familiar.

In short, nobody I've ever met has felt completely comfortable with all the math on the SAT. I teach test-taking strategies for a living, I can answer and explain every single question in the Blue Book, and I still don't feel like I know a lot of math. Don't let it bother you!

But that's not all—mastering the key mathematical concepts that can appear on the SAT still won't guarantee a high score. In fact, you probably know some students who are "math geniuses" who still don't make perfect scores on the SAT Math section. You might even be one of those students yourself.

For those students—and for most students, actually—there's something missing when it comes to SAT Math. There's a key idea that they haven't realized yet.

What idea is that? It's the fact that the SAT Math test is NOT a math test, at least not in the sense that you're probably used to. The SAT Math section has very little to do with actual mathematical knowledge. Think of it as a logic test, or as a bunch of problem-solving exercises. Actually, the better you get at SAT Math, the more you'll come to realize it's just a game—and the more you come to see it as a game, the better you'll get at it.

The truth is that the SAT Math section is primarily a test of your knowledge and application of mathematical definitions and properties. The calculations themselves aren't complicated, as you'll see when we go through some real test questions. The SAT could have made the calculations difficult, but the calculations themselves are always fairly easy, even on so-called "hard" questions. The only thing that makes SAT Math questions difficult is figuring out what they're asking you to do in the first place.

So natural test-takers do better on "SAT Math" because they focus on setting problems up, rather than automatically relying on formulas. Unfortunately, most test-takers never realize how different SAT Math is from school math, so they spend too much time trying to find complicated solutions to the problems on the SAT, as though the SAT were like a regular math test in high school. This is very frustrating, and results in low scores. It's like trying to cook an omelet with a hammer.

Studying this book will help you use the techniques that natural test-takers use to score well on SAT Math. More importantly, this Black Book will help you come to see the SAT "Math" test for what it really is: a reading and problem-solving test that happens to involve numbers!

The Big Secret Of SAT Math

Before we go any further, it's important that you be in the right frame of mind when you approach SAT Math questions. As I've mentioned a couple of times so far, most SAT Math questions aren't really "math" questions at all, at least not in the way you probably think of math questions. It's important for us to understand why this is.

Put yourself in the College Board's position for a moment. If you're the College Board, your goal is to provide colleges and universities with useful, reliable data on their applicants' abilities. It wouldn't really make sense to have those applicants take a traditional test of advanced math, for two reasons:

1. Not all applicants will have taken the same math classes, so a traditional test wouldn't be able to distinguish students who had never learned a certain type of math from students who had learned it and were bad at it.
2. More importantly, the high school transcript already does a pretty good job of indicating a student's ability to answer traditional math questions.

A traditional test of advanced math wouldn't let the College Board provide very useful data to colleges and universities. And it wouldn't make any sense to come up with a traditional test of basic math, either, because far too many test-takers would do very well on that, and the results would be meaningless.

The College Board's solution to this problem is actually kind of clever. They make sure that SAT Math questions only cover basic math topics, but they cover those basic topics in non-traditional ways. In this way, the College Board can be fairly certain that every test-taker has the potential to answer every question correctly—but only by thinking creatively, which keeps the results of the test interesting for colleges and universities.

In fact, let me say that last part again, in all caps, and centered, because it's super important:

SAT MATH QUESTIONS TEST BASIC MATH IDEAS IN STRANGE WAYS.

That idea is the thing that most test-takers don't realize. It's the thing that causes so many people to spend so much time practicing math for the SAT with so little result. The way to get better at SAT Math isn't to learn advanced math, because advanced math ideas don't appear on the test. The way to get better is to learn to take apart SAT Math questions so you can understand which basic ideas are involved in each question.

For this reason, you'll often find that the most challenging SAT Math questions can't be solved with any of the formulas you normally use in math class. In general, SAT Math questions avoid formal solutions. If anything, you might even say that answering SAT Math questions is kind of a creative process, because we never know exactly what the next question will involve, even though we can know the general rules and principles underlying its design.

The Two Critical Components of SAT Math Success

Since the SAT Math section is all about basic math ideas presented in strange ways, there are two key areas of knowledge we'll need to do well on the test:

1. Basic knowledge of arithmetic, geometry, and algebra (including some basic graph-related ideas)
2. A thorough understanding of the SAT's unwritten rules, patterns, and quirks.

So you will need *some* math knowledge, of course, but you won't need anything like trig, stats, or calculus, and you won't have to memorize tons of formulas. Like I keep saying (and will continue to say), it's much more important to focus on how the test is designed than to try to memorize formulas.

In a moment we'll go through the "Math toolbox," which is a list of math concepts that the SAT is allowed to incorporate when it makes up questions. After that, we'll get into the SAT's unwritten rules of math question design.

SAT Math Toolbox

In a moment, we'll talk about how to attack the SAT Math section from a strategic perspective. But first, it's important to make sure we know all the mathematical concepts the SAT is allowed to test (don't worry, there aren't that many of them).

If you already know all the concepts below, then you don't need to go over them again. Instead, go to the next section and start learning how to attack the test.

If you're not familiar with some of the concepts below, then take a few minutes to refresh yourself on them.

This concept review is designed to be as quick and painless as possible. If you feel that you'd like a little more of an explanation, the best thing to do is find somebody who's good at math (a teacher, parent, or friend) and ask them to spend a little time explaining a few things to you.

This concept review might seem easier to you than the actual SAT Math section. That's because the difficulty in SAT Math really comes from the setup of each problem, not from the concepts that the problem involves. The concepts in this review are the same concepts you'll encounter in your practice and on the real test, but the real test often makes questions look harder than they really are by combining and disguising the underlying concepts in the questions.

For SAT Math, it's not that important to have a *thorough* understanding of the underlying concepts. All you need is a quick, general familiarity with a few basic ideas. So that's all we'll spend time on.

Please note that this list is similar in some ways to chapters 14 through 18 of the College Board publication *The Official SAT Study Guide*, but my list is organized a little differently and presents the material in more discrete units. In addition, my list explains things in plainer language and omits some concepts that are redundant, making it easier to study.

As you're going through this list, you may see concepts that aren't familiar. Before you let yourself get confused, make sure you've read this list through TWICE. You'll probably find that a lot of your confusion clears itself up on the second reading.

Also, please try to remember that the material in the Math Toolbox is pretty dry and technical, and that it's not the focus of the proper strategic approach to the SAT. It's just a set of basic ideas that need to be refreshed before we get into the more important stuff.

Properties of integers

An integer is any number that can be expressed without a fraction, decimal, percentage sign, or symbol.

Integers can be negative or positive.

Zero is an integer.

Example:

> These numbers are integers: -99, -6, 0, 8, 675
>
> These numbers are NOT integers: pi, 96.7, 3/4

There are even integers and there are odd integers.

Only integers can be odd or even—a fraction or symbolic number is neither odd nor even.

Integers that are even can be divided by 2 without having anything left over.

Integers that are odd have a remainder of 1 when they're divided by 2.

Example:

> These are even integers: -6, 4, 8
>
> These are odd integers: -99, 25, 675

An even number plus an even number gives an even result.

An odd number plus an odd number gives an even result.

An odd number plus an even number gives an odd result.

An even number times an even number gives an even result.

An even number times an odd number gives an even result.

An odd number times an odd number gives an odd result.

Some integers have special properties when it comes to addition and multiplication:

Multiplying any number by 1 leaves the number unchanged.

Dividing any number by 1 leaves the number unchanged.

Multiplying any number by 0 results in the number 0.

Adding 0 to any number leaves the number unchanged.

Subtracting 0 from any number leaves the number unchanged.

It's impossible, for purposes of SAT Math, to divide any number by 0.

Word problems

SAT word problems are typically simple descriptions of one of the following:

Real-life situations

Abstract concepts

Example:

> **An SAT word problem about a real-life situation might look like this:**
>
> **"Joe buys two balloons for three dollars each, and a certain amount of candy. Each piece of the candy costs twenty-five cents. Joe gives the cashier ten dollars and receives twenty-five cents in change. How many pieces of candy did he buy?"**
>
> **An SAT word problem about an abstract concept might look like this:**
>
> **"If *x* is the arithmetic mean of seven consecutive numbers, what is the median of those seven numbers?"**

To solve SAT word problems, we have to transform them into math problems. These are the steps we follow to make that transformation:

Note all the numbers given in the problem, and write them down on scratch paper.

Identify key phrases and translate them into mathematical symbols for operations and variables. Use these to connect the numbers you wrote down.

Example:

> **In the phrase "two balloons for three dollars each," the *each* part means we have to *multiply* the two balloons by the three dollars in order to find out how much total money was spent on the two balloons. 2 * 3 = 6. Six dollars were spent on the two balloons if they cost three dollars each.**

After the word problem has been translated into numbers and symbols, solve it like any other SAT Math problem (see the SAT Math Path in this chapter for more on that).

Number lines

A number line is a simple diagram that arranges numbers from least to greatest.

The positions on a number line can be labeled with actual numbers or with variables.

Example:

This number line shows all the integers from -7 to 4:

On the SAT, number lines are drawn to scale and the tick marks are spaced evenly unless the question notes otherwise.

To determine the distance between two numbers on a number line, just subtract the number to the left from the number to the right.

Example:

> **On the number line above, the distance between 1
> and 3 is two units, which is the same thing as
> saying that 3 − 1 = 2.**

On a number line, there is a DIFFERENCE between the distance that separates two numbers and the number of positions between them.

If you're asked how many positions are BETWEEN two numbers on a number line, remember that you CANNOT answer this question by simply subtracting one number from the other—that's how you would find the distance. You should actually *count* the positions—you'll find the number of positions is one less than the difference you get when you subtract.

Example:

> **On the number line above, there are NOT two
> positions between the numbers 2 and 4, even
> though 4 − 2 = 2. There is only one position between
> the numbers 2 and 4, which is one less than the
> difference we get when we subtract the number 2
> from the number 4.**

On the SAT, the positions on a number line don't have to represent whole numbers. They might represent groups of five numbers at a time, or hundredths, or any other consistent amount.

A number's absolute value is the distance of that number from zero on the number line.

Example:

> **-4 and 4 both have an absolute value of 4. We signify
> the absolute value of a number with vertical lines
> on either side of the number:
> |-4| = |4| = 4.**

Squares and square roots

To square a number, multiply the number by itself.

Example:

> **Five squared is five times five, or 5 * 5, or 25.**

To find the square root of a number, find the amount that has to be multiplied by itself in order to generate the number.

Example:

> **The square root of 25 is the amount that yields 25
> when it's multiplied by itself. As we just saw, that
> amount is 5. So the square root of 25 is 5.**

When you square any number, the result is always positive. This is because a positive number times a positive number gives a positive result, and so does a negative number times a negative number.

Square roots on the SAT are always positive.

The SAT never asks about the square root of a negative number.

The SAT likes to ask about the squares of the numbers -12 through 12. Here they are:

Number	Square
-12 or 12	144
-11 or 11	121
-10 or 10	100
-9 or 9	81
-8 or 8	64
-7 or 7	49
-6 or 6	36
-5 or 5	25
-4 or 4	16
-3 or 3	9
-2 or 2	4
-1 or 1	1
0	0

While I don't recommend using a calculator on the SAT if you can help it, remember that you can always find the square root of a number very easily on a good calculator.

Fractions and rational numbers

A fraction is a special type of number that represents parts of a whole.

Fractions are written this way:

[number of parts being described in the situation]
[number of parts that the whole is divided into]

Example:

> Imagine that we're sharing a six-pack of soda cans. I really like soda, so I drink five of the cans. In this situation, I've had five of the six cans that make up the six-pack—I've had 5/6 of the six-pack.

The number above the fraction bar is called a *numerator*.

The number under the fraction bar is called a *denominator*.

When the numerator of a fraction is less than the denominator, the value of the fraction is less than 1.

When the numerator of a fraction is greater than the denominator, the value of the fraction is greater than 1.

Example:

> 1/2 is equal to one half, which is less than 1. 6/3 is equal to 2, which is greater than 1.

Any integer can be thought of as having the denominator 1 already underneath it.

Example:

> **7 is the same thing as 7/1.**

A reciprocal is what you get if you switch the numerator and the denominator of a fraction.

Example:

> **The reciprocal of 2/3 is 3/2. The reciprocal of 7 is 1/7.**
> **(Remember that all integers can be thought of as**
> **having the denominator 1.)**

To multiply two fractions, first multiply their numerators and write that amount as the numerator of the new fraction; then, multiply the denominators and write that amount as the denominator of the new fraction.

Example:

> **4/7 x 9/13 = 36/91**

To divide fraction *a* by fraction *b*, we actually multiply fraction *a* by the RECIPROCAL of fraction *b*.

Example

> **4/7 divided by 9/13 = 4/7 x 13/9 = 52/63**

Multiplying a non-zero integer by a fraction that's less than 1 (that is, by a fraction where the numerator is less than the denominator) will give a result that is closer to zero on a number line than the original integer was. (Read this item again if you need to!)

Examples:

> **6 x 3/5 = 18/5, and 18/5 falls between 0 and 6 on a**
> **number line.**
>
> **-7 x 2/9 = -14/9, and -14/9 falls between -7 and 0 on a**
> **number line.**

Fraction *a* is equal to fraction *b* if you could multiply the numerator in *a* by a certain number to get the numerator in *b*, and you could also multiply the denominator in *a* by the same number to get the denominator of *b*.

Example:

> **3/5 is equal to 18/30 because 3 x 6 = 18 and 5 x 6 = 30.**
> **Here's another way to write this: 3/5 x 6/6 = 18/30.**
> **Notice that 6/6 is the same thing as 1 (six parts of a**
> **whole that's divided into six parts is the same thing**
> **as the whole itself). So all we really did here was**
> **multiply 3/5 by 1, and we know that doing this will**
> **give us an amount equal to 3/5.**

For more on fractions, see the discussion of factors and multiples below.

Factors
The factors of a number *x* are the positive integers that can be multiplied by each other to achieve that number *x*.

Example:

> The number 10 has the factors 5 and 2, because 5 * 2 = 10. It also has the factors 10 and 1, because 1 * 10 = 10.

"Common factors," as the name suggests, are factors that two numbers have in common.

Example:

> The number 10 has the factors 1, 2, 5, and 10, as we just saw. The number 28 has the factors 1, 2, 4, 7, 14, and 28. So the common factors of 10 and 28 are 1 and 2, because both 1 and 2 can be multiplied by positive integers to get both 10 and 28.

Multiples

The multiples of a number x are the numbers you get when you multiply x by 1, 2, 3, 4, 5, and so on.

Example:

> The multiples of 4 are 4, 8, 12, 16, 20, 24, 28, 32, 36, 40, 44, 48, 52, and so on.

Remainders

Remainders are what you get when you divide one number by another number and have something left over (this assumes you don't use fractions or decimals to write the answer to your division problem).

Example:

> If we divide 30 by 4, we see that it doesn't work out evenly. 4 * 7 = 28, which isn't enough, and 4 * 8 = 32, which is too much. So if we divide 30 by 4, one way to state the answer is to say that 30 divided by 4 is "7 with a remainder of 2," because 4 * 7 = 28 and 28 + 2 = 30.

The remainder in a division problem must be less than the number we're dividing by.

Example:

> It doesn't make any sense to say that 30 divided by 4 is "3 with a remainder of 18," because 18 is bigger than 4 and 4 will still go into 18 a few more times.

As a reminder, when you first learned to divide, you were probably taught to use remainders.

Most calculators don't give remainders when solving division problems—instead, they give fractions or decimals.

Prime numbers

A prime number is a number that has exactly two factors: 1 and itself.

Example:

> **17 is a prime number because there are no positive integers besides 1 and 17 that can be multiplied by other integers to generate 17. (Try to come up with some—you won't be able to.)**
>
> **24 is NOT a prime number because there are a lot of positive integers besides 1 and 24 that can be multiplied by other integers to generate 24. For example, 2, 3, 4, 6, 8, and 12 can all be multiplied by other integers to generate 24.**

All prime numbers are positive.

The only even prime number is 2.

1 is NOT a prime number because it has only one factor (itself), while prime numbers must have exactly two factors.

Ratios, proportions, and percentages

Ratios, proportions, and percentages are all ways to express a relationship between two numbers.

A ratio is written as a pair of numbers with a colon between them.

Example:

> **If you make 5 dollars for every 1 dollar Bob makes, then the ratio of *your pay* to *Bob's pay* is *5 : 1.***

A proportion is usually written as a fraction, with a number in the numerator compared to the number in the denominator.

Example:

> **If you make 5 dollars for every 1 dollar Bob makes, then your pay can be compared to Bob's pay with the proportion 5/1. (Or, if we wanted to compare what Bob makes to what you make, that proportion would be 1/5.)**

A percentage is a special proportion where one number is compared to 100.

To determine a percentage, first compare two numbers with a proportion, and then divide the top number by the bottom number and multiply the result by 100.

Example:

> **If Bob makes 1 dollar for every 5 dollars you make, then the proportion that compares Bob's pay to your pay is 1/5. If we divide 1 by 5 and multiply by 100, we see that Bob makes 20% of what you make.**

Ratios can be set equal to each other and "cross-multiplied." (If you don't already know how to do this, don't worry—it's just a short cut around regular algebraic techniques. You don't have to know how to do it for the SAT.)

If the relationship between two quantities is the kind where increasing one quantity results in an increase in the other quantity, then we say those two quantities "vary directly" or are "directly proportional."

Example:

> If I make 1 dollar for every 5 dollars you make, then when I make 4 dollars you make 20 dollars— increasing my pay to 4 leads to an increase in your pay to 20. That means our two rates of pay are in direct proportion.

If two quantities are related so that increasing one decreases the other, then we say those two quantities "vary indirectly" or are "inversely proportional."

Example:

> If we have two quantities x and y set up so that $xy = 20$, then x and y are inversely proportional—every time one increases, the other one decreases, and vice-versa. So if x starts out as 10 and y starts out as 2, changing x to 5 means we have to change y to 4— as one decreases, the other increases.

Sequences

Sequences are strings of numbers that follow a rule, so that knowing one number in the sequence allows us to figure out another number in the sequence.

Sequence questions on the SAT will rarely operate in exactly the same way that a question about an arithmetic or geometric series would work in a math class, though the College Board often tries to mislead you by making a sequence question look deceptively similar to a traditional question about a series.

SAT sequences can either go on forever or stop at some point, depending on the setup of the question.

There are two common types of SAT sequences, and we can classify them by the rules that are used to figure out which numbers go in the sequence. Let's look at the different types of SAT sequences:

Example:

> The sequence 3, 5, 7, 9, 11, 13, . . . follows a very simple rule: to get the next number in the sequence, just add 2 to the number before. So the next number in this sequence would be 15, then 17, and so on.

The sequence 3, 15, 75, 375, . . . also follows a simple rule: to get the next number, multiply the previous number by 5. The next number here would be 1,875.

The Math section MIGHT ask you to figure out:

- The sum of certain terms in a sequence.
- The average of certain terms.
- The value of a specific term.

If you studied sequences in school, they were probably a lot harder in your math class than they will be on the SAT. For example, there's no sigma notation on the SAT. (If you've never heard of sigma notation, don't worry about it.)

Set theory

Sets are collections of things.

Sets on the SAT are usually groups of numbers.

Example:

> **The set of factors of 24 is {1, 2, 3, 4, 6, 8, 12, 24}.**

On the SAT, the things in a set can be called "members" of that set or "elements" of that set.

The "union" of two or more sets is what we get when we combine all of the members of those sets into a bigger set.

Example:

> **The set of factors of 24 is {1, 2, 3, 4, 6, 8, 12, 24} and the set of factors of 36 is {1, 2, 3, 4, 6, 9, 12, 18, 36}. That means the union of those two sets is the set {1, 2, 3, 4, 6, 8, 9, 12, 18, 24, 36}.**

The "intersection" of two or more sets is the set of members that the two sets have in common.

Example:

> **Given the sets {1, 2, 3, 4, 6, 8, 12, 24} and {1, 2, 3, 4, 6, 9, 12, 18, 36}, the "intersection" is {1, 2, 4, 6, 12}, because those members are common to both sets.**

Counting problems

On the SAT, "counting problems" are problems where you're asked to give the total number of ways that two or more events might happen.

If you've studied these types of problems in math class, you probably called them "permutation and combination" problems.

The general, basic rule of these types of problems is this: when you have two events, and the first event might happen in any one of x ways, and the second event might happen in any one of y ways, then the total number of ways that both events could happen together is given by xy. (That might sound a little complicated—let's do an example.)

Page 131

Example:

> Imagine there are three roads between your house and your friend's house, and there are 6 roads between your friend's house and the library. If you're driving from your house to your friend's house and then to the library, how many different ways can you go?
>
> There are 3 ways to get from your house to your friend's house. So the event of you getting to your friend's house can happen in any one of 3 ways. Then there are 6 ways to get from your friend's house to the library, so the event of going to the library from the friend's house can happen in any one of 6 ways. This means the total number of paths you could travel from your house to your friend's house and then on to the library is given by 3 * 6, which is 18.

The key to solving these types of problems is making sure you correctly count the number of possible outcomes for each event.

Example:

> Imagine that there are 3 roads between your house and your friend's house. You're going to visit her and then return home. For some reason, you can't travel the same road twice. What's the total number of ways you could go from your house to your friend's house and back?

Well, the total number of ways to go from your house to your friend's house is 3, and the total number of ways to come back home is ONLY 2. Why can you only come back from your friend's house in 2 ways? *Because the problem says you're not allowed to use the same road twice, and when you go back home you will already have used one of the three roads to visit your friend in the first place.* So the right way to answer this is to multiply 3 * 2, NOT 3 * 3. That means the answer is 6, NOT 9.

Operations on algebraic expressions

Algebraic expressions are figures that include variables.

Algebraic expressions, just like the regular numbers they represent, can be added, subtracted, multiplied, and divided—but sometimes there are special rules that apply.

We can add or subtract two algebraic expressions when they involve the same variable expressions.

Example:

> We can add $5x$ and $19x$ to get $24x$, because the $5x$ and $19x$ both involve the same variable expression: x. We can subtract $17xyz^2$ from $100\ xyz^2$ and get $83xyz^2$ because they both involve the variable expression xyz^2.
>
> But if we want to add $5x$ to $17\ xyz^2$, we can't combine those two expressions any further because they have different variable expressions. So we would just write "$5x + 17xyz^2$" and leave it at that.

We can multiply any two algebraic expressions by multiplying all the terms in the first expression by all the terms in the second expression.

Example:

> $$5x * 7y = 35xy$$
>
> $$(5a + 2)(4b + 9) = 20ab + 45a + 8b + 18$$

We can divide any algebraic expression by another algebraic expression when they share factors. (See the discussion on factoring algebraic expressions.)

Example:

> $$26xy/13x = 2y$$

When multiplying two algebraic expressions on the SAT, we can often use the "FOIL" technique. "FOIL" stands for "First, Outer, Inner, Last," and refers to the order in which the terms of the two expressions are multiplied by one another.

You have probably used FOIL in your math classes, but if you used some other technique there's no need to worry.

Example:

> To multiply the expressions $(5x + 7)$ and $(3x + 4)$, we can use FOIL.
>
> The "First" pair in the acronym is the $5x$ and the $3x$, because they are the first terms in each expression. We multiply these and get $15x^2$.
>
> The "Outer" pair in the acronym is the $5x$ and the 4. We multiply these and get $20x$.
>
> The "Inner" pair in the acronym is the 7 and the $3x$. We multiply these and get $21x$.
>
> The "Last" pair in the acronym is the 7 and the 4. We multiply these and get 28.
>
> Now we just add up all those terms and we get the expression $15x^2 + 20x + 21x + 28$, which we can simplify a little bit by combining the two like x terms, giving us:
>
> $15x^2 + 41x + 28$
>
> So $(5x + 7)(3x + 4) = 15x^2 + 41x + 28$

If this seems a little complicated now, don't worry about it. You'll get it with practice—and there isn't that much of it on the SAT anyway.

Factoring algebraic expressions

On the SAT, factoring an algebraic expression involves breaking the expression down into two other expressions that could be multiplied by each other to give the original expression.

Example:

> If we have an algebraic expression like $(8x + 4)$, we can break that down into the factors 4 and $(2x + 1)$, because $4(2x + 1) = 8x + 4$.

On the SAT, there are three types of factoring situations you'll need to recognize:

1. recognizing common factors
2. doing "FOIL" in reverse
3. recognizing a difference of squares

Recognizing common factors involves noticing that every term in a given expression has a common factor, as we did in the last example.

Example:

> In the expression $(21xy + 7x)$, both of the terms in the expression have a common factor of $7x$, so we can factor the expression like this: $7x(3y + 1)$.

Factoring polynomials basically involves doing the "FOIL" process in reverse. Trust me, it's not as hard as it looks. It just takes a little practice.

Example:

$$9x2 - 21x + 12 = (3x - 3)(3x - 4)$$

$$5x2 - 3x - 2 = (5x + 2)(x - 1)$$

When we factor the difference of two squares, there's a shortcut we can use—the difference of two squares can be factored as the product of the sum of the square roots of the two squares times the difference of the square roots of the two squares. Let's see an example.

Example:

$$9x^2 - 4 = (3x + 2)(3x - 2)$$

Exponents

An exponent of a number is what we get when we multiply the number by itself a certain number of times.

Example:

> $x * x * x = x^3$ is an example of an exponential expression. The 3 in this example is the exponent, and the x is called the "base."

Exponents can be positive or negative.

When an exponent is positive, we multiply the base by itself as many times as the exponent indicates, just like we did in the above example.

When an exponent is negative, we treat it just like a positive exponent EXCEPT that we take the reciprocal of the final amount (take another look at the discussion of reciprocals on page).

Example:

$$x^5 = x * x * x * x * x$$

$$x^{-5} = 1/(x^5)$$

We can multiply exponent expressions by each other when the bases are identical. To do that, we just add the exponents:

Example:

$$(x^6)(x^4) = (x * x * x * x * x * x) (x * x * x * x) =$$
$$x * x * x* x * x * x * x * x * x * x = x^{10}$$

$$(x^7)(x^{-4}) = x^3$$

We can also divide exponent expressions when they have the same base. For that we just subtract the exponents:

Example:

$$(x^8)/(x^2) = x^6$$

Finally, we can raise exponential expressions to other exponents by multiplying the first exponent by the second one:

Example:

$$(x^4)^5 = x^{20}$$

Note that raising any number to an exponent of zero gives you the number 1.

Example:

$$y^0 = 1$$

Using equations

On the SAT, an equation is a statement that involves an algebraic expression and an equals sign.

Example:

> $5x = 20$ is an equation, because it involves the
> algebraic expression $5x$ and an equals sign.

Solving an equation means figuring out how much the variable in the equation is worth. We can solve equations just like you learned in algebra class—by multiply, dividing, adding, or subtracting both sides of the equation by the same amounts until we're left with a value for the variable.

Example:

$$5x = 20$$
$$5x/5 = 20/5$$
$$x = 4$$

On the SAT, we can often use equations to answer a question *even when we can't solve the equation for each variable individually*.

Example:

> We might be told that $(a + b)/10 = 15$. How can we
> figure out the value of $a + b$? In school, you might
> try to figure out a first, and then b, and then add
> them together. But we don't have enough
> information to do that. So what can we do? Well, we
> just solve for the entire amount $a + b$. In this
> situation, we can do that by multiplying both sides
> by 10, so $a + b = 150$. In this case, even though we
> can never know the individual values of a and b, we
> can know the sum $a + b$.

On the SAT, we can also solve equations "in terms of" one particular variable. To do this, we just isolate the target variable on one side of the equation.

Example:

> What if we have to solve this expression in terms of
> n?
> $$4n + 7y = 2a$$
> $$4n = 2a - 7y$$
> $$n = (2a - 7y)/4$$
> $$n = (2a - 7y)/4$$

Sometimes you'll have a "system" of equations. A system of equations contains two or more equations with the same variables.

Example:

> **This is a system of equations:**
>
> $x + y = 5$
>
> $2x - y = 7$

The easiest way to solve a system of equations is to solve one equation in terms of one variable, like we just did before. Then we substitute in the second equation and solve.

Example:

> **First, we'll isolate the y in the first equation, giving us that equation in terms of y: $y = 5 - x$. Now that we know y is the same thing as $5 - x$, we just plug in $5 - x$ where y appears in the second equation:**
>
> $2x - (5 - x) = 7$
>
> $2x - 5 + x = 7$
>
> $3x - 5 = 7$
>
> $3x = 12$
>
> $x = 4$
>
> **Now that we know x is 4, we just plug that back into the first equation, and we'll be able to solve for y:**
>
> $4 + y = 5$
>
> $y = 1$

Inequalities

On the SAT, inequalities are statements that show a particular amount may be greater than or less than a second amount. They use these symbols:

The symbol < means "less than."

The symbol > means "greater than."

The symbol ≤ means "less than or equal to."

The symbol ≥ means "greater than or equal to."

You solve an inequality the same way you solve an equation, with one difference: when you multiply by -1 to solve for a variable, you have to switch the direction of the inequality symbol.

Example:

$$-x/4 = 10 \qquad\qquad -x/4 \leq 10$$
$$-x = 10(4) \qquad\qquad -x \leq 10(4)$$
$$-x = 40 \qquad\qquad -x \leq 40$$
$$x = -40 \qquad\qquad x \geq -40$$

Solving quadratic equations by factoring

A quadratic equation is an equation that involves three terms:

1. one term is a variable expression raised to the power of 2.
2. one term is a variable expression not raised to any power.
3. one term is a regular number with no variable.

Example:

$x^2 + 3x = -2$ is a quadratic equation because it involves a term with x squared, a term with x, and a regular number.

There is only one way to solve quadratic equations on the SAT, and that is by factoring. (See the discussion of factoring above).

To solve a quadratic equation by factoring, we have to make one side of the equation equal to zero, and then factor the other side of the equation (the quadratic part).

Example:

$$x^2 + 3x = -2$$
$$x^2 + 3x + 2 = 0$$
$$(x + 1)(x + 2) = 0$$

Now that we know $(x + 1)(x + 2) = 0$, what else do we know? We know that one of those two factors has to equal zero—either $x + 1 = 0$ or $x + 2 = 0$. How do we know this? Remember that the only way to multiply two numbers and get zero is if one of the numbers is zero. So if we can multiply $x + 1$ by $x + 2$ and get zero, then either $x + 1$ is zero or $x + 2$ is zero.

Once we've factored, we solve for the variable by creating two small sub-equations in which each factor is set equal to zero.

$$x + 1 = 0 \quad \text{or} \quad x + 2 = 0$$
$$x = -1 \quad \text{or} \quad x = -2$$

So in the equation $x^2 + 3x = -2$, x can equal either -1 or -2.

Quadratic equations can have multiple solutions, as we've just seen.

Functions

Functions are formulas that tell you how to generate one number by using another number.

Functions can be written in a lot of ways. On the SAT, they'll usually be written in $f(x)$ notation, also called "function notation."

Example:

$f(x) = x^3 + 4$ is a function written in function notation.

When we write with function notation, we don't have to use $f(x)$ specifically. We could write $g(n)$, $a(b)$, or whatever.

Don't confuse function notation like $f(x)$ with the multiplicative expression $(f)(x)$, which means "f times x"!

When we evaluate a function for a certain number x, it means that we plug the number x into the function and see what the $f(x)$ is.

Example:

If our function is $f(x) = x^3 + 4$ and we want to evaluate the function where $x = 2$, then we get this:

$f(x) = x^3 + 4$

$f(2) = (2)^3 + 4$

$f(2) = 8 + 4$

$f(2) = 12$

So for our function, when x equals 2, the $f(x)$ equals 12.

The "domain" of a function is the set of numbers on a number line where the function can be evaluated.

Example:

In the function $f(x) = x^3 + 4$, the domain is all the numbers on the number line, because we can put any value from the number line in for x and get a result for $f(x)$.

In the function $f(x) = \sqrt{x}$, the domain is only those numbers that can have a square root. Remember that, on the SAT, you can't take the square root of a negative number. That means the domain for the function $f(x) = \sqrt{x}$ is the set of non-negative numbers.

The "range" of a function is the set of numbers that $f(x)$ can come out equal to.

Example:

> The function $f(x) = x^3 + 4$ has a range of negative infinity to positive infinity—by putting in the right thing for x, we can get any number we want as $f(x)$.
>
> The function $f(x) = \sqrt{x}$ has a range of only non-negative numbers, because there is no way to put any number as x and get a number for $f(x)$ that's negative.

Linear functions

A point can be plotted on a graph in (x, y) notation if we take the x number and make it the horizontal separation between the point (x, y) and the origin $(0, 0)$, and then we make the y value the vertical separation between (x, y) and $(0, 0)$.

A linear function is a function in which the $f(x)$ is replaced with a y, and all the (x, y) pairings form a straight line when they're plotted on a graph.

Example:

The function $f(x) = (x/2) + 1$ is linear, because all of the (x, y) pairings that it generates fall in a straight line when they're plotted as lines on a graph.

Here's a chart that shows some (x, y) pairings for the function $f(x) = (x/2) + 1$:

x	y
0	1
1	1.5
2	2
3	2.5
4	3
5	3.5
6	4
7	4.5
8	5
9	5.5
10	6
11	6.5
12	7
13	7.5
14	8
15	8.5
16	9

When we plot these points on a graph, we see that they fall in a straight line:

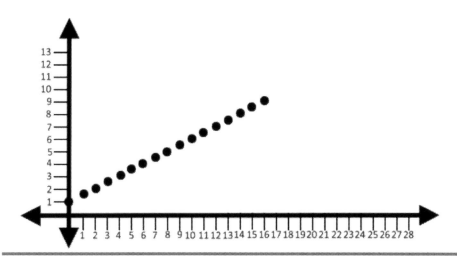

Of course, the points plotted on the graph are only the (x, y) pairings when x is a positive integer. But isn't the domain for f(x) = (x/2) + 1 all the numbers on the number line? That means that there must be an f(x) even where x equals 1.135623, or 8.4453, or any other number at all. For every value on the x axis, there's a corresponding f(x) value on the y axis. We could "connect the dots" on our graph above, and extend the line of our function infinitely in either direction. Let's do that:

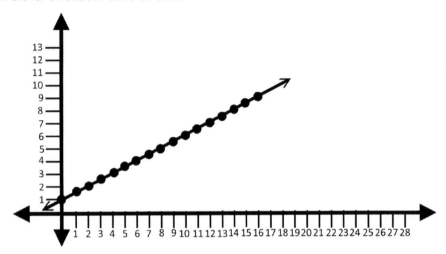

The "slope" of a linear function is a fraction that shows you how steeply the line is tilted. To find the slope of a line, choose any two points on the line. Measure the vertical separation between the two points, *starting from the left-most point*. The vertical separation number goes in the numerator of the slope fraction. Then measure the horizontal separation between the two points, again starting from the left-most point. The horizontal separation goes in the denominator of the slope fraction.

Example:

> In our graph above, we can pick any two points on the function line to determine the slope. Let's pick (2,2) and (8,5). The vertical separation here is the difference between 2 on the left-most point and 5 on the right-most point. So the vertical separation here is 3, and we put a 3 in the numerator of the slope fraction for this line. Now we determine the horizontal separation between 2 on the left and 8 on the right, which is 6. So a 6 goes in the denominator of the slope fraction. Now we have the numerator and the denominator of the slope fraction, and we see that the entire slope fraction is 3/6, or 1/2. So the slope of f(x) = (x/2) + 1 is 1/2. (Keep reading for a much easier way to figure out slope.)

The equation for a line will often be written in this format: y = mx + b. In fact, our function from the previous example was written in that way: f(x) = (x/2) + 1. (Remember that y and f(x) are the same thing for the purposes of graphing a function, and that "½ x" can be re-written as x/2.)

This y = mx + b format is called "slope-intercept format." We call it that because it shows us two things right away: the slope of the function, and the "y-intercept" of the function.

The m coefficient of the x variable will be the slope.

The *b* constant in the function will be the point where the linear function crosses the *y* axis.

Example:

> In the linear function $f(x) = 9/7\ x + 14$, the *m* in the *y* = *mx* + *b* notation is 9/7, and the *b* is 14. This means the slope of the function is 9/7, and the point where the line crosses the *y*-axis is 14.
>
> In the linear function $y = -3/2\ x + 2$, the slope is -3/2 and the *y*-intercept is 2.

When two linear functions have the same slope, they are parallel.

When you can multiply the slope of one linear function by the slope of another linear function and get -1, the two linear functions are perpendicular to one another.

The SAT will never ask you to graph a linear function. It will only ask you to use graphs to figure out other information, or to identify an answer choice that correctly graphs a function.

Quadratic functions

A quadratic function is a function where the *x* variable has an exponent of 2.

Example:

> $y = x^2$ is a quadratic function.

Quadratic functions are NEVER linear.

The SAT never asks you to draw the graph of a quadratic function. It will only ask you to use given graphs to answer questions, or to identify which answer choice correctly graphs a given function.

Quadratic functions always extend infinitely in some direction (up or down).

Example:

> The graph of $y = x^2$ extends "up" infinitely, and looks like this:

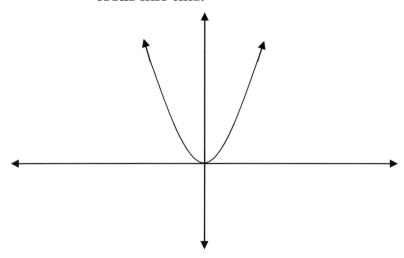

The graph of $y = - (x^2)$ extends "down" infinitely, and looks like this:

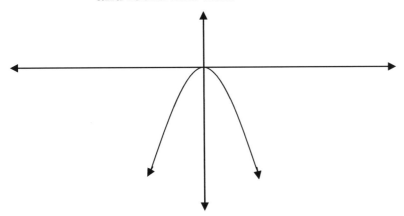

Note that the "direction" of the graph of a quadratic equation is really just a question of its range. When the range extends to negative infinity, the graph "opens down." When the range extends to positive infinity, the graph "opens up."

When a quadratic function "opens down," its highest point is the (x, y) pair that has the greatest y value.

When a quadratic function "opens up," its lowest point is the (x, y) pair that has the lowest y value.

Sometimes you'll be asked to find the "zeros" of a quadratic function. The zeros are the points where the graph of the function touches the x-axis. To find the zeros, just set $f(x)$ equal to zero, and then solve the resulting equation by factoring, just like we did above.

Example:

To find the zeros of $f(x) = (x^2)/3 - 3$, we set $f(x)$ equal to zero and then solve for x by factoring:

$$0 = (x^2)/3 - 3$$

$$3 = (x^2)/3$$

$$9 = x^2$$

$$x = 3 \quad or \quad x = -3$$

So the zeros of $f(x) = (x^2)/3 - 3$ are 3 and -3.

Geometric notation

The SAT likes to use what it calls "geometric notation" to describe lines, rays, angles, and so on. You've probably seen this notation in your classes, but don't worry if you haven't—it's not hard to learn.

AB means the distance from A to B.

$\overleftrightarrow{AB}$ means the line that goes through points A and B (note the little arrows on the ends, which indicate an infinite extension into space.)

$\overline{AB}$ means the line segment with endpoints A and B. (The lack of arrowheads on the symbol indicates that the given segment does not stretch on to infinity.)

$\overrightarrow{AB}$ means the ray with endpoint A that goes through B and then stretches on infinitely.

$\overrightarrow{BA}$ means the ray with B for an endpoint that goes through A and stretches on infinitely.

∠ABC means the angle with point B as a vertex that has point A on one leg and point C on the other.

∠ABC = 60° means that the measure of the angle with point B as a vertex, and with point A on one leg and point C on the other, is 60 degrees.

△ABC means the triangle with vertices A, B, and C.

▱ABCD means the quadrilateral with vertices A, B, C, and D.

$\overline{AB} \perp \overline{BC}$ means that the line segments AB and BC are perpendicular to each other.

Points and lines

A unique line can be drawn to connect any two points.

Between any two points on a line, there is a midpoint that is halfway between the two points.

Any three or more points may or may not fall on the same line. If they do, we say the points are collinear.

Angles in the plane

Degrees are the units that we use to measure how "wide" or "big" an angle is.

Example:

This is a 45-degree angle:

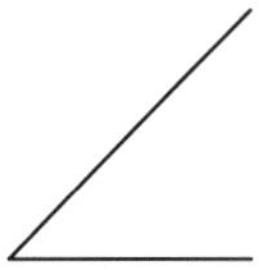

This is a 90-degree angle, also called a "right angle:"

This is a 180-degree angle, which is the same thing as a straight line:

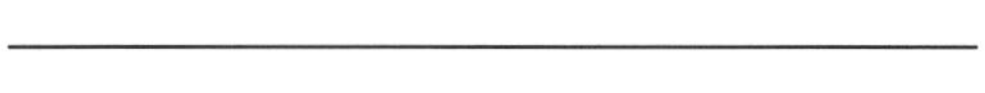

Sometimes angles have special relationships. The two types of special relationships that the SAT cares about the most are vertical angles and supplementary angles

Vertical angles are the pairs of angles that lie across from each other when two lines intersect. In a pair of vertical angles, the two angles have the same degree measurements as each other.

Example:

Angles ∠ABC and ∠DBE are a pair of vertical angles, so they have the same degree measurement. Angles ∠ABD and ∠CBE are also a pair of vertical angles, so they have the same measurements as each other as well.

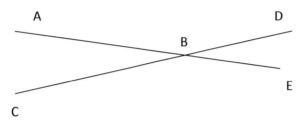

Supplementary angles are pairs of angles whose measurements add up to 180 degrees. When supplementary angles are next to each other, they form a straight line.

Example:

∠ABC and ∠ABD are a pair of supplementary angles, because their measurements together add up to 180 degrees—together, they form the straight line CD.

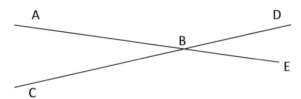

Triangles

The SAT loves to ask about triangles.

The sum of the measures of the angles in any triangle is 180 degrees, the same as it is in a straight line.

In any triangle, the longest side is always opposite the biggest angle, and the shortest side is always opposite the smallest angle.

In an "equilateral" triangle, all the sides are the same length.

In an equilateral triangle, all the angles measure 60 degrees each.

Example:

In the equilateral triangle △EQI below, all the sides are of equal length, and all the angles are 60 degrees.

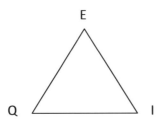

In an "isosceles" triangle, two of the three sides are the same length as each other, and two of the three angles are the same size as each other.

Example:

In the isosceles triangle △ISO below, side IS is the same length as side SO. Also, ∠SIO and ∠SOI have the same degree measurement as each other.

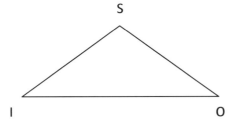

A "right" triangle is a triangle that includes a ninety-degree angle as one of its three angles.

A special relationship exists between the measurements of the sides of a right triangle: If you take the lengths of the two shorter sides and square them, and then add those two squares together, the resulting amount is the square of the length of the longest side.

Example:

In the right triangle below, $a^2 + b^2 = c^2$

The expression of this relationship, $a^2 + b^2 = c^2$, is called the "Pythagorean Theorem."

A "Pythagorean triple" is a set of three numbers that can all be the lengths of the sides of the same right triangle. Memorizing four of these sets will make your life easier on the SAT.

Example:

> **{3, 4, 5} is a Pythagorean triple because**
> $3^2 + 4^2 = 5^2$.
>
> **{1, 1, √2} is a Pythagorean triple because**
> $1^2 + 1^2 = √2^2$
>
> **{1, √3, 2} is a Pythagorean triple because**
> $1^2 + √3^2 = 2^2$
>
> **{5, 12, 13} is a Pythagorean triple because**
> $5^2 + 12^2 = 13^2$

When we multiply each number in a Pythagorean triple by the same number, we get another Pythagorean triple.

Example:

> **If we know {3, 4, 5} is a Pythagorean triple, then we also know {6, 8, 10} is a Pythagorean triple, because {6, 8, 10} is what we get when we multiply every number in {3, 4, 5} by 2.**

In a {1, 1, √2} right triangle, the angle measurements are 45°, 45°, 90°.

In a {1, √3, 2} right triangle, the angle measurements are 30°, 60°, 90°.

Two triangles are "similar triangles" if they have all the same angle measurements.

Between two similar triangles, the relationship between any two corresponding sides is the same as between any other two corresponding sides.

Example:

> **Triangles △ABC and △DEF below are similar. Side AB has length 8, and side DE has length 24, so every side measurement in △DEF must be three times the corresponding side in △ABC.**

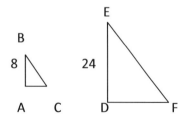

The formula for the area of a triangle is given in the front of every real SAT Math section.

In every triangle, the length of each side must be less than the sum of the lengths of the other sides. (Otherwise, the triangle would not be able to "close.")

Parallelograms

A parallelogram is a four-sided figure where both pairs of opposite sides are parallel to each other.

In a parallelogram, opposite angles are equal to each other, and the measures of all the angles added up together equal 360.

Example:

In □ABCD below, all the interior angles taken together equal 360°, and opposite angles have equal measurements.

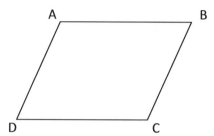

Rectangles

Rectangles are special parallelograms where all the angles measure 90 degrees. In a rectangle, if you know the lengths of the sides then you can always figure out the length from one corner to the opposite corner by using the Pythagorean theorem.

Example:

In the rectangle below, all angles are right angles, and we can use the Pythagorean theorem to determine that the diagonal AC must have a length of 13, since $5^2 + 12^2 = 13^2$.

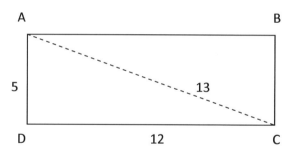

Squares

Squares are special rectangles where all the sides have equal length.

Area

The area of a two-dimensional figure is the amount of two-dimensional space that the figure covers.

Area is always measured in square units.

All the area formulas you need for the SAT appear in the beginning of each Math section, so there's no need to memorize them—you just need to know how to use them.

Perimeters (squares, rectangles, circles)

The perimeter of a two-dimensional object is the sum of the lengths of its sides or, for a circle, the distance around the circle.

To find the perimeter of a non-circle, just add up the lengths of the sides.

The perimeter of a circle is called the "circumference."

The formula for the circumference of a circle appears in the beginning of every real SAT Math section. It's C = 2*pi*.

Other polygons

The SAT might give you questions about special polygons, like pentagons, hexagons, octagons, and so on.

The sum of the angle measurements of any polygon can be determined with a simple formula: Where *s* is the number of sides of the polygon, the sum of the angle measurements is (*s* – 2) * 180.

Example:

> A triangle has 3 sides, so the sum of its angle measurements is given by (3 – 2) * 180, which is the same thing as (1) * 180, which is the same thing as 180. So the sum of the measurements of the angles in a triangle is 180 degrees. (Remember that we already knew this!)
>
> A hexagon has 6 sides, so the sum of its angle measurements is (6 – 2) * 180, or (4) * 180, which is 720. So all the angles in a hexagon add up to 720 degrees.

To find the perimeter of any polygon, just add up the lengths of the sides.

To find the area of a polygon besides a triangle, parallelogram, or circle, just divide the polygon into smaller triangles, polygons, and/or circles and find the areas of these pieces. A real SAT math question will always lend itself to this solution nicely.

Circles (diameter, radius, arc, tangents, circumference, area)

A circle is the set of points in a particular plane that are all equidistant from a single point, called the center.

Example:

> Circle *O* has a center point *O* and consists of all the points in one plane that are 5 units away from the center:

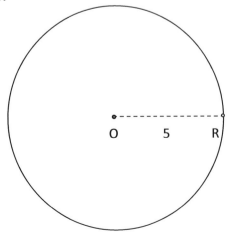

A radius is a line segment drawn from the center point of a circle to the edge of the circle at point R.

Example:

> **In the circle above, the line segment OR is a radius because it stretches from the center of the circle (O) to the edge of the circle**

All the radii of a circle have the same length, since all the points on the edge of the circle are the same distance from the center point.

A diameter is a line segment drawn from one edge of a circle, through the center of the circle, all the way to the opposite edge.

Example:

> **LR is a diameter of circle *O* because it starts at one edge of the circle, stretches through the center of the circle, and stops at the opposite edge of the circle.**

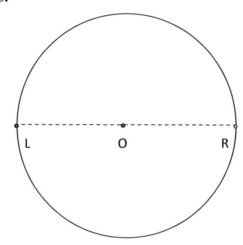

Because a diameter can be broken into two opposite radii, a diameter always has a length equal to twice the radius of the circle.

A diameter of a circle is the longest line segment that can be drawn through the circle.

A tangent line is a line that intersects a circle at only one point.

A tangent line is perpendicular to the radius of the circle that ends at the one point shared by the tangent and the circle.

Example:

> **Circle *O* has a tangent line TS that intersects the circle at point R, and is perpendicular to radius OR.**

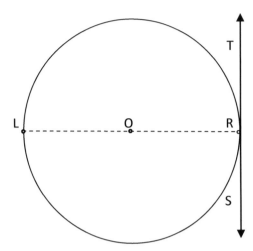

The circumference of a circle is the length around the circle, similar to the perimeter of a polygon.

An arc is a portion of a circle. We can measure an arc by drawing radii to the endpoints of the arc, and then measuring the angle formed by the radii at the center of the circle.

Example:

> **Circle *O* has a 90° arc *PR*, which we can measure by measuring the angle formed by radius *PO* and radius *RO*.**

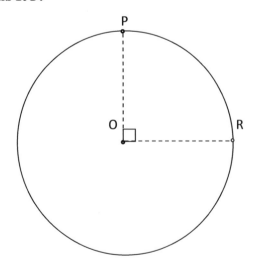

The formulas for area and circumference of a circle appear in the beginning of all real SAT math sections, so there's no need to memorize them if you don't already know them.

Solid geometry
On the SAT, solid geometry may involve cubes, rectangular solids, prisms, cylinders, cones, spheres, or pyramids.

All necessary volume formulas will be given to you, so there's no need to memorize them.

The surface area of a solid is the sum of the areas of its faces (except for spheres or other "rounded" solids, which you won't have to worry about on the SAT).

Statistics

The arithmetic mean of a set of numbers is the result you get when you add all the numbers together and then divide by the number of things that you added.

Example:

> **The average of {4, 9, 92} is 35, because**
> **(4 + 9 + 92)/3 = 35.**

The median of a set of numbers is the number that appears in the middle of the set when all the numbers in the set are arranged from least to greatest.

Example:

> **The median of {4, 9, 92} is 9, because when we**
> **arrange the three numbers from least to greatest, 9**
> **is in the middle.**

If there is an even number of elements in the set, then the median of that set is the arithmetic mean of the two numbers in the middle of the set when the elements of the set are arranged from least to greatest.

Example:

> **The median of {4, 9, 11, 92} is 10, because the**
> **number of elements in the set is even, and 10 is the**
> **average of the two numbers in the middle of the set.**

The mode of a set of numbers is the number that appears most frequently in the set.

Example:

> **The mode of {7, 7, 23, 44} is 7, because 7 appears**
> **more often than any other number in the set.**

Probability (elementary and geometric)

The probability of an event is a fraction that describes how likely the event is to happen. If the fraction is closer to 1, the event is more likely to happen; if the fraction is closer to zero, the event is less likely to happen.

To determine the fraction, you first calculate the total number of possible outcomes and place this number in the denominator of the fraction; then, you determine the number of outcomes that satisfy the event's requirements, and place this number in the numerator of the fraction.

Example:

> **The probability of rolling a 3 on a normal 6-sided die is 1/6. There are 6 possible outcomes, so 6 goes in the denominator of the fraction. Out of those 6 outcomes we only want one, the one where a 3 comes up, so 1 goes in the numerator of the fraction.**

The probability of rolling an odd number on a normal 6-sided die is 3/6. Again, there are 6 possible numbers we might roll, so 6 is our denominator. But now, since we want any odd number, the numbers 1, 3, and 5 all satisfy the requirements of our event, so there are 3 possible outcomes that we'll be happy with—that means 3 goes in the numerator.

Probability fractions can be manipulated just like any other fractions.

To find the probability of two or more events happening in a sequence, we just find the probabilities of each event by itself, and then multiply them by each other.

Example:

> **The probability of rolling double-sixes on two normal 6-sided dice is 1/36, because the probability of rolling a six on either die is 1/6, and (1/6)(1/6) = 1/36.**

Conclusion

We've just covered all the math concepts that the College Board will allow itself to cover on the SAT. As I mentioned at the beginning of the Toolbox, it's important to keep in mind that simply knowing these concepts is not enough to guarantee a good score on the SAT. It's much more important to focus on the design of the SAT Math section and learn how to take apart challenging questions.

And that's exactly what we'll start talking about on the next page . . .

Unwritten Rules of SAT Math

The rules for SAT Math problems are pretty much the same whether you're looking at Multiple Choice questions or Student-Produced Response questions.

SAT Math Rule 1: You Have To Know The Words

In the Writing and Critical Reading sections of the SAT, you can usually 'fake' your way past a few unfamiliar words in a particular question by using the proper technique. But if an SAT Math question asks you about the number of prime factors in a set, there's typically no way to answer the question without knowing what prime factors and sets are. The questions typically don't have any context in the way the questions on the Critical Reading section might. You pretty much have to know the terminology, which is why we discussed all the concepts in the Math Toolbox.

SAT Math Rule 2: Formulas Aren't That Important

You DON'T have to know any geometric formulas, but you do have to know when to use particular formulas that the College Board provides. For example, the SAT may want you to realize that you need to find the area of a triangle, but it won't ask you to know the formula. The test provides every single geometry formula that you need to answer every question (even though it might not always seem that way to the untrained eye). These formulas either appear in the resource box at the beginning of each SAT Math section, or they appear in the question itself.

SAT Math Rule 3: SAT Calculations Are Relatively Easy.

All the math on the SAT Math section is relatively easy.

In advanced high school math problems, the solution to one problem might involve complex graphs, trigonometric expressions, fraction bars, and pi; they're very complex problems, and they have very complex answers.

On the SAT, the solution is much more likely to be a plain old number like 12, because the actual calculations that we do for an SAT Math question are usually very basic. The most challenging part of an SAT Math question will typically be figuring out what the question is asking you to do in the first place; actually doing it usually isn't that hard after that.

If that sounds a little confusing right now, don't worry—it'll make a lot more sense after we look at some examples of real SAT Math questions together.

SAT Math Rule 4: The Drawings Are Usually Accurate

You can assume that every drawing is done to scale EXCEPT when the test specifically says otherwise. This is a very useful fact, because it sometimes lets you answer questions just by measuring things, or even eyeballing them— you don't need any math at all.

SAT Math Rule 5: Limited Subject-Matter

In the Math Toolbox, we went over every single mathematical concept the SAT might throw at you. You'll probably find that you're familiar with most of them, if not all of them, and the rest are relatively straightforward. Once you know these concepts, you can rest assured that they will be enough to answer *every single real SAT Math question*.

SAT Math Rule 6: 30 Seconds or Less

Perhaps the most important rule of all, from a strategic perspective, is that EVERY SINGLE MATH QUESTION can be answered in less than 30 seconds.

This doesn't mean that you're going to get the question wrong if it takes you longer—it just means you aren't going about answering the question in the easiest way. When you're looking for a way to solve the problem, just remember that every single question is simple, no matter how complicated it may seem at first. When we run into questions we can't figure out at first, which is guaranteed to happen to everyone, we need to train ourselves so that our instincts are to try to make things simpler, not more complex.

SAT Math Rule 7: All Necessary Information

Unless one of the answer choices is that the question hasn't provided enough information, each question must have all the information you need to choose the correct answer choice—no matter how much it might seem like that isn't true on some questions.

SAT Math Rule 8: Wrong Answers Are There For A Reason

The College Board puts a lot of thought into the wrong answers that it offers you for every multiple-choice question. Those wrong answers aren't just randomly generated. Instead, each one is the result of certain mistakes that the College Board thinks students will make on a particular question. Imagine that you try to solve an SAT Math question and end up with the number 15 as your answer. Then you look at the answer choices and see that they only include 10, 12, 18, 24, and 30. In that case, you would know right away that you had made a mistake on the question, and you'd be able to start over and try to solve the question correctly. From the College Board's standpoint, this would be like letting you get away with a free mistake, because you'd be able to realize what you'd done wrong and fix it.

To keep that from happening, the College Board does its best to include 4 wrong answers to each question that try to anticipate the mistakes that you're likely to make.

This might seem pretty mean-spirited on the part of the College Board, but we can actually use it to our advantage as test-takers. Since the College Board tries to come up with wrong answers to tempt us into making mistakes—and since it has to do this in standardized, repetitive ways, just like everything else it does—then we can learn to use the concepts and relationships that appear in the answer choices to get an idea of what the question is actually asking about.

This will make a lot more sense after we talk about common patterns that we'll encounter in the answer choices, and after we go through some solutions from the Blue Book together. We'll cover some of those common patterns starting on the next page, and then we'll do the Blue Book solutions a few pages after that.

Hidden Test Design Patterns of SAT Math Questions

Most of the hidden patterns on the SAT math section have to do with using the answer choices to help you check your answers, where that's possible. Looking at the answer choices can reassure you that you have the right answer (or help show you your mistakes so you can correct them).

Many students are surprised to find out that these patterns appear reliably and consistently in real SAT Math questions from the College Board, because they really have very little to do with actual math rules—they're purely related to the test-design principles required by the standardization of the test. So before we get into these patterns, I'd like to take a moment to remind you why they're a part of the SAT.

As we discussed at the beginning of this book, it's important to remember that the SAT is not a normal test. It has a very specific purpose and must, therefore, follow very specific rules to make sure that questions are designed to test the same skills in the same underlying ways, without actually repeating the questions. It's also important to remember that the SAT is predominantly a multiple-choice test, and that the multiple-choice format only requires a test-taker to separate right answers from wrong answers, rather than requiring you to provide correct answers on your own. This means that the relationships among right answers and wrong answers must remain constant for all real tests, because changing those relationships would involve changing the nature of the multiple-choice questions and breaking the standardization rules of the test.

Keep these things in mind as we discuss the patterns in the SAT Math section, and as you encounter real SAT Math questions in the future.

Hidden Pattern 1: Halves and Doubles

Very often, one of the wrong answer choices will be twice as much as the right answer choice, or half as much as it. This is especially true when the problem involves multiplying or dividing an amount by 2. If you solve a problem and get an answer like 18, a wrong answer choice like 36 might reassure you that you're right.

Remember that this pattern is an indication that you're probably right, not a confirmation that you're definitely right. Also, it's important not to get it backwards—in the same hypothetical example, the right answer might be 36, and the wrong answer might be 18! Be very aware of this useful pattern, but don't rely on it exclusively.

Hidden Pattern 2: Right Answer, Wrong Time

One of the ways that the SAT will try to confuse you is by giving you a problem that involves two or three steps. When it does that, one of the wrong answers will often be the number that you would get if you stopped after one of the earlier steps. For example, a problem might ask you to find the price for pens by giving you the prices for different combinations of pencils and erasers. The problem might require you to figure out the price of pencils in order to figure out the price for erasers, and one of the wrong answer choices would be the price of pencils. Because this wrong answer is actually a number that you found in the process of solving the problem, seeing it in as a wrong answer can reassure you that you're on the right track.

Hidden Pattern 3: Substitution

As I said before, the SAT likes to give you problems that look complicated but have very simple solutions. The test often does this by showing you a rather complicated expression that you can simplify by substituting one thing for another. If you start looking for substitution opportunities, you'll find them all over the test, and they'll make your life easier. For example, the SAT will often reward you for substituting a difference of squares like $x^2 - y^2$ with the expression $(x - y)(x + y)$. On the other hand, it might also reward you for going in the other direction, and realizing that $(x - y)(x + y)$ can be restated as $x^2 - y^2$.

Don't worry if this sounds a little vague right now. We'll see several examples of it when we go through real SAT questions from the College Board in a few pages.

Hidden Pattern 4: Try To Avoid Firsts And Lasts In A Series

Sometimes some or all of the answer choices in a math question will form a series. These series might be pretty easy to recognize in some cases, like if the answer choices are 7, 8, 9, 10, and 11. In other cases, the series might be less obvious, and it might be related to a concept in the question: if the question is talking about dividing some quantity by 4, then the answer choices might contain the series 3, 12, 48, because each number in the series is one fourth of the next number in the series.

The College Board seems to include series in the answer choices when it hopes that you'll make a mistake and repeat a step in the solution one time too many or too few, ending up with one of the wrong answers in the series. In other words, if a question involves finding the perimeter of a triangle with sides of 5 units each, the answer choices might include the series 10, 15, 20, because the College Board is hoping you'll either add 5 one time too few (ending up with 10) or one time too many (ending up with 20).

For this reason, when a series is involved in the answer choices, we'll typically find that the correct answer isn't the first or last number in the series. The College Board seems to like to put the correct answer near the middle of the series in order to allow you to make a mistake in either direction and still find a wrong answer that reflects your mistake.

Remember, as with the other patterns in this section, that this isn't an unbreakable rule. So I'm not saying that we'll never, ever find the right answer at the beginning or the end of a series; sometimes we will. I'm just saying that it's more common to find it in one of the middle positions of a series, and that it helps to be aware of that.

Hidden Pattern 5: Wrong Answers Try To Imitate Right Answers

The College Board likes to create wrong answers that incorporate elements of correct answers, probably in an attempt to make it harder for you to eliminate answer choices on the basis of a partial solution. In other words, if you're working on a question where the answer choices are all algebraic expressions and you figure out that the correct answer should include the expression $2r$ along with some other stuff, then you'll often find that a majority of the answer choices include $2r$. This way, the College Board can try to force you to figure out the rest of the question in order to identify the correct answer.

While this can be an annoying thing for the College Board to do, you'll find that you can actually use it to your advantage in many cases: after you think you've solved a question, if you see that the wrong answers seem to include a lot of the elements in common with the choice that you like, you can often take that as a good sign that you've thought about the question correctly.

In other words, if the wrong answers seem to be imitating parts of the right answer, that's typically a sign that you've understood the question correctly. (Notice I said, "typically," and not "always.")

We'll see several examples of this, and of the other SAT Math patterns, when we go through some questions from the Blue Book in a few pages.

Special Math Technique: Learning From Diagrams

Many math questions on the SAT will involve diagrams. You probably already knew that. But you might not know that SAT diagrams can actually give away a lot of information about the best ways to attack a particular question.

When an SAT diagram is drawn to scale, you can often extract important information from it just by looking at it. For example, you can eyeball the relative sizes of angles and the relative lengths of line segments.

But when a diagram isn't drawn to scale—or simply isn't provided at all—you can often learn even more.

When the College Board decides to leave out a diagram or to include a diagram that isn't drawn to scale, they make this decision because including an accurate diagram would give away the answer to the question you're being asked. In these situations, it's often helpful to try to draw your own scaled diagram in the test booklet if you can.

Similarly, the College Board will sometimes show you a diagram and then provide a further explanation of that diagram in the written portion of the question. Again, the reason for this is simple: If the written information had been labeled directly on the diagram in the first place, the answer to the question would have been a lot easier to figure out.

So if you want to maximize your score on the SAT Math section, you're going to need to practice using diagrams. Whenever you see a diagram on the test, be very alert to the things that are left out of it. Always be prepared to augment the given diagram (or provide a substitute diagram of your own). You may be surprised at how many questions become much, much easier once you catch on to this.

The Recommended Math Path

Now that we've explained the rules and patterns that you'll find on the SAT Math section, we can look at the process that I recommend for those questions. I call it the "Math Path," mostly because that rhymes.

The Math Path is a set of guidelines to help us figure out how to attack tough questions. You won't need to use it on every question, and you can modify it as you keep practicing. I'm teaching it to you because it's a good way to keep all of the elements of SAT Math questions in mind. If you practice with these ideas, you'll find that they become second nature.

1. Read the question carefully.

This might sound kind of strange, but if you asked me to pick the single mistake that costs people the most points on the Math part of the SAT, I'd say it's the mistake of not reading the questions and the answer choices carefully.

In fact, we should really think of the entire SAT, including the Math portion, as an extended test of reading skills. Most of what we do on the Math portion of the test will depend on our ability to notice key phrases and details in each question.

By the way, because of the way SAT Math works, if you know the meanings of every word in a particular question, then you know enough math to be able to answer that question. Trust me on this—we'll see proof of it as we continue.

2. Read the answer choices if there are any.

Most students ignore the answer choices in a Math question until they're basically done with the question. They typically read a question, try to figure out the answer on their own, and look for that answer (or a similar answer) in the answer choices. Now, if you could successfully do that for the course of an entire test without making a single mistake, it's true that you wouldn't miss any questions. But so many questions become so much easier to answer when we consider the answer choices as part of the question from the very beginning.

Remember that the College Board likes to play little games in the answer choices of the SAT Math section. We talked about some of those "games" a few pages ago when we covered the hidden patterns of these questions. Sometimes wrong answers will include elements of the right answer, for instance, or sometimes they'll form a series, and so on. Sometimes, simply noting that all the answer choices are one-digit numbers can be enough to help you realize how to approach a question.

So after you read the main part of the question, look over the answer choices and see what kind of options the test is giving you. Try to figure out why the test is presenting the answer choices that way—look at the values in the choices, but also look at the *relationships between those values*, and try to think about how those relationships might be important to the question.

I said earlier that it's important to remember that every SAT Math question can be answered in less than 30 seconds each if we're really on our game. Often, a large part of finding these super-fast solutions involves thinking about how the answer choices relate to the question from the very beginning.

So remember to think of the entire question, including the answer choices, as one big system of ideas. We'll see several examples of how this works when we look at some real SAT questions from the College Board's blue book in a few pages.

3. Consider diagrams, if there are any.

As we discussed earlier, there are two questions you should always ask yourself when a math question includes a diagram:

1. Is this drawn to scale?

2. Are any dimensions of the diagram left out of the diagram itself but included in the text underneath it?

If a diagram is drawn to scale, we can often (but not always) find the answer to the question just by looking at the diagram itself.

If the diagram is not to scale, the reason is almost always that drawing it to scale would have given away the correct answer. So if we re-draw the diagram to scale, we'll often be able to figure out how to answer the question pretty easily.

Any dimensions that are left out of the diagram itself but included in the text of the question will probably be the basis for the first step in the solution to the question.

4. Think about what areas of math might be involved.

Now that you've read the question and the answer choices, and considered the diagram if there is one, you should have a pretty good idea of which specific math terms and concepts are mentioned in the question.

Many test-takers overlook the fact that the solution to a question can only involve concepts that are immediately related to the concepts in the question. It sounds kind of obvious once it's pointed out, but everything in math proceeds in a step-by-step fashion, with each step building on the previous one.

When most people get stumped on the SAT Math section, they panic and try to call to mind every single math concept they know in the hope that one of those concepts will miraculously reveal the answer. Instead, we want to narrow our focus and confine our thought process to the concepts in the question and the concepts that are related to them.

For example, if an SAT Math question involves words like "degrees" and "radius" and "center," then it must be a question about circles, and there are only a few circle-related concepts that the SAT is allowed to ask us about (look back at the toolbox if you don't remember what they are). That means that the solution to the question must somehow involve those circle-related concepts, so we should focus our attention on them.

5. Look for a 30-second solution.

In this step, we try to use everything we've already figured out (the clues from the diagrams, the clues in the answer choices, and the relevant mathematical concepts) to help us string together the right basic math ideas that will let us connect the prompt to the correct answer choice. And don't forget—the best solutions will take you less than 30 seconds to work out.

Of course, as I said before, you can still get the question right even if you can't find a solution in under 30 seconds. But it's a good idea to get in the habit of looking for fast, simple solutions, because the majority of the difficulty that people have on the SAT Math section comes from not catching small details in a question, and wasting a lot of time and effort as a result.

6. Solve the problem.

After you have read the question, considered the answer choices, considered the diagram, considered the likely areas of math to be involved, and decided on a straightforward solution, you've finally earned the right to go ahead and solve the problem. IF YOU TRY TO SOLVE THE PROBLEM WITHOUT GOING THROUGH THE EARLIER STEPS, YOU'LL PROBABLY JUST WASTE YOUR TIME.

This is one more way that SAT Math questions differ from the math questions you encounter in school. In school, the questions on a math test are basically just like the questions you've been doing for homework and the questions your teacher has been doing in lectures, so you build up a kind of instinctive, automatic approach to doing math, in which you memorize formulas and then automatically apply a certain formula in a certain situation.

But that won't work on the SAT Math section, where questions seem to be specifically written so that formulas are of little help. If you read a math question on the SAT and dive right into it without thinking about it first, you're probably doing something wrong. Don't try to solve the problem until you've read it and thought about how it fits the SAT's patterns and rules.

7. Re-check the answer choices.

One of the best ways to double-check your work is to look at all the choices you think are wrong and see if you can figure out why some of them are included. In other words, if you can figure out the mistakes that the College Board wanted you to make for some of the wrong choices, then there's a pretty good chance that you've handled the question correctly. But if you look back over the wrong answers and you don't have any idea why any of them are there, that's typically a sign that you misunderstood the question. Be on the lookout for hidden patterns like the ones we talked about.

If you're fully satisfied that you know why your answer is right and why at least a few of the other answer choices are present as wrong answers (for multiple-choice questions), mark your answer and move on to the next question. AS ALWAYS, IF YOU'RE NOT COMPLETELY SURE THAT YOU HAVE THE RIGHT ANSWER, SKIP THE QUESTION. DON'T GUESS! If you don't remember why you shouldn't guess, go back and look at our earlier discussion of the problems with guessing.

SAT Math Path Conclusion

The important thing about SAT Math questions is that you shouldn't try to solve them without reading them carefully and setting them up first. Taking a few seconds to get your bearings will make answering the question a lot easier. Remember to keep the solution to every problem as simple as possible.

It may seem like this process is pretty long or complicated, especially for questions that seem obvious when you first look at them. But it's important to remember that you don't have to use this process on every question—only on the ones that you can't figure out at first. And you can modify it as you see fit, depending on the question and your own preferences.

The important thing is to be aware of all the elements involved in the Math Path (careful reading, considering the answer choices, evaluating diagrams, identifying relevant concepts, trying to find the simplest possible solution, and catching your mistakes). Try to implement them in your practice sessions, so they can become second nature when you see challenging questions on the test.

What About Grid-In Questions?

Many students wonder if the Student-Produced Response questions (or "grid-in" questions) require a different approach from the multiple-choice questions. For the most part, the Math Path process that we just discussed is the process I would follow for the grid-in questions (with the obvious exception that we won't have any answer choices to consider in deciding how to attack the question.

There are a few special considerations we should keep in mind for the grid-in questions, though.

If The Question Refers To The Possibility Of Multiple Solutions, Make Sure You Understand Why

The grid-in format allows the College Board to ask more open-ended math questions, which is one of the reasons it exists on the SAT in the first place. So be aware that you might see questions that offer more than one valid solution. Such a question will often use a phrase like "one possible value," as in, "If X has a value between 3.9 and 4, what is one possible value of X?"

If you realize that you're dealing with a question that refers to the possibility of more than one valid response, make sure you can figure out why. In other words, if you can only think of one possible answer for such a question, then you've probably misunderstood it in some fundamental way, and there's a very good chance that the answer you're thinking of is wrong.

I'm not saying that you actually need to work out more than one solution in order to know that you've got the question right; I'm just saying that you need to understand where other solutions might come from. For instance, in the hypothetical question I just mentioned, you might say, "I know that 3.91 is between 3.9 and 4, and I know they used the phrase 'one possible value' because there's an infinite number of numbers between any two numbers." You wouldn't necessarily have to work out that 3.92 and 3.93 are also valid solutions in order to be certain you understood the question correctly.

Don't Be Afraid To Guess, But Don't Expect Much To Come Of It

You aren't penalized for missing a grid-in question, so you should never leave a grid-in question blank. On the other hand, since there are thousands of possible ways to fill out the answer grid for each question, the chance of guessing right is extremely small—which is why they don't penalize you in the first place.

If you do decide to guess on a grid-in question, make that decision as quickly as you can so that you don't waste any more time on the question than necessary. I would recommend guessing either 0 or 1, if those answers seem like they have any chance of being correct, just because I feel like I see those answers appearing more frequently than any other individual number. But the advantage of that, if there even is one, is extremely slight, and your chance of being correct on a random guess is basically zero anyway.

The Last 2 or 3 Questions Might Seem Extra Weird

We'll often find that the strangest questions on the whole SAT Math section appear as questions 16, 17, and/or 18 on the grid-in section. We won't always find exceptionally weird questions in these positions, but if there are going to be exceptionally weird math questions on a particular test, this is probably where they'll appear.

These questions must still follow the same rules and patterns that the rest of the test follows—they still can't involve trigonometry, for instance, and they must still be answerable in under 30 seconds and without a calculator. It's just that sometimes they seem noticeably weirder than other questions on the SAT Math section.

Unfortunately, simply knowing that this might happen doesn't do much to help us answer these questions. I just wanted to mention that we sometimes see extremely strange questions in these positions so that you know to look out for them, and so that you don't think the test is suddenly changing dramatically and begin to doubt yourself.

Conclusion

We've just discussed a few special considerations for the grid-in questions, but remember that we want to approach them in basically the same way we would approach any other SAT Math question: by reading carefully, paying attention to details, thinking about which areas of math might be involved, looking for the simplest possible solution, and so on.

Sometimes You Can't Solve For Every Variable

We've seen several examples of the way the College Board likes to make questions more challenging by handling things differently from the way they're handled in school. One of the best examples of this is the way the test sometimes asks questions that involve multiple variables.

In school, if you have a question that involves four variables, you're usually supposed to figure out the individual values of each variable. But the SAT often asks questions in which it's unnecessary—or even impossible—to work out values for individual variables.

This doesn't mean that questions with multiple variables are impossible to figure out on the SAT. It's just that sometimes it's possible to know the value of an expression that involves several variables even if you can't know the values of the variables themselves.

For instance, if I tell you that $ab^2 - 7 = 53$, and then ask you for the value of ab^2, you can still figure out that ab^2 is 60, even if it's impossible to know the values of a or b individually.

One of the test's main signals that it might not be possible to solve for every variable in an expression is when they ask you for the value of an expression that contains multiple variables, rather than asking for the value of an individual variable within that expression. In the ab^2 example I just gave, I couldn't ask for a or b individually because there wasn't enough information about them; that's why I had to ask for the entire expression ab^2.

So if you see a question that asks for the value of $x + y$ or some other expression with more than one variable, don't make the mistake of assuming that you have to find x and y individually. It may be more expedient to try to solve for the entire $x + y$ expression all at once.

One example of a question that involves multiple variables that can't be approached individually is question 16 from page 919 in the second edition of the College Board's Blue Book. My explanation for that question appears later in this book, when I go through a selection of challenging SAT Math questions.

It's Not School Math—Your Work Doesn't Matter

Lots of test-takers experience significant difficulty on the SAT Math section for a reason that might seem strange to a lot of people: they try to approach each question in a formalized way that would satisfy a math teacher.

But by now we know that the SAT doesn't reward the same things that school rewards. And the SAT Math section is no different.

The bottom line is that the SAT doesn't care what kind of work you do to arrive at the answer that you choose. The SAT only cares if the answer that you choose is correct. That's it.

This fact has two very important implications for us as test-takers. First, it means that we can, and should, get in the habit of looking for the fastest, most direct route to the answer, even if that route doesn't involve solving a formal equation (or even writing anything down at all). Second, it means that we have to make sure we don't make any small mistakes in our solution that might lead us to mark the wrong answer even if our overall approach is formally sound, because the College Board will never know what our approach was. For the College

Board, a wrong answer is a wrong answer no matter how solid the approach to the question was, and a right answer is a right answer no matter what you did to arrive there.

So remember that the SAT Math section often features questions where formulaic solutions are literally impossible to use.

In the parts of this book where I provide solutions to real SAT Math questions from the College Board's Blue Book, you'll often see that the approach I recommend wouldn't be acceptable to most math teachers, because it's not formal. This isn't because I'm not good at math; it's because I'm very, very good at *SAT Math*, and in SAT Math there's no value in approaching things formulaically. In fact, there's usually a lot more value in abandoning formulaic math whenever possible.

So try to get in the habit of finding the most direct approach to a question that you possibly can, and remember that the only thing that matters to the College Board is that you mark the correct answer!

Avoid Decimal Expressions Unless A Question Uses Them

In high school and college math classes, we're often encouraged to use decimal values rather than fractions. For instance, we might write "0.8" instead of "4/5."

On the SAT, it's usually a bad idea to express things in terms of decimals, unless the answer choices are also in decimal form. When we work with decimals, we often miss opportunities to simplify and reduce expressions that are much easier to see when we keep everything in fraction form.

For instance, if a question involves multiplying 4/5 by 5/6, then using fractions might help me see right away that the 5's cancel out and I'm left with 4/6, which is the same thing as 2/3. If I had to enter that into a calculator, I'd probably lose time, and I'd also run the risk of hitting the wrong key or something. In general, we'll have a much better chance of finding the shortest possible solution if we get in the habit of avoiding decimal expressions on the SAT.

The only real exception to this comes when a question involves decimal expressions in its answer choices. When the College Board sets a question up like that, they're usually trying to get us to realize that we can simply approximate the answer, often by using the scale of a diagram or some other clue in the question, and that the correct answer choice will be the only one that's close to our approximation. In these situations, it can be very helpful to use the decimal approximation to solve the question—but in just about every other situation, it'll be smarter to stick with fractions.

Ignore The So-Called "Order Of Difficulty"

Test-takers are often encouraged to believe that the questions on the SAT Math section get harder as the section goes on. But I would recommend ignoring that idea.

It's true that the College Board assigns difficulty-level rankings of 1 through 5 to each question, and that we'll typically see that the earliest questions in an SAT Math section are ranked 1 or 2, while the last questions are 4's and 5's.

But that shouldn't mean anything to us, as trained test-takers. Let me explain why.

The difficulty ranking is simply an indication of the percentage of the test-taking population who miss a particular question. In other words, if a question has a difficulty ranking of 1, then the vast majority of people who see it will get it right; if it has a difficulty ranking of 5, then the vast majority of people who see it will answer it incorrectly.

The difficulty ranking has nothing to do with the number or type of math concepts that appear in a particular question. Sometimes a question that's based on the definition of the word "even" might be ranked as a

1, and sometimes it's ranked as a 5. The deciding factor is simply the percentage of test-takers who get it right or wrong.

And here's the important thing to keep in mind: the vast majority of SAT-takers have no idea at all of how to take the test. They do almost everything wrong. If you're familiar with the concepts in this Black Book, you'll be looking at SAT Math questions the right way, and the percentage of regular test-takers who get a question right has nothing to do with whether you, yourself, will get that question right.

We'll generally find that questions near the end of an SAT Math section tend to be more abstract or conceptual, while questions towards the beginning of a section tend to be a little more similar to the kinds of things you might be asked about in school. But that doesn't mean the later questions are always harder. In fact, we'll often find that questions towards the end of a section are more likely to be things you can solve without actually doing any calculations (because they'll rely on things like properties and definitions of terms). This can often mean that we can answer later questions much more quickly than earlier questions, if we're approaching them correctly.

But this cuts both ways. Just as we shouldn't be intimidated by later questions, we also shouldn't take earlier questions for granted. Remember that doing well on SAT Math is a question of reading carefully and thinking carefully, and that wrong answer choices are often designed to attract students who make small mistakes. This means that we have to be alert to possible mistakes at all times, even when a question might seem extremely easy.

In fact, when I work with students who are trying to score a perfect 800 on the SAT Math section but who might be missing one or two questions per test, I find that they nearly always miss questions in the first half of the section because of small mistakes—usually because they've been incorrectly taught that those questions are always "easy" and that they don't have to pay full attention to them.

So here's the bottom line: you should ignore the idea of an order of difficulty, because it serves no purpose. Instead, treat each question as a separate event. Don't be afraid of any questions, and don't take them for granted either.

The Math Path In Action

To demonstrate how this approach to SAT Math questions works, and to help you improve your understanding and execution of that approach, we'll go through an SAT Math section from the second edition of the College Board's Blue Book, *The Official SAT Study Guide*. (Remember, the Blue Book is the only book I recommend for practice questions, because it's the only book whose questions are totally guaranteed to play by the College Board's rules.) I've chosen the first practice-test section that includes both Multiple Choice problems and Student-Produced Response problems. It starts on page 413 of the Blue Book.

Page 413, Question 1

You really have to be careful on a problem like this—it's the kind of thing that most test-takers will feel they can't possibly miss because it seems so simple. But it's very easy to overlook a couple of small details on this question and end up with a wrong answer.

The question asks us to figure out how many new houses were built from 1961 to 1990. To answer that question, we have to look at the relevant years on the chart. The first row shows the houses built from 1961 to 1970; the next row shows the houses from 1971 to 1980; the third row shows us the houses from 1981 to 1990. There are 2 house icons in the first row, 4 in the second row, and 8 in the third row. That makes a total of 14 house icons.

Notice that choice (A) reflects a mistake that would be pretty easy to make here: if we assumed that each house icon represented one house, then we'd think (A) was right. But each icon represents 2,000 houses, so the right answer is 28,000. That makes (E) right.

As always, I'd also try to think about where some of the other wrong answers might have come from. In this case, (B) is what we'd get if we counted all the icons in the entire chart (including 1991 – 2000) *and* also made the mistake of thinking each icon only represented one house. (C) is what we'd get if we correctly realized that each icon represented 2,000 houses but accidentally only counted the third row. Finally, (D) is what we'd get if we didn't count the second row for some reason.

I always try to figure out where some of the wrong answers are coming from because it helps me be sure I've understood the question. It's not necessary to figure out *every* wrong answer, even though we were able to do that in this question. But if you can't figure out where any of them are coming from at all, then there's a very good chance you made a mistake, and you should re-check your work.

Also note that, in this case, 3 out of the 5 choices are numbers in the tens of thousands. This strongly suggests (BUT DOES NOT GUARANTEE) that the right answer should be one of those 3. If we had accidentally overlooked the information about each icon counting for 2,000 houses, then noticing that most of the answer choices are huge numbers should have helped us realize we might have missed something.

This is a perfect example of the kind of question that you should absolutely lock down, double-check, and be done with in well under a minute, possibly in as little as 10 seconds. It's important to work quickly and efficiently through questions like this in order to save time for questions where you might have more difficulty gaining a foothold.

One last thing: note that this question, like many SAT Math questions, is primarily a critical reading question at heart. The major way people will make mistakes here is by misreading the question or the chart, not by failing to multiply the numbers 14 and 2,000.

Page 413, Question 2

This question presents us with a type of drawing that we might not ever have encountered before. But that's fine: remember that this question, like all SAT Math questions, can only be made out of the same basic math ideas that were in the Math Toolbox earlier in this book. So let's see what we can figure out.

We know the diagram is drawn to scale, because it doesn't say that it's not. But the answer choices are so close to one another that it would probably be hard to answer this question by eyeballing the drawing and using the scale.

So let's think in terms of geometry. We know that we can fill in the measurements of the angles opposite the labeled angles, because opposite angles are identical. So the angle opposite the 35-degree angle is also 35 degrees, and the one opposite the 45-degree angle is also 45 degrees.

Now it looks like we're getting somewhere: once we label those opposite angles, we can see that w is the third angle in a triangle, and that the other two angles are 35 degrees and 45 degrees.

That means w + 35 + 45 = 180. So w + 80 = 180, which means w is 100 degrees. So (B) is right.

Notice that (B) is in the middle of a 3-term series in the answer choices, with the other two terms differing by 10. This should alert you to the fact that it would be very easy to be off by 10 in this question if we forgot to carry a digit during the addition or the subtraction. So we should go back and check to make sure we didn't mess that up.

Still, it's very reassuring that we like the answer choice in the middle of this range, because typically the College Board likes to make the number in the middle of the range be correct. (As we discussed in the section on patterns, they do this because it gives us the option to be off in either direction and still find an answer choice reflecting our mistake.)

This is another question that probably should take less than 30 seconds to do. We want to answer it quickly, check to make sure we're right, and move on.

Page 414, Question 3

A lot of students ask me about this question because they can't figure out how to set it up algebraically.

But this is the SAT—we don't have to do it algebraically! In fact, in most cases I prefer not to use algebra on the SAT, because it often takes longer and it increases the chance that we'll make a mistake.

So let's just think about this. (There's no magical way to "just think about" a question—all we do is dive in somewhere and then see what adjustments, if any, we need to make.)

If each of the 19 tables had 4 people, then there would be seats for 76 people, because 4*19 = 76. We need to find seats for 84 people, though, which is 8 more than 76.

So 8 of the tables will need to have an extra seat, which makes (E) the right answer.

Notice that this isn't really the kind of question you would probably ever be asked in a math class, and the solution I just gave isn't the kind of solution your math teacher would ever accept. This is normal for the SAT, and we need to get used to it.

Also notice that the answer choices form a series in this question, and the correct answer happens to be the largest number in the series, which is something that I said doesn't happen often. I was right—it doesn't happen often—but that doesn't mean it never happens. In this case, when I see that the answer I like is the last number in a series, I'd just double-check my work and make sure I hadn't made a mistake, and move on.

One more thing—you might ask how I knew to start out by multiplying 4 and 19. But I didn't "know" that would lead to the answer right away until I tried it. On the SAT Math section, we have to be willing to play with questions like this, and we have to get away from the idea of following established formulas.

Page 414, Question 4

This question often overwhelms test-takers who think in terms of school math, because it has two variables in it, and one of those variables (m) is actually impossible to solve for. In school math, it might be a problem if we couldn't solve for a variable, but this is SAT Math. The SAT often gives us questions in which it's impossible to work out the value of a particular variable.

Since the question asks which answer choice would be equal to the original expression when a equals 4, and since every answer choice has 4's in it instead of a, I would start out by plugging 4 in for a, and determining that the original given expression equals $4m^2 + 4m + 4$. Then we can go through each answer choice and distribute the 4 in each one, until we end up with a choice that also results in $4m^2 + 4m + 4$ as an answer.

The answer choice that fits the bill is (D).

Notice that the choices here fit a pattern we discussed earlier in this book: the elements of the right answer appear very frequently in the wrong answers.

In other words, in this case, the correct answer has the parenthetical expression with m^2, m, and 1. Notice that 3 out of the 5 choices have m^2 somewhere in them, 4 out of 5 have m, and 4 out of 5 have 1 in them. Also notice that 4 out of 5 don't have a 4 in the parentheses, and 4 out of 5 don't involve squaring the expression in parentheses (like choice (B) does).

So if we were going to try to predict the right answer, based purely on the answer choices, we'd probably want the choice with these attributes:

- includes m^2
- includes m
- includes 1
- doesn't have a 4 in the parentheses
- doesn't square the expression in parentheses

We'd want that answer choice because those are the most popular features in the field of answer choices. The choice that satisfies all of those conditions is (D), which is the right answer in this case.

Just to be completely clear, let me point out that I would never, ever recommend that you answer a question based only on figuring out which choice has the most popular features. That will work a whole lot of times, but it doesn't work every time, and my goal is for us to be correct on every single question. So this idea is a pattern to be considered, not a rule to be followed unfailingly.

In this particular question, if we accidentally misread (E) and thought it was correct, being aware of the imitation pattern might let us realize that none of the other answer choices have a 4 inside the parentheses, which is probably a bad sign. If we liked (A) for some reason, then noticing that the other choices were all highly similar to one another and that none of them had m^3 might help us realize we needed to re-evaluate our conclusion.

Notice that we answered the question without ever finding out what m represents. This kind of thing is normal for the SAT. On the SAT, we need to get away from the idea that we have to solve for every variable we see in a question.

Page 414, Question 5

This question frustrates a lot of students because they've never seen a diagram like this in their math classes. But we have to remember that this kind of thing is standard on the SAT: no matter how much you practice, you're going to encounter things on test day that don't look like anything else you've ever seen, at least on the surface. We have to learn how to attack these kinds of situations systematically, and confidently.

In this case, they're asking us for the area of the shaded portion. As trained test-takers we know two things:

They have to give us all the geometry formulas we need.

They didn't give us a formula for the area of a portion of a square.

That means there must be a way to figure out the area of this shaded region without having a formula uniquely for that purpose.

We do have a formula for the area of a circle, though. And we could use that formula to find the area of the whole circle altogether, and then divide the area of the circle up to find the area of the shaded region.

So now we have to figure out how to find the area of the circle. On the SAT, there's only one way the College Board can ask us to do that: we have to use $A = pi(r^2)$, where A is the area and r is the radius. (Again, this formula is provided at the beginning of the math section if you don't remember it.)

How can we find the radius? In this case, we use the only number provided anywhere in the diagram: we look at the fact that the side length of the square is 2 units, and we realize that this corresponds to the diameter of the circle. If the diameter is 2, then the radius is 1. So the radius of the circle is 1 unit, which makes the area *of the entire circle* $pi(1^2)$, which is just pi.

Now we have to figure out what portion of the circle the shaded area represents. There are two ways to do this. Since the diagram is drawn to scale, we could just eyeball it and realize that the shaded area is one-quarter of the circle. If we want to be more precise, we could realize that the angle at point O must be a 90-degree angle, since O is the center of the circle and the center of the square. And 90 degrees is one-quarter of 360 degrees, so, again, the shaded area must be a quarter of the circle.

That means the correct answer here is pi/4. Again, pi is the area of the entire circle, and the shaded region is 1/4 of the circle, so its area is pi/4. And (A) is correct.

There are a lot of ways to mess this question up, and most of them will involve either thinking that the radius is 2 or accidentally thinking that the shaded portion is 1/2 of the circle (this can happen if a person tries to work out the area mathematically and makes a mistake in the process, instead of just looking at the picture). Notice that both mistakes are reflected in the wrong answer choices. In fact, (E) is what you'd get if you made both mistakes together.

This is a question I would definitely double-check, or even triple-check, for several reasons. The first reason is that the answer choice patterns aren't really pointing to (A) being right, even though it is. The patterns are really suggesting that (B) would be right (it's in the middle of a geometric series with (A) and (C) and (E), and there are more 2's in the answer choices than 4's). Also, even apart from the answer choices, this is a question where it would be very easy to make a simple mistake and be off by a factor of 2 or 4, and the answer choices are clearly waiting for that.

This is a great example of the kind of question that causes the most trouble for the most test-takers. It's something the vast, vast majority of test-takers have the skills and knowledge to answer correctly, but it's also something where a simple mistake or two can easily be made, wrecking the question. If you want to improve your SAT Math score, this kind of question is where you should probably focus your energy first. Most people would significantly increase their scores if they just stopped giving away points on questions like this, rather than focusing on questions that seem harder.

Page 415, Question 6

This question asks about perpendicular lines. We need to know that when two lines are perpendicular to one another, their slopes are opposite reciprocals (this was an idea discussed in the toolbox earlier in this book). This idea is crucial to solving this question (at least when it comes to the way most people will solve it), but notice that the idea is a *property* of perpendicular lines, not a *formula*. Remember that challenging math questions on the SAT rely much more heavily on properties and definitions than on formulas.

To solve this question in the most straightforward way, it would probably be best to get the expression for the original line into slope-intercept format (the one that looks like $y = mx + b$). If we do that, we get this:

$x + 3y = 12$

$3y = -x + 12$ (get the *x* on the right-hand side)

$y = -x/3 + 4$ (isolate *y*)

So the slope of the given line is -1/3.

A line perpendicular to this must have a slope that is the opposite reciprocal of -1/3, which is 3. So (C) must be correct, because it gives a coefficient of 3 for *x* in the $y = mx + b$ format, where *m* is the slope.

Note that we have the usual kinds of wrong answers we'd expect on an SAT Math question. The slope of (B) is the opposite of the correct slope, and we can probably imagine how a person might make that mistake. The slope of (D) has the right sign (it's positive) but uses 1/3 instead of 3, and, again, that's an understandable mistake.

Notice, also, that there's no other slope in the answer choices that has both its reciprocal and its opposite in the choices. This is a manifestation of the imitation pattern, and it's a good sign that (C) is, indeed, correct.

A less straightforward way to answer this, but one that wouldn't require knowing that perpendicular slopes are opposite reciprocals, would be to use your calculator. You could graph the original line on your calculator, and then graph each answer choice. This would let you see on your own which choice generated a perpendicular line. Of course, this would be a little time-consuming, and you'd have to make sure you didn't key in the graphs wrong. But it could be a viable way to solve the question if you had forgotten perpendicular lines have slopes that are negative reciprocals of each other.

Finally, note that the *y*-intercepts don't matter here. The question asks about perpendicular lines, and that idea only requires us to consider the slopes, not the intercepts. This question provides yet another example of a situation in which we must consider the answer choices as part of the question, rather than hoping to predict the correct answer choice completely from scratch—in this case, there are an infinite number of valid *y*-intercepts that could be part of a line perpendicular to the given line.

Page 415, Question 7

This question bothers a lot of people—but, as we often see on the SAT Math section, it really just comes down to basic properties and definitions. In this case, we need to know what a triangle is. (In case you've forgotten, it's a closed three-sided figure.)

If we go through each choice and imagine trying to draw it, we'd see that they can all be drawn except for (E)—if you try to draw a triangle with two sides of 5 units and a third side of 10 units, you end up with just a line segment of 10 units, because in order to reach the endpoints of the long 'side,' the two short 'sides' have to open up completely to make a straight line.

We could also think of this in terms of the so-called "triangle inequality," which says that the length of any side of a triangle must be less than the sum of the other two sides. But I deliberately wanted to talk about it without referring to that idea because, as I keep saying, it's very important to learn to attack SAT Math in an informal way.

There's another important element here, too. Notice that the question uses the word "EXCEPT." I can't tell you how many times people have missed questions like this because they overlooked that word, and ended up just choosing the first answer choice that would work under normal circumstances. This is one more example of how important it is to read everything on the SAT very, very carefully. It's also a good example of the importance of checking over the other answer choices before you move on—if you overlook the word "EXCEPT" and choose (A) because it's the first thing you see that works to make a triangle, you can hopefully catch your mistake if you glance through the other choices and notice that (B), (C), and (D) also work.

Page 415, Question 8

There are a ton of things we can learn from this question, especially. Please, *please* read this whole description and pay attention!

First, this question is rated 5 out of 5 for difficulty by the College Board. In other words, this is a question that a ton of people miss. But, as we'll see in a moment, it only involves basic arithmetic. In fact, it involves a specific application of an idea from arithmetic that has possibly never, ever come up in a normal math class before. What it does NOT involve is any kind of formula, or any way that a calculator is likely to be helpful. Remember, this is SAT Math, and it's likely to involve tricks and misdirection more than formulas.

I'd also like to point out, before we even get started, that this is a question in which several of our reliable answer-choice patterns would have allowed us to predict the correct answer without even seeing the question, just from the answer choices alone. I am NOT saying that you should ever try to answer a question just from the answer choices—I'm just saying that the answer choices are hinting very strongly at (C) being the right answer, if we know how to read them. The fact that so many people missed this question shows us that most people aren't paying any attention to the answer choices, which is part of the reason why most people have a really hard time on the SAT Math section.

This question, then, is a positively classic example of the way most test-takers throw points away for no reason on the SAT Math section. People don't miss this question because they don't know basic arithmetic. They miss it because they don't pay attention to details and they don't check over the other answer choices and think about SAT patterns.

In other words, they miss this question because of a lack of SAT-specific skills. Don't be like them.

Okay, enough preamble. Now let's actually answer the question.

The question asks what percent of the votes were cast for Candidate 1 given that Candidate 1 received 28,000 more votes. Most people will try to solve this by figuring out that 28,000 is 1% of 2.8 million. So far, so good. Then they'll assume that this must mean Candidate 1 got 51% of the vote. They'll choose (D), and they'll move on to the next question without giving this a second thought.

And they'll be wrong.

Here's the mistake: if Candidate 1 pulls 51% of the vote, than Candidate 2 must pull 49%, and *51% is 2 percentage points more than 49%, not 1 percentage point more*. So in order for Candidate 1 to have a 1 percentage-point margin over Candidate 2, the correct split isn't $51 - 49$.

It's 50.5 to 49.5.

That's why (C) is correct.

Notice that there are 3 answer choices that end in a 5, and only 2 that end in a 1. This goes along with the imitation pattern, and it strongly suggests that the correct answer should end in a 5. Also, notice that 3 out of the 5 choices involve decimals, which also suggests that 51% isn't correct. We could even say that 50.5% is the middle entry in a series of sorts, where the other numbers are 50.05 and 55—it's not a traditional series in the mathematical sense, but there's a clear progression with reference to the decimal places, and (C), the right answer, is in the middle of that progression.

This is yet another great example, then, of the tremendous importance of thinking about the answer choices as part of the question. They're not just there to take up space—the College Board uses them deliberately, in ways that we can exploit.

Page 416, Question 9

Sometimes people make this question a lot harder than it needs to be, by coming up with a decimal approximation for √18 or by converting it to 3√2. But it's much easier just to start by squaring both sides, so we get 2p = 18. That means p = 9.

Remember that SAT Math gets a lot easier if we look for ways to keep it simple.

Page 416, Question 10

This question, like many SAT Math questions, is really just a matter of knowing definitions and doing basic arithmetic.

When we round the given number to the nearest whole number, we get 2. When we round it to the nearest tenth, we get 1.8. Since 2 – 1.8 is 0.2, the answer is just 0.2.

Notice that this question is pretty impossible to answer if we don't understand the concept of rounding, or if we don't know which decimal place represents tenths. Also notice that the math is incredibly basic, but people will still miss this question because of its strange presentation.

Page 417, Question 11

As is often the case, there are many ways to answer this question. We could do it with pure algebra, letting x be the number of towels and writing 6 = 2x/5. But that would be a little more formal than I like to be on the SAT Math section.

So let's just think through it instead. If 6 towels represents 2/5 of all the towels, than 3 towels must represent 1/5 (because 3 is half of 6 and 1/5 is half of 2/5). So if 3 towels are 1/5 of the towels, then there must be 15 towels, because 3*5 is 15. So the answer is 15.

Just to be clear, there's nothing inherently wrong with doing it algebraically, as long as you feel comfortable with that and you set it up correctly and don't make any mistakes. I'm just more comfortable with mental math, and I find that it tends to work a lot better on the SAT, so I encourage it in my students as much as possible.

Page 417, Question 12

This question is very difficult for a lot of test-takers. But if we just remember to read carefully and pay attention to details, we can figure this out.

The question describes 5 points on a line, like this: A B C D E.

We know that AD is 4.5, and BE is 3.5. Why not try to plot that out?

When we do try to plot it, we realize that we don't have enough information yet. If AD is 4.5 and BE is 3.5, there's an infinite number of ways we could draw that. For instance, it might look like this:

```
_____
A      BD    E
```

Or it might look like this:

```
_____
A   B    DE
```

Or anything in between.

At first, this uncertainty might seem troubling, but we have to remember that this is an SAT Math question, and that SAT Math questions often deal in uncertainty. So there's no need to panic—we just need to figure out how it can be possible that the test is allowing there to be multiple arrangements here.

One clue is the phrasing of the question: it asks for "one possible value" of the BC length. As trained test-takers, we know that the College Board only uses that phrase in a question when there are multiple possible values involved. So it's clearly okay for us not to be sure exactly where A, B, D, and E are relative to one another in every case. We only need to work out one single possible arrangement. So let's pick the one where D and E are very close together, like this:

_____

A   B   DE

Now the question tells us that CD is 2 units. So if we put C in between B and D, and 2 units away from D, we get something like this:

_____

A   BC   DE

In other words, if we put D and E basically right next to each other, and B is 3.5 units away from E, then let's say it's 3.49 units from D. If C is 2 units from D, then B is 1.49 units from C, because $3.49 - 2 = 1.49$.

Now, there are other possible answers here, so your work doesn't have to look exactly like mine. What's most important, I think, is not to get too thrown off by the fact that more than one outcome can be correct. For a question like this, we don't have to figure out the entire range of possible solutions, as we might do in a math class in school. We just have to find one possible value and realize that there are other possible values out there.

Note that this question is fairly challenging for a lot of test-takers even though it only involves the most basic arithmetic (addition and subtraction) and the most basic geometry concepts (points on a line). This is the kind of thing you have to look out for on the SAT: simple concepts presented in strange ways.

Page 417, Question 13

This is yet another question that can't really be set up with a typical algebraic formula. So let's just think about it.

If the ratio of rainy days to sunny days is 3 to 2, then we can think about the days in terms of "blocks" of 5 days, because every 3 days of rain requires 2 days of sun, and $3 + 2 = 5$.

So if we're dealing with blocks of 5 days, and we have a 30-day month, then there can be 6 blocks of days in that month, because $6*5 = 30$.

That means that there will be 6*3 rainy days, and 6*2 sunny days. So there will be 18 rainy days and 12 sunny days. (Just to be sure we haven't made a mistake, at this point I'd probably quickly add 18 and 12 in my head to confirm that it's 30, just like it needs to be.)

Now we have to be very careful at this point. The question is asking how many more rainy days there were than sunny days—the question is NOT asking how many rainy days there were, nor how many sunny days there were. It's asking for the difference between those two numbers.

I'm sure a lot of people either answer 18 or 12 to this question, because they forget what it was asking, but the real answer is 6.

This is yet another example, then, of the critical role that reading comprehension and attention to detail will play in your SAT preparation.

Page 417, Question 14

Again, we have to be sure to read carefully. And we should probably try to avoid using traditional, formal series notation on this question. As is usually the case, this question will probably be a lot easier if we just think about it and figure it out using basic reasoning.

The gap between the 3rd term and the 6th term is exactly 3 terms (because $6 - 3 = 3$). In terms of units, the same gap is 60 units, because $77 - 17 = 60$.

So a difference of 3 terms corresponds to a difference of 60 units. That means each term is a difference of 20 units, because $60/3 = 20$. (The fact that the actual arithmetic has been pretty easy so far is a good sign that we're approaching the question correctly.)

We can confirm that each term is 10 more than the one before it by filling in the gaps in the original sequence: 17, 37, 57, 77.

So if each term is 20 units and the 6th term is 77, then we know the 7th term is 97 and the 8th term is 117.

Remember: read carefully, and don't be afraid to think about basic math concepts in new ways. There's a reason the College Board made the numbers fairly easy to work with here: they didn't want you to have to use a formula. They wanted to give you the chance just to sit back for a second and think about the question, and count stuff out if you needed to. They could have asked for the thousandth term, or they could have made the difference between terms equal 13.4 instead of 20, or who knows what, but they didn't. Instead, they made the arithmetic part fairly easy once we figured out what was going on.

Page 418, Question 15

In this question, the phrase "least value" indicates that there are at least two values that x might have. We need to keep that in mind as we work through the question.

We could choose to do this in a formal algebraic way. That would look like this:

$|x - 3| = 1/2$

$x - 3 = 1/2$ OR $x - 3 = -1/2$ (create the two absolute value possibilities)

$x = (1/2) + 3$ OR $x = (-1/2) + 3$ (isolate x)

$x = 3.5$ OR $x = 2.5$ (simplify the right-hand side)

Then we'd know that 2.5 is the correct answer, because it's the lower of the two possible values.

Instead of the algebra, we could also just look at the expression in the question and realize that it's basically just telling us that x is 1/2 a unit away from 3 on a number line. The two numbers that are 1/2 unit away from 3 are 2.5 and 3.5, and the smaller one of those is 2.5, so that's the answer.

(If that second approach didn't make any sense, don't worry about it. It was just another way to go, that's all. The algebra works fine too, of course.)

Page 418, Question 16

This is a question that many test-takers don't even understand when they first read it, because it sounds quite odd—usually we don't describe a "four-digit integer" with a string of capital letters like *WXYZ*. But in these cases we should always trust that the College Board will explain what it means—it has to, or else the question can't be asked. So let's keep reading.

The question says that each capital letter represents a digit in the number, and then it tells us some things about the relationships of the values of those digits. Our job is to figure out what the values are.

Many people will try to approach this question like a system of equations. I suppose that might be possible with a lot of effort, but it won't come easily to anyone.

Another popular (but largely unsuccessful) approach is to try picking numbers for each digit and play around with it until you hit on a working arrangement.

Let's try something else, though. Let's just look at what's going on and try to think about what it says. And, above all, let's remember not to panic just because this is a weird question. By now we know that the SAT likes to try to scare us by asking questions that look weird. No big deal.

One thing that I'd notice is that X is clearly the biggest number, because it's the sum of all the other numbers. Okay, that might come in handy.

What's a little less obvious, but still clear, is that Z is the smallest number. We know this because rule 2 tells us that Y is 1 less than W, but rule 3 tells us Z is 5 less than W.

So, since Z has to be the lowest digit out of these 4 digits, why not see what happens if we make it equal zero, which is the smallest digit possible? If we try setting Z equal to zero and it works, great! If it doesn't work, we'll probably figure out some more information about the question as we try to use 0 for Z. So let's give it a shot and see what happens.

If Z is 0, then rule 3 tells us that W is 5.

If W is 5, then rule 2 tells us Y is 4.

Plugging all of that into rule 1, we would get that X equals 5 + 4 + 0, or 9. That makes sense, since we said before that X must be the biggest digit.

So the answer will be that WXYZ corresponds to 5940.

You might wonder how I knew to start with the idea of Z being 0. But I didn't know beforehand that 0 would work; it was just an informed hunch. If I had started with Z as 2, I would have seen my mistake, adjusted, and tried again. And I didn't even have to start with a value for Z. I might have started with W being 8 or something. In any case, the important thing isn't to try to nail the question on the first guess; the important thing is to be willing to play around with the results until you get something to work.

And let me make something else extremely clear about this question: the lesson to be learned here is not how to approach future SAT Math questions about mysterious 4-digit numbers whose digits have particular relationships to one another. The chance of you ever seeing a question like this on the test again is basically zero. The much more important thing to try to pick up on is the general thought process—the way we read carefully, think about what the words mean, avoid using formal solutions whenever possible, and just kind of experiment with the question until we find an answer. That underlying skill set is critical on the SAT.

Page 418, Question 17

This question, like so many others, manages to be challenging even though it only involves a simple idea—in this case, the idea of equilateral triangles. As will often be the case on the SAT, there is no way to apply a formula or use a calculator. Instead, we just have to think about it.

One thing that we should note right away is that the diagram is not drawn to scale. We'll want to focus on the part that doesn't seem to be to scale and see if we can figure out what's going on there.

Another important feature of this question is that it gives us information about the dimensions of the diagram in the text, but that information isn't labeled on the diagram itself. This means that the information about those dimensions will be the key to solving the problem.

So let's see what happens when we put all of that together. If CD is 10, and DE is also 10, and EF is also 10, then we know that each of the overlapping triangles has side lengths of 20. In other words, before they were overlapping, the two triangles were both 20 units on every side. And if DE is 10 units, then all the sides of the small triangle are also 10 units, because the two big triangles are equilateral. So a more accurate representation of the situation would be something like this:

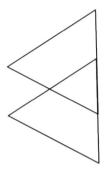

With that in mind, let's just work our way around the figure, starting with C and going clockwise.

CD is 10 units.

DE is 10 units.

EF is 10 units.

FA is 20 units.

From A to the indented corner on the left is 10 units. (Remember, the diagram in the original question isn't drawn to scale.)

From the indented corner on the left to B is 10 units.

BC is 20 units.

So if we add that all up, we get 10 + 10 + 10 + 20 + 10 + 10 + 20 = 90 units.

So the answer is 90.

Notice, once more, that none of the arithmetic in this question was difficult. The difficulty came from figuring out what was being asked, and we did that by reading carefully and knowing to pay attention to the way the College Board draws diagrams.

Page 418, Question 18
The diagram in this question is drawn to scale, so we want to take note of that. Unfortunately, it doesn't have any kind of scale labeled on it, but we may be able to work around that if it turns out we need to.

The question is also talking about 3 different variables: x, k, and a. This will give a lot of people trouble, because most test-takers who treat SAT Math like school math will think they need to figure out the values of those variables.

But if we look carefully, we see that there's not enough information to figure out k. Instead of worrying about that, we just realize that k must not matter in the question. Easy enough.

Let's focus on the end of the question. It asks for the value of a, but all we know about a from the rest of the question is that it's positive and that $g(a - 1.2) = 0$.

A lot of people will want to plug $a - 1.2$ in for x in the original function equation, because that's the typical knee-jerk reaction that would be appropriate in a school situation. But if we consider that move for a moment, I think we'll see that it's not likely to help us very much. We'd end up with this expression, which would be very ugly:

$$g(x) = k((a - 1.2) + 3)((a - 1.2) - 3)$$

This doesn't really look promising, from an SAT Math standpoint. (Now, it's true that the last question on the grid-ins is often more complicated than other SAT Math questions, but I'd still be reluctant to go about expanding and condensing that hideous expression unless absolutely necessary.)

So let's try a different tack.

One thing that's kind of interesting is the fact that we were told the value of $g(a - 1.2)$ is *zero*. Zero is a unique number with unique properties, particularly when it comes to functions and graphs. On a graph, the zeros of a function are the points where the function crosses the x-axis; in a function equation, we find the roots of an expression by setting the factors of the expression equal to zero.

So let's think about that for a second. In the equation, the ways to make $g(x)$ come out to zero are to set either $(x + 3)$ or $(x - 3)$ to zero. (k can't be zero, if it were, every single $g(x)$ value would also be zero, and that isn't what the graph shows.)

So if either $(x + 3)$ or $(x - 3)$ is zero, that means the $g(x)$ value would be zero when x is either -3 or 3. And that fits with the graph, because the places where the function equals zero seem to be at $x = -3$ and $x = 3$. So we know that $g(-3) = 0$, and $g(3) = 0$. And that should be kind of our eureka moment: if $g(-3)$ and $g(3)$ are both zero, and $g(a - 1.2)$ is zero as well, than that must mean that $(a - 1.2)$ is the same thing as either (-3) or (3)!

That means that a is either 4.2, or -1.8. But the question tells us a must be positive, so that means it's 4.2.

Once again, the College Board has created a misleading question out of very basic ideas. In this question, we needed to know that the x-intercepts of a graph are the places where its y-value is zero; we needed to know that 4.2 is bigger than zero but -1.8 is not; we needed to know that $4.2 - 1.2$ is 3. That's about it, from a math standpoint, and none of those ideas is very complicated on its own. I would bet that over 90% of the people who took this test knew every single one of those facts, but they missed the question because they didn't realize it was asking about those facts in the first place.

So the challenge came from the sheer weirdness of the question, and we had to use our reading skills to understand what was being asked, and our thinking skills to realize that the idea of the zeroes of the function was very important.

Conclusion

By now, you're probably beginning to develop a strong appreciation for the strange way the College Board designs SAT Math questions. In the next section, we'll continue to develop your understanding by exploring a large selection of questions from the Blue Book that most people have some trouble with.

Video Demonstrations

If you'd like to see videos of some sample solutions like the ones in this book, please visit http://www.SATprepVideos.com. A selection of free videos is available for readers of this book.

A Selection of Challenging Questions

At this point we've taken a look at a variety of Math questions, but you're probably interested in seeing more. I understand where you're coming from with that, and I'm about to show you some more Math solutions, but . . . before I do, I want to make sure I reiterate what you should be learning from each solution.

I am NOT doing these solutions in an effort to show you something formal that you should memorize and then expect to repeat on future SAT Math questions, as we would normally do for a math class in school. Remember that the SAT Math section will show you very strange combinations of very basic ideas, and specific questions and questions 'types' are not repeated for the most part. The odds are that when you take the SAT for real, you'll see a whole test full of math questions that don't look like any other SAT Math questions you've ever seen before, at least not on the surface. And this will be the case no matter how many practice SAT Math questions you work on beforehand. Every test combines the same basic stuff in new ways.

You may have noticed I'm repeating this idea a lot. There's a reason for that:

It's very important, and most people ignore it.

So if you want to get better at SAT Math, the goal is to learn the underlying process, and to practice using it against real SAT Math questions written by the College Board. That's why I've included these solutions: to give you an idea of the right general approach so you can continue to refine your instincts, not to give you cookie-cutter instructions for specific question types, because specific question types basically don't exist on the SAT Math section, practically speaking.

With that important reminder out of the way, let's take a look at some of the SAT Math questions that students have typically asked about.

As with other question explanations in this book, you'll need a copy of the second edition of the College Board's *Official SAT Study Guide* (otherwise known as the Blue Book) to follow along. Let's get started.

Page 399, Question 11

As with many SAT Math questions, there are basically two ways to do this: we can pick a concrete number that satisfies the requirements for k and then look to see what happens to $k + 2$, or we can think in the abstract about properties relating to the concept of remainders. In general, abstract solutions will be faster to reach but harder for many students to execute, while concrete solutions will give most students added confidence but end up taking more time. For this particular question, though, the amount of time spent on each solution is likely to be roughly the same.

If we go the concrete route of picking a number to be k, we have to make sure that it satisfies the setup. In this case, a number like 13 would work, because 13 divided by 7 gives a remainder of 6. So then we'd look to see what happens when we divide 15 by 7, since 15 is 2 more than 13; the result is a remainder of 1.

The other way to do this is to think in the abstract: if k has a remainder of 6 when it's divided by 7, then k is 6 more than some multiple of 7, and $k + 2$ will be 8 more than that multiple of 7. We know that 8 is more than 7, so one more 7 will "fit in" when $k + 2$ is divided by 7, and we'll be left with a remainder of 8 - 7, or 1.

Either way, (B) is the right answer.

Of course, you wouldn't need to do both solutions on test day. I'm just doing both of them to show that there are a variety of ways to attack this question successfully, as will be the case for most SAT Math questions.

Page 400, Question 17

This is one of those questions that lets us work on identifying a whole variety of the patterns and rules we talk about in this book.

First, we'd want to notice that the diagram is drawn to scale. That means that we might be able to figure out the answer by eyeballing the diagram—or, at the very least, we want to make sure that our final answer makes sense in the context of the scale of the diagram.

Also notice that the diagram and the answer choices have a lot of expressions with √2 in them. We know that √2 relates to 45°-45°-90° triangles, which seems relevant to the question since ABC, ADB, and BDC are all 45°-45°-90° triangles.

There are a variety of ways we could try to figure out the area of the shaded region. The most straightforward way is probably to work out the distance of EF, along with the distance from F to the base of the figure, and then multiply those two things together, since they would represent the length and the height of the rectangle. We might do that by realizing that BE and BF are each 5√2 units long, and that they are each the legs of a 45°-45°-90° triangle with EF as its hypotenuse. Since the ratio of the sides of a 45°-45°-90° triangle is 1:1:√2, the distance of EF is 5√2(√2), which is 10.

Since the shaded region is divided into two squares, we know that the distance from E or F to the base of the figure must be 5. So the shaded area is 50, because we multiply 10 (the length) by 5 (the height) to find the area. So (C) is correct.

There are other ways to get this answer, as well. We could also realize that AC must be 10√2(√2), or 20 (again because of the 1:1:√2 ratio for sides of a 45°-45°-90° triangle). Then we could realize that the height of triangle ABC must be 10 (because BD is one of the legs for which BC is a hypotenuse, and this is another 45°-45°-90° triangle for which the 1:1:√2 ratio applies). That means the area of the entire triangle ABC must be 100 units. The shaded region represents 1/2 of the area of ABC (we know this either by eyeballing the scaled diagram, or by realizing that the four unshaded small triangles are the same total area as the shaded rectangle).

Now let's turn to the answer choices. An awareness of the patterns that frequently appear in answer choices on the SAT Math section would help us to realize that 50 looks like a very likely option to be the correct answer. It fits the halves-and-doubles pattern and it's also the middle number in a series (the series is 25, 50, 100). It also doesn't have √2 in it, which is probably good because 3 out of the 5 choices don't have √2.

Page 423, Question 11

Like most SAT Math questions, this one rewards us for reading very carefully and thinking about the definitions and properties of basic terms.

We're told that 2 of the faces are black and the rest are white; this means there must be 4 white faces, since the total number of faces on any cube is 6.

If the total area of the white faces of the cube is 64 square inches, and if there are 4 white faces, then the total area per face is 64/4, or 16.

That means each face is 16 square inches. And since the dimensions of a cube are all identical, that means each face is a 4 x 4 square, which means the cube is 4 inches in each dimension.

The volume of the cube, then, is 4 x 4 x 4, or 64. So the correct answer is (A).

Notice that some of the answer choices differ from the correct answer by a factor of 2 or 4. This is a strong, strong reason to go back over your work and check it for small mistakes. If we misread the setup, or if we accidentally mis-multiplied or mis-divided, we can easily be off from the right answer in a way that will be accounted for in the answer choices. Also notice that (B) is 5 x 5 x 5, and (D) is 6 x 6 x 6. This reinforces our belief that we should find the correct answer by cubing something, but it also means we have to make sure we were right to cube 4 instead of 5 or 6.

Page 424, Question 14

As will often be the case on the SAT, there are multiple valid approaches to this question. If we wanted to use a simple permutation solution, we could realize that there are 5 options for one color, and 4 options for the other color (there are only 4 options for the second color because we're not allowed to repeat the selected color—otherwise there would be 5 options for both). 5 x 4 = 20, so there would be 20 possible arrangements.

But the SAT doesn't make us do things like this in the formal way—the SAT doesn't care how we get the answer, as long as it's right. So, if we want, we can just list out the different possible arrangements and then count them up. (To be clear, this list-and-count approach will take a good bit longer than we would normally like to spend on a question, but it can be a very concrete way to arrive at the answer if you don't feel comfortable with permutations. Remember, too, that the reason we try to go through most questions as quickly and efficiently as possible is so that we can have more time if we need it on questions like this.)

So if we call the colors a, b, c, d, and e, and then list things out, here are the different arrangements:

zone 1 / zone 2
a/b
a/c
a/d
a/e
b/a
b/c
b/d
b/e
c/a
c/b
c/d
c/e
d/a
d/b
d/c
d/e
e/a
e/b
e/c
e/d

That means there are 20 different arrangements, so (B) is correct.

Page 457, Question 20

Most people try to approach this using some variation on the slope formula (which is $(y_2 - y_1)/(x_2 - x_1)$, not that I recommend it here).

But we have to remember that this is the SAT, and the College Board often likes to leave short cuts hidden in the questions for people who think to look for them.

Instead of going through the hassle of working out the slope of the original line, the slope of the perpendicular line, and the missing y-value that would make the whole thing work out correctly, let's take a second and actually notice the answer choices for a minute.

Remember that we always want to check out the answer choices before we commit to a course of action. They'll help us understand a lot of stuff in a lot of questions if we just pay attention to them a little.

In this case, I'm noticing that the answer choices are kind of falling into 3 different groups, in a sense. We have negative numbers, then we have 2 and 3, and then we have 5. Hmmmm.

Let's try actually plotting line *l* and see what it looks like. Here's a rough approximation of the situation described in the question:

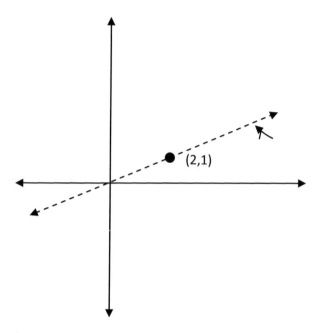

If we plot the points (0,0) and (2,1), and then think about the options offered by each of the answer choices, we might start to notice something. (A) and (B) clearly don't work if you're trying to draw line that would go through either value and (2,1), and be perpendicular to the existing line:

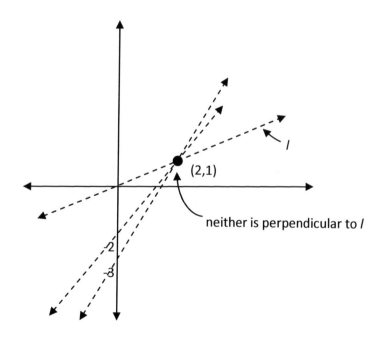

The values for (C) and (D) don't work, either:

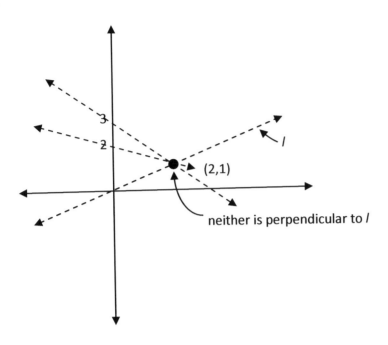

neither is perpendicular to *l*

Only (E) is in anywhere near the proper place to create a line that passes through (2,1) and is perpendicular to the original line *l*. So (E) must be right:

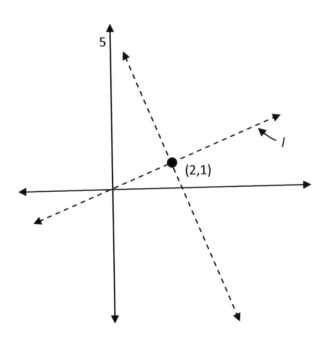

(I realize that none of the diagrams I supplied is exactly to scale, but the diagrams you would draw for yourself in your test booklet would also be out-of-scale. During the test, the point isn't to create a perfectly scaled drawing, but to get a solid idea of where the different elements of the question would be relative to one another.)

So, as we've just seen, it's possible to solve this question, which is the last one in the section and which was missed by a lot of people, without ever using any kind of formula or consulting a calculator or even adding two single-digit numbers. All we had to do was remember to notice the answer choices, plot a few points (or even just think about plotting some of them), and then realize that only one answer choice was close to working.

Notice that the College Board could have made this question much harder by including wrong answers that were closer to the right answer, or by changing the overall scale of the question. But they didn't. They left a shortcut for alert test-takers to seize. Remember that, and look for these kinds of things on other questions.

Page 464, Question 6

People mess this question up all the time, but it's really just a pretty straightforward application of the concept of slope. We know that for two reasons: the first one is that the diagram shows a diagonal line with its horizontal and vertical changes marked off, and the second reason (perhaps a bit more obvious) is that the question includes the word "slope."

Remember that slope, by definition, is the ratio of the vertical change to horizontal change. That means that, in this case, for every 7 units of vertical change there are 16 units of horizontal change. If we only have 3.5 units of vertical change, then we need 8 units of horizontal change to maintain the ratio, because 3.5 is half of 7 and 8 is half of 16. So the correct answer is (A).

Notice that one of the wrong answers is 32, which is what we get if we accidentally double 16 instead of cutting it in half.

Page 468, Question 15

I often talk about how the College Board likes to mislead you by making questions seem to be something they're not. This question might be one of the all-time best examples of that technique. It starts out looking like a classic probability question, one of those situations where somebody has a certain number of things in a bag and you have to calculate the chance that they'll pull a certain kind of thing out of the bag at random.

But that's not what it is at all. Instead, it's much simpler than that, but it's unlike anything that any test-taker has probably ever seen before.

This is one more example of why you can't take anything for granted on the SAT. Everything needs to be read carefully.

Ari starts out with 3 red things and 4 green things. If he takes 13 more pieces and we need to end up with more reds than greens, we might imagine that the 13 is made up of 7 reds and 6 greens, just as a place to start; if that's the case, then there would be 10 red and 10 green, which doesn't satisfy the requirements of the question. So in order to end up with more reds than greens, Ari would need to pull out at least 8 reds, so the answer is 8.

Again, there's absolutely no formula for this, and it has nothing to do with probability. It's just reading and thinking. Most SAT Math questions are just reading and thinking.

Page 468, Question 16

A lot of people who see this question immediately start worrying about the word "tri-factorable," as though it were a real math term instead of something that the College Board made up specifically for this question.

There are two ways that we can figure out that the word "tri-factorable" was just made up for this question. The first way is that the question tells us what the word means: a tri-factorable number is one that is the product of 3 consecutive numbers. (If this were a real math term, the College Board wouldn't bother to define it. For slope questions, they don't say, "What is the slope of this line, if slope is defined as blahblahblah," because you're supposed to know what slope is, because slope is a real math concept.)

The second way that we can know this is a made-up word is to be familiar with what the SAT is allowed to ask us about when it comes to math. The SAT can only ask about the concepts in the toolbox in this book, and the toolbox doesn't cover tri-factorability.

So it must just be that we're supposed to figure out what the word means from reading the question. If we know what the words "product" and "consecutive" mean, then we know what a tri-factorable number is. Remember, as always, that the most important skill on the SAT is reading carefully.

Now, let's proceed.

We know that all of these questions can be answered in less than 30 seconds, and we know that it would clearly take a lot longer than 30 seconds to attempt to tri-factor each of the first 1,000 integers.

So there must be another way to go.

It's important to remember that we can always just list out the answers to these kinds of questions that ask how many numbers in a certain set satisfy a certain condition. Either we'll start listing them and realize there's only a small number of them, or we'll start listing them and realize there's a certain pattern they all follow, and then we can predict the final number from the pattern.

So how can we figure out a tri-factorable number? Since they're made by multiplying consecutive integers, I'd start with the smallest positive integer and see what happens:

1 * 2 * 3 = 6

So if we start with 1 as the first positive integer, we arrive at the product 6, which must be the first tri-factorable number.

The next tri-factorable number will start with 2:

2 * 3 * 4 = 24

From there we can basically get on a roll:

3 * 4 * 5 = 60

4 * 5 * 6 = 120

5 * 6 * 7 = 210

6 * 7 * 8 = 336

7 * 8 * 9 = 504

8 * 9 * 10 = 720

9 * 10 * 11 = 990

10 * 11 * 12 = 1320

Oops—notice that that last number is bigger than 1000! So there are 9 numbers that work: the one I get when I multiply three consecutive numbers starting with 1, the one I get when starting with 2, starting with 3, with 4, with 5, 6, 7, 8, and finally 9, and that's it.

Notice that this question, like so many other 'challenging' SAT Math questions, involves nothing more than careful reading, basic arithmetic, and a willingness to play around with familiar concepts in strange ways. This is typical for the SAT, as we've seen many times by now and will see again.

Notice also that there are many ways to mess this question up. We might miscount, or accidentally overlook one or more of the tri-factorable numbers. Any one of those tiny mistakes will cause us to miss the question completely.

Page 468, Question 17

This is another one of those questions that we could try to answer in a few different ways. Many people will attempt an algebraic solution, or you could also try guessing and checking. There's also another approach we'll talk about after I go over the algebraic one.

For call A, the cost will be $1 + $0.07($t$-20).

For call B, the cost will be $0.06($t$).

So just set them equal and solve:

$1 + $0.07($t$-20) = $0.06($t$)	(initial setup)
$1 + .07t - 1.4 = .06t$	(distribute $0.07 on the left)
$1 - 1.4 = -.01t$	(combine like terms)
$.4 = .01t$	(simplify the expression on the left)
$40 = t$	(isolate t)

The faster approach is a little more holistic, and would probably not be tried by most test-takers, even trained ones. Still, I thought we should talk about it. To work this problem out without really writing out any algebra, we could realize that the $1 for the first 20 minutes works out to 5 cents per minute, which is one cent per minute less than the other rate. After those 20 minutes are up, the rate goes to 7 cents per minute, which is one cent per minute more than the other rate. So to get everything to equal out, you'll need 20 more minutes of talking at the higher rate after the initial 20 minutes of talking at the lower rate. 20 + 20 is 40, so 40 is the answer.

Just to be clear, both approaches are equally valid, of course. I just wanted to introduce the second one as an exercise of sorts, to keep calling your attention to the fact that the College Board usually sets up SAT Math questions so that they can be attacked quickly and easily if we know how to look at them.

Page 468, Question 18

This question is rated 5 out of 5 for difficulty, but, of course, we know that that doesn't mean much. All it means is that a lot of untrained people missed it. As we'll see in this explanation, this is yet another SAT Math question that requires nothing more than careful reading and careful thinking.

We're told the perimeter is p, and we know that each square has a side of k. The perimeter consists of 16 sides, so the perimeter's length is $16k$.

The area of each square must be k^2, and there are 10 squares. So the area is $10k^2$.

Since the question says that p and a are equal, we know that

$16k = 10k^2$

Solving, we get

$16 = 10k$	(divide through by k)
$1.6 = k$	(isolate k)

And that's all. Notice that this question only required us to know the definitions of the word "perimeter" and "area," and basic algebra. There was no formula involved, apart from the formula for the area of a square, which the test provides for us at the beginning of the section. There was also no real need for a calculator, since the question only involves dividing by 10, which we can accomplish by moving the decimal point.

Again, these attributes are pretty typical of the 'hardest' SAT Math questions.

Page 483, Question 8

This question stumps a lot of people. In my experience, almost everybody who misses it does so because they don't read it carefully, or they don't notice the answer choices.

If the probability of choosing red is 3 times that of choosing blue, that means that there are 3 times as many red beads as there are blue beads. Since there are 12 red beads, then, there must be 4 blue beads. Further, the number of glass beads altogether is 4 times the number of wooden ones, so if there are 16 total glass beads (12 red and 4 blue), then there are 4 wooden ones. Adding that all up, we get that there are 20 beads.

That's the more mathematical way to approach this.

But an easier way to think about this might be to realize that there are more red beads than anything else, and there are only 12 of those, so 45 is already way too big of a number, and anything bigger than 45 is obviously also way too big. That means the only answer choice that can possibly work is (A).

Remember to pay attention to details and answer choices!

Page 485, Question 12

This is another SAT Math question that a lot of people struggle with, even though it only involves one of the simplest ideas in all of geometry: the idea that there is an infinite number of points in a circle (or in any geometric figure).

I think the easiest way to approach this is to say that every single point on the circumference of the circle could be a point that served as the corner of a rectangle like the rectangles in the original diagram. So there is an infinite number of rectangles with perimeter 12 that can be inscribed in the circle. Since infinity is bigger than 4, we know that the answer is (E).

Page 486, Question 15

For this question, once more, I would just read the question carefully and think about what it's describing.

20% of Tom's money was his spend on the hotel. He spent $240 overall, so he spent $240 * 0.2 = $48 on the hotel.

If he only paid for 1/4 of the hotel, then the hotel cost $48 * 4, or $192.

The fact that the last three answer choices all differ from one another by $48 should alert us to the fact that we need to be really careful here, because there are ways to misread or miscalculate and end up on either wrong answer. The far most common mistake is to misread the thing about sharing with 3 *other* people, and treat it like it just says the room was split among 3 people.

This is one more situation in which paying attention to the relationships among the answer choices can alert us to mistakes that the College Board wants us to make, and can reassure us that (D) is the correct answer.

Page 486, Question 16

Like many other SAT Math questions, this is one that manages to be fairly challenging even though it only involves basic arithmetic. It's also a question that will require very careful reading, and a question for which there is no ready-made formula. In other words, it's a typical SAT Math question.

So let's just think about what the question is describing, and how we might figure out what it's asking us.

One approach would be to try to make a square board that would have a number of border tiles somewhat near each answer choice, and see if only one answer choice can be made to work like that. This will be a little tedious, and probably extremely time-consuming, but it will work if we do it right:

(A) doesn't work--if there are 10 on the boundary, it couldn't be 3 x 3 or 4 x 4.

(B) doesn't work either. 7 x 7 would give you 24.

(C) doesn't work because 9 x 9 would give you 32.

(D) doesn't work because 11 x 11 would give you 40.

(E) works because if the board is 14 x 14 there are 52 tiles on the border.

Another approach, possibly slightly faster, is to try drawing out a few small game boards to see if we can figure out some kind of pattern that would help us eliminate all the wrong answer choices.

If, for instance, $n = 2$, then the square would look like this:

In this case, the number of things on the boundary would be 4.
If n is 3, then the board looks like this:

In that case, the k number is 8.

And so on. Now we need to try and understand what's going on here. Basically, k must always end up being a multiple of 4. So we need an answer choice that's a multiple of 4. Only (E) is.

There are other valid approaches here as well, but I think those two will be the ones that most people find.

This question presents me with another opportunity to remind you of what's important to take away from these discussions. The goal of going over this solution is not to teach you a formal way to approach questions that ask about the border tiles on square game boards, because there will never be another SAT Math question that asks about the border tiles on square game boards.

Instead, the goal of going over this question is to deepen your understanding of the principles of SAT Math in general. There's no way to predict exactly what kinds of things you'll see on test day, but if we come to understand the importance of reading carefully, thinking about the answer choices as part of the question, and so on, then you'll be able to take apart whatever weird combinations of basic facts the SAT presents you with. So it's not about memorizing rigid steps for certain types of questions. It's about developing a general feel, and confidence that you can work out whatever they throw at you by relying on the test's design principles.

Page 518, Question 17

Just about everyone panics for a second when they run into this question, because it seems to be asking us to figure out the area of a shape we've never seen before. This is one of those moments when knowing the unwritten rules of the test really comes in handy. Remember that the College Board can only ask you to find the areas of rectangles, triangles, and circles, and it gives you the formulas for those areas at the beginning of each SAT Math section.

So if a question looks like it's asking for the area of something else without giving you another area formula to use, then that something else can always be expressed in terms of rectangles, triangles, and circles. Always.

In this case, it's probably pretty clear that we can't use triangles and rectangles, because there are no corners in this figure. So we'll have to figure out the area of these figures as though they were circles.

But how can we do that?

I think the easiest way is to imagine reversing the bottom half of the big circle from left to right, so that the bottom half of the circle becomes just a reflection of the top half, and we're left with 3 circles, all tangent to each other on their left-most points. It would look something like this:

So now we have to find the areas of those circles, and add and subtract them appropriately. If AD is 6, then each of those dots is 1 unit from the dot before it or after it. That means the radius of the smallest circle is 1, so its area is pi. The radius of the biggest circle is 3 units, so its area is 9pi. The radius of the medium circle, the unshaded one, is 2 units, so its area is 4pi.

So we want the amount equal to the area of the biggest circle minus the area of the medium circle plus the area of the smallest. So it's 9pi – 4pi + 1pi, or 6pi. Which means (C) is correct.

This is just one more example of a question that seems a lot more exotic than it is. If you remember the rules the College Board has to play by, then you'll find a lot of things much easier than most people will. An untrained test-taker will throw up his hands in frustration over this question, but a trained test-taker knows how to turn it into a simple question about circles, and then solve it using the basic formula provided in the beginning of each SAT Math section.

Page 519, Question 18

For this question, I would just draw 6 points out so that no 3 are on a line together, and then try connecting them: basically, each of the 6 points connects to the other 5. We can count the lines up after drawing them out, or we can try doing a little multiplication.

If we multiply, it might seem like there should be 30 lines, since 6 * 5 = 30, but we have to remember that each line touches two of the points. So there aren't actually 30 lines, because each line counts as a connection for both of the points. In other words, if we call the points A, B, C, D, E, and F, then the line from A to B is the same line as the one from B to A.

So we want to divide the 30 apparent connections by 2 in order to compensate for the fact that each line serves as one connection between 2 points, so we don't double-count the lines. That gives us 15 for our final answer, so (A) is correct.

Note the patterns in the answer choices: 15 is half of 30, and there's also 36 and 18 (36 would be 6 x 6 instead of 6 x 5, and 18 is half of that). Once more, the answer choices help point us in the right direction and make us aware of potential mistakes that could be easily made.

Page 519, Question 19

This question often blows people away because it seems much more complicated than it actually is—which, as we've said many times, is typical for SAT Math questions in general. As usual, we'll approach this by reading carefully and thinking carefully.

First, it's important to realize that the question tells us that a and b are equal, so $f(a)$ and $f(b)$ must also be equal.

We also want to remember that questions with roman numerals for answer choices are often based on abstract properties.

Finally, we want to remember that we don't need to know what the actual function is. All we need to know is that it has the property that $f(x + y) = f(x) + f(y)$.

So now let's try to reframe each Roman numeral in terms of that property, and see if we can do it:

For I, $2f(a) = f(a) + f(a) = f(a + a) = f(a + b)$. We can substitute b for a at the end to arrive at $f(a + b)$.

For II, $f(a) * f(a)$ has nothing to do with what the question told us about; the question only told us about an additive property of the functions, not a multiplicative one. So we can't substitute or manipulate anything further here.

For III, $f(2a) = f(a + a) = f(a) + f(a) = f(b) + f(b)$. So this one works too.

So we can see that (C) works because roman numerals I and III are valid statements given that $f(x + y) = f(x) + f(y)$.

This is a question that won't allow us to use a concrete example (unless you get *extremely* lucky in making up a function for f). The only practical way to approach it is to make substitutions and follow the rules of algebra to see which roman numerals contain valid equations.

For most test-takers, this will be one of the hardest questions. So this is a good time for me to remind you that your primary goal probably shouldn't be trying to improve your performance on the occasional tough question like this; it's much more important to make sure you lock down all the questions that seem easier first. Once you get to a point where you never make any 'careless' errors, you should feel free to start worrying about questions like these. But if you try to tackle these kinds of questions without first making sure that you're executing correctly on the questions you can handle more comfortably, you'll just be wasting your time, and your score won't improve.

I'm not saying that a question like this can't be answered, or that if follows different rules. This question can be solved with basic math and careful thinking, just like every other SAT Math question. I'm just saying that it's important to focus on eliminating mistakes before you focus on figuring out questions that seem more challenging to you.

Page 519, Question 20

This question really helps drive home the importance of considering the answer choices along with the rest of the question.

When we look at the answer choices, we can see that they all involve y, with no x. That means we need a way to express x in terms of y. The only way to do that is to realize that x times y is 4000, since that's the area of the rectangle. So x is $4000/y$.

Furthermore, the total length of rope needed is $y + 4x$, because there are 4 vertical line segments with length x in the diagram.

We can re-write $y + 4x$ as $y + 4(4000/y)$, which is the same as $y + 16000/y$. So (B) is correct.

When I look back over the other answer choices, I would definitely want to notice that more of the answer choices include $3y$ than just y in the denominator, and that would worry me for a second, because I know that elements of the correct answers tend to appear in wrong answers in questions like this. So I would double-check my work again.

Page 527, Question 8

Despite my general dislike of algebra for the purposes of SAT Math solutions, sometimes it can't be avoided, and I think this question represents one of those times for most test-takers. This question is also one of those questions that can be expected to take most test-takers more time than usual. It's because of questions like this that we have to try to work through other questions as quickly as possible without sacrificing accuracy.

For most people, the obvious first step will be to multiply out the expression on the left (using FOIL), which gives us this:

$(x-8)(x - k) = x^2 - kx - 8x + 8k$

In terms of what we would normally get from FOIL-ing out two binomials, this expression is a little odd, because it has two terms with x instead of one. (This is because the original binomials involved more than one unknown value—they had a k in addition to the x-es.) So let's try to fix that by combining $8x$ and kx:

$(x-8)(x - k) = x^2 - kx - 8x + 8k$

$(x-8)(x - k) = x^2 - (8 + k)x + 8k$

Now it looks a bit more normal—we're still stuck with that weird k, but at least now we have one term with x^2, one term with just x, and one term with no x at all, which is our normal arrangement after FOIL-ing out two binomials.

So now our entire equation looks like this:

$x^2 - (8 + k)x + 8k = x^2 - 5kx + m$

Now we realize that $(8 + k)x$ must correspond with $5kx$, and that $8k$ corresponds with m. In other words, the two x terms on both sides must correspond, and the two terms on both sides with no x at all must also correspond. So we can solve for k, and then use k to solve for m:

$(8 + k)x = 5kx$ (deal with the k terms on both sides first)

$(8 + k) = 5k$ (divide both sides by x)

$8 + k = 5k$ (simplify)

$8 = 4k$ (combine like terms)

$2 = k$ (isolate k)

and, therefore:

$m = 8k$ and $k = 2$

$m = 8(2)$ (substitute 2 for k)

$m = 16$ (simplify)

So (B) is correct.

That's the algebraic approach. It's kind of ugly, at least by SAT standards, but it works.

There's another approach we can use that will probably be a little easier on our brains, though it might not be any faster. That would be to look at each answer choice and try to solve backwards; only one of the choices will make this possible.

For instance, if we want to test out choice (A), we would see what has to happen if m is 8. Since m is the product of 8 and k, according to FOIL, then we know that k would have to be 1 if we made m be 8. But if we FOIL out the expression on the left with k equal to 1, the rest of the expression doesn't end up matching with the rest of the expression on the right.

Then we could try with (B), (C), and so on. We would see that the process can be made to work when m equals 16, but not for any other choice.

Another way to go, which is probably faster, but which requires a bit more awareness of algebra, is to notice the relationship between m and $8k$, and the relationship between $8x$, kx and $5k$. Basically, we can see that k must be a value such that $8+k$ and $5k$ are equal, which means k must be 2, as we figured out before. And that would mean that m has to be 16.

Again, this is one of the ugliest questions in the book, but we can work out the answer if we stick to the fundamentals of algebra, and if we're willing to play around with an unfamiliar presentation of those fundamentals.

Depending on the approach you take, this question might eat up a little (or a lot) more time than the average SAT Math question. While we should always try to find the most efficient solutions during practice sessions, remember that it's normal for some questions to take longer than others on test day. Questions like this one are a big part of the reason why it's so important to try to save time on questions that seem easier to you. That way, you have enough time left to play around with the harder questions, or to go back over your work and check your answers.

Page 530, Question 18

This question is a little complicated for an SAT Math question, but, as trained test-takers, we expect that we might see a little more complication in the last question or two of the grid-in section. As always, we'll pay close attention to what the question is asking and see what we can figure out.

This question asks about the value of a, and the only place in the whole question where we can find any reference to a is in the expression $y = ax^2$. So that means we're going to need values for y and x that we can plug in to that expression, so we can solve for a.

Apart from (0,0), which won't help us figure out a, there are only two points on the graph that have (x,y) coordinates we can probably figure out: points Q and R, which are also in square $PQRS$.

We're told that $PQRS$ has an area of 64. We know this is an important dimension to be aware of because it was included in the text of the question after being omitted from the diagram itself. If the area is 64, that means each of the square's sides is 8 units long. And that, in turn, means that point R is located at (4,8), because OS is half of PS.

Now we have values for x and y that we can plug in for point R, which is on the graph of $y = ax^2$:

$y = ax^2$	(given equation for the graph)
$8 = a(4^2)$	(substitute x and y values for the point (4,8))
$8 = 16a$	(simplify expression on the right)
$8/16 = a$	(divide both sides by 16 to isolate a)
$1/2 = a$	(simplify expression on the left)

Notice that all of the ideas in this question are relatively simple ideas on their own; the trick was to trace the proper approach back through the wording of the question to figure out how to string together the relevant ideas.

Notice, also, that this question is actually very similar to question 18 on page 717 of the College Board's Blue Book. (The two questions aren't identical, but the only real difference between them is that *ABCD* isn't a square in that other question, and the function in this question isn't a parabola.) Do not be misled by this coincidence into assuming that the College Board frequently repeats a limited number of question types in each SAT Math section. On the contrary, in the entire Blue Book these two questions are among the only examples of question material being repeated so closely on the SAT Math section.

Page 547, Question 13

When you have a question like this where the answer choices are all relatively small numbers, that's a sign from the test that counting the options is the best way to go. On the other hand, if the number of options was much higher, that would be a sign that there's a solution where you don't actually have to count things.

From the beginning, though, we want to notice that each answer choice is only one more than the choice before it, so if we make a very small mistake and end up overlooking one of the possible combinations, or accidentally counting a combination twice, there will be a wrong answer choice waiting for us. Remember that it's always very important to pay attention to small details on the SAT, but it's especially important on questions like this.

So at this point I would go ahead and list the possibilities systematically, to make sure I don't skip anything. In this case, I would start with the smallest-value tokens and then work up from there.

- Seventeen 1-point tokens
- Twelve 1-point tokens and one 5-point token
- Seven 1-point tokens and two 5-point tokens
- Seven 1-point tokens and one 10-point token
- Two 1-point tokens and three 5-point tokens
- Two 1-point tokens, one 5-point token, and one 10-point token

So the answer is (E), six.

Normally I would be suspicious of liking the largest answer choice in a series, because the College Board usually likes to make the correct answer be somewhere in the middle of a series if one appears in the answer choices. So I would double-check my counting to make sure that everything I listed was really valid.

I'd also like to reiterate that this question is a great example of how SAT math can be "tricky" rather than really difficult. There's no advanced math concept or common formula involved here or anything, just a simple arithmetic issue where it's very easy to get mixed up and overlook some options.

Page 548, Question 16

This question involves a lot of geometric concepts, but as long as we think through them carefully we should have no problem navigating it—after all, since this is the SAT Math section, all of the individual concepts involved must be fairly simple on their own, even if they're combined in ways that might be strange.

The first idea mentioned in the question is that of a cube with volume 8. If the volume is 8, then the side length of the cube must be 2, because 2 cubed is 8.

Then we're told that the cube is inscribed in a sphere. That's a hard thing to represent with a diagram on a two-dimensional page, so let's describe it with words instead: think of a throwing die stuck inside a ping-pong ball so that it can't move.

Now the question asks for the diameter of the sphere. Since we were only given one numerical measurement in the entire question (the volume of the cube), it must be possible to figure out the diameter of the sphere from some measurement related to the cube.

At this point, we need to realize that the distance from one corner of the cube to the very opposite corner of the cube (in other words, the distance to the corner on the other side of the center of the cube) is the same as the diameter of the sphere. I'll make a diagram and leave the sphere out of it so you can see the distance I'm talking about. The dashed line is the distance we want to find:

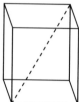

To find this distance, we have to use the Pythagorean theorem twice. First, we'll use it to find the distance of the diagonal across one of the faces of the cube; next, we'll use that diagonal as a leg to find the actual corner-to-opposite-corner distance we're looking for. So here's step 1:

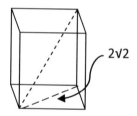

That diagonal across the bottom face is the hypotenuse of a 45°-45°-90° triangle with legs of length 2, so its length is 2√2.

Notice that the diagonal of 2√2 now forms the leg of another right triangle whose hypotenuse is the distance we're looking for, and whose other leg is one of the vertical edges of the cube.

This new triangle then has legs of 2√2 and 2, which means the hypotenuse is the square root of the sum of $2\sqrt{2}^2$ and 2^2. That sum is 12, so the hypotenuse is the square root of 12, which we can simplify like this:

√12 = √4 * √3

= 2√3

So (D) is correct.

I would like to add that I have always felt like there is a much simpler way to approach this question, but I don't quite see it. Note that the values in the answer choices are all pretty well spread out from one another, for the most part—I'm pretty sure there's something we're supposed to be able to notice from the setup that might let us realize that the correct answer must be a value between 3 and 4 or something. The reasoning would go something like this: 2 is much too small to be the distance across the cube because it's already the side-length of the cube, and 4 is much too big, because it's twice the side-length. I feel like there must somehow be a way to tell that 2.5 is also too small. Otherwise, I don't see any reason for the College Board to have included the decimal approximations in choice (B) and choice (D), because the College Board only seems to include these approximations when there's some kind of rough reckoning that can be used to rule out certain choices.

So if you'd like a little mental exercise, see if you can figure out a way to eliminate values of 2.5 or smaller in this question without doing the actual math. I'm pretty sure that will leave you with the fastest possible solution to the question.

(If, like me, you can't see a way to do that, there's no real problem—we should still have plenty of time left over from answering most of the other questions as quickly and efficiently as possible.)

Page 586, Question 20

This question offers a classic example of the kinds of information we can glean from a question by thinking of the answer choices from the very beginning.

Most test-takers will try to answer this question by coming up with an algebraic expression on their own and then looking in the answer choices to find a match. That approach can work if you do it perfectly, but it's very challenging for some people.

What I would recommend instead is to think about the similarities and differences in the answer choices and how they might be relevant to the concepts in the question.

If we look at the elements in the answer choices, we see that each choice is a fraction, with either n or $100n$ on the top, and either $n + 75$ or $2n + 75$ on the bottom (choice (C) also has 100 on the bottom).

So we basically only need to figure out the answers to these questions:

1.   Should 100 be involved in the correct expression? If so, in the numerator or in the denominator?

2.   Should the denominator contain the expression $n + 75$ or $2n + 75$?

Let's think about that. As for the issue with 100, we'd want to realize that the question is asking for a percentage but the answer choices are all fractions. Ideally, thinking about the percentages-versus-fractions issue along with the idea of 100 should remind us that we have to multiply fractions by 100 to turn them into percentages (because fractions describe a portion of a single unit, and percentages describe a portion of 100 units). So we should have 100 in the correct expression, and it should be in the numerator because we're multiplying by it.

Now, should the denominator have n or $2n$? For a lot of people, the temptation is to say that $2n$ doesn't make any sense, because it doesn't appear in the text of the question. But there are a couple of clues in the answer choices that should make us re-examine that assumption. For one thing, if $2n$ were just some pointless, random mistake, we wouldn't expect to see it repeated across multiple answer choices; instead, we'd expect that other choices would have other random values like $3n$ or $4n$. On top of that, $2n + 75$ actually appears *more often* in the denominator than just $n + 75$, which would suggest, according to the answer choice patterns we talked about for the SAT Math section, that $2n$ is actually the correct version. (Just to be clear, there's no guarantee that $2n$ is correct just because it shows up more often, but in general the elements that show up more often will tend to be part of the correct expression.)

So we really want to revisit this idea of $2n$. Is there any way it could make sense—either as the correct answer, or as an understandable mistake?

Actually, it makes sense as the correct answer when we realize the question is asking us to compare the number of male students to the entire number of students in the whole college. So the number in the denominator needs to reflect both the male and female students together. We know that the number of female students is given by $n + 75$, and the number of male students is given by n. So the sum of the female and male students will be $n + 75 + n$, or $2n + 75$.

That means (E) must be correct.

(Notice, by the way, that 100 appears in 3 of the 5 answer choices, which strongly suggests it's part of the right answer. In those 3 appearances, it shows up twice in the numerator, which suggests—but, again, does NOT guarantee—that it ought to be in the numerator in the correct answer.)

Page 595, Question 8

I remember being asked about this question for the first time in a live class I was teaching literally the first weekend after the second edition of the Blue Book came out. I had never seen the question before and for some reason I completely panicked in front of my students (which I almost never do). I had to admit sheepishly that I wasn't seeing whatever I needed to be seeing, and ask the students to allow me to give them the solution over lunch break when I would have time to think more clearly. (This, by the way, is the only time in my life I ever needed to do that. But sometimes these things happen. As it would turn out, all of my troubles were caused by straying from my normal game plan because I let myself get stressed out. More on that in a moment.)

The difficulty in this question, for most people, arises from the fact that it looks like the small triangle at the top of the figure has a nearly horizontal base. We really want that base to be horizontal, because then it will be parallel to the base of the large triangle, and then c would just be 180 - a - b, like choice (C) says.

Unfortunately, the base of that top triangle just isn't horizontal, no matter how we look at it, which means (C) can't be right. And this is where panic mode might start to set in.

When we panic on the SAT Math section, our normal reaction is to try to make things as complicated and advanced as we can, because that kind of thing usually works on math in school. But on the SAT we want to try to have the opposite reaction, actually—we want to try to look at the question in a simpler, more basic way.

On the day that I panicked in front of my students, for some reason I completely abandoned this principle and started writing out extremely complicated algebraic expressions trying to relate the different measurements of the various angles to one another. It was a mess. In general, if you find yourself writing out gigantic algebraic expressions to solve an SAT Math question, you're probably doing it wrong. At the very least, you're doing it in a much, much more complicated way than necessary.

So anyhow, when I looked back at the question a second time over my lunch break, I immediately saw the solution—and it was much, much easier than anything I had previously thought of. In fact, it took about 5 seconds to do, and didn't even involve picking up a pencil.

The fast solution comes from noticing that the 3 small triangles with angle measurements marked in them all combine to form a quadrilateral, and the angle measurements in a quadrilateral add up to 360°. So we can find the value of c by beginning with 360° and subtracting out all the other angle measurements, giving us 360 - 2a - 3b, which is what (E) says.

There's a very big lesson in the mistake I made on this question when I first saw it—it's one I apparently needed to be reminded of at the time, and one you need to learn now if you want to do well on the SAT Math section. Remember that questions on this test can be answered quickly and usually pretty simply. Remember that having to write out long algebraic expressions or go through 15 steps to get an answer means you're not looking at the question in the best way. Remember to look at the answer choices (I would have seen that 360 appears twice in the choices, which should have been a dead giveaway that a 4-sided figure might be involved, since there are clearly no circles in the question). Remember, above all, that this is the SAT, and the typical school approaches to math just don't work here most of the time.

Page 598, Question 18

At first glance, this question might look like a normal permutation question. But when we read closely, we realize that this question has a unique aspect that makes it different from typical permutation questions. In this question, one of the cards is forbidden to appear in two of the five positions.

So we can't use a standard factorial calculation here, because the factorial wouldn't take into account the limitations on the gray card. The factorial would tell us the total number of arrangements if every card could appear in every position.

But we can use the underlying logic that makes the factorial work, and modify how we apply it so that it fits the current situation. I can think of two ways to do that.

For the first way, we'll start with the idea that we're going to figure out the number of cards that can appear in each position, and then we'll multiply all the possibilities for each position together so we arrive at the total number of possible outcomes for all five positions together.

Since we have to make sure we don't end up with the gray card last, I'd figure out the number of possibilities for the end positions first, and then the number of possibilities for the middle positions.

For the first end position, we can put any one of 4 cards (any of the non-gray cards).

For the second end position, we can put any one of 3 cards (there are 3 non-gray cards left after we use the first one for the first end position).

For the first non-end position, we can put any one of 3 cards (there are 2 non-gray cards left, plus the possibility of the gray card).

For the second non-end position, we can put any one of 2 cards.

Finally, for the last non-end position, there will only be one card remaining.

So multiplying the number of possibilities at each position gives us 4 * 3 * 2 * 1 * 3, or 72.

Another way to go would be to figure out the number of possible arrangements if the gray card could go anywhere, and then subtract out the possibilities with the gray card at either end.

If we didn't care about where the gray card went, there would be 120 possible arrangements of the cards, because there would be 5 possible cards for the first slot, 4 for the second slot, 3 for the third, 2 for the fourth, and 1 for the fifth, and 5 * 4 * 3 * 2 * 1 = 120.

Now we have to subtract out the situations in which the gray card is at the first position or the last one. Since there are 5 cards, it stands to reason that each card is in each of the five positions for 1/5 of the 120 arrangements. We don't want to count the 1/5 of 120 where the gray card is first, and we don't want to count the 1/5 of that 120 where it's last. So we want 120 - 2/5(120), or 120 – 2(24), or 120 – 48, or 72.

Either of these approaches is perfectly valid, and there are probably other ways you could choose to tackle this question as well. I would probably advise against trying to list out all of the possible outcomes here, for two reasons. First of all, there are too many things involved, so it would probably take too long. Secondly, there are no answer choices, so if you miscounted by even one possible arrangement you'd end up with the wrong answer (if there were answer choices and you ended up differing from one of the choices by only one, you could probably assume that you had miscounted, but without answer choices that will be harder to catch).

This question is one more great example of why we don't really need to use formulas very often on the SAT. There's no formulaic way to attack this question that the average high school student will be familiar with in advance; instead, we have to think about the bizarre situation it presents us with, and then figure out a way to respond to that.

Page 642, Question 17

Students ask about this question all the time. It's probably one of the most time-consuming questions in the entire Blue Book.

For this one, we have to realize that we need the equation for line ℓ, so we can plug t and $t+1$ in for x and y, and then solve.

In order to figure out the equation, we need two things: the y-intercept, and the slope.

It may seem hard to figure out the y-intercept for line ℓ, because we don't seem to have enough information. But, as always, we need to remember that the SAT gives us enough information to answer questions, and we need to remember that careful reading is very important. We actually can figure out the y-intercept for line ℓ, because we're told that the line goes through the origin, which means that its y-intercept is 0. So now we just need the slope.

We can find the slope because it must be the negative reciprocal of the slope of the other line, since the two lines are perpendicular. Since the other line has a slope of -4, line ℓ has a slope of 1/4.

Now we know that line ℓ has the equation $y = (1/4)x$, so we just plug in t and $t + 1$ and solve:

$t + 1 = (1/4)t$ (original equation with t and $(t + 1)$ subbed for x and y)

$4t + 4 = t$ (multiply both sides by 4)

$3t = -4$ (combine like terms)

$t = -4/3$ (isolate t)

So (A) is correct.

Looking at the other answer choices, I would be a little worried because it looks like the choices are trying to distract me from choice (E)—choice (E) is the only one with both its reciprocal and its opposite in the answer choices. So I would double-check my work to make sure that I hadn't accidentally switched my signs or something.

Page 643, Question 20

Test-takers miss this question all the time, even though it only involves basic arithmetic. This is just one more example of how important it is to pay attention to details on the SAT, and really make sure we lock down every question we can.

If we're familiar with the definitions and properties of words like "remainder" and "factor," we can work this out logically. If we were going to think about it in the abstract, we'd realize that if the remainder is going to be 3, then we know that we're looking for factors of 12 that aren't also factors of 13, 14, and 15, because 15 - 12 is 3. The factors of 12 are 1, 2, 3, 4, 6, and 12. But 1, 2, and 3 don't work, because they're all factors of either 14 or 15, so we're left with 4, 6, and 12, and the answer is that there are three possible values for k.

The more concrete way to do this would be to list all the numbers of from 1 to 15, and then write down the remainders when 15 is divided by each of them:

15/1 = 15 r 0

15/2 = 7 r 1

15/3 = 5 r 0

15 / 4 = 3 r 3

15/5 = 3 r 0

15/6 = 2 r 3

15/7 = 2 r 1

15/8 = 1 r 7

15/9 = 1 r 6

15/10 = 1 r 5

15/11 = 1 r 4

15/12 = 1 r 3

15/13 = 1 r 2

15/14 = 1 r 1

15/15 = 1 r 0

So we can see that there are three numbers that produce a remainder of 3, and they are 4, 6, and 12.

So (C) is correct.

When people get this wrong, it's either because they've forgotten the meaning of the word "remainder," or because they've miscounted the number of things that produce a remainder of 3. Both of these are elementary math mistakes—exactly the kind of thing that you can't let happen on the SAT Math section.

Page 655, Question 18

Most test-takers will try to apply the distance formula here (or else they'll fail to remember the distance formula and then just take a guess at the answer based on nothing).

The distance formula would ultimately work here, but I prefer to think in terms of the Pythagorean theorem—and, after all, the distance formula is just one specific application of the Pythagorean theorem anyway.

(The Pythagorean theorem says that, in a right triangle, the square of the hypotenuse is equal to the sum of the squares of the legs: $a^2 + b^2 = c^2$, where c is the hypotenuse and a and b are the legs. If you forget the Pythagorean theorem, you can always go to the beginning of any SAT Math section and find it in the box of provided formulas.)

Some people would choose to diagram this question. Let's work it out mathematically first, and then we'll see what a diagram might look like.

If we're thinking in terms of the Pythagorean theorem, the distance between the two points will be the hypotenuse in the theorem, and the horizontal and vertical changes between the two points will be the legs in the theorem.

We know that the hypotenuse, or the distance, is 17.

We know that the separation in the y axis is 15, because point B has a y value of 18 and point A has a y value of 3, and 18 - 3 is 15. We're looking for one possible value of x, so we need to know how big the separation in the x-axis must be in order for it to be true that $a^2 + b^2 = c^2$ when a is 15 and c is 17. So let's figure it out. 15^2 is 225, and 17^2 is 289. So that gives us this:

$225 + b^2 = 289$ (Pythagorean theorem)

$b^2 = 64$ (combine like terms)

$b = 8$ or -8 (isolate b)

So we know that the separation in the x-axis must be 8. (Don't make the mistake of thinking that 8 is the answer to the question! 8 is just the length of the separation in one axis, but the question is asking for an actual coordinate in the x-axis.)

Since the x-axis separation is 8 units and the x-value for B is 10, we know that the x-value for point A must be either 2 or 18. So the answer can be either 2 or 18.

Now let's take a look at what we might get if we decide to diagram this. First, let's get a rough idea of where point B is:

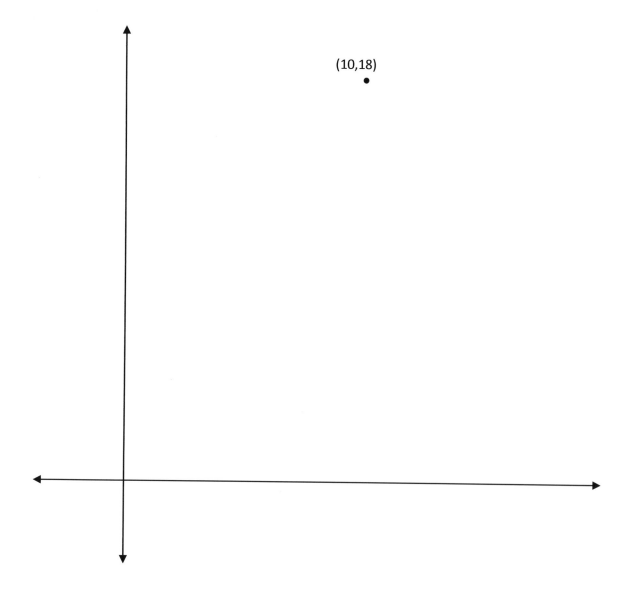

When we try to plot point *A*, we start to see the difficulty in the question: we have one coordinate for *A*, but not the other, so we can't plot it. All we can do is say that *A* must lie somewhere on the line of *y* = 3, because its *y*-value is 3.

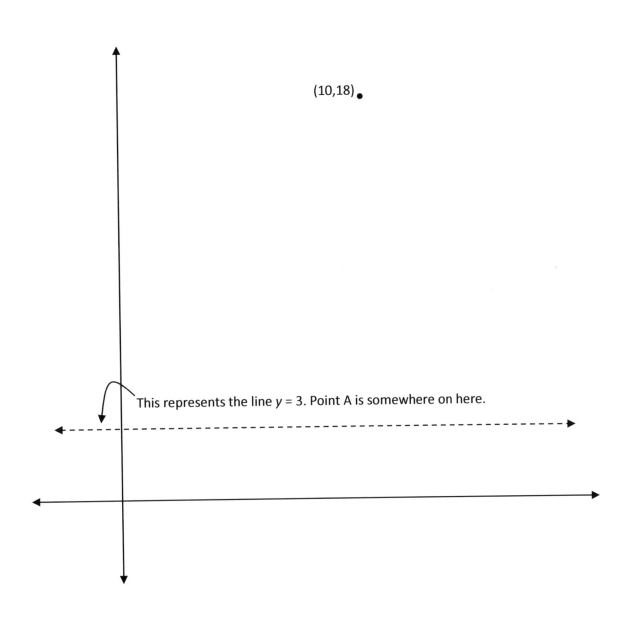

(10,18)

This represents the line *y* = 3. Point A is somewhere on here.

So now the issue is that *A* is 17 units away from *B*, and *A* is also somewhere on the dashed line in the diagram. So we have to figure out exactly where *A* can go. At this point, I would draw a circle (or part of a circle) showing the points that are 17 units away from *B*. *A* must be on a point where this circle intersects the line *y* = 3 above.

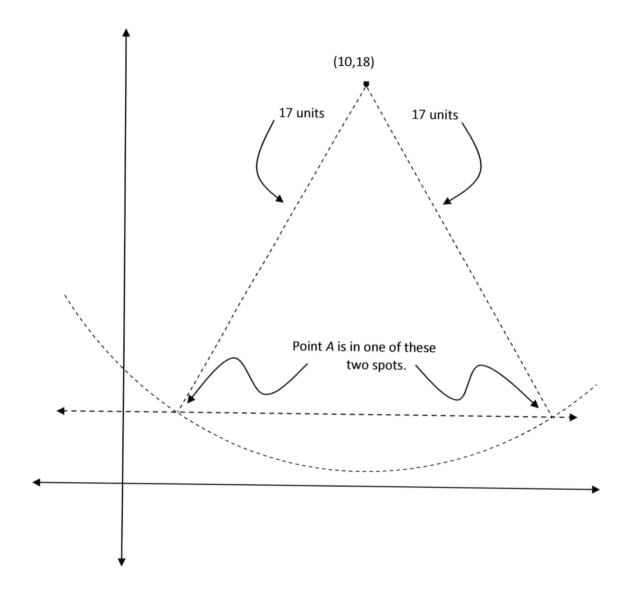

Now, all we have to do is figure out the *x*-value of either one of those two spots where *A* could be. For this, we'll want to use the Pythagorean theorem. The separation between the *y*-values of the two points will be one leg in our right triangle. The separation between the *x*-values of the two points will be the other leg. And the hypotenuse will be the 17-unit straight-line distance between the two points:

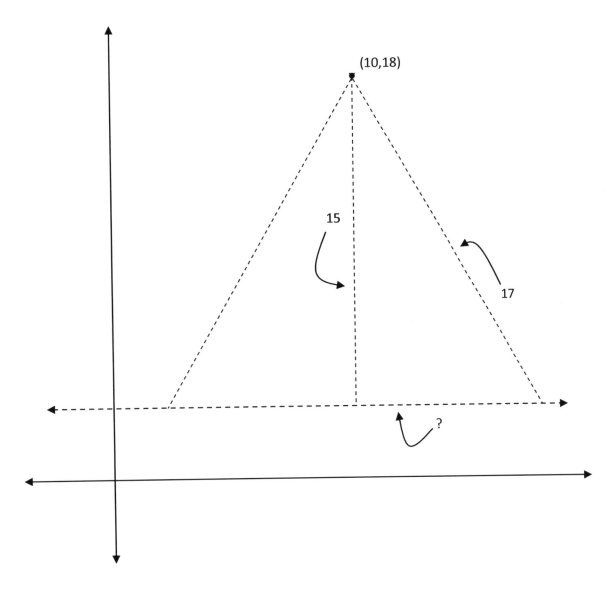

From here, we can apply the Pythagorean theorem as we did in the other approach, and realize that the horizontal leg in the triangle must have a length of 8 units, which means that the *x*-value for point *A* must be either 2 or 18.

Again, we could have done this in a more formal way by using the distance formula:

$$d = \sqrt{(y_2 - y_1)^2 + (x_2 - x_1)^2}$$

But, in general, I advise you to avoid formulaic thinking on the SAT, because there are so many instances on the average SAT Math section in which a formula might seem appropriate when it actually isn't. And even when a formula might work on a particular question, it's almost always going to take more time and energy than a non-formulaic approach, and it will also typically increase the likelihood of a mistake on your part.

Also, in the case of the distance formula, I find that it's much easier for most people to remember and apply the Pythagorean theorem than to recall every detail of the distance formula correctly. And since the SAT doesn't care how you arrive at the answer, I generally advise people to work in whichever way seems easiest at the time.

Page 671, Question 15

For this question, the key thing is understanding what the idea of modeling the data means. We're looking for the line that provides the best match to the general trend of the data points. Since the data doesn't increase or decrease as you move from left to right, the only thing that works is (A).

Note that (B), (C), and (D) would all have to go through the point (0,0), which clearly isn't appropriate here. Lastly, (E) would be increasing as it went to the right—it would pass through (0,44) and (5,49). We don't want that kind of positive slope because if we look at the plotted points we can see that the values are not increasing overall as we move left-to-right. The highest value is in the second trial, and one of the lowest values is in the 5th.

This is one more example of a question that's fairly easy if we read carefully and pay attention, but that many test-takers will miss anyway.

Page 671, Question 16

As with many SAT Math questions, there are a lot of ways to go about this one. The easiest approach, I think, is to convert either 12L or 10L to W, and then figure out the number of L x W rectangles, since that's what the question asks for.

The only way to convert L to W is to notice that 2L = 3W, which we know because 2L and 3W both correspond to the height of the big rectangle in the diagram.

If 2L is 3W, then 12L is 18W.

That means the area being covered can be expressed as 18W x 10L, or 180LW. Since LW is the size of each tile, that means we would need 180 tiles. So the answer is (E).

Notice that one of the wrong answers, (B), is 1/5 of the right answer. This makes sense, because a lot of people might accidentally determine the number of times that the big rectangle in the diagram could fit into the 12L x 10W region.

Page 703, Question 14

Most students I've worked with on this question have ultimately arrived at the right answer, but they often don't see the easiest way to get there.

Most of them try to figure out the median slope by determining the slope of every single line segment in the question, and then trying to arrange them from least to greatest (which they usually do by converting them all to a common denominator). It's quite time-consuming.

The much easier thing is to pay attention to the diagram and to think about what the concept of slope means in the first place. The slope of a line is a measurement of how slanted it is, in a manner of speaking. So the line segment with the median slope will be the one whose 'slantiness' puts it in the middle of all the other segments.

In other words, we can tell that line segment OC is the one with the median slope just by looking at the diagram. Now all we have to do is determine the slope of OC, and we're done. Since OC starts at the origin and point C is at (4,3), that means it goes up 3 units and over 4, for a slope of 3/4. So (C) is right.

Notice that all the other answer choices are the slopes of the line segments, which allows test-takers to make all kinds of mistakes and still find a wrong answer that they'll like. Remember to pay attention to details!

Page 705, Question 19

This question is one more excellent example of how we always have to be ready to apply basic math ideas in non-traditional ways. In this case, we're asked to find equivalent proportions even though every proportion involves 4 variables and we're never told the values of any of those variables. How is that possible?

In situations like this, it's often helpful to fall back on the idea of trying to identify concepts related to the things that appear in the question. In this case, pretty much the only usable concept we have in front of us is the idea of cross-multiplying.

As it turns out, if we cross-multiply each answer choice, we'll see that choice (A) gives us $ac = bf$, but all the other choices give us $af = bc$.

That means choice (A) is the one that's not equivalent to the others.

So, in the end, we never learned the values of any of these variables, and we never did anything more complicated than cross-multiplying to answer the question. Many, many test-takers must have missed this question, but when I talk to students who've missed it I've never met one who didn't know what cross-multiplying was. Remember that the challenge on the SAT Math section is to identify the basic concepts that will solve the problem.

Page 705, Question 20

Remember that these questions with roman numerals are typically going to be based on some kind of abstract property of the concepts in the question. If we can figure out what that property is, answering the question will usually be pretty straightforward.

For instance, the question tells us that roman numeral I will work out to $ab - b$. So we have to ask ourselves if there are any conditions in which that might be equal to zero.

That should raise the question, "when can subtracting one thing from another give us zero?"

The answer is that subtracting one value from another can only result in zero when the two values were equal to start with. This is a property of zero.

So $ab - b$ can only equal zero if ab and b are equal to each other.

And that leads to another question: when can ab and b be equal? When can we multiply something by a and have it equal our original starting value, in this case b?

We can only multiply something by a without changing its value if a equals 1. This is a special property of the number 1.

So, in the end, $ab - b$ can only equal zero when a equals 1, because if a is 1 then the expression $ab - b$ is the same as the expression $b - b$, which must be zero.

So that means that the expressions in each of the other answer choices can only come out to be zero if the part of the expression before the box can possibly equal 1, like a could in roman numeral I.

For roman numeral III, then, it's pretty clear that the value can work out to be zero if we just make a be 1 again.

But what about roman numeral II?

The $(a + b)$ expression at the beginning of roman numeral II could work out to be 1 if a and b could be fractions or even if one could be negative. But the question tells us that a and b must be positive integers, which means the lowest possible value for $a + b$ is 2. And that can't work.

So the correct answer here is (E): only roman numerals I and III can work.

Notice that this question has really no resemblance to anything that ever happens in the average math class in school. Notice that with this solution we never really needed a calculator, or even a pencil. Notice, also, that there's no other question in the entire book that calls for the same specific approach to that this one calls for. In other words, the lesson to learn from this question is NOT the idea of specifically attacking roman numeral questions by looking to see what kinds of subtraction can result in zero, because you'll probably never see a question that tests that concept in this exact way again. Instead, the lesson to take away from this is, as always, that we need to practice thinking about SAT Math questions in terms of basic principles, definitions, and properties. We need to read everything carefully. And we have to learn to be flexible in our thinking in the way that the SAT Math section rewards over and over again.

Page 714, Question 8

This question is a marvelous example of how important it is to be aware of the limitations of what the SAT Math section can ask you. Most people try to approach this question by taking the 6th root of both sides of the equation, but, as trained test-takers, we need to know that the SAT can never ask us to take any root besides the square root. So taking the 6th root isn't going to be the easiest way to go here (and anyway, the 6th root of 432 is an irrational number).

So now what?

Well, as is often the case, there are two basic ways to go here. We can try a kind of backsolving, brute-force sort of approach, or we can try using algebraic principles. The first kind of approach requires less familiarity with math but will be a bit more time-consuming for most people, since it's basically just trying a whole bunch of hit-or-miss combinations of a and b values. The second approach will go a little faster but will be harder for most test-takers to think of or pull off.

If we were going to do the first approach (the hit-or-miss approach), we'd start out by listing all the factors for the quantities in the answer choices. Notice, by the way, that the choices have a lot of factors in common, since they're all multiples of 6. That would suggest that concentrating on numbers like 2, 3, and 6 might not be a bad way to start.

Anyhow, to start working through our options, we'd take an answer choice like (A), figure out its factors (they're 1, 2, 3, and 6), and then get out our calculators and start plugging in combinations of those factors for a and b in the original expression to see if we could come up with a value of 432.

This will be made more challenging and time-consuming by the fact that, to be really thorough, you have to try each factor for a and again for b, since they aren't treated the same in the expression.

But it's made a little easier by the fact that some combinations of factors will prove to be too small or too large, which might help you adjust your guessing and hit on the right answer more quickly. A lot of people who try these kinds of backwards solutions like to start with (C), since it's the value in the middle, see how that goes, and then adjust up or down. In general I think that's a fine approach, but in this case it might result in more work because the larger numbers probably also have more pairs of factors to work with. So it's a toss-up, in my opinion—start where you like.

The second approach, as I mentioned, is a bit more mathematical, and is the one I would probably employ (not that that matters).

I would start out by realizing that I can simplify the expression on the left-hand side of the equation, so that the whole equation reads like this:

$a^3b^2 = 432$

Now that's starting to look like something we might have seen at some point in algebra class—it's starting to look a bit like a prime factorization, with *a* and *b* being the possible factors of 432.

So at this point, I'd break down 432 into its prime factors. I'd do this by using what my algebra teacher, Mrs. Turner, used to call a "factor tree." They look something like this:

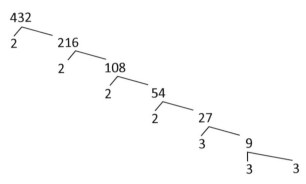

From this, we can see that the prime factorization of 432 is $2^4 * 3^3$.

That's almost what we're looking for, except for one small problem: 432 is the same thing as $2^4 * 3^3$, but we're looking to express it as $a^3 b^2$. It looks like the *a* can match up with the 3 in our factorization, because they're both cubed, but how do we get b^2 to match up with 2^4? We'll have to realize that 2^4 is 16, and 16 is 4^2.

That means that $a^3 b^2$ is 432 when *a* is 3 and *b* is 4. And that, in turn, means *ab* is 12, so (B) is correct.

As far as our answer choices are concerned, we see that we have a series of multiples of 6. In this situation we'd expect the right answer not to be a value on either end of the series—maybe that's not a ton of help here, but at least it doesn't suggest we're wrong.

Page 717, Question 17

A lot of people get nervous when they see this question, because they've never encountered a shape like the one in the diagram. But as trained test-takers, we have to remember that we're always going to see new stuff on the SAT, and our job is to figure out how to apply basic math knowledge in these new situations.

In this case, as in many other questions, it's just a matter of reading carefully. The only line segments that will be on edges are the ones to the vertex directly to the left of V, directly to the right of V, and directly underneath V. That means that the lines to the other 8 vertices aren't on the edges of the figure.

Like many of the SAT Math questions that most test-takers struggle with, this question involves no formula and no chance to use a calculator. It's just a matter of reading carefully and then subtracting 3 from 11 and arriving at 8 as the answer.

Page 717, Question 18

This question challenges many test-takers, usually because the drawing looks so complicated. But if we think carefully and work through the question, we'll find that it only relies on basic math at its core, just like all SAT Math questions.

The question asks us to find *p*. Since the only mention of *p* in the whole question is in the equation $y = px^3$, that's pretty much where we'll have to start.

The only way we can get *p* out of $y = px^3$ is to know the values for *y* and *x*. So that means we need to be able to identify the *x* and *y* values for some point on the graph of the function.

Apart from (0,0), which would be useless for us here, the only clear points that the function passes through are the ones labeled *A* and *C*.

Since *C* has *x* and *y* values that are positive, let's focus there. We know that *C* is at (1/2,*c*). So now we need to figure out the dimensions of triangle *ABCD*.

Since we know the area of *ABCD* is 4, and the diagram shows its width is 1 unit based on the *x*-coordinates, then we know that *ABCD* has a height of 4.

This means that point *C* is at (1/2 , 2). Now we just plug those *x* and *y* values into $y = px^3$:

$2 = p(1/2)^3$ (plug in 1/2 for *x* and 2 for *y*)

$2 = p(1/8)$ (simplify on the right)

$16 = p$ (isolate *p*)

This question was a bit more involved than many SAT Math questions. We know to expect that some time near the end of the grid-ins. But the solution still only involved a bizarre combination of basic facts—something else we've come to expect from SAT Math questions in general.

The real lesson to take away from this question is the idea of tracing the solution back through the concepts in the question. Here, they asked about *p*, so we looked in the question for a statement that was relevant to *p*, then we thought about things that were relevant to that statement, and so on. This general approach will come in handy on other SAT Math questions, even though this particular question will never appear on a real test in the future.

Notice, also, that this question is actually very similar to question 18 on page 530 of the College Board's Blue Book. I'll repeat here what I said earlier in the explanation for that question: do not be misled by this coincidence into assuming that the College Board frequently repeats a limited number of question types in each SAT Math section. On the contrary, in the entire Blue Book these two questions are one of the only examples of question material being repeated so closely on the SAT Math section.

Page 732, Question 14

Many students get nervous over this question because they don't like things that deal with ranges and inequalities, but it's important to remember that we don't have to do these questions in ways that we could defend to a math teacher. We just need to find the answer any way we can.

I would start by multiplying the smallest and greatest values of *x* and *y* together, and then seeing how those things relate back to the answer choices. The smallest and greatest values of *x* are 0 and 8, while the smallest and greatest values of *y* are -1 and 3. So:

0 * -1 = 0

0 * 3 = 0

8 * -1 = -8

8 * 3 = 24

So our range of possible values for *xy* at least needs to include -8 and 24.

That means (E) is the only choice that works.

If we look at the answer choices, it's a good sign that many of the choices end in 24. It's not a great sign that only one choice ends in -8, but we could easily pause to double-check the validity of -8 by realizing that 8 * -1 is, indeed, -8.

In fact, from a certain way of looking at it, once we're positive -8 is a valid option we can actually stop doing any further work, because only one choice includes it.

(Now, if you're a math teacher or a strong math student you might be shaking your head at my approach here, which is quite informal. In fact, you might shake your head at a lot of what we do in the Black Book because of its informality. But my goal isn't to show my students how to attack SAT Math questions formally, because formal solutions to SAT Math questions are typically slower and more difficult than the simple, direct approaches I want my students to follow. I'm not teaching math in this book; I'm teaching how to answer SAT Math questions. The distinction is important.)

Page 770, Question 8

Many test-takers miss this question, even though it involves nothing more than careful reading and basic arithmetic.

The question says that the new average is equal to the median number of siblings per student. That means we need to figure out what the median number of siblings is, and then figure out how to make the new average number of siblings equal to that median number.

So let's start by figuring out the median number of siblings.

We see there are 3 students with 0 siblings, 6 students with 1 sibling each, 2 students with 2 siblings each, and 1 student with 3 siblings. So if we arrange the number of siblings for each student in a row from least to greatest, we'll get this:

0,0,0,1,1,1,1,1,1,2,2,3

So the median number of siblings is 1, because the numbers in the middle of that series are both 1.

So when the new kid joins the class, the average number of siblings that everyone has is going to equal this median number of 1. When the new kid joins the class, there will be 13 total students in the class, which means the total number of siblings for all the kids in the class must also be 13 (because 13/13 is 1).

So now we add up the numbers of siblings of existing students, so we can see how far we are from a total of 13 students:

0 + 0 + 0 + 1 + 1 + 1 + 1 + 1 + 1 + 2 + 2 + 3 = 13

So actually, it turns out that the 12 students already in the class have a total of 13 siblings already, which means that the 13th student needs to have zero siblings in order for the average number of siblings in the class to be 1.

That means (A) is correct.

Now let's review the math ideas that were necessary to answer this question. We had to know how to read a relatively simple table. We had to know what the words "median" and "average" meant. We had to arrange a lot of single-digit numbers from least to greatest. We had to figure out that a lot of single-digit numbers added up to 13. We had to know that 13/13 is 1. And we had to know that 13 + 0 is 13.

None of that would probably qualify as advanced mathematical knowledge at your school, but test-takers miss this question very, very often. We should ask ourselves why that is, so we can make sure we don't make their mistakes.

In my experience, people who miss this question (or just give up on it in the first place) do so because they don't understand what it's asking when they read it. This is why I often say that critical reading skills are the most important thing on the entire SAT. And it's because of the great number of questions like this—questions that present bizarre combinations of simple math ideas—that test-takers who try to prepare for the SAT by learning advanced math usually don't see any improvement.

Page 773, Question 17

For this question, as for many abstract questions on the SAT Math section, there are two ways to go: we can come up with concrete values for the variables described in the question and run a test, or we can think about the question in the abstract. The concrete approach tends to take more time but will often feel more comfortable, while the abstract approach is faster but will be harder for many test-takers to manage.

In this explanation, I'll start with a concrete example and then show the abstract one. You could use either on the test, of course, without bothering to think about the other.

Let's assume that p is 3, r is 5, and s is 7, as those are three different prime numbers greater than 2, like the question asks us for.

In that case, n is 3 * 5 * 7, or 105.

Now let's figure out what the factors of n are:

1, 3, 5, 7, 15, 21, 35, 105

There are 8 of them, so the answer to the question is 8.

Now, if we wanted to think about this in the abstract, we'd note that since n is the same as prs, and since p, r, and s don't have any other factors besides 1 (since they're prime), then the factors of prs will include every possible combination of p, r, and s, like this:

p, r, s, pr, ps, rs, prs

. . . plus, of course, 1.

That also makes for a total of 8 factors.

(Notice that the concrete example we did follows our abstract thinking perfectly if we substitute 3 for p, 5 for r, and 7 for s.)

Page 785, Question 2

People often miss this question, even though it's fairly early in the section and doesn't really involve any math. When they miss it, it's usually as a result of not having read it carefully. Most people choose (A) because the figure in that choice has a line of symmetry, and they're rushing through the question. They don't notice that 3 other choices also have a line of symmetry, which might help them realize their mistake.

If we read carefully and realize we're looking for a figure with 2 lines of symmetry, then we realize that (D) has one line of symmetry going vertically straight down its center and another line going horizontally straight through its center.

It's a real waste to miss a question like this! Make sure you pay proper attention to every single question on the entire test. Even the so-called 'easy' ones can trip you up if you rush.

Page 789, Question 18

This is one of those questions in which knowing the unwritten rules of the SAT Math section comes in especially handy.

Most people who try to answer this question will either use some version of a summation formula or they'll actually try to add up every integer starting from -22 until they hit a running total of 72.

Either approach could conceivably work, but neither is very fast, nor very easy.

Instead, we want to remember that there must be some way to do this question in under 30 seconds relying only on some combination of basic arithmetic, algebra, and/or geometry.

One thing that would jump out at me right away is that we're looking for a *positive* sum, but we're starting by adding up some *negative* numbers in the beginning of our series. That means we'll have to add quite a few numbers before our running total becomes positive, because at the beginning of our series (-22, -21, -20, . . .), the running total will just become increasingly negative.

So wait a second . . . when does the running total start to creep towards a positive balance?

Well, that won't happen until we start adding in some positive numbers, of course. So our series will have to go past zero, for sure.

And when it passes zero, for a while, each positive number added to the running total will only serve to erase one of the negative numbers already added to it. Positive 1 undoes -1, for instance, and positive 2 undoes -2, and so on.

If we think about it, then, we'll see that every number from -22 to positive 22, added together, gives a sum of zero, because every positive number in the series is outweighed by a negative number and vice-versa.

So all the numbers from -22 to positive 22 add up to zero. Then what happens?

We add in positive 23, positive 24, and positive 25, and we've reached our grand total of 72.

That means that all the numbers from -22 to positive 25 add up to positive 72. So (B) is the answer.

Notice some of the wrong answers here. (C) is the sum of the two numbers in the original question, while (E) is the difference. (A) is the first positive number that produces a positive value when added to the running total, so some test-takers will probably accidentally choose it because they've realized it marks the beginning of the positive running total without remembering what the question was actually asking.

Page 799, Question 14

People often get frustrated by this question because they can't figure out the values of *b* and *c*. In school math classes, we're often programmed to find the values for every variable in a question, but on the SAT Math section we often have to let go of that. Sometimes there's not enough information in a question to figure out the value of every variable, but the question can still be answered anyway. One of the clearest signs of that situation is when the question involves multiple variables but doesn't actually ask you for each one of their values.

For questions about function graphs, I often like to look at the intercepts. In this case, we know that *c* is positive, so the *y*-intercept must also be positive, because the *y*-intercept is what we get when *x* = 0.

Only (E) has a graph with a positive *y*-intercept, so only (E) works.

Page 800, Question 15

I often resist the idea of identifying 'types' of math questions on the SAT Math section, because I want you to realize that you'll basically have to figure out stuff you've never seen before when you take the SAT. But if there were going to be a type of question that I might specifically train somebody for, it would be the kind of thing described in this question. (By the way, this comes up less than once per test in the College Board's Blue Book. The odds that it will ever come up for you on a real test are less than 50%. And, even if it does come up, it'll probably only count for one question. These are the kinds of reasons why I generally avoid thinking in terms of question types.)

Anyway, for these questions that ask you about the distance from one point of a 3-dimensional figure to another point, you basically have to apply the Pythagorean theorem twice.

Let's label the corner underneath point B as point Q, and let's label the corner to the right of point A as point T.

So then triangle ATQ has legs of 1 and 2 units, which means that AQ has a distance of √5.

So now we can use AQ, which was the hypotenuse of ATQ, as a leg in the triangle ABQ. Using the Pythagorean theorem again, we get this:

$AB^2 = √5^2 + 1^2$

$AB^2 = 5 + 1$

$AB^2 = 6$

$AB = √6$

So the answer is (D).

Note that one of the wrong answer choices is √5, for people who forget to finish the question.

Page 800, Question 16

This is a question with a made-up function. For these kinds of things, it's always very important to read and follow directions very carefully.

In this case, people often fail to realize that the right-hand side of the equation should be $(a-2)^2 - (a-2)$. We have to apply the oval function to the whole expression inside the oval, and the whole expression inside the second oval is $(a-2)$.

Once we do that correctly, all that remains is to solve:

$a^2 - a = (a-2)^2 - (a-2)$	(substitute the starting values from the question)
$a^2 - a = (a^2 - 4a + 4) - a + 2$	(FOIL the expression on the right)
$a^2 - a = a^2 - 5a + 6$	(combine like terms on the right)
$-a = -5a + 6$	(subtract a^2 from both sides)
$0 = -4a + 6$	(combine a terms)
$4a = 6$	(separate a term from constant)
$a = 6/4$	(isolate a)
$a = 3/2$	(simplify)

So (C) is correct.

As we might expect, one of the wrong answers is twice as much as the right answer. The other wrong answers seem to reflect what we might have ended up with if we had handled the algebra incorrectly.

By the way, another approach to this question, which would probably take longer but would avoid so much algebra, would be to take each answer choice and plug it in to the original expression until you find one choice that results in a true mathematical statement. But even if you do the question in this way, you still need to make sure you handle the substitution properly by reading the question very carefully.

Page 835, Question 18

To answer this one we have to think about what we're given and what we're asked for. We're given the averages of the two groups and asked for the ratio of their sizes. Note that it's impossible to know the actual number of people in each group—one major clue to this is the fact that the test asks for the ratio.

Many test-takers try to approach this question by figuring out individual values for *p* and *n*, but it literally can't be done. It is possible, however, to figure out the value of *p/n*.

We'll figure out the ratio by using the definition of the term "average," which tells us that if *p* students have an average of 70, then the total number of points scored by those *p* students is 70*p*.

Similarly, the total number of points scored by the *n* students is 92*n*.

Using the definition of average, again, we find that the average of all the *n* students' scores plus the *p* students' scores must be $(70p + 92n)/(n + p) = 86$. Then we solve:

$70p + 92n = 86p + 86n$	(multiply both sides by $n + p$)
$6n = 16p$	(combine like terms)
$6n/16 = p$	(isolate *p*)
$6/16 = p/n$	(isolate *p/n* since the question asks for it)
$3/8 = p/n$	(simplify)

Page 848, Question 6

Many test-takers miss this question because they mistakenly think that a square yard is the same thing as 3 square feet. But a square yard is 9 square feet, because a square yard is 1 yard x 1 yard, or 3 feet x 3 feet, or 9 feet[2].

Once we know that, it becomes easier to realize the correct answer is 12 * 18 / 9, or 24.

Another way to approach the situation is to convert the dimensions of the floor to yards right from the beginning, so that we calculate 4 yards by 6 yards, again getting 24 yards[2].

So (C) is correct. Note that (A) is there for us in case we divide by 3 one time too many, and (E) is there in case we accidentally find the square footage instead of the square yardage. Things like this are why it's always so important to read carefully on the SAT Math section.

Page 851, Question 15

This question often frustrates people, but it's actually not as hard as people often think. The question asks for the shortest distance between the center of the cube and the base of the cube. If we visualize the cube, we'll see that the distance from its center to its base is the same as the distance from the center of one of its sides to the base—or, in other words, if you looked at the cube straight on it would look like this:

where *C* is the center of the square/cube and the bottom line of the square/cube is the base.

If the volume of the cube is 8, then the sides are all length 2, which means the distance from the center to the base is 1 (because it's half the distance from the base to the top side of the cube). So the answer is (A).

Page 852, Question 18

This question provides one more terrific example of the difficulty that the College Board can manage to infuse into an SAT Math question without actually using any math.

This question throws a lot of people. But, as always, all we really need to do here is follow what the text says, alternately switching the left or the right wire with the center wire. So the pattern goes like this:

step 1: BAC
step 2: BCA
step 3: CBA
step 4: CAB
step 5: ACB
step 6: ABC

So the answer is (D). Notice that it's possible to end up with the wrong answer of 7 if we accidentally count the "Start" as a step. One more moment when critical reading skills really come in handy on the math part of the SAT.

This is also a great example of an SAT Math question for which no formula exists. There's no way you could use a calculator on this question; there's not even any real way you could use basic arithmetic. This question is literally about braiding, but untrained test-takers in advanced calculus classes miss it frequently in practice.

Page 852, Question 19

Like the previous question, this one ends up involving no actual math. All we need to do is think carefully about the definition and properties of the term "median."

If you double the value of each number or increase each number by 10, you must end up changing the median number (because you either double it or increase it by 10, as the case may be).

In other words, if the 11 numbers are 1, 2, 3, 4, 5, 6, 7, 8, 9, 10, 11, then doubling them all makes the median 12 and adding ten makes it 16. The median is the value in the middle--that's the definition of the term. Changing the number that's in the middle of the range of numbers changes the median.

(C) or (D) might also end up affecting the median, if we increase the smallest number by such an amount that it becomes greater than the original median, or if we decrease the largest number by such an amount that it becomes less than the original median.

Only (E) has no possibility of changing the median. Increasing the largest number still causes it to remain the largest number, so the number in the middle of the series can't change.

Page 861, Question 16

Many students try to use some kind of formula here, but that's a mistake, of course. For one thing, the SAT can't ask us to find the area of a trapezoid because it doesn't give that formula in the beginning of the math section or in the question itself. So there must be some other way to solve the problem that is easier and more direct.

If you draw out the rectangle and the trapezoid, we'll see that the trapezoid takes up 3/4 of the area of the rectangle, like so (I dashed in some other lines so you can see that *ABED* takes up 3/4 of *ABCD* more clearly):

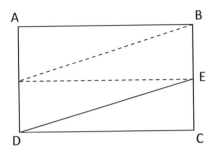

So that means that we can do this:

ABED = 3/4(ABCD)
2/3 = 3/4(ABCD)
8/9 = ABCD

This means that the answer is (C).

Notice that one of the wrong answers is 3/4. This is a good sign for us, because it indicates that we were probably on the right track when we figured out that ABED was 3/4 of ABCD.

Page 888, Question 8

This question is often frustrating for untrained test-takers because it seems at first as though it will be impossible to figure out the product of the slopes if we don't know the slopes themselves, and the question doesn't tell us the slopes.

But if we remember the definition of the term "rectangle" and the properties of perpendicular lines in a coordinate plane, then we can realize that the slopes of lines that are perpendicular to one another are opposite reciprocals (like, for instance, 2 and -1/2), so they'll have to multiply together to give us -1.

There are two pairs of perpendicular sides, in a rectangle, so the final product of all of these slopes is 1, because -1 * -1 is 1. (For instance, if the slopes were 2, -1/2, 2, -1/2, they would multiply together to make 1.) So (D) is the right answer.

So, in the final analysis, this question really just involved knowing that rectangles have 2 pairs of perpendicular sides, knowing that perpendicular lines have slopes that are opposite reciprocals, and knowing that -1 * -1 is 1. Each of those facts is pretty basic on its own, but most people who look at this question never realize that those facts are involved in answering it. This is why it's so important to develop the instincts for taking these questions apart by reading carefully, thinking about definitions and properties, and ignoring formulas and calculators for the most part.

Page 906, Question 12

This question basically hangs on the definition of the term "directly proportional." We need to know that when n is directly proportional to q, $n = kq$, where k is some unknown proportional constant that we usually need to figure out.

So, in this case, if y is directly proportional to x^2, then $y = k(x^2)$.

So let's substitute and see what happens:

$1/8 = k(1/2)^2$ (plug in the given values for x and y)

$1/8 = k(1/4)$ (simplify on the right)

$4(1/8) = k$ (isolate k)

$1/2 = k$ (simplify)

Now that we know what k equals, we can plug it in with a y value of 9/2, to find our new x:

$9/2 = 1/2(x)^2$ (plug in values for y and k)

$9 = x^2$ (combine like terms)

$3 = x$ (isolate x)

So the answer is (D). Notice that our other answer choices include 9, which is what we'd get if we accidentally solved for x^2 instead of x, which is a mistake people often make on this question.

It's not common for the SAT to test a math concept as obviously as it's testing direct proportionality in this question—the only wrinkle in this question is the idea of being proportional to x^2 instead of x. I think this particular question is so direct because direct proportionality is a concept that many algebra teachers no longer cover for some reason. (This is just a theory on my part, but I think it matches the evidence. Math concepts that are more commonly encountered on the SAT aren't usually tested this directly.)

At any rate, if you saw this question and realized that you had forgotten (or never been taught) the idea of direct proportionality, it would be a good idea to review it. The odds of it coming up on test day for you are relatively slim, but it's such a simple concept that it can't hurt to take a few moments to memorize it.

Page 907, Question 18

For this question, as for most SAT Math questions, we simply need to read carefully and look for ways to apply basic math ideas.

If there are 18 arcs of each length in the circle, and if the circle has a circumference of 45 units, then we can write this:

$18(2 + b) = 45$

That means that $36 + 18b = 45$, which means that $18b = 9$, so $b = 1/2$ unit.

If b is 1/2 unit and there are 45 units in the circumference of the circle, then 45 units corresponds to 360 degrees of arc. This means that each of the 45 units in the circle's circumference accounts for 45/360 degrees, or 8 degrees; since b is 1/2 of a unit, b must be 4 degrees, and the answer is (A).

Notice, as is often the case, that the answer choices represent mistakes that can be easily made. 16 degrees is the arc measurement of the 2-unit arcs, and 20 degrees is the arc measurement of a $(2 + b)$ combination.

Page 908, Question 20

This question, like many questions near the end of an SAT Math section, is actually much easier than it might look. It's also an especially clear example of a few of the SAT Math rules and patterns from this book, all wrapped into one test item.

One of the first things I'd want to notice is that the diagram isn't drawn to scale. That means I should think about re-drawing it to scale. To figure out how to do that, I have to look at the text of the question, which mentions that each of the five line segments are congruent (which is just a fancy way to say they're all the same length). That means that this diagram should show two equilateral triangles that share a side, like this:

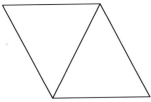

The text of the question also includes another piece of information that was left out of the original diagram, which is the existence of line segment AC. So I'll add that in:

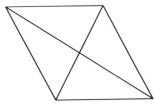

Another fundamental thing that we should pay attention to is the set of answer choices. Notice that they all involve either √3 or √2 (choice (E) actually involves both).

We should ask ourselves what kinds of math concepts are related to the concepts we've encountered so far. We know the diagram involves two equilateral triangles, and we know equilateral triangles are 60°-60°-60° triangles. We also know that the answer choices involve √3 and √2; √3 is related to 30°-60°-90° triangles and √2 is related to 45°-45°-90° triangles.

At this point, we'd want to realize that line AC cuts the two 60°-60°-60° triangles in half, creating 4 new triangles, and *each of these new triangles is a 30°-60°-90° triangle.*

We know that the ratio of the legs of a 30°-60°-90° triangle is 1: √3, with √3 representing the long leg. (This is something we'd want to have memorized, but even if you forget it momentarily you can always look at the given information at the beginning of any SAT Math section).

The question asks for the ratio of AC to BD. AC includes two long legs of 30°-60°-90° triangles, while BD includes two short legs of 30°-60°-90° triangles. That means the ratio is 2√3:2, which is the same thing as √3:1, which is what (B) says, so (B) is correct.

Surveying all the answer choices, we'll see that most of them start with √3, which is a good sign that starting with √3 is probably the correct option. But more of them end with something related to 2, not 1, so I would double-check myself to make sure that I hadn't made a mistake in simplifying the ratio.

Page 919, Question 15
Most untrained test-takers will see this question and assume that they need to figure out the actual measurements of each angle in the answer choices, because that kind of solution might seem similar to something we would do in a trigonometry class. But, as trained test-takers, we'd want to realize that it's possible to figure out which angle is smallest without figuring out their actual measurements—and, anyway, trig isn't allowed on the SAT, so there has to be another way.

Since the two endpoints of each angle are the same (always X and Y), the farther away the vertex is, the smaller the angle will end up being. Since D is the farthest point from X and Y, XDY is the smallest angle, even if we never figure out its actual measurement. So (D) is the correct answer.

Page 919, Question 16

Most untrained test-takers will try to identify the actual values of x and y, because that's what we would typically have to do in school if we saw a math question with multiple variables. But on the SAT, we'll frequently be asked questions in which the variables don't need to be identified, and this is one of those questions. (One of the major clues that we don't need to identify the variables is that we weren't asked to find either variable's individual value; we were only asked to find the value of a complex expression that involves both variables.)

As always, it's important to think about the answer choices, and how they relate to the concepts and quantities in the question. Notice that every answer choice has a clear relationship to the quantities 7 and 5 from the question:

(A) is the difference of 7 and 5, so it would make sense as the right answer if $x^2y - y^2x$ were the same thing as the difference between xy and $x-y$

(B) is the sum of 7 and 5, so it would make sense if $x^2y - y^2x$ were the sum of xy and $x-y$.

(C) is twice the sum or 7 and 5, which also doesn't make any sense here.

(D) is the product of 7 and 5, so it will be the right answer if $x^2y - y^2x$ is the same thing as the product of xy and $x-y$. Which is exactly what it is, so (D) is correct.

(E) is twice the product of 7 and 5.

As I've mentioned many times, we really want to get in the habit of thinking of the answer choices as part of the question itself, not as an afterthought. Looking for ways that the choices relate back to the text of the question can really help you increase both your speed and your accuracy. This question is one of the most frequently missed questions in this section (we can tell this from the College Board's difficulty ranking), but it can literally be answered without even picking up a pencil if we notice what's going on in the answer choices. This question ultimately boils down to paying attention, knowing what 7 * 5 is, and knowing how to multiply simple expressions in algebra.

Page 953, Question 17

This is a grid-in question that asks us to find "one possible value of the slope" of a line that intersects line segment AB. Remember that when a question like this asks us to find "one possible value," then there must be more than one value possible—whenever a question refers to the possibility of multiple values, there are multiple values.

In this case, any slope value of any line whatsoever that intersects AB will be fine. If a line (8,3) hits point A exactly, then a line through (9,3) must intersect AB. The line through (9,3) will have a slope of 3/9, or 1/3. So that's one possible value.

Another way might be to try to cut AB in half. To do that, we could imagine a line through (8,1.5), or through (16,3) (that would be the same line, determined at two different, collinear, points). Either one would create a line with a slope of 3/16.

Yet another way to create a valid answer might be to realize that a line with a slope just barely over horizontal would have to intersect AB since point B lies on the x-axis. So we could pick a slope of 1/10 or .001 or something.

Any of these approaches could work, as could a wide variety of others.

Page 969, Question 16

I once saw a YouTube video of a guy who explained how to attack this question in the most complicated way I could possibly imagine. He began by identifying the curve in the graph as a parabola, and then tried to figure out what the equation for the parabola would be (after trying to figure out the coordinates of various points on the parabola, like the vertex, the intercepts, and so on). Once he had the equation of the parabola worked out, he set it equal to 0, solved it, and then found his answer.

It worked, of course, but it created a ridiculous amount of extra work for no reason—and let's not even mention the extra opportunities for error it created by drawing the solution out unnecessarily.

Unfortunately, that kind of approach is what most test-takers would try on this question, because they're programmed to answer questions on the SAT Math section the same way they would answer questions in school.

There's a much easier way to approach this question, which relies on simply understanding the properties and definitions of concepts relating to the graphs of functions.

We should recognize that the places where $h(a) = 0$ will be the places where the graph of $h(a)$ crosses the x-axis.

We should also recognize that the graph is drawn to scale, which means we can eyeball it relative to the provided values and figure out where the graph crosses the axis from there.

If we look at the answer choices, we'll see that (A) must be correct, because where $x = -1$ on the given graph, we find $h(a)$ crossing the x-axis.

Some students are tempted to choose 4 as the answer to this question, because it kind of looks like the right-hand x-intercept of the graph might be at $x = 4$. But if you look carefully, you'll see it's at a position much closer to $x = 5$. Remember how important it is to pay attention to details!

If we read carefully, look at the graph carefully, and remember to think in terms of things like intercepts, we can answer this question in about 10 seconds, without even picking up a pencil.

Page 981, Question 15

A lot of test-takers drop the ball on this question because they don't look for the ways to simplify the algebraic expressions involved, or they try to assign values to n and k without making sure that those values satisfy the original requirements of the given equation.

I would start off by simplifying the expression on the left-hand side of the equation, dividing by n/n and 'eliminating' an n from the top of first fraction and the bottom of the second fraction. Then it's a little easier to see that the whole thing could be combined to this:

$n/(n^2 - 1)$

(Notice that $(n - 1)$ can be multiplied by $(n + 1)$ to create the difference of squares $(n^2 - 1)$. This is something we'd want to be able to do in our heads, without needing to foil it out manually.)

So now our equation looks like this:

$n/(n^2 - 1) = 5/k$

This means that n corresponds to 5, and $(n^2 - 1)$ corresponds to k.

If n is 5, then $(n^2 - 1)$ is 24, so the answer is (C).

In our wrong answers, we see the value of n, which helps reassure us that we attacked the question correctly, because it suggests that the College Board is hoping some test-takers will correctly realize that n is 5 but then forget the question was asking for k. We also see a series that goes 24, 25, 26, which might seem odd at first, because normally we'd expect the right answer to be in the middle of a series like that. But there's a certain logic to it here, because in order to arrive at 24 we have to square 5 and subtract 1; in this case, the wrong answers reflect squaring 5 and *adding* 1, and squaring 5 while forgetting to add or subtract. We can see there's a certain symmetry the College Board is going for here, in trying to give test-takers a variety of ways to mess this question up. And that can reassure us that squaring 5 and then subtracting 1 was, indeed, the right way to go.

Conclusion

We've just looked at a whole bunch of SAT Math questions, and we never really broke a sweat! We did this by sticking to our simple process, and by looking for quick and easy answers. As we saw, the hardest part of each problem was the setup. The actual calculations didn't present much of a problem, as long as we had our basic concepts in order.

On the next page, you'll see a brief, one-page summary of the main ideas to keep in mind on the SAT Math section. After that, we'll dive into the SAT Writing section. You'll see that the Writing section, like the SAT Math section, is a lot easier to attack if you're familiar with a core set of basic principles.

Video Demonstrations

If you'd like to see videos of some sample solutions like the ones in this book, please visit http://www.SATprepVideos.com. A selection of free videos is available for readers of this book.

SAT Math Quick Summary

   This is a one-page summary of the major relevant concepts. Use it to evaluate your comprehension or jog your memory. For a more in-depth treatment of these ideas, see the rest of the section.

The Big Secret: SAT Math tests very simple things in very strange ways.

The concepts in the SAT Math section must be limited because of standardization. No trig or advanced stats—just arithmetic, algebra, and geometry. Refer to the SAT Math Toolbox if necessary.

Focus on the definitions and properties of the concepts in each question, not on formulas.

All SAT Math is "easy," and each question can be done in 30 seconds or less if you find the fastest solution. If your solution is very complicated, you're probably doing the question wrong.

Look for shortcuts, things that cancel out, equivalent terms, etc. Leave expressions as fractions and radicals, instead of decimals, for easier canceling and substitution.

Diagrams are assumed to be to scale unless the question says otherwise. Taking a close look can often help to eliminate wrong answers or even point to the right one without doing any math.

Diagrams that aren't drawn to scale often yield important information if you redraw them to scale.

Every question contains all the information you need to answer it (unless "not enough information" is an answer choice, in which case there may not be enough information), even if it doesn't seem like that. If you understand every word in the question, then you know enough to mark the right answer.

Some common wrong answer patterns include choices that are:

- half or double the right answer
- in a series with the right answer
- a number that you have to find "on the way" to the answer
- similar in appearance to the right answer

I recommend a step-by-step process called the Math Path for questions that are hard to figure out:

1. Read the question carefully and consider the words. This is the most important step.
2. Consider any diagrams—scale, missing dimensions, etc.
3. Consider answer choices (if there are any)—relationships with each other and with question.
4. What areas of math are involved? What can the SAT test in those areas? (Math Toolbox.)
5. In light of steps 1 - 4, look for a solution that would take 30 seconds or less, ideally.
6. Solve the problem.
7. Check your work with the answer choices. "Carelessness" costs more people more points than any other single thing does.

Note that we think about the question holistically before we actually start solving it.

Ignore the order of difficulty, which is based on people who don't know what they're doing. You can make careless mistakes on any question, and every question has a simple, direct solution.

See the example solutions in this Black Book for demonstrations of these ideas.

The SAT Essay

"You only fail if you stop writing."
- Ray Bradbury

Overview and Important Reminders For The SAT Essay

The SAT Essay is supposed to evaluate your ability to produce what the College Board calls "good writing." The College Board's intention here is commendable, but the essay test it has come up with is an awful tool for measuring writing ability. In other words, while a good writer might score well on this writing exercise, it's very possible to score well without being a good writer at all, and some hallmarks of good writing might actually hurt you. In fact, in a widely publicized *New York Times* article from 2005, Dr. Les Perelman, a director of undergraduate writing at MIT, described the writing skills necessary for a good SAT score as "exactly what we don't want to teach our kids."[1]

To score well on the SAT Essay, all you have to do is completely ignore the official scoring rubric on page 105 of the College Board's *The Official SAT Study Guide* and just imitate (almost copy) the features of the high-scoring sample essays from the *Study Guide*. In the coming pages, you'll see what really sets apart a high-scoring essay, and exactly how to construct one of your very own.

(While you should do your best to imitate high-scoring sample essays and copy their techniques, you should NEVER plagiarize ANYTHING, ever. I'm not suggesting that you recycle any passage from anyone else's work as your own. For one thing, since SAT Essay topics aren't repeated, it's unlikely that an exact passage from a high-scoring sample essay will help you much; more importantly, though, passing off another person's work as your own is one of the most intellectually reprehensible things anyone can do. So don't do it.)

---

[1] Michael Winerip, *New York Times*. "ON EDUCATION; SAT Essay Rewards Length And Ignores Errors Of Fact." 4 May 2005.

Unwritten Test Design Rules of the SAT Essay

Believe it or not, even essay tests have rules. You have to learn them if you want to do well. But be careful! The SAT Scoring Guide that appears on page 105 of the College Board Publication *The Official SAT Study Guide* isn't very useful if you're trying to figure out exactly what to do on the test.

It might sound strange to say this, but most of the College Board's advice on how to write the SAT essay is very, very bad, in the sense that many people who make an effort to follow it still end up with lower scores on the SAT Essay than they would like. Instead of following the rules that the College Board states explicitly, we'll do something much smarter—we'll figure out the rules that are implicitly revealed in the high- and low-scoring sample responses provided by the College Board in *The Official SAT Study Guide*. Remember that these are the rules revealed by actual high- and low-scoring sample essays released by the College Board. As such, they may be very different from the stated rules that you'll find on page 105, and elsewhere, in the College Board's Blue Book, the *Official SAT Study Guide*. Here are the real rules:

SAT Essay Rule 1: Open-Ended Prompts

The prompts that appear on the SAT Essay are all open-ended and fairly vague about what they want you to write. This gives you a wide degree of latitude in deciding which side of an argument to defend, and in supporting your position, which can be a good thing if you don't let it overwhelm you.

SAT Essay Rule 2: Talk About Whatever You Want

When you plan your answer, you don't have to worry about being politically correct or trying not to offend your reader. As an example, take a look at page 197 of the College Board publication *The Official SAT Study Guide*. You'll see a perfect-scoring essay that talks favorably about how the Confederate Army was "defending its way of life" during the Civil War when it fought to defend slavery.

Now, nobody is suggesting that you go out of your way to discuss something controversial or offensive. All I'm trying to point out is that there's no need to be worried that you might say the wrong thing. As the essay on page 197 demonstrates, the graders are interested in how well you develop an argument that answers the question in the prompt—they don't really care what the argument actually is.

SAT Essay Rule 3: Make Up Any Proof You Want

When you're looking for examples to support your argument, the SAT allows you to draw from anything at all. Some high-scoring essay-writers choose to draw examples from history and literature, but some of them draw examples from their own lives. In fact, the high-scoring essay on page 200 of *The Official SAT Study Guide* uses two personal examples that are almost certainly made up.

Many test-takers are surprised to learn that you don't get extra consideration for using more academic examples, but it makes sense if you put yourself in the College Board's shoes. The College Board is always nervous about being accused of elitism; if the SAT Essay rewarded historical and literary examples over personal ones, then people might complain that the scoring process was too heavily influenced by the quality of a test-taker's education rather than by innate writing ability. So the College Board accepts non-academic examples in an effort to avoid this kind of criticism.

It's also okay to make up facts, or to make mistakes in your presentation of historical or literary details if you decide to use academic examples. This isn't like a history test in school, where the teacher would probably take points off for historical inaccuracies in addition to poor writing. On the SAT Essay, the accuracy of the facts simply doesn't matter. (This is one of the things that Dr. Perelman was referring to when he complained that the test rewards the wrong things.) All that matters is that the examples you cite *would* support your thesis if they were true. Whether they actually *are* true is irrelevant.

Again, the reasoning behind this bizarre policy starts to make a little sense when we think about it from the College Board's standpoint. Since they have to standardize the grading of the essay, if they were going to penalize you for writing something false, they would have to fact-check every single statement in every single essay, which would take a ton of time and money, particularly since writers can cite personal examples. So the only real solution for the College Board is to avoid doing any kind of fact-checking at all. Instead, the graders are simply looking to determine whether your examples would support the thesis if they were true.

This means that the SAT Essay allows you to make up any facts you want, as long as they would support the thesis if they were true.

SAT Essay Rule 4: Some Imperfect Grammar Is Okay

The high-scoring essays that appear in *The Official SAT Study Guide* have many mistakes that would qualify as errors for the Identifying Sentence Errors portion of the Writing Section. For example, the high-scoring essay on page 120 of the College Board's book improperly shifts from the present tense to the past tense, uses the incorrect word *alright*, and incorrectly starts a sentence with the conjunction *however*. So you can get away with a few grammatical mistakes and still make a perfect score.

SAT Essay Rule 5: The Longer, The Better

All the high-scoring sample essays included in *The Official SAT Study Guide* are fairly long and well-developed, while the low-scoring sample essays are much shorter. But be careful—an essay's score seems to correlate with its length, but that doesn't mean that writing garbage just to fill up space is a good idea. What it means is that if you've written a short essay, your chances of scoring high seem to be just about zero.

For proof of this, check out the sample essay on page 210 of *The Official SAT Study Guide*. You'll notice that it's one of the better-written sample essays provided by the College Board, at least in terms of grammar, diction, and style, and that it does a better job of following the scoring guide on page 105 than the other sample essays do. You'll also notice that it received a 3 out of 6 because it's too short.

SAT Essay Rule 6: Vocabulary Isn't That Important

On page 105 of the Blue Book, the College Board says it looks for a "varied, accurate, and apt vocabulary" in high-scoring essays. But the essays that receive the highest possible scores demonstrate very little in the way of vocabulary skills. The biggest word in the sample high-scoring essay on page 120 is *dumbfounded*, and, as already mentioned, that essay also uses the non-word *alright*. The other high-scoring essays have similarly unimpressive vocabularies.

I often see essays in which test-takers have tried to use big words they didn't actually understand in an effort to impress the reader. But the reader truly doesn't care about your vocabulary; the reader only cares how well you support your position and how long the essay is, as we see from the grades that real essays get. Be aware, though, that poorly used vocabulary words can hurt you if the reader notices them. The safest way to avoid any potential difficulties is simply to stick to words you actually know, since trying to use words you're not certain of can't help, and might hurt.

SAT Essay Rule 7: There's No Set Format (But Use The 5-Paragraph One)

The high-scoring essays in *The Official SAT Study Guide* use a variety of formats. Some seem to use variations on the standard five-paragraph essay; all of them use an opening paragraph and a closing paragraph, both of varying lengths. So, in theory, just about any format seems acceptable.

Most of the top-scoring essays I've seen, though, have followed something similar to the 5-paragraph format: intro paragraph, three example paragraphs, conclusion paragraph. The number of example paragraphs might vary, and sometimes there isn't a conclusion paragraph, but in general the top-scoring essays seem to favor this 5-paragraph format. It's the format I use, and the one I advise all of my students to use.

SAT Essay Rule 8: Clearly State Your Thesis, Preferably In The First Sentence

Whether you use the 5-paragraph format or not (again, I highly recommend it), make sure you have a clearly stated thesis in the essay. One of the things that graders really seem to pay attention to is how well you support your position (which makes sense, right?). If they can't find a clearly articulated statement of your position right away, it becomes more difficult for them to tell if you did a good job of supporting that position. So make it easy on them and include a clear thesis.

I'd also recommend putting that thesis as the first sentence in your essay, even though that's not the common place for a thesis in the standard 5-paragraph essay format. For an example of an essay that does this, check out the essay on page 197 of *The Official SAT Study Guide* again. Note that the prompt asks, "Is deception ever justified?" The first sentence of the essay on 197, which got a perfect score, is "Deception is sometimes justified"—a clear statement of the thesis for the rest of the essay to support.

I think readers react well to a thesis in this position because it makes it very clear what you're trying to prove, which makes it easy for them to determine whether you go on to prove it or not. (Of course, in order to get a good score, you do need to support the thesis in the rest of the essay. Stating it clearly is just an important first step.)

Recommended Step-By-Step Approach to the SAT Essay

This process is an effective way to organize your thoughts and write a response that closely imitates known high-scoring essays. Feel free to use it or adapt it to fit the situation—but make sure any adaptations you make are still in line with the rules for the SAT Essay in this book.

1. Watch the clock from the beginning.

You only have 25 minutes to plan and write an essay. If you kill just 5 minutes day-dreaming or panicking, you've wasted twenty percent of your time! Do NOT let time get away from you here. Remember that it's crucial to fill as much of the given space as possible, because the single largest factor in your score will be the length of the essay. So plan to hit the ground running.

2. Develop a one-word response to the question.

Before you can write this essay, you have to know what you're going to be saying. It sounds simplistic, but you need to focus yourself before you can make effective, efficient use of your time.

This one-word answer will often simply be "yes," "no," or "maybe," but it could just as easily be anything else. Remember that there is no correct answer to an SAT Essay question—you can't get this step wrong. The goal is simply to focus your mind on the point you're trying to make in your essay.

3. Find or make up three facts that illustrate your position. Use personal experiences if you want.

Remember that the SAT scorers don't care whether the examples that illustrate your position are factually true or false, or whether they're academic or personal. All they care about is whether you can put together ANY example at all that would support your point.

So if you decide to make these examples up out of thin air, then be sure the relationship between the examples and your position is clear and direct. Don't invent an example that's only vaguely related to your answer. This is a blank check—come up with something relevant. It will make your score higher, and make the rest of your writing easier.

In general, test-takers seem to have an easier time using personal examples than academic ones. But if academic examples are what come to mind more naturally for you, then feel free to use them—just make sure they're relevant (if they're not, feel free to change the facts until they are).

4. Begin your essay with a one-sentence statement of your answer to the prompt.

The SAT scorers aren't big on subtlety. Start your essay with a flat statement of the point you intend to prove. (For examples of top-scoring essays that did this, see pages 123, 197, and 200 of the College Board book *The Official SAT Study Guide*.) Refer to your one-word answer in Step 2 if you've forgotten what you were trying to say.

5. Fill in a sentence or two that relate to your thesis.

At this point, we're really just trying to add some length to the essay. If you know what your examples are likely to be, then feel free to refer to them. If you're not so sure, then just expand on the thesis a little.

6. Finish the first paragraph with a sentence that gives a strong introduction to your examples.

Make the last sentence in the first paragraph a simple transitional sentence that introduces the examples you thought of in Step 3. To finish the imaginary first paragraph that we started in Step 6, we might write a sentence like

Three episodes from my personal experience serve as compelling examples of this fact.

See? Nothing too fancy. At this point, you're finished with the first paragraph—the groundwork has been done, and the hardest part of the essay is behind you!

7. Begin the second paragraph with a general statement that introduces your first example.

This first sentence of the second paragraph serves to introduce your first example. Make it something general. See the sample essay on page 200 of the College Board publication *The Official SAT Study Guide* for an example—the first sentence of its second paragraph is *Sometimes deception occurs in the form of white lies*, and then the rest of the first paragraph is a (probably made-up) example from the author's life in which deception took the form of a white lie.

8. In 3-5 sentences, tell the story that goes with your first example.

In the middle of the second paragraph you'll insert the story that goes with your first example. Don't draw any lessons or anything at this point—just set the stage and explain what happened. Make sure the story is clearly relevant to the thesis.

9. Use a sentence or two to relate the story of your first example to the thesis.

Now that you've told the story, you need to re-connect it to the first sentence you wrote so you can close out this paragraph and move on. So write one or two sentences in which you point out the way the examples demonstrate the thesis—and make sure it really relates to the first sentence in your essay!

10. Repeat these steps for the third paragraph with your second example.

The first example is out of the way. Now you'll just go through the second example in the same way, and that will provide your third paragraph.

11. Repeat the steps for the fourth paragraph with your third example.

Remember, we're just cranking out paragraphs that illustrate our main point. Don't forget to relate everything back to the main point at the end.

12. Begin the final paragraph with a sentence that relates all of your examples back to the thesis.

At this point you're starting to close the essay, so you want to wrap everything up. The first sentence of your last paragraph is going to put your three examples back into the context of the main point you're trying to make.

13. Finish the essay with a sentence that rephrases the first sentence in the essay.

The last thing that remains is to cap off your essay with a sentence that re-establishes the main point of your essay. Of course, you probably don't want to use the exact same wording that you used in Step 4, but you do want to make roughly the same point with this sentence that you made in Step 4.

Conclusion

Believe it or not, this simple process will help you crank out winning essays with just a little bit of practice. You'll notice that it doesn't give you much room to be creative, but creativity isn't the point. All we want is a reliable, predictable way to get a top score every time.

You've probably also noticed that this formula is very repetitive—it restates the main point of the essay often. Don't let that bother you. The readers go through your essays so quickly that they won't even notice you banging them over the head with the same point. And besides, as the high-scoring sample essays in the Blue Book demonstrate, this is the way the SAT rewards you for writing anyway.

Now that you've seen that the SAT Essay doesn't reward the same kind of writing that you're expected to do in school, let's take a look at the multiple-choice questions on the Writing section. You'll see that they don't necessarily reward the same things that your teachers in school reward, just as the type of essay-writing you do for high school also turned out to be bad for the SAT. In fact, this is a common theme that you'll observe in all question types as we proceed.

An Analysis Of Top-Scoring SAT Essays From The Blue Book

Since there are many ways to write the SAT Essay while still respecting the correct rules and patterns, I think one of the best ways that we can see what a top-scoring SAT Essay really does is to analyze the four SAT Essays in the Blue Book that are provided as examples of the "perfect" SAT Essay. The Blue Book lists the scores for these essays out of 6 points, so a 6-out-of-6 corresponds to a perfect 12 on the real SAT. These essays appear on pages 120, 123, 197, and 200 in the Blue Book.

The Essay From Page 120 Of The Blue Book

Length

This essay is provided with the original handwriting, and it takes up all of both pages, which is typical for an SAT Essay that receives a score of 6 out of 6 (or 12 out of 12).

Thesis

There is no real thesis statement in this essay, with the arguable exception of the last two sentences in the entire essay ("So is perfectionism a vice or a virtue? It depends on whom you are talking to"). This is very abnormal for an SAT Essay that makes a perfect score. It shows that SAT Essays can succeed without having a thesis statement clearly articulated in the first paragraph, even though a typical top-scoring SAT Essay would normally have a clear thesis statement, as we'll see in a moment.

Structure

This essay has no real structure, which is also abnormal for a top-scoring SAT Essay. Most of them use a variation of the 5-paragraph format as I explained earlier, but this essay demonstrates that it's possible to score high with a loose narrative structure. The other "perfect" essays in the Blue Book use something closer to the classic 5-paragraph format.

Type of examples

The examples in this essay are purely personal, and might even be made up. This is something we regularly see in top-scoring SAT Essays.

Vocabulary

All of the words in this essay are used appropriately, which is normal in a top-scoring SAT Essay. The words are fairly basic, which is also normal in a top-scoring SAT Essay. The only long words in the essay are "dumbfounded" and "perfectionism," which aren't very advanced.

Grammar

The grammar in this essay is okay but not great, with several noticeable mistakes, including the use of "which" instead of "that," switching from "one" to "his or her" in a sentence, and incorrectly using an apostrophe in a word that's not a possessive or a contraction, among other things. It's very normal to see that top-scoring SAT Essays occasionally have a few mistakes like this.

The Essay From Page 123 Of The Blue Book

Length

This essay is presented in a standardized handwriting font, so we can't see exactly how long it was in the actual test booklet. But we can compare it to the other essays in the Blue Book and see that it's among the longest in there, which suggests that it probably filled up most or all of the allotted two pages when it was hand-written on test day.

Thesis

The first sentence in this essay is a direct reaction to the prompt, and a clear thesis statement that the rest of the essay will support. This is the way that I recommend you begin your own SAT Essay, because a large percentage of the top-scoring SAT Essays I've seen have used this kind of opening.

Structure

This essay uses what we might call a modified 5-paragraph format. It includes very obvious introductory and concluding paragraphs, but the four paragraphs in the middle provide an extended historical example with a lot of "howevers" in them, rather than providing a series of unrelated examples. Overall, it's fairly typical for what we'll see from top-scoring SAT Essays, though the example paragraphs in other top-scoring essays tend to be unrelated to one another.

Type of examples

As I just noted, this essay uses an extended analysis of a single historical event. It's common to see top-scoring SAT Essays draw their examples from history, but a large portion of top-scoring SAT Essays also draw their examples from other types of sources.

Vocabulary

The words in this essay are very well-chosen and perhaps a little more advanced than they will tend to be in most top-scoring SAT Essays. Still, the only noticeably advanced words in the essay are probably "embryo" and "ameliorated."

Grammar

For the most part, the grammar in the essay is quite sound. There are a couple of missing commas, but nothing major. Like the vocabulary, the grammar is probably slightly above-average relative to most other SAT Essays that would score a 6 out of 6.

The Essay From Page 197 Of The Blue Book

Length

This essay is provided in the original handwriting, so we can see that it takes up both pages available in the test booklet. This is typical for top-scoring SAT Essays.

Thesis

The first sentence of the essay is a direct response to the prompt and also a clear thesis for the rest of the essay. This is very common in SAT Essays that score a 6 out of 6.

Structure

This essay uses a slight variation on the typical 5-paragraph format that we'll find in most top-scoring SAT Essays, because it only uses two example paragraphs instead of three. Remember that the number and type of examples don't really matter; all that matters is that the examples are relevant and that the essay takes up both pages.

Type of examples

Two examples are included—one historical, and one literary. This is a common thing to see in top-scoring SAT Essays, though we also see plenty of top-scoring SAT Essays that avoid historical or literary examples. There's also a one-sentence mention of Enron in the last paragraph, but it's so short I wouldn't be surprised if the graders didn't even see it.

Vocabulary

The vocabulary in this essay is pretty unremarkable, with the possible exception of the words "protagonist" and "mendacity."

Grammar

The sentences in this essay are fairly simple and straightforward. This is typical for top-scoring SAT Essays: nothing remarkable in terms of grammar or sentence structure, but the sentences are generally well-executed.

The Essay From Page 200 Of The Blue Book

Length

The essay is presented in a standardized handwriting font, so we can't see exactly how much of the two pages in the test booklet it would have taken up. But if we compare it to other essays in the Blue Book we can see that it's pretty long compared to them, which is a rule for scoring high on the SAT Essay.

Thesis

The first sentence of the entire essay is its thesis, but this thesis is a little bit more grammatically complex than many of the thesis statements we'll see in top-scoring SAT Essays.

Structure

This essay uses a structure that's closer to the classic 5-paragraph structure typical of many top-scoring SAT Essays: introduction paragraph, three example paragraphs, and conclusion paragraph. In this case, the last example paragraph is more of a list of hypotheticals than a single episode.

Type of examples

The examples in this essay are all personal, and sound like they might also have been made up. Remember that the SAT Essay-graders don't care if your examples are academic or personal, or even if they're factually accurate. All the graders care about is whether your examples would support your thesis if they were true.

Vocabulary

The wording is pretty basic, but everything is used properly. This is typical for top-scoring SAT Essays.

Grammar

The last sentence of the essay is grammatically incorrect (the word "a" needs to be removed), but otherwise the essay is free of errors. It's normal to see an SAT Essay receive a perfect score like this one did even if it contains a couple of small grammatical mistakes.

Conclusion

We've just analyzed the four SAT Essays from the Blue Book that each scored 6 out of 6 (which is the same as a perfect 12 on the rest test). These examples make it clear that most SAT Essay-writing advice out there has no basis in reality, and they show us what actually works instead. The only consistent feature in all top-scoring SAT Essays is their length. Essays that use personal examples can make perfect scores, just like essays with more academic examples. The basic 5-paragraph format, or some variation of it, will be found in most top-scoring SAT Essays, but isn't strictly necessary. Top-scoring essays typically don't demonstrate advanced vocabularies or flawless grammar.

So the next time somebody tries to tell you differently (and people will), have them look at the actual top-scoring essays in the Blue Book :)

SAT Essay Quick Summary

This is a one-page summary of the major relevant concepts. Use it to evaluate your comprehension or jog your memory. For a more in-depth explanation, see the rest of the section.

The Big Secret: The SAT Essay isn't graded like a school essay, and shouldn't be written like one.

State your position on the prompt clearly, and support it with three examples.

Factual accuracy doesn't matter, as long as your examples would support your thesis if they were true.

Personal, historical, and literary examples are all equally valid. Go with what's easiest for you.

Some imperfect grammar is okay. Showing off your vocabulary won't help. Just say what you mean.

Length is the most important thing. Plan on 1.5 pages at a bare minimum. Closer to 2 is best.

Format:

There's no set format you must follow to get a good score, but I find it's best to stick to the standard 5-paragraph format: intro, 3 example paragraphs, conclusion. Since it's familiar, structured, and repetitive, it will be easy to write in the time allotted, and it will be easy for the grader to read and understand quickly.

Remember that you're not trying to stand out and write a 'special' essay. You want to write one that's just like all the other high-scoring essays, so the grader can quickly read it, recognize that it's a good essay, give you a good score, and then move on.

Here's the process:

1. Read the prompt and quickly pick a side.
2. Intro paragraph: Start your essay with a simple thesis statement, just a clear and direct response to the prompt. Briefly mention your three supporting examples. Restate your answer to the prompt in a sentence or two. Pad out the first paragraph (which is a more polite way of saying "BS it").
3. 1st example paragraph: In a few sentences, explain your first example. Finish the paragraph with a sentence or two relating this example back to the first sentence of the essay.
4. 2nd example paragraph: Repeat the previous step with your second example.
5. 3rd example paragraph: Repeat the previous step with your third example.
6. Conclusion: Start with a sentence or two relating all your examples back to the first sentence of your essay. Finish by rephrasing the first sentence of the essay. Pad this out, too ;)

As I said, this is not the only possible way to get a high score on your essay, but in my experience it's the easiest and most reliable. Just make sure it's long, and your examples support your position.

There's probably no need to plan your essay, since you can make up whatever examples you want anyway. A lot of people don't plan at all. They just make up each example as they come to it, and use the time they save so they can write more, because length is the primary indicator of the score.

Refer to the example essays in the Blue Book to see what high-scoring essays look like.

SAT Writing Multiple Choice

"The greater part of the world's troubles are due to questions of grammar."
- Michel de Montaigne

Overview and Important Reminders for SAT Writing Multiple-Choice

The remaining three SAT question types are all part of the Writing Section of the SAT. We'll get into the specifics of each question type in a minute, but first we need to clear up a few misconceptions that often keep people from doing as well on SAT Writing as they could.

Let's get started.

The Big Secret(s) Of SAT Writing Multiple-Choice Questions

There are a lot of important things about this part of the SAT that you probably don't know. We'll start with the biggest one, which is that you may not even need to worry about the SAT Writing section at all.

Many Schools And Scholarship Programs Don't Even Consider The Writing Section

The Writing section is a relative new-comer to the SAT, since it was only added to the test in 2005. (It has existed on the PSAT for longer than it has on the SAT, and there used to be an SAT Subject Test in Writing, but the Writing section as we know it on the SAT 1 has only existed since 2005.)

Many schools don't like the SAT Writing section for a couple of reasons. The SAT Essay is widely thought to be a terrible measurement of writing ability, for one thing. And we also have to remember that the entire point of the SAT is to allow colleges to make meaningful comparisons among current applicants and the applicants from previous years; since colleges only have a few years of data from the Writing section, as opposed to decades of data for the other two sections, many schools trust the Writing scores a lot less than they trust the other two scores.

With each passing year, it stands to reason that more and more colleges will start to feel comfortable enough to trust the Writing section. Even now, it's definitely trusted a lot more than it was when it debuted in 2005. Still, between the section's relatively poor design (which we'll talk about in the rest of this section) and the relative lack of historical data, I would expect that there will be plenty of schools that ignore the SAT Writing section for the foreseeable future.

If you're wondering whether your target schools care about the Writing section, the best thing you can do is track down their admissions statistics on the Internet, or even call up the admissions office of each school and ask directly if they consider the SAT Writing section. You can do the same thing for any SAT-based scholarships you might be competing for. If it turns out that none of your target schools or programs cares about this part of the test, then you can focus even more intently on raising your scores in the other sections, and leave this part of the test alone.

Generally speaking, the larger state schools seem to be the ones that place less emphasis on the Writing section, though there are plenty of more selective private schools that also say they don't care about it very much. And, just anecdotally, I can tell you that I've been called on by prestigious admissions consultants to help students raise their Reading and Math scores in a last-ditch effort to get them up before an application deadline, but no admissions professional has ever asked me to do that for a client's Writing score, even when the client's Writing score was only average.

Again, these things can change from year to year and from school to school, so you should always verify on your own whether your target schools will care about your Writing score. I just want you to be aware that many seem not to.

The SAT Writing Section Doesn't Always Reflect The Way Anyone Actually Speaks

The approach that most people take to the Writing section is to trust the way a sentence sounds to them. If they think it sounds like something they would say, they're happy. If not, they try to find a way to change it that would bring it more in line with how they talk.

The problem with this should be obvious if you've been reading this book straight through from the beginning: the SAT doesn't do much of anything the way regular people do it.

So we'll find a bunch of arbitrary rules and patterns on the Writing section, just as we do on the other two sections. (Remember that being "arbitrary" isn't the same thing as being "unpredictable" or "pointless." When I say the rules are arbitrary, I mean that the College Board had to make some arbitrary decisions in setting up the rules that the Writing section would follow. But the rules are totally predictable and consistent from one test date to the next. They're just not always based on the way educated people actually speak or write.)

For example, as we'll see in a few pages, the College Board wouldn't be okay with a sentence like this:

They said it was going to rain today.

This is a totally normal English sentence, but it breaks a certain SAT rule about the use of the pronouns "it" and "they." I'll cover that rule when we talk about Identifying Sentence Errors questions.

This next sentence would also not be acceptable on the SAT Writing section, even though it's a perfectly grammatical English sentence:

My house is much bigger than John.

That sentence would break the SAT's unwritten rule about comparisons needing to be made between similar things. Again, we'll talk about that rule when we discuss the Identifying Sentence Errors questions.

For now, I just want to make it clear that there are specific test-design principles that SAT Writing questions must always follow, and those principles don't always line up with our natural instincts as speakers of English.

And this talk of different question types brings me to my next big secret.

There Are Two Different Standards For Correct Sentences On The SAT Writing Section

Most test-takers assume that every question on the SAT Writing section follows the same standards. But this is not the case.

There are two major types of multiple-choice questions on the Writing section of the SAT: the Identifying Sentence Errors questions, which are numbers 12 through 29 on the large Writing sub-section in each SAT, and the Improving Sentences questions, which are numbers 1 through 11 on the large Writing sub-section and numbers 1 through 14 on the short sub-section at the end of the test. (There's also a third question type that is basically a hodgepodge of the other two, with some ideas from the Passage-Based Reading questions thrown in as well. Those are the Improving Paragraphs questions, and they run from numbers 30 to 35 on the large Writing sub-section.)

The Identifying Sentence Errors questions only test your knowledge of the rules of SAT grammar. They test things like subject-verb agreement, the correct formation of irregular verb tenses, making sure you use "nor" with "neither," and so on. But they *don't* test the "awkwardness" of a sentence at all.

In other words, they only test whether the strict rules of grammar are being followed in the sentence; they don't test whether the sentence could be expressed in a more pleasing way apart from its grammatical mistakes.

The Improving Sentences questions, on the other hand, *do* reward you for creating a sentence that is both grammatically acceptable and as pleasing to the College Board's ear as possible. This means you will sometimes see Improving Sentences questions with more than one grammatically acceptable answer choice, and your job will be to choose the grammatically acceptable choice that also does the best job of following the SAT's style guidelines. (These style guidelines are never spelled out by the SAT, but I've figured them out by looking at a whole bunch of real questions from the College Board and looking for patterns over the years. I'll share them with you when we get to our discussion of the Improving Sentences questions a little later.)

So the Identifying Sentence Error questions are purely about SAT grammar, while the Improving Sentences questions combine SAT grammar and SAT style.

This means that some phrases that would be acceptable in correctly phrased Identifying Sentence Error questions are incorrect for the Improving Sentences questions. This can happen if the phrase is grammatically correct but still "awkward" in the eyes of the College Board.

Conclusion

Now that we've talked about some of the most important parts of the SAT Writing section that come as a surprise to most people, I'd like to explain how I think you should try to improve your score on this section. In some ways it's a little different from what I recommend you do on the other two sections.

How To Improve Your Score On The Writing Section

Most people try to improve on the Writing section by memorizing a lot of grammatical rules and then looking for opportunities to apply them to the test.

This doesn't work, for reasons we just discussed. For one thing, the rules of "SAT grammar" aren't always the same as the normal rules of grammar that you might learn from an English teacher or find on the Internet. For another thing, we have to keep in mind that different question types on the Writing section reward different things: some are only concerned with SAT grammar, while others rely on SAT grammar and SAT style together.

So I usually advise my students to learn what the SAT rewards on the Writing section by becoming very familiar with real SAT Writing questions written by the College Board, which we can find in the Blue Book. If you work with those real questions and pay attention to the principles of SAT grammar and style that I share with you in this book, you'll quickly develop strong instincts about what the College Board rewards and punishes on this part of the test.

I used the word "instinct" in that last sentence very deliberately, because over the years I've seen that most test-takers aren't very familiar with formal English grammar. This is especially true for native speakers of American English, because most American schools don't teach grammar. For most American students, the only grammar they've ever formally studied is the grammar of the foreign language they take, and that grammar may not bear much resemblance to English grammar.

I don't think it's important to develop any technical knowledge of the names of different parts of speech, different semantic roles, and so on. The Writing section is different from the Math section in this regard. The Math section will use technical math words like "hypotenuse" or "integer" in its questions, so you need to know those words if you want to score high. But the Writing section never asks you to identify a helping verb or subordinating conjunction by name, so we don't actually have to know any of that jargon to be able to identify correct answers consistently.

In other words, if you can tell that a particular phrase on the Writing section is something that the College Board won't like, because similar phrases have always been wrong in the questions you've analyzed in the past, then it doesn't matter what label you would put on the mistake.

As an example, I often work with students who use the word "parallelism" to refer to a wide variety of situations—everything from normal subject-verb agreement (which isn't really an instance of parallelism) to a properly formed corollary conjunction (which is kind-of-maybe parallelism). But as long as their understanding of parallelism lets them answer questions correctly, nothing else matters as far as the SAT is concerned.

Conclusion

Instead of trying to learn formal English grammar, I would advise you to try to develop the right instincts for this section, without worrying about identifying and classifying different types of phrases.

You can develop those instincts by reading the rest of this section, paying attention to the rules and patterns I explain, and to the sample solutions I provide. If you take those things to heart and then try your hand at some practice questions from the Blue Book on your own, you should see improvement. The more questions you encounter and the more you practice implementing the ideas in this book, the higher your score will go.

Of course, if you would like a formal explanation of SAT grammar that uses words like "gerund" and "copular," you can find my Writing Toolbox as an appendix at the end of this book. It gives you a formal explanation of all the points of SAT grammar. But you'll probably find that you don't need it.

Now let's dive into the question types on the Writing section in more detail. We'll start with the Identifying Sentence Error questions.

Overview and Important Reminders for Identifying Sentence Errors On The SAT

Like the rest of the Writing questions, the Identifying Sentence Errors questions on the SAT test a limited number of concepts over and over. But, as I mentioned earlier, these questions are purely about SAT grammar, with no consideration of style. These questions are also unique in that they don't ask you to rephrase anything—they're only interested in your ability to identify bad SAT grammar. You don't have to worry about fixing any of the problems you see.

Each of these questions will present you with a single sentence. Several of the words and phrases in the sentence will be underlined. Your job is to find the part of the sentence that contains an error according to the SAT's idea of grammar. If any one of the underlined portions of the sentence contains something that the SAT considers to be bad grammar, you're going to mark it as the correct answer choice. If nothing is grammatically wrong with the sentence according to the College Board's rules of grammar, you'll mark (E).

You'll find that the same handful of issues accounts for a majority of the question. Things will start to seem very repetitive after you practice a little bit. So let's get started!

Unwritten Test Design Rules of Identifying Sentence Errors on the SAT

There are only a few rules for these questions that are worth pointing out, but they're very important, so don't forget them!

SAT Identifying Sentence Errors Rule 1: No Style Points

For these questions, you should think ONLY about grammar—don't worry about style at all. *That means you can't mark an answer choice just because you have a vague notion that there might be a better way to say it!* Actually, there often IS a better way to say most of the things that appear in these questions, but your job is still only to find the things that are clearly grammatically wrong as far as the SAT is concerned.

SAT Identifying Sentence Errors Rule 2: No Deletions Except In Rare Cases Of Redundancy

Sometimes you may be tempted to mark an answer choice because you think it should be deleted entirely.

You can't just delete phrases because you don't like them, though. You can only choose to delete an entire underlined phrase when the phrase is redundant. There aren't usually a lot of questions that test redundancy—in the entire second edition of the College Board Blue Book, there's only a handful of questions that test it. One of them is question 29 on page 535, which is discussed later in this book.

Let me repeat that, because it's important: you can't just mark an answer choice on this part of the test because you think it sounds weird. You can only mark it if you think it's breaking an actual rule of SAT grammar.

SAT Identifying Sentence Errors Rule 3: "He," "She," "It," And "They" Must Always Be Replaceable Within A Sentence

If the College Board uses the words "he," "she," "it," or "they" (or any form of those words, like "its" or "them"), then there MUST be a noun somewhere else in the sentence that indicates what that pronoun is referring to.

This rule might sound like it's not that important, but students often choose wrong answers when they forget about it, because this rule actually means that *many common English expressions would be wrong on the SAT.*

Whenever you see the word "it," there must be a phrase somewhere in the sentence that could be plugged in *exactly* in place of the word "it" in order to make the sentence work. For instance, this sentence would be fine:

This book says it was printed in 1934.

In that sentence, the phrase "this book" could be plugged in exactly where the word "it" is, and the sentence would still make perfect sense:

This book says this book was printed in 1934.

Similarly, if you have the word "they" in a sentence, there must be a plural phrase somewhere in the sentence that could be plugged in where the word "they" is. So this would be okay:

The dogs whimpered because they were hungry.

This works on the SAT because we could plug "the dogs" in where "they" is:

The dogs whimpered because the dogs were hungry.

But, as I mentioned earlier, the following sentence would NOT be okay on the SAT, even though it's a normal English sentence:

*They said it would rain today.

There are no words or phrases in this sentence that could be plugged in directly for the words "they" and "it," so the College Board would call this a grammatically incorrect sentence.

Make sure you keep this rule in mind, because test-takers forget it all the time. If you see the word "they" or the word "it" underlined, you have to make sure there's a phrase somewhere in the sentence that can be plugged in exactly for that word. If there's not, then the College Board will say the usage is incorrect.

SAT Identifying Sentence Errors Rule 4: Verb Tenses Can Only Be Wrong If They're Formed Wrong, Or If They're Impossible

It's possible for the tense of a verb to be grammatically incorrect on the SAT Writing section, but only in two situations.

- The verb is conjugated incorrectly.
- The verb creates an impossible situation when combined with other verbs in the sentence.

Let's talk about incorrect conjugations first. Basically, you have to be on the lookout for sentences like this:

*My neighbor forgived me for being so loud.

In that case, the irregular verb "forgive" should have been used in its proper past-tense form, which is "forgave."

The other way a verb can be incorrect is when it creates an impossible situation in the context of other verbs in the same sentence.

Here's what I mean by that. Each of these sentences has an acceptable verb tense by itself, because there are no other verbs in the sentence that could possibly interfere:

The tree fell over.

Lightning will strike the tree.

But this next sentence would be incorrect on the SAT Writing section, because it combines two verbs with two different tenses in an impossible way:

*The tree fell over when lightning will strike it.

The problem here is that the word "when" indicates that the two events in the sentence happened at the same time, but the word "fall" is in the past and the phrase "will strike" is in the future. Two events can't happen at the same time if one of them was in the past and one of them will be in the future.

So unless a sentence contains a poorly formed conjugation or some kind of impossibility, then the verb tense in the sentence can't be wrong.

SAT Identifying Sentence Errors Rule 5: You Can Only Compare Similar Things, And Only In Similar Phrases

The multiple-choice questions on the SAT Writing section will only allow you to make comparisons between things of the same kind, and the ideas being compared need to be stated in similar ways.

Let's start by talking about the first half of that rule: the idea that the SAT only lets us make comparisons between similar concepts.

For example, we're not allowed to choose a sentence like this on the SAT:

My house is bigger than John.

Even though this is a perfectly grammatical and logical sentence (because a house is typically bigger than a person), it would be incorrect on the multiple-choice portion of the SAT Writing section because it compares two things of different types. On this part of the test, we'd be allowed to compare a house to another house, or we could compare a person to a person, but we can't compare a house to a person. So either of these sentences would be okay:

I am bigger than John.

My house is bigger than John's house.

This means that you always need to be alert when two things are compared, so you can make sure they're two things of the same type.

Now let's talk about the second half of this rule, which is the idea that the things being compared need to be phrased in similar ways (many students refer to this as "parallelism").

So, for instance, this would be an incorrect sentence on the SAT:

There are more people living in Germany than Hawaii.

The College Board wouldn't like that because "Germany" has the word "in" before it, but "Hawaii" doesn't. So this would be one way to fix that problem:

There are more people living in Germany than in Hawaii.

By the way, you can often recognize that these issues might be relevant to a sentence when you see words like "more," "less," "than," or "as" in the sentence, or words that end in -er, like this:

I am bigger <u>than</u> John.

I am <u>as</u> big <u>as</u> John.

SAT Identifying Sentence Errors Rule 6: The SAT Tests Prepositional Idioms, But Rarely

The word "idiom" is used incorrectly by a lot of SAT tutors and websites to explain solutions to multiple-choice questions on the SAT Writing section. In fact, the College Board itself even misuses the word on its website to describe phrases that aren't idioms.

Let me explain, because knowing what an idiom actually is will come in handy if you decide to go online for help with this part of the test (which is something I don't recommend, but people do it anyway). Technically, an idiom is a phrase that doesn't follow the broad rules of a language. It's a phrase that you can only know and understand if you've encountered it before. But if you look at the College Board's own explanations for SAT Writing questions on its SAT Question Of The Day web site, you'll see that the College Board uses the word "idiomatic" to refer to almost any phrase it deems correct, even when that phrase follows rules that other phrases also follow. Which is just one more reason not to pay too much attention to the College Board's explanations of SAT questions.

The reason I mention this is that the SAT does occasionally test your knowledge of idioms that involve prepositions. On average, you'll see these kinds of questions a couple of times per test.

A prepositional idiom is a phrase that includes a particular preposition for no reason other than the fact that native speakers always use that phrase with that particular preposition. (A preposition is a short word like "in," "on," "to," or "from." For a full explanation of what a preposition is, see the Writing Toolbox in the appendix.)

For instance, it's appropriate to say, "I listen <u>to</u> music," but not to say "I listen <u>towards</u> music" or "I listen <u>at</u> music." The preposition "to" is okay in that phrase, but the prepositions "towards" and "at" are not. We would call this phrase an idiom because there's no general rule about the words "towards," "to," and "listen" that would have told us beforehand that "listen to" is okay but "listen towards" is not.

Contrast this situation with a rule-governed process like a verb conjugation. When we conjugate a verb, we know that there are broad rules that are applied to different classes of verbs to generate verb forms with predictable endings. The College Board (along with other sources) sometimes refers to a correctly conjugated regular verb as "idiomatic," but such situations don't involve idioms at all; they involve rules. Keep this in mind if you decide to read the College Board's explanations for some SAT Writing questions, or you might accidentally end up thinking that almost every question involves an unpredictable idiom.

But let's get back to our prepositional idioms like "listen to." A few times per test, the College Board may include a Writing question with an underlined preposition, and the underlined preposition may be inappropriate because it doesn't fit with an idiom that the College Board thinks you should know.

So you should be aware that these types of mistakes can appear on the test as errors that you need to correct. The rough part for us test-takers is that there are thousands and thousands of prepositional idioms, so you can't really try to memorize them all—and even if you wanted to, I have no idea where you would find a complete list of them.

But the good news is that you don't have to worry about the prepositions on every single question, because there can only be one error per question, and in many cases you'll realize there's some other error in the sentence that has nothing to do with any prepositions. You only need to pay attention to underlined prepositions if you can't find any other errors in a sentence.

In that case, if a preposition feels a little weird to you, then you may want to mark it as the error for the sentence. As you practice, keep track of how accurate your instincts are with these prepositional idioms. Some people are very good at noticing them, and some aren't. If you're not, then you may want to err on the side of choosing (E) or omitting questions when you're not sure if a preposition is incorrect.

As I mentioned before, there won't be more than a few questions like this, at most, on any given test. So the damage from these questions will be limited, even if you never answer a single one correctly. But that only makes it all the more important that you focus on every question and make sure you don't make any "careless" mistakes on other questions.

SAT Identifying Sentence Errors Rule 7: No Substitute For "And"

The College Board never lets you substitute a phrase like "in addition to" or "as well as" for the word "and." So if you're looking at an answer choice that says something like "I like pizza, hot dogs, as well as sushi," that choice is wrong on the SAT, because the SAT wants you to use the word "and" instead of "as well as."

Hidden Test Design Patterns of Identifying Sentence Errors on the SAT

Just like every other question on the SAT, the Identifying Sentence Errors questions have patterns that will make it easier to find the right answer. Here they are:

Hidden Pattern 1: The Intervening Phrase

Very often on these questions, you'll see that a descriptive phrase comes between a noun and its verb. Instead of agreeing with the correct word, the verb might incorrectly agree with something in the descriptive phrase. A lot of students miss these questions because the verb does agree with the noun that's closest to it—the issue is that it doesn't matter how close together two words are in a sentence. Never forget that a verb has to agree with the thing that's actually doing the action.

Consider the following sentence, for example:

This list of names takes a long time to read.

The intervening phrase here is "of names," and the word "takes" agrees with "list," so that the core part of the sentence would be "This list takes." The phrase "of names" is just a way to describe the list. So it would be wrong to say it this way:

*This <u>list</u> of names <u>take</u> a long time to read.

Because then you'd be making "take" agree with "names," as though the core of the sentence were something like "names take."

Here's another sentence where the intervening phrase is longer:

Our neighbor from across the street with the loud dogs who spend all night barking wants to know if we can watch her house while she's away.

The core of this sentence is "neighbor wants," but the phrase "from across the street with the loud dogs who spend all night barking" is inserted between the words "neighbor" and "wants." It would have been wrong to write the sentence this way:

*Our <u>neighbor</u> from across the street with the loud dogs who spend all night barking <u>want</u> to know if we can watch her house while she's away.

So when you read a sentence on the SAT Writing section, ignore these intervening phrases and focus on the core relationship in the sentence to make sure the appropriate words agree with one another. We'll see several examples of this in a few pages when we look at solutions to real Blue Book questions.

(I realize this might be considered a grammatical rule—in fact, I even talk about it in the Writing Toolbox in the appendix. But it's so important, and it comes up so often on these questions, that I thought it was worth mentioning separately here.)

Hidden Pattern 2: Singular vs Plural

By far, the largest broad issue that comes up on the Writing section is the distinction between the singular and plural forms of different kinds of words. This can come up in a lot of ways, and you should learn to keep a sharp eye out for all of them. The example I gave in Hidden Pattern 1 involved the singular and plural forms of a verb, but you might also see the singular word "it" used incorrectly to refer to a plural noun. You might even see an incorrect sentence that says something like, "My brother and my sister both want to be a dentist," when the correct version would be "My brother and my sister both want to be dentists," since two people can't become a single dentist.

So keep your eyes open for these singular/plural mismatches. They're all over the Writing section, and they can show up in a variety of ways.

Hidden Pattern 3: The Last Few Sentences Will Be Convoluted

The last few questions in the Identifying Sentence Errors section will involve the same kinds of issues that appear in the other Identifying Sentence Errors questions, but the word-order of these last few sentences is often pretty odd. So it's important to pay careful attention to the relationships among nouns, adjectives, verbs, and the other parts of speech, to make sure that you're not missing anything just because the words are in a bizarre order. When you're checking out a sentence to see if a word or phrase is in the proper form, remember that you have to look both before and after the underlined phrase, because subjects might appear after verbs, or antecedents might appear after pronouns, and so on. (This is true for every sentence on the SAT Writing section, but it comes up most often on questions 25 - 29 of the big Writing sub-section.)

The Recommended Step-By-Step Approach For SAT Identifying Sentence Errors

This is the process I recommend you follow when you're attacking SAT Identifying Sentence Errors questions.

1. Read the entire prompt sentence.

You need to be able to place the underlined portions of the sentence in their proper context, so you have to read the entire sentence before you do anything else.

2. Focus on the underlined portions of the prompt sentence.

Remember that only the underlined portions of the text can have something wrong with them—and, on top of that, only ONE underlined portion per sentence can be wrong. Remember, too, that we're not just looking for phrases that you would change if you could, just to make things sound better in your opinion; we're looking for phrases that specifically violate the College Board's grammar rules.

3. Think about how each underlined word relates to the other words in the sentence. Consider drawing lines from each underlined word to the other words it is related to, if that helps you keep track.

This step will help you see the relationships among the various parts of the sentence. For example, if the pronoun "she" appears in an underlined portion of the sentence, you could draw a line connecting the word "she" with the noun that it's referring to. Then draw another line connecting "she" with the verb that goes with it. If you want, you can use the basic grammatical concepts outlined in the appendix to see which words in a sentence are related to each other—for example, a pronoun is related to the noun (or nouns) that it stands for, and a verb is related to its subject. On the other hand, you can probably develop an instinct for these relationships just by reviewing and digesting the sample solutions in this Black Book.

4. Look for a word that doesn't fit properly with the words it is supposed to be related to.

Now that we've identified all the relationships between underlined and non-underlined words in the sentence, we check all those relationships to find the one relationship where a word doesn't fit the words it should be related to. For example, if the singular pronoun "she" is supposed to go with the underlined word "were," then we know that "were" needs to be "was."

5. Consider that there may be nothing wrong with the sentence.

Remember that not every sentence will contain an error. If you've considered all the underlined portions of the sentence and you haven't found one that has an error, then mark (E) and go on to the next question.

Don't forget that (E) will be the right answer as frequently, or infrequently, as it would in any other section; the SAT distributes correct answers randomly in every section. For more on that, see the discussion of SAT Misconception 6 in the section of this book called "8 Things You Thought You Knew About The SAT Are Wrong."

6. Re-read the sentence and mark your answer.

Re-read the entire sentence to double-check yourself, and then mark the answer you think is right and move on.

Conclusion

We've just seen an entire approach to the Identifying Sentence Errors portion of the SAT Writing Section. Now, to show you that the process works, and to help you build up your instincts for the Identifying Sentence Errors questions, we'll try it out against actual SAT questions published by the College Board in the Blue Book. Let's get started!

The Step-By-Step Approach To Identifying SAT Sentence Errors In Action

Now we'll try our hand at some real SAT questions from the Blue Book, which is the College Board publication *The Official SAT Study Guide*. As you follow along with these explanations, remember that the goal is to build up your instincts for handling these kinds of questions.

Page 409, Question 12

(C) is wrong because two people can't become one thing. A correct form would be "entomologists." The College Board's favorite issue to test, broadly speaking, is the difference between singular and plural phrases, so this is the kind of thing we want to get used to looking out for.

Page 409, Question 13

Nothing is grammatically wrong with this sentence, so (E) is the answer.

Page 409, Question 14

(A) is wrong because the form "badly" makes it sound like the casserole is doing a bad job of smelling—that is, it makes it sound like the casserole has a nose and isn't using that nose very well. A correct form would be "surprisingly bad." The College Board sometimes tests the difference between adjectives and adverbs, so whenever we see an adjective or an adverb underlined we have to make sure it's the appropriate form. (For a thorough explanation of the difference between adjectives and adverbs, check out the Writing Toolbox in the appendix of this book.)

Page 409, Question 15

(C) doesn't work because the word "whenever" indicates that the verb "learned" and the verb in (C) need to be the same tense. A correct form for (C) would be "sought out" or "would seek out." Remember that we can only say a verb tense is wrong when the given tense makes the sentence logically impossible, as it does here.

Page 409, Question 16

(D) is wrong because in a situation like this we would have to say "thought it wise to suppress."

Page 409, Question 17

(C) is the grammatical flaw in this sentence because it needs to be an adverbial form, because it's modifying the verb "has risen." A correct form would be "noticeably." This is basically the same issue we just saw in question 14 from this page, except that in 14 the adverb needed to be an adjective, and in this question the adjective needs to be an adverb.

Page 409, Question 18

(A) needs to be "nor," to match "neither." The issues of "neither + nor" and "either + or" are probably the most basic and easily identified issues on the entire SAT, but for some reason test-takers miss them frequently, usually because they don't read the question carefully enough. This is just one more example of how important it is to read EVERYTHING carefully.

Page 409, Question 19

(C) is wrong because "his or her" needs to be "their" in order to match the plural "passengers." Again, the single most frequently tested issue is the difference between singular and plural phrases, and it's something we always have to look out for.

Page 410, Question 20

Nothing is grammatically wrong with this, so (E) is the correct answer. Some students like to choose (B) because they think "or older" should be "and older," but a single person can't be both 65 *and* older than 65; he can only be either 65 *or* older, so (B) is okay the way it is.

Page 410, Question 21

This one contains a bad comparison: on the SAT, we either have to compare painters to painters or we have to compare paintings to paintings. We can't compare paint*ings* to paint*ers*. So a correct form for choice (B) might be "to the paintings of Rauschenberg." Whenever you see a question on the Writing section of the SAT that involves comparing two things, you should check to make sure the two things are of the same type.

Page 410, Question 22

A lot of students don't like the way this sentence is written, but there's nothing grammatically wrong with it, so the answer is (E).

Most people who miss this choose (C) incorrectly, but "at too great a distance" is an acceptable phrase, because it doesn't break any rules:

- "distance" is a noun
- "great" is an adjective, so it can be used to describe a noun
- "too" is an adverb, so it can be used to describe the adjective "great"
- "at" is an appropriate preposition for the word "distance"

This one is a good example of how important it is to remember that we're only concerned with SAT grammar for Identifying Sentence Errors questions; it doesn't matter if we think we could rephrase the sentence in a way that would be more stylistically pleasing.

Page 410, Question 23

For this one, (C) is the problem because "is released" needs to be "are released" in order to agree with "spears," which is plural. Once more we see that the College Board is trying to get us to overlook a mis-match between singular and plural phrases. Remember how repetitive the SAT is, and how important it is to read everything carefully!

Page 410, Question 24

A lot of test-takers think something is wrong with this sentence, but if we read it carefully we'll see that everything in it is actually okay, so (E) is the answer. Test-takers are often worried about (D) being in the passive voice, but the College Board doesn't consider the passive voice to be a grammatical mistake, as this question (along with many others) clearly demonstrates.

Page 410, Question 25

The correct phrase should be "capable of distinguishing," so (C) is the mistake here. This question is an example of the kind of prepositional idiom that the College Board occasionally tests. Unfortunately, there's not much we can learn from this question, because it's unlikely that the College Board will revisit this particular idiom when you take the test for real, since there are thousands of prepositional idioms and different ones show up on each test.

Page 410, Question 26

Though most people would say a sentence like this in real life and not think twice about it, the word "their" is plural, which doesn't work because the town's name is technically singular. A correct phrase would be "its residents," so (D) is the mistake. This is one more case of the College Board hoping you won't notice a mismatch between singular and plural phrases. It's also a good example of how a sentence can be incorrect on the SAT even though it would seem perfectly normal to an educated speaker of English in real life.

Page 410, Question 27

Nothing is wrong with this sentence, though students often think there is. The phrase "long since forgotten" is acceptable, and the phrase "crafted by artisans" is also okay, even though it's in the passive voice, because the College Board doesn't consider the passive voice to be a grammatical problem. (E) is the correct answer.

Page 410, Question 28

Here, the word "requires" should be "require," in order to agree with "grades," so (D) is the answer. This is another example of the College Board hoping you won't notice that a singular verb has been paired with a plural subject.

Page 410, Question 29

The problem with the original version of the sentence is that it compares a "story" to a person, "Hank Aaron." Remember that the College Board requires us to compare stories to stories or people to people, but it doesn't let us compare stories to people, so (D) is the mistake. A correct form might have been "than the story of baseball's great hitter," because then we'd be comparing one story to another story.

Conclusion

As you can see, the key to doing well on these Identifying Sentence Errors questions is to train yourself to look for the same handful of grammatical issues over and over in a variety of settings. It's also very important to think only in terms of actual rules being broken, rather than in general terms of "awkwardness," because the critical issue in any question is going to be a specific rule of SAT grammar, not a loosely defined concept like awkwardness.

Video Demonstrations

If you'd like to see videos of some sample solutions like the ones in this book, please visit http://www.SATprepVideos.com. A selection of free videos is available for readers of this book.

A Selection of Challenging Questions

We've now completed an entire section of Identifying Sentence Error questions. Let's take a look at some of the more challenging questions from the second edition of the College Board's *Official SAT Study Guide*, the Blue Book.

As we've seen with every other question type on the SAT, we'll find that these questions simply recycle the same basic concepts that all other questions of the same type use.

Of course, you'll need a copy of the Blue Book to follow along. I strongly advise you to follow along with these solutions as a way to continue to improve your instincts for answering Identifying Sentence Errors questions.

Page 471, Question 18

Many test-takers get hung up on the verb phrase in choice (A), because they wonder if it would sound better as "evaluated." But we have to remember that it's not our job to think about what would sound better; it's our job to identify grammatical errors. Since "was evaluating" and "evaluated" are both in the past, even if they're in slightly different forms, there's no way for one form to be grammatically acceptable and the other one to be unacceptable in the context of this question.

The actual issue is something we should always be on the lookout for: the word "they" in choice (C) is plural, but it's referring to the singular noun "tax." Remember that the College Board will test you on the singular/plural issue more frequently than on any other single issue!

Page 472, Question 29

For a lot of test-takers, this sentence just kind of 'feels' like it has something wrong with it—but we have to remember that we can only mark answers on this section if there are specific grammatical issues we can identify in the underlined phrases. In this case, there aren't any issues. (A) is okay because "herself" can refer to the accountant. "To help" goes fine with "offered." "As they were" might seem a little odd, but it's actually totally fine: "as" is okay, "they" refers to the plural word "accounts," and "were" is okay as a past-tense plural verb with "accounts" as the subject. "By" is also okay as a pronoun used in this passive-voice construction (remember that the passive voice is not a grammatical error on the SAT). So the correct answer is (E).

Page 533, Question 13

Some test-takers think the mistake in (D) is the odd phrase "than did X," but that isn't actually the issue here. It would have been okay to write "than did Jim's science project."

The mistake is actually that the SAT doesn't let us compare things of different types. So we can compare a science project to another science project, or we can compare a person to another person, but we can't compare a science project to a person on the SAT.

Remember that it's always very important to figure out the exact reasoning behind a right or wrong answer on the Writing section (or for any other part of the SAT, really). That way you can be sure you're getting the maximum benefit from your practice sessions.

Page 534, Question 22

This is a question test-takers often miss, even though the idea being tested here is the most commonly tested issue on the entire test: the difference between singular and plural.

The word "they" is plural, but it's referring to the singular "gecko," which the College Board doesn't like. So (A) is the correct answer.

Remember that you must ALWAYS be on the lookout for things that change from singular to plural or from plural to singular.

In this case, I think a lot of test-takers miss the question because the pronoun appears before the noun, instead of in its usual position after the noun. Remember that you have to consider all the words in the entire sentence to make sure phrases are agreeing with one another properly.

Page 534, Question 24

Test-takers often miss this question because they overlook the verb tense issue in (A).

Remember that verb tenses can be potential errors for Identifying Sentence Errors questions on the SAT, but only when they lead to logically impossible situations.

In this case, (A) leads to a logical impossibility because the sentence says that the people "decided" to do something "after" the verb in (A)—but (A) is in the present tense (yes, the present tense—I'll get to that in a minute).

It's a logical impossibility to say that something that happened in the past (the decision) happened "after" something in the present (the completion of the leading). The past must come before the present, not after it.

You may be wondering how I can say that (A) is a verb in the present tense, since many English teachers would describe "has led" as a past-tense form. But from a technical perspective, "has led" is a verb in the present tense with something called "perfect aspect"—in other words, it's a verb in the present tense that indicates that an action has already been completed. In this case, it indicates that the action of leading has been completed in the present moment.

In this sentence, an acceptable form for (A) might have been either "led" or "had led."

You may be thinking that this is all a bit complicated right now, and I don't blame you. Luckily, there's a relatively easy way to keep it all straight. When you see a compound verb in English, the tense of the helping verb is the same as the tense of the overall verb phrase. So, in this case, we can tell that "has led" is a present-tense verb because the helping verb "has" is a present-tense verb.

Don't worry about the issue in this question too much. For one thing, it's fairly easy to identify the tense of a verb phrase using the helping-verb method I just described. For another thing, there aren't a ton of questions that test verb-tenses as sneakily as this one does. So it's fairly unlikely that you'll see something like this on test day, and, even if you do, it's not that hard to focus on the tense of the helping verb anyway.

Page 535, Question 29

This is one of the relatively rare SAT Writing questions that tests the idea of redundancy. In this case, (D) restates the idea of the word "annually" from earlier in the sentence, so we should remove it because it's redundant according to the rules of the College Board. Notice that "annually" isn't underlined as well, because, if it were, there would be no way to say whether "annually" or the phrase in (D) should be removed to fix the redundancy.

Page 601, Question 19

Test-takers frequently miss this question because they don't like the phrase "in which," and would like to change it to something like "where" or "whose."

But we have to remember that we can only choose answers that represent verifiable grammatical mistakes, and "in which" is not a grammatical mistake. "Which" is referring back to the word "cities;" since "which" can refer to either singular or plural words as long as they aren't people, it's fine here. And "in" is an okay pronoun to use with "cities," since cities are physical locations and it's possible to be located inside them.

People sometimes also want to pick (C) or (D) because of the passive-voice construction they create, but, as always, we have to remember that the College Board doesn't consider the passive voice to be a grammatical mistake. So the answer is (E), because the College Board doesn't see anything wrong with any of the phrasing in this sentence.

Let this question serve as an important reminder to look only for grammatical mistakes and ignore everything else!

Page 602, Question 27

This question, like many others, tests your ability to recognize a mismatch between singular and plural phrases. In this case, the singular verb "was" needs to agree with the plural phrase "the proposed health clinics and the proposed center," so (A) is the answer. If (A) had been the word "were," it would have been fine.

Even though test-takers should know to look out for mismatches between singular and plural phrases, many people miss questions like this because the word-order is a little abnormal (since the verb comes before the noun). Remember that underlined phrases might have to agree with words that come before them or after them, and always consider the entire sentence when looking for mismatches!

Page 659, Question 25

This is one of those questions that people often miss if they aren't familiar with some of the College Board's more idiosyncratic grammatical rules. We have to remember that the SAT doesn't allow us to substitute words like "with" where the word "and" could have worked, so (C) needs to read "and a decrease." (Of course, it's okay to use the word "with" in other contexts on the SAT. We just can't use it as a replacement for "and.")

This is a rule that tends to be tested more frequently on the Improving Sentences questions, but, as this question demonstrates, we'll sometimes see it tested in the Identifying Sentence Errors questions.

Page 720, Question 16

Test-takers often miss this question because they think that "its" should be "their," but if we read carefully we'll see that "its" is actually correct. The thing doing the eating is technically the word "each," which is singular. So the answer here is (E).

This question demonstrates how critical it is that we pay very careful attention to the details of the sentences we encounter. Remember that paying attention to details is one of the most important skills to have for the entire SAT!

Page 721, Question 25

For this question, we have to think very carefully about the meanings of the words "results" and "as." The verb "results" indicates that a process has finished and an outcome has been achieved, but the word "as" indicates that something is still going on. We would need to change "as" to a word like "when" or "after" in order for this to work. So (C) is correct.

This question is one that students ask about pretty frequently, and it really helps to demonstrate how important it is to read things carefully and to think about them carefully. Most people who read this sentence end up feeling that it's a little odd, but they don't scrutinize the sentence carefully enough to realize where the mistake lies.

Page 721, Question 28

This is another question that test-takers often struggle with, but the issue here is actually very simple: "neither" has to be followed by "nor," not by "or." So (D) is the mistake. Remember that the last few sentences in the

Identifying Sentence Errors questions might have bizarre word orders, but they test the same basic concepts as the rest of the questions.

Page 838, Question 19

This is a sentence that probably sounds pretty normal to speakers of American English, but we have to remember that the SAT is interested in whether sentences follow its grammar rules, not in how they sound. For the College Board, the problem here is the use of "your." Since the reader can't possibly be a person living in an ancient society, "your" isn't appropriate in the eyes of the College Board. It might have been okay to replace "your" with "their" (referring to the word "people" at the beginning of the sentence). So (D) is correct.

Page 839, Question 26

This question is a great example of the way the College Board can keep testing the same basic concepts in subtle ways that sometimes go unnoticed by test-takers.

In this case, we need to remember that the College Board only lets us use the word "it" when the rest of the sentence contains a singular noun that "it" can refer to. If we look carefully, we'll see that this sentence has no singular noun that "it" can refer to—the phrase "to relive the moment" is a verb phrase, not a noun phrase. So (D) is the mistake here.

If we wanted to correct this sentence, we could change "do it" to "do so." (Of course, you don't have to correct anything on this part of the test, but I wanted to explain the correct version of this phrase because many students aren't familiar with the idea of using "to do so" when referring to a verb phrase.)

As we can see from this question, it's very important that we always remember to check the rest of the sentence for an appropriate singular noun whenever we see the word "it" underlined! It's also important to remember that SAT grammar sometimes deviates from normal American speech, especially when the words "it" or "they" are involved.

Page 894, Question 15

Even though this sentence is pretty long, the issue being tested is fairly simple. The word "which" can't be used to refer to people; the correct form would have been "who." So (B) is the right answer. Remember to take each sentence phrase-by-phrase, and not to let yourself get overwhelmed just because a particular sentence is very long.

Page 895, Question 23

This question involves two of the College Board's favorite things to include in an Identifying Sentence Errors question: a mismatch between singular and plural phrases, and an intervening prepositional phrase designed to keep you from noticing that mismatch.

The plural verb-form "show" in choice (A) needs to be "shows," in order to match with the singular noun "observation" at the beginning of the sentence, because the observation is what's doing the showing. Notice that the phrase "of diverse animal species" has been placed between the subject and the verb, in an attempt to get you to forget that the subject was singular by the time you get to the verb.

As always, it's important to read everything very carefully and not to get sidetracked by the College Board's tricks!

Page 956, Question 17

In this question, "are" needs to be "were" in order to match the past-tense verb phrases "were watching" and "feared" in the rest of the sentence. So (D) is the correct answer.

We know that the verbs' tenses need to match in this question because the phrase "just when" indicates that all the verbs are happening at the same time. Remember that verb phrases on the SAT Writing section can't create situations that are logically impossible.

Page 957, Question 26

The College Board only lets us use "she" or "he" when the word is clearly referring to a singular noun phrase somewhere in the sentence. In this case, "she" could refer either to the manager or to Ms. Andrews, so it's not okay, and (C) is the correct answer.

Page 957, Question 28

Once more, we have a sentence in which the College Board switches from the plural to the singular—as I've mentioned repeatedly, this is the College Board's favorite mistake to test. In this case, the word "they" is plural but the phrase "a candidate" is singular. We would need to change "a candidate" to "candidates" in order to make this acceptable to the College Board, so (A) is correct.

Conclusion

We've now seen how to handle the Identifying Sentence Errors questions on the SAT Writing Section. We've learned all about the rules, patterns, and processes for these questions, and we've seen real solutions worked out to real SAT questions published by the College Board in the Blue Book.

As is the case with every other question type on the SAT, the more you work with these questions, the better you'll be able to answer them!

The following page offers a brief summary of the major ideas for these Identifying Sentence Errors question. After that, we'll move on to the questions that deal with both SAT grammar and SAT style: the Improving Sentences questions.

Video Demonstrations

If you'd like to see videos of some sample solutions like the ones in this book, please visit http://www.SATprepVideos.com. A selection of free videos is available for readers of this book.

Identifying Sentence Errors Quick Summary

This is a one-page summary of the major relevant concepts for Identifying Sentence Errors questions. Use it to evaluate your comprehension or jog your memory. For a more in-depth treatment of these ideas, see the rest of the section.

The Big Secret: Awkwardness doesn't matter. <u>All that matters are the rules of "SAT grammar."</u> SAT grammar is often similar to the way people talk but differs in certain ways.

Rules and patterns:

You can pick up the fine points of SAT grammar by going through the Blue Book solutions in this Black Book, or by reading the appendix in this Black Book. Apart from those, here are the rules and patterns unique to ISE questions:

- <u>Style doesn't count.</u> You can only pick something if it actually breaks a rule, not just because you think you could make it sound better.
- You can't pick an underlined phrase because you think the *whole phrase* should be deleted, except in cases of redundancy (which are rare on the SAT).
- <u>You'll often see unnecessary descriptive phrases inserted between two words that should agree.</u>
- The issue of "<u>singular vs plural</u>" is the single most commonly tested concept.
- <u>Questions 25 - 29 or so tend to be more convoluted</u> than the other questions.
- <u>Comparisons can only be made between similar things, and only in similar ways.</u>
- <u>No substitutes for the word "and"</u> (you can't use "with," "in addition to," "as well as," and so on).
- <u>Verb tenses can only be wrong if they're misconjugated or impossible in context.</u>
- <u>Prepositional idioms might be tested a couple of times</u> or so. Only an issue for questions with no other errors.

Here's the Identifying Sentence Errors process:

1. Read entire prompt sentence.
2. Focus on underlined portions of prompt sentence.
3. Think about how each word in the underlined portions relates to other words in the sentence (draw lines if it helps).
4. Look for an underlined word that doesn't agree with a word it's related to.
5. Consider that there might be nothing wrong with the sentence.
6. Re-read the sentence and mark your answer. Remember there must be a broken SAT grammar rule.

For examples of these concepts in action, see the sample Blue Book solutions in this Black Book.

Overview and Important Reminders for Improving Sentences on the SAT Writing Section

The Improving Sentences questions on the SAT Writing section are relatively straightforward and repetitive once you develop a feel for the rules and patterns we'll talk about in the next couple of pages. Each question presents you with a sentence that has an underlined word or phrase. The answer choices then provide you with several possible versions of the underlined portion of the prompt sentence. Your job is to choose the version of the underlined phrase that fits best according to the College Board's ideas of grammar and style.

Don't worry! You'll find that these questions test a fairly limited number of concepts, and—like everything else on the SAT—you'll be able to answer them pretty mechanically with a little practice. Let's get started.

Unwritten Test Design Rules For Improving Sentences on the SAT

We don't need to talk about that many rules for these questions, because there's very little variation from question to question. Here are the 4 rules you'll need.

SAT Improving Sentences Rule 1: Grammar Still Matters

I mentioned earlier that the Improving Sentences part of the SAT Writing section involves some stylistic considerations, while the Identifying Sentence Errors questions only test SAT grammar. That's still true, but it's important to remember that the Improving Sentences questions ALSO test grammar in addition to style.

The correct answer to every single Improving Sentences question will always follow the grammar rules on the SAT. So you can always feel safe eliminating an answer choice that is grammatically incorrect according to the College Board.

SAT Improving Sentences Rule 2: Style Counts, Especially When The Underlined Portion Is Longer

Sometimes you'll have Improving Sentences questions in which two or more answer choices would be grammatically acceptable, in the sense that none of them breaks a rule of SAT grammar. In these cases, you have to pick the choice that is the most stylistically acceptable to the College Board.

In other words, sometimes the difference between a wrong answer choice and a correct answer choice is an issue of knowing which one just "feels" better to the College Board.

This might upset you at first—how are you supposed to know what the SAT thinks is good writing style? Don't worry. The stylistic choices that the College Board prefers may have been originally chosen in an arbitrary way, but they have to be consistent from test to test just like every other part of the SAT. That's what makes the test standardized, after all.

In a couple of pages, I'll give you a list of 3 style patterns that the College Board rewards on the Improving Sentences questions. All you need to do is pick the answer choice that is grammatically correct and does the best job of following those patterns.

Don't worry if that sounds a little weird or intimidating. The patterns are pretty easy to apply, and we'll see plenty of examples of solutions that use them when we look at some questions from the Blue Book later on.

By the way, style is more likely to be an issue in the answer choices when the underlined portion is longer than 4 words. When the underlined portion is under 5 words long, the question will typically (but not always) be purely grammar-based, which means that there will probably be only one answer choice that is grammatically acceptable. Of course, any time a question only has one grammatically acceptable answer choice, that choice is the right answer because of Rule 1.

SAT Improving Sentences Rule 3: Don't Make Trouble

The correct answer choice must do more than fix any mistakes in the underlined portion of the prompt sentence—it also has to avoid creating new mistakes.

Sometimes students zero-in on a problem in the prompt sentence and then choose the first answer choice that gets rid of that particular problem. But this isn't good enough! The correct answer choice must not have ANY mistakes. So it's important to consider each answer choice in its entirety before settling on an answer.

SAT Improving Sentences Rule 4: (A) Is The Same

This isn't really worth mentioning from a strategic perspective, but it's probably still worth pointing out—the first answer choice in each Improving Sentences question is an exact restatement of the underlined portion of the prompt sentence.

I thought I should mention this just in case, because some students skip the instructions to each section and get confused when they can't see a difference between the prompt sentence and choice (A).

Hidden Test Design Patterns of Improving Sentences On The SAT

Combining an awareness of SAT grammar with an understanding of the following patterns will allow you to answer all the Improving Sentences questions that you'll ever see on a real SAT. (Of course, you'll have to read questions and their answer choices carefully in order to apply those ideas.)

In some cases, more than one answer choice will satisfy one of the patterns below. If that happens, the answer choice that satisfies the most patterns will be the right one. We'll see a lot of examples of how this works when we look at some solutions to Blue Book questions in a few pages.

Hidden Pattern 1: Shorter is Better, All Else Being Equal

The correct answer choice for SAT Improving Sentences questions is very often the shortest answer choice. (This is probably because the best way to fix the kinds of stylistic errors that appear on these questions is usually to cut things out.)

When the correct answer choice is NOT the shortest one, it's very often the longest one. This is because the other common way to fix the kinds of errors that appear in this section is to add words and phrases.

This is NOT the same thing as saying that you should always pick the shortest or longest answer. That would be an idiotic thing for me to say. All I'm saying is that the correct answer is very often the shortest or longest answer choice. Knowing this helps us start to take apart the Improving Sentences questions, because it calls our attention to the fact that the best solutions to these questions often involve cutting as much as possible from, or adding as much as possible to, the given sentence.

This pattern is very powerful, and it's important for us not to forget it. In fact, if the shortest answer choice is grammatically correct (according to the SAT's idea of correct grammar), then it's always the right answer.

By the way, when I refer to the shortest answer choice I'm talking about the choice that takes up the least linear space on the page, not necessarily about the choice that has the fewest words. In other words, I'm talking about the answer choice that would be shortest if you measured all the choices with a ruler.

Hidden Pattern 2: It's Better To Have Fewer "-ed" and "-ing" Words, All Else Being Equal

One of the College Board's favorite ways to make an answer choice stylistically undesirable is to introduce participles or gerunds where they don't need to exist. So we'll often find that the answer choice with the fewest of those types of words is the correct one.

Those words are easy to identify in English because they tend to end in "-ed" or "-ing."

Be especially careful around the words "being" and "having," as those are often found in incorrect answer choices. (Of course, it's possible for an answer choice to be correct while having either of those words in it, so I'm not saying you should automatically eliminate any answer choice that has them. I'm just saying that, in general, those words tend to indicate that a choice is incorrect.)

Hidden Pattern 3: It's Better To Have Fewer Short Words, All Else Being Equal

In order to make its wrong answers longer and more awkward, the College Board often has to insert things like prepositions, conjunctions, relative pronouns, regular pronouns, helping verbs, and so on. You could spend a lot of time learning about all of these grammatical categories if you wanted . . . or you could just exploit the happy coincidence that, in English, these words are typically less than 5 letters long.

The correct answers, then, will tend to have the fewest words that are less than 5 letters long—the fewest words like "of," "as," that," "and," "to," "it," "have," "by," and so on.

Just to be clear, I'm not suggesting that the correct answer will never contain any of these words. I'm saying that if you have one answer choice with only 3 words like this, and all the other choices have 5 short words, then, all else being equal, we'd expect the choice with only 3 short words to be the right answer.

Hidden Pattern 4: Wrong Answers Tend To Imitate Elements Of Right Answers

We'll often find that phrases from the correct answer to a question are repeated in some of the incorrect answers, because the College Board wants to trick you. This means that you can often get an idea of which elements of an answer choice are likely to be correct by seeing which ones are repeated more throughout the answer choices. As an example, imagine a questions where 3 of the 5 answer choices begin with the word "but," and 3 out of the 5 end with the word "always." All other things being equal, we would expect the correct answer choice to begin with the word "but" and to end with the word "always."

You may remember that the answer choices in certain SAT Math questions feature similar patterns, and for similar reasons. Just like in the Math section, it's important to remember that I'm NOT saying that an answer choice will ALWAYS be correct if it includes all the most popular phrases from the other choices. I'm just saying that this happens very often, and it's something we should be aware of as we work on Improving Sentences questions.

The Step-By-Step Approach To Improving SAT Sentences

Here's the process I recommend for SAT Improving Sentences questions.

1. Read the entire prompt sentence.

The first step in attacking these questions is to read the entire sentence, since you need to know the context of each element in the sentence.

2. Eliminate answer choices that make grammatical mistakes according to the SAT.

As we noted before, the correct answer choice must be grammatically acceptable, so any choice that breaks the SAT's grammar rules is automatically wrong. On some questions, only one answer choice will be grammatically acceptable, so that choice must be right, and you don't need to think about anything else. On other questions, the shortest answer choice will be grammatically acceptable, and that also automatically means that choice is right.

On many questions, though, more than one answer choice will be grammatically acceptable, and the shortest choice will not be among them, so you'll need to consider a few other things.

3. Look for the 3 most important patterns in the answer choices that are grammatically acceptable: the length of the answer choice, the number of words ending in "-ed" or "-ing," and the number of words that are less than 5 letters long.

Remember the rules for this section—we can only change things that are underlined, and we can only change them in the ways that appear in the answer choices! You have to focus on the underlined portion of the sentence. Without trying to rewrite it on your own, look for the patterns we frequently encounter on the Improving Sentences questions.

4. Determine which choice follows the most patterns.

Assuming that you've read correctly and that you've correctly eliminated the choices with bad SAT grammar, the correct answer choice will be the one that fits the most of the 3 hidden patterns we talked about for Improving Sentences questions.

5. Read the entire sentence with your favorite answer choice inserted in place of the underlined portion.

It's important to remember that the correct answer needs to fit back in the sentence. Sometimes test-takers forget some key element of the sentence when they've been reading through the answer choices, and they don't realize that an answer choice they like might actually create a grammatical problem when re-inserted in the sentence. So it's always critical to consider the entire sentence again before marking an answer choice.

6. Re-examine all the other answer choices.

Remember—you never answer an SAT question without considering all the answer choices, and the Improving Sentences questions are no exception. When you look back through the other answer choices, you should be able to identify issues in those choices (whether grammatical or stylistic) that would prevent them from being correct on the SAT. If you don't see anything wrong in one of the other answer choices, then you need to reconsider the question.

If you've done everything correctly up until this point, you should have one answer choice that is grammatically acceptable on the SAT and looks stylistically ideal, and four answer choices with identifiable issues that make them wrong, either because they're grammatically unacceptable or because they don't follow the style patterns as well as the choice that you like does.

7. Mark your answer or skip the question.

If you decide that one of the answer choices is clearly correct, then mark it with confidence and move on. If you can't decide which answer choice is correct, consider skipping the question for the time being and returning to it later, so that you can move on and correctly answer questions that are easier for you to do.

Conclusion

You've now seen the entire process for Improving Sentences questions on the SAT Writing section. In the next section, I'll show you the process in action against real SAT questions published by the College Board in the Blue Book!

The Step-By-Step Approach To Improving SAT Sentences In Action

To demonstrate how the Improving Sentences process works against real test questions, and to help you get a feel for the practical application of that process, I'll go through all the Improving Sentences questions that start on page 407 of the first sample SAT that appears in the College Board's Blue Book (the *Official SAT Study Guide*).

Page 407, Question 1

This is a question in which the underlined portion is very short, suggesting that the issue is likely to be grammatical, rather than stylistic. Sure enough, the correct form ("by falling") indicates grammatically that the method by which the drivers cause accidents is "falling asleep."

(A) is a run-on sentence.

(B) is a correctly punctuated compound sentence, but it's not as short as (C).

(C) is correct.

(D) is grammatically incorrect—if we were going to use "and," the following verb would need to be in the past tense to match "caused."

(E) is also a run-on sentence.

Page 407, Question 2

In this question the underlined portion is longer, suggesting that the question might involve stylistic elements. The original has "is being," something the College Board almost always dislikes. The correct form, (C), is also the shortest one, as we would frequently expect. Remember that when the shortest answer choice has no grammatical issues as far as the College Board is concerned, it will be the correct answer choice.

(A) doesn't work because of "is being."

(B) has a few different things wrong with it, but the biggest problem is the use of the word "is" in conjunction with the phrase "as a result of."

(C) is correct.

(D) "hard studying" doesn't work, because if we insert that phrase in the sentence we end up with a statement equating "the depths" with "studying." Notice, by the way, that more answer choices begin with "to study," which often suggests—but doesn't guarantee by itself—that that form is likely to be correct.

(E) again, "hard studying" doesn't work.

Page 407, Question 3

The original version of the question isn't a full sentence because of the word "which," which demotes the following phrase to a dependent clause. To be a full sentence while retaining the word "which," the question would have to say something like "Several of the fires, which were caused by carelessness, burned out of control." The correct version is (B), which omits the "which" and provides a verb in the past tense. Note that the correct answer choice features the passive voice, which is okay on the SAT because the College Board has no problem with the passive voice.

(A) creates a sentence fragment.

(B) is correct.

(C) also creates a sentence fragment.

(D) doesn't work because "are" is in the present tense, while "occurred" is in the past tense.

(E) doesn't work because we can't say "happened from." Also, the word "being" tends not to appear in correct answers on Improving Sentences questions.

Page 407, Question 4
This question has a short underlined portion, suggesting a grammatical issue. The correct answer is the only one that matches the form of the verb "showed" in the phrase "when she showed." So (C) is correct, because it has the verb "disproved" in the simple past tense, just like the word "showed."

Page 407, Question 5
Here, we need a conjunction that indicates that the two ideas being discussed are opposite to one another. "And" won't work, so (A) and (B) are out. (C) and (D) are out because of "extending." (E) is correct because it's the only sentence with a negating conjunction ("however") and an acceptable form of the verb "extend."

Page 408, Question 6
(A) works fine.

(B) doesn't work because of the word "that."

(C) doesn't work because of "culminating."

(D) doesn't work because of "beginning" and "culminating"—remember that the correct answers to Improving Sentences questions tend to avoid words ending in "-ing" if possible.

(E) has a couple of problems. The biggest one is that the phrase "as a child" makes it sounds as though the actual memoirs themselves are a child, which is impossible.

Page 408, Question 7
For this question, the correct answer is the shortest answer choice, as we will often find. Really, that should be enough analysis for you to be certain you have the right answer: when the shortest answer choice is grammatically acceptable, it's the correct answer. But let's look at the other choices anyway:

(A) doesn't work because the word "it" makes it seem as though the uniform itself is the thing that is "dressed in a uniform."

(B) doesn't work because the "efficient manner" is the thing "dressed in a uniform," grammatically speaking.

(C) doesn't work because the word "that" turns the entire string of words into a sentence fragment.

(D) is grammatically correct and it's the shortest answer choice, so it works automatically.

(E) is a sentence fragment.

Page 408, Question 8
Here, again, the shortest answer choice is grammatically correct, which means the College Board will say it's the correct answer.

(A) is the shortest choice and it's grammatically correct, so it's right.

(B) has a lot of problems, the biggest of which is that in this version the scientists themselves are the "cure for some kinds of cancer." Remember that the College Board's grammar rules state that when a descriptive phrase is stuck to the beginning of a sentence with a comma, then the first noun after the comma is the noun being described by the phrase—in this case, "a cure for some kinds of cancer" is the descriptive phrase and "scientists" is the first noun after the comma.

(C) creates a sentence fragment.

(D) creates a comma splice.

(E) creates a sentence fragment.

Page 408, Question 9

(A) doesn't work because "and" is a conjunction that indicates two similar ideas, but the ideas of being confusing and melodious aren't similar.

(B) doesn't work because of "by having," two words the College Board tends to avoid placing in the correct answer to an Improving Sentences question.

(C) has the word "and," just like (A) does, and is wrong for the same reason.

(D) doesn't work because it would be saying that the review, not the symphony, had a melodious movement.

(E) is correct because the conjunction "but" indicates we're joining two ideas that are dissimilar.

Page 408, Question 10

Many test-takers will find this question confusing because it has so many underlined words. One of the easiest ways to approach a question like this is to focus on individual parts of the answer choices—remember that even a single mistake in the answer choice causes the whole thing to be wrong, so once we identify a flaw in a choice we can stop worrying about it. In other words, if we take each choice on its own and discard it as soon as we run into a problem with it, then we don't have to keep five different versions of a 19-word phrase in our heads at once.

(A) doesn't work because the "consumption" would be "building new farms," which is impossible.

(B) doesn't work because the word "it" can't be directly replaced with a singular noun phrase in the sentence, which is a requirement of SAT grammar (even if it's not a requirement of English grammar in real life).

(C) is the correct answer because it's grammatically correct and it's the shortest answer choice—remember that when the shortest answer choice is grammatically acceptable, it's always correct.

(D) doesn't work because the word "it" doesn't refer to a noun phrase elsewhere in the sentence.

(E) is grammatically okay (though a little awkward sounding), but it loses to (C) because (C) is the shortest choice and it's also grammatically correct.

Page 408, Question 11

This question often frustrates students, because it often sounds to them like two or three of the choices are all equally acceptable. At times like this, it's very important to remember that there is ALWAYS a single correct answer, and that the reasoning behind the correct answer must be consistent with the reasoning behind all other real SAT Writing questions.

In this case, the issue boils down to one of parallelism: since the original sentence says "in northern England," our sentence needs to end with "in the Highlands." Only one answer choice also contains "in," and that's (E), so (E) is correct.

We can learn a lot from this question, actually. Most test-takers will see this question, get frustrated, and just pick whatever sounds best to them. But a well-trained test-taker never forgets that EVERYTHING on the SAT follows certain basic rules and patterns, and there is ALWAYS one answer choice that is predictably correct. If we don't see what separates the right answer from the other answers, then we must have overlooked some important detail somewhere, and it's our job to find that detail before we answer the question—in this case, of course, the detail is the word "in."

Conclusion

As you can see, being aware of the unwritten rules and patterns that the College Board uses when constructing the Improving Sentences questions makes answering them a lot easier. Now let's look at some of the questions from the Blue Book that students have typically asked about most.

Video Demonstrations

If you'd like to see videos of some sample solutions like the ones in this book, please visit www.SATprepVideos.com. A selection of free videos is available for readers of this book.

A Selection of Challenging Questions

Now that we've gone through a complete section of Improving Sentences questions, let's take a look at a sample of some of the more challenging questions from the Blue Book, the College Board's *Official SAT Study Guide*.

These questions are some of the ones that students have asked me about the most over the years. Of course, they still follow the same rules and patterns as other questions, but sometimes test-takers have a harder time identifying those things in certain situations. So these questions aren't really doing anything different from any other questions; it's just that they're sometimes a bit more subtle about what they're doing.

As with other question explanations in this book, you'll need a copy of the Blue Book to follow along. Let's get started.

Page 430, Question 9

I wanted to single out this question for consideration because it's a good example of the way that questions can often be misinterpreted by test-takers as they prepare for the SAT.

Many people incorrectly assume that (E) is correct because it avoids the passive voice constructions that appear in (A), (B), and (C), but that isn't actually the reason that (E) is correct. In other words, if we assume that passive voice is a problem on all SAT questions, then we'll find ourselves getting questions wrong when the correct answer happens to use the passive voice.

It's important to understand that the reason (E) is correct has nothing to do with the passive voice. (E) is correct simply because it is the shortest answer, and it has no grammatical mistakes.

Many test-takers end up making the Writing section much more difficult for themselves than it needs to be because they reach incorrect assumptions about the test's reasoning on certain issues, and the passive voice is one of the best examples of this type of misunderstanding. If you want to do well on the SAT, it's not enough to know about reading, grammar, and math in real life—you have to know the rules the College Board actually follows, many of which might seem odd or counterintuitive to most test-takers. That's what this Black Book is all about!

Page 470, Question 7

There are a lot of ways to approach this question, but the easiest one is probably to realize that (C) is the shortest answer choice and is also grammatically acceptable, so it must be right.

Just like on the previous question we talked about, many people will assume that the correct answer here is somehow related to the fact that many of the wrong answers use the passive voice. This is a tempting conclusion to reach, but it's wrong—there are many correct answers in the College Board's book that include the passive voice.

Remember: if the shortest answer choice has no grammatical issues, it's right.

Page 470, Question 10

The College Board sometimes tests your awareness of idioms, and that's what this question is doing. In fact, the issue is simply that "for all their talk" is a grammatically acceptable phrase in English.

(If "for all their talk" doesn't make sense to you, think of it this way: the sentence is a bit like saying "even though they always talk about ecology, major companies have [blah, blah, blah].")

The good news on this question is that an awareness of the three major patterns of Improving Sentences questions would have helped us answer this correctly, even if we didn't know the idiom. (A) is the shortest choice, for one thing, which is often a good sign; it's also one of the only two choices without any -ing or -ed words. It does have more short words than (C) and (D), but those two choices have weird conjunctions for this sentence—neither "besides" nor "in addition to" really makes a lot of sense in this context.

So it would be possible to work out that (A) is correct even without actually knowing the idiom being tested. It won't always happen that knowing the patterns of the SAT can save us from not recognizing an idiom, but it will happen sometimes, clearly. I wanted to talk about this question so I could make it clear that we always have to be alert to the patterns in the answer choices, even when all hope might seem lost in the beginning.

Page 492, Question 10

This question is a good example of how important it is to read carefully and be very familiar with the test's rules.

Many test-takers incorrectly choose (D), usually because the first part of the answer choice seems very clear and direct. But they overlook the fact that (D) ends with the word "and," which isn't an effective conjunction here—the SAT is picky about making sure that conjunctions are used appropriately.

People often shy away from (A) and (B) because they start with the word "because," but we have to remember that it's actually okay to begin a sentence with the word "because" as long as the rest of the sentence includes a portion after the comma that could stand on its own as a sentence. In other words, any time that you could create a valid sentence with the structure "X, because Y," then it's also okay to write "because Y, X" as long as the X part could be a sentence on its own.

So if you could say "Measuring beforehand is good because the recipes don't allow for interruption," then you can also say "Because the recipes don't allow for interruption, measuring beforehand is good." Note that everything after the comma could be set aside as a sentence on its own.

That means (B) must be right, because it's the only choice without any grammatical issues in the eyes of the College Board.

Note that (A) has the word "having," which often indicates a wrong answer, and (C) has the phrase "being that," which is also often found in incorrect answers. Further, (E) has many, many short words, which is also often a sign of an incorrect answer.

Again, it's very, very important to read things carefully and to keep the design of the test in mind!

Page 532, Question 10

This question often confuses people who think it would be more natural to use the pronoun "their." The problem with the word "their" is that it's a plural pronoun, but the word "band" is singular in American English—even though the band involves multiple people, the band itself is a single thing according to the SAT's grammar rules. So we have to use the word "its." So (A) is correct.

Some people aren't comfortable with the word "its" because they aren't sure if it should be spelled with an apostrophe. But that isn't anything we need to worry about on the SAT—the SAT doesn't try to mislead you by testing spelling. (The ACT, on the other hand, *does* try to mislead you with those kinds of issues, so if you're going to take the ACT make sure you're aware of that distinction.)

Page 532, Question 11

The College Board likes to insist on a kind of parallelism in these kinds of questions, so we have to make sure that we pick the exact right words to satisfy the SAT's grammar rules.

In this case, the phrase "twice as many" is the first half of the structure "twice as many X as Y." So we need an answer choice that begins with the word "as."

That gets us down to (A) and (B). Now it's time to complete the parallel structure: note that the original sentence says the birds "inhabit" something. That makes (B) correct.

Another way to approach this question would be to say that the College Board requires comparisons like "twice as many X as Y" to be made between similar things. Since the first half of the sentence is talking about the number of birds that inhabit an area, the second half of the sentence must also mention those words.

Page 554, Question 10

This is yet another example of a question that will needlessly confuse many test-takers who get intimidated by the number of words in each answer choice.

If we jump right to the shortest answer choice, which is (B), we see that it's grammatically acceptable, which means it must be correct. (Remember, as I've mentioned repeatedly, that it's okay for a sentence to begin with the word "because" if the words after the comma could stand on their own as a sentence.)

One other thing: it's not okay to say something like "because X is the reason why . . ." in the way that the original version of this sentence does. In those cases, you should just say, "X is the reason why," or "because X," as choice (B) does. (A), (C), and (E) all violate this principle in various ways.

Page 599, Question 1

This is another of the College Board's comparison questions, so we should look very carefully to make sure that similar things are being compared in the correct answer.

The first half of the sentence talks about visiting places "in Great Britain," so the second half needs to talk about things "in Canada"—this way, both phrases contain the word "in." So (E) is correct.

Remember that the answers will always be clear if we keep the test's rules in mind and read carefully.

Page 599, Question 3

Test-takers are often surprised to find that (B) is grammatically correct, because the phrase "as does" strikes them as odd.

But we should remember that the College Board requires a certain kind of parallelism with the word "as" when we're comparing two things, so the underlined portion will need to include that word (since the first half of the sentence uses it). That gets us down to (A) and (B). From there, we should recall that the test requires us to compare similar things—in this case, the campus "newspaper" must be compared to the hometown "newspaper," not to the hometown itself. So (B) is correct.

Page 600, Question 6

There are a lot of subtle things that we need to make sure we catch in order to answer this question correctly.

One of the most often overlooked issues with this question is the fact that the first verb in the correct answer needs to agree with the word "reasons," not with the word "process." So the verb needs to be "are," not "is."

That means (A) and (D) are out.

From a grammatical standpoint, we could actually say that (C) is the only grammatically correct option, since the two "reasons" need to be noun phrases, and since putting the word "that" in front of a verb phrase makes it into a noun phrase. In other words, the phrases "that they have . . ." and "that they work . . ." actually function as nouns in (C).

Other people might try to appeal to a sense of parallelism to explain why (C) is correct, but I think it's important to avoid appealing to parallelism whenever possible on the SAT—I try to limit its use in my explanations to questions that involve comparing two or more things. (The reason for this is that students can get kind of obsessed with the idea of parallelism and try to apply it everywhere, with disastrous results, if I'm not very careful about laying down strict rules.)

Page 600, Question 9

There are a lot of important things to note in this question.

One of the most important is that choice (A) is only wrong because the phrase "as well as" appears in a position where the word "and" could have been used, and the College Board doesn't like that.

It's also worth pointing out that (E) is the only choice without an "-ing" word, which is one of the ways we might realize it's correct.

Finally, (E) begins with the word "because." Again, there's nothing wrong with starting a sentence that way as long as the words after the comma could stand as a sentence on their own. (In this case, everything from the word "George" could stand as a sentence on its own.)

Page 657, Question 10

On this question, if we're pretty good with grammar we can tell that (A) is the only grammatically acceptable choice, so it must be right.

But the phrase "which duration" will throw off a lot of people. In this case, though, it's still possible to arrive at the right answer by following those three patterns I mentioned earlier. Let's take a look at how things break down:

(A) has 2 words ending in "-ed" or "-ing," and 6 short words.

(B) has 2 words ending in "-ed" or "-ing," and 8 short words.

(C) has 2 words ending in "-ed" or "-ing," and 10 short words.

(D) has 2 words ending in "-ed" or "-ing," and 7 short words.

(E) has 3 words ending in "-ed" or "-ing," and 6 short words. (It's also the shortest choice, but it isn't grammatically correct because of the word "making.")

So we can see that (A) is the most ideal option, just by counting up the types of words the College Board likes to avoid and then picking the choice with the fewest of those words.

(This type of analysis will make a lot of English teachers very upset, but I don't care. Because of the SAT's poor design, these patterns can get you out of a lot of tough situations if you remember to use them. Of course, you have to read and count carefully to do it correctly.)

Page 677, Question 7

This is yet another question in which the shortest answer choice is grammatically acceptable, and is therefore the correct answer. So (E) is correct.

I'd also like to point out that the original version of the sentence might sound very natural to a lot of test-takers, but it's no good from an SAT standpoint because it uses the word "it" to refer to the verb phrase "if you represented." Remember that the College Board only lets us use the word "it" to refer to singular noun phrases.

Page 739, Question 5

Many test-takers accidentally choose (A) on this question, because it seems to make a strong sentence.

But we always have to remember to consider each answer choice and make sure we can find something wrong with the choices we're not picking! That's the only way to be sure you're not making any mistakes.

In this case, (D) is the shortest answer choice and has no grammatical mistakes. That means the College Board will say (D) is the right answer.

(Notice also that (D) includes the passive voice construction "is highly motivated," but it's still correct.)

Page 775, Question 5

If we read the answer choices carefully, we'll see that only choice (C) is grammatically acceptable. (A) doesn't work for a couple of reasons, but the most obvious is that the word "their" is referring to the singular noun "literature." (B) doesn't work because "direct" and "fresh" need to be in their adverb forms in order to modify the word "speaking." (D) has the same problem as (B). And (E) uses "they," just like (A) does.

Test-takers often miss this question, and questions like it, because they get caught up in what sounds best to them rather than sticking to the simple and repeatable rules of SAT grammar.

Page 775, Question 11

This is a question that most test-takers would be well advised to skip, because most of them won't be able to arrive at a single answer choice that seems to follow all the rules and patterns the College Board likes.

The reason they won't be able to reach a solid conclusion on one answer is that most test-takers don't know the phrase "at once X and Y," which is an expression that indicates that something has two attributes that might often be thought of as opposites. (For instance, we might say that the Eiffel Tower is "at once imposing and delicate.")

If we know that that phrase exists, then we can probably tell that (E) is correct, because (E) starts with "and" and also includes the "because of" structure that's in the first part of the prompt sentence.

By the way, even if we weren't sure that "and" was the right way to start off this phrase, it might have helped us to realize that 2 answer choices start with "and," while no other word appears at the beginning of the answer choices more than once. This doesn't always indicate that the correct answer should start with "and," but it strongly suggests that the correct answer *probably* starts with "and."

Page 803, Question 13

This is yet another example of a Writing question that incorrectly compares two things of different types. If we read carefully, we see that the things being compared in the original sentence are "the *number* of alligators" and "the Gila monster." In other words, the original sentence is comparing a number to an animal. But on the SAT, we have to compare things of similar kinds. So in this case, we either need to compare an animal to an animal, or a number to a number.

The only answer choice that fixes this problem is (E), which talks about "a comparison of the numbers of [both animals]." The fact that the word "numbers" is plural means that we're talking about the number of alligators and the number of Gila monsters.

As is often the case, being aware of the College Board's rules helps us cut right to the heart of the matter and identify the only answer choice that will be grammatically acceptable on the SAT.

Page 803, Question 14

This is probably the single Improving Sentences question that I get asked about the most.

Part of the difficulty for most students stems from the fact that the answer choices all involve such long phrases, and that so many of the phrases in the different choices are so similar to one another.

In these situations, it's very important not to get overwhelmed by details. We should just pick a part of the answer choices to focus on and start there, and see what happens.

My inclination would be to start with the shortest answer choice—if that one is grammatically okay, then we know it's the right answer. Unfortunately, in this case the shortest answer choice, (E), would result in an incomplete sentence, because it uses the word "being" instead of "are" or "were." So it's wrong, and we're going to have to work a bit more to answer the question. Oh well.

We could also start with the original version of the underlined phrase, which we'll find in choice (A). (A) really doesn't seem too bad from a grammatical standpoint, but since it's not the shortest answer choice we'll need more than just acceptable grammar. One thing that puts me off about (A) is the phrase "that of the" at the end— that's a lot of short words in a row, and they don't seem to be necessary. At any rate, let's hold on to (A) and keep moving.

We might as well look at (B) next. (B) seems grammatically weird because of the phrase "there were" after the comma.

(C) might seem tempting to a lot of students, but it makes one of the most common (and subtle) errors that the College Board likes to test us on: it switches from plural to singular when it talks about "instruments" at the beginning of the sentence but then switches to the singular verb "was."

(D) is actually going to be the clear winner here when we take everything into consideration. It's grammatically acceptable and it also avoids the short words "that" and "of" that appeared in choice (A). In fact, if we look carefully, (D) has all the same major phrases from (A) but in a slightly different order, and it omits those short words, so it's the best choice.

Since we can clearly articulate a problem with each of the other choices, and since (D) follows the patterns that correct answers tend to follow, we know it's the right choice. As you can see, this type of analysis isn't that hard to do if you just take it step by step, but it does definitely require you to read carefully and pay attention to the text—just like the rest of the SAT does!

Page 837, Question 5

Many students incorrectly choose (E) for this question, because it's the shortest choice and they think it's grammatically okay. But we can't say "emphasize how" in this context; we need to go with "emphasize that." (As is often the case, there are more choices that begin with the word "that" than the word "how," indicating that "that" is probably the correct option.)

The other issue in this question is the incorrect use of "their," which is plural, to refer to the singular noun "woman" in the original sentence. (B) fixes this issue without introducing any "-ing" words like (C) does, so (B) is the right answer.

Page 837, Question 9

This question is another good example of the way zeroing in on a key issue often helps us identify the right answer immediately, without getting bogged down in extraneous stuff.

In this case, the structure "X rather than Y" requires us to put X and Y in the same grammatical form (at least in terms of SAT rules). Since the first half of the sentence has "to appeal and persuade," we need another option with "to" in it. Only (E) has that, with "to educate and inform."

Another way to identify that (E) is correct is to note that it's the shortest answer choice and that it has no grammatical mistakes.

Page 893, Question 8

This question provides us with a good opportunity to observe several of the College Board's patterns and rules in action.

First, since the underlined portion is short, we can expect that the question is probably meant to test grammar alone, which turns out to be the case.

We might also be tempted to assume that the correct answer would avoid the word "in," since the first 3 answer choices start with "either" and only 2 start with "in." But notice that 4 of the choices actually include the word "in" at some point, which suggests that we might want to include it.

Of course, it becomes clear that we need to include "in" when we realize that the question is comparing two things, and that the first part of that comparison is the phrase "in poetry."

That might get us down to (D) and (E). How do we know that (D) is correct? Well, as always, we arrive at that conclusion by thinking carefully about the elements of the question. In order for the phrase "either X or Y" to work on the SAT, X and Y must be two phrases of similar types. If we choose "either fiction or in drama," then X would be "fiction" and Y would be "in drama," which doesn't work on the SAT since one phrase is just a noun and the other begins with the preposition "in." So (D) is the way to go.

Page 925, Question 8

This question stumps a lot of test-takers because most of the answer choices sound pretty decent to most people. This is why it's so important to know the rules of the test. If we know that the shortest answer choice is always correct if it has no grammatical mistakes, we can say with confidence that (C) is the answer choice that the College Board will say is correct.

Page 986, Question 4

This question, like many Improving Sentences questions, is much more straightforward than it probably seems to most untrained test-takers.

(A) is the shortest answer choice and it has no grammatical mistakes, so (A) is automatically correct. That's all there is to this one.

Let this question and the many questions like it remind you of how important it is to know the rules of the test and to read carefully!

Conclusion

We've now discussed all the rules, patterns, and strategies for Improving Sentences questions in the SAT Writing section, and you've seen them in action against a wide variety of actual SAT questions published by the College Board in the Blue Book.

After they've done a lot of Improving Sentences questions, many of my students often remark that these questions just seem to be repeating the same basic ideas over and over again. They're exactly right to think that. And while it might seem frustrating to repeat the same basic steps for 2 dozen questions or so on each test, we have to remember that this repetition is what makes the SAT so beatable once we understand how the game is played. (In fact, the whole point of this Black Book is to show you how to exploit the repetitive nature of the SAT.)

We want to get very familiar with the rules and patterns of every type of SAT question so we can always identify correct answers and incorrect answers. This way, when a question goes well we'll be able to realize that we've found the right answer, and when a question seems not to have a right answer that fits the patterns of all the other questions, we'll know that we've made a mistake somewhere, and we can fix the mistake.

Video Demonstrations

If you'd like to see videos of some sample solutions like the ones in this book, please visit www.SATprepVideos.com. A selection of free videos is available for readers of this book.

On the next page, you'll find a quick summary of the main ideas for Improving Sentences questions. Then we'll tackle the Improving Paragraphs questions after that. They're basically a combination of the SAT grammar and style ideas we've covered already, with some ideas from the Critical Reading section thrown in.

Improving Sentences Quick Summary

This is a one-page summary of the major relevant concepts. Use it to evaluate your comprehension or jog your memory. For a more in-depth treatment of these ideas, see the rest of the section.

The Big Secret: There are 3 bizarre patterns that help us identify the correct answers in situations where it's not clear.

Here are the rules for these questions:

* The SAT grammar concepts from the Identifying Sentence Errors questions still apply to these questions. The right answer must be grammatically okay.
* But SAT style also counts on these questions. Sometimes you'll have two or more choices that are grammatically okay, and then you'll need the style patterns (see below).
* Don't pick a choice that fixes one problem but creates another.
* Choice (A) is always the same as the sentence.

Here are the 3 patterns:

1. Shorter is better, all other things being equal.
2. Fewer words ending in "-ed" or "-ing" is better, all other things being equal.
3. Fewer words that are under 5 letters long ("that," "and," "as," "in," "by," how," and so on) is better, all other things being equal.

Here's the general Improving Sentences process:

1. Read entire prompt sentence.
2. Read the answer choices and eliminate any with grammatical mistakes.
3. If you're not instinctively sure which choice has the best SAT style, then determine which choice follows the most of the 3 patterns above.
4. Read the entire sentence with your preferred answer choice in place of the underlined portion to make sure it's good.
5. Mark your answer or skip the question.

For examples of these principles in action, please see the Blue Book solutions in this Black Book.

Overview and Important Reminders for Improving Paragraphs on the SAT Writing Section

For these questions, you'll be given a short, poorly written composition, and asked questions about how the composition could be improved. In general, the questions will ask about changes that could be made to individual sentences, ways to combine two sentences into one, or additions or subtractions that could be made to individual paragraphs.

The Unwritten Test Design Rule For Improving Paragraphs on the SAT

For the most part, the rules for Improving Paragraphs are essentially the same as the rules for Improving Sentences, because most of these questions are questions that could have appeared as Improving Sentences questions. The only questions you'll have to deal with in this section that are really new are the ones about adding and deleting sentences, so the rule below bears mentioning:

SAT Improving Paragraphs Rule: Ideal Paragraphs

According to the SAT Writing section, the best paragraphs mention each concept in the paragraph more than once.

So whenever you're asked if a sentence should be deleted from a paragraph, choose to delete a sentence if the sentence introduces a topic that isn't mentioned elsewhere in the paragraph. And whenever you're asked if a sentence should be added, choose to add the sentence that will restate the most ideas in the original paragraph, or that introduces the fewest new concepts to the paragraph.

Recommended Step-By-Step Approach To Improving Paragraphs On The SAT

This is the recommended process for SAT Improving Paragraphs questions. Note that it incorporates the processes for the other SAT writing multiple-choice questions, and has some similarity to the Passage-Based Reading process.

1. Identify the type of question you're dealing with.

Remember that the Improving Paragraphs questions are sort of a combination of Improving Sentences questions and Passage-Based Reading questions. Many of the questions are almost exactly like Improving Sentences questions, and those can be answered using almost exactly the same approach as the normal Improving Sentences questions.

2. Consider the Improving Sentences approach, but be careful of small changes.

Use the Improving Sentences approach on the appropriate questions, but be careful—there are certain things you have to look out for. For example, there may not be an underlined portion of the sentence to fix; instead, any portion of the sentence might be changed, or the entire sentence could be replaced with a similar sentence that has the same effect. Still, the goal with these questions will be to find the optimal "SAT-ideal" sentence: the one that avoids the most "bad" patterns and uses the most "good" patterns. So you're looking for things like correct grammar, fewer short words, and so on.

There's another very important difference you need to be aware of! For Improving Paragraphs questions, the best way to deal with a sentence may be to delete the sentence entirely. If the question asks you to add or delete a sentence from a paragraph, remember that the "SAT-ideal" paragraph repeats each concept at least once. This means you should choose to delete (or not to add) sentences that discuss concept that aren't anywhere else in the paragraph, while sentences that stick to the same concepts as the rest of the paragraph should be added or kept.

3. Consider using the Passage-Based Reading Approach to answer the question.

Questions that ask about an author's goal or strategy, or questions that ask about the relationships between one part of a composition and another, can be handled in the same way that we attacked the Passage-Based Reading questions. (As a quick refresher, remember that we NEVER succumb to subjectivity in answering these types of questions, no matter how the prompt for the question is written!)

4. Use the appropriate basic concept to answer the question.

Based on your assessment of the question, answer it by using the appropriate approach from the Improving Sentences of Passage-Based Reading processes.

Conclusion

You've probably noticed that the recommended process for answering these questions types is fairly short. That's because these questions are often extremely similar to the Improving Sentences and Passage-Based Reading questions, so we were able to incorporate the process for those questions in Steps 2 and 3.

At any rate, let's take a look at these processes in action against real SAT questions published by the College Board!

The Recommended Step-By-Step Approach To Improving SAT Paragraphs In Action

In this section, we'll apply what we've learned to some real SAT questions from the College Board's Blue Book, *The Official SAT Study Guide*. I strongly advise you to follow along with these explanations in your copy of the Blue Book to help you learn how to apply these concepts.

Page 411, Question 30

For this question, we need to think about the College Board's idea of the ideal paragraph. (C) will be correct because the paragraph mentions palaces and explains what castles are, but doesn't explain what palaces are. Adding information about what a palace is doesn't introduce a new topic to the paragraph, so the College Board will prefer this answer.

(A) is wrong because medieval history isn't already mentioned in the paragraph.

(B) is wrong because word origins are irrelevant to the passage.

(C) is correct.

(D) doesn't work because sentence 7 isn't talking about the same things as sentence 1.

(E) doesn't work because sentence 3 is relevant to sentence 2, so the College Board won't want us to delete it.

Page 411, Question 31

For this question we need an answer that includes elements of sentences 3 and 4. We can think of this question as something similar to a Passage-Based Reading question, where our job is to find the answer choice that restates elements of the text.

(A) doesn't work because labor isn't mentioned in either sentence.

(B) doesn't work because drawbridges are only mentioned in sentence 3.

(C) works because "obstacles" restates the idea of "stone walls, moats, iron gates, and drawbridges" in sentence 3, while archers shooting out the windows in sentence 4 correspond to the word "peril" in this answer choice.

(D) doesn't work because neither kings nor property nor feudalism appears in sentences 3 and 4.

(E) doesn't work because the word "still" would indicate a contrast to the idea of "marauding plunderers" and "hostile armies," but sentence 4 goes right back to the idea of shooting at "intruders." So neither sentence 3 nor sentence 4 mentions the idea of people coming without "hostile intentions."

Page 411, Question 32

Students often struggle with this question. The correct answer to this question will be the one that produces a sentence in accordance with the College Board's reading comprehension ideas and its grammar and style rules for Writing multiple-choice questions, which we discussed earlier in this section.

(A) doesn't work because the word "because" makes it seem as though the reason that castles had dark dungeons was that palaces had more comforts.

(B) doesn't work because of the phrase "compared to," which makes it seem as though the comforts are being compared to the palaces.

(C) doesn't work because it's technically comparing two things of different types, which the College Board doesn't like. At first, it seems to be comparing castles and palaces, which are both large medieval structures, and which should be fine for the SAT. But if we read carefully, we see that it's technically comparing "medieval castles" to "many comforts," since those two phrases are the beginnings of their parts of the sentence.

In other words, it might have been okay to say this:

While medieval castles offered only dungeons, royal palaces offered many comforts.

But it's not okay to say this on the SAT:

*While medieval castles offered only dungeons, many comforts were in palaces.

In the first version, "medieval castles" are compared to "royal palaces," but the structure of the second version makes us compare "medieval castles" to "comforts."

This is one more example of the supreme importance of reading everything on the SAT very carefully and keeping the rules of the test in mind.

(D) doesn't work because the original text says that castles had dungeons and drafty living quarters "instead of" comforts. But this choice would be saying that castles didn't offer comforts outside of dungeons and drafty quarters. In other words, this choice is saying that there are some comforts to be found in dungeons and drafty quarters, instead of saying that those things exist instead of comforts.

(E) is correct because it says that castles offered few comforts, and that castles had dungeons and drafty quarters, and that some comforts could be found in royal palaces.

Again, this is a very good example of the way we sometimes need to read very carefully to be able to separate a wrong answer from a correct answer.

Page 411, Question 33
For this question, we need a word that demonstrates the relationship among the ideas in sentence 9. Since sentence 9 talks about keeping people away and about attracting visitors, we want a word like "ironically," so (C) is correct. (Remember that the College Board uses the word "ironic" to describe a situation in which two ideas contradict one another—in this case, the idea of keeping people away contradicts the idea of attracting people.) (D) doesn't work because it would establish a contrast between sentence 8 and sentence 9, not a contrast between the ideas in sentence 9 itself.

Page 412, Question 34
For this question, we need to insert an idea that restates concepts from the paragraph. (D) is correct because it restates ideas from sentence 12, since "crumbling away" goes with "decaying," and "relative obscurity" goes with "ordinary street." No other answer choice restates ideas from the paragraph. (A) comes close when it mentions the idea of being "obsolete," but (A) says that there are some castles that aren't obsolete, while sentence 8 says that "castles were made obsolete." In other words, (A) contradicts the text.

Page 412, Question 35
Again, we want a sentence that restates a concept from sentence 12, almost as though this were a Passage-Based Reading question. Choice (B) is correct because the word "there" in the answer choice goes with "in one village," "medieval austerity" in the answer choice goes with "castle," and "modern comfort" in the answer choice goes with "cozy . . . houses."

Conclusion

This was pretty small set of questions, but that's because there are only 6 of these questions on each test anyway. We'll move on to some of the harder ones from the Blue Book in the next section. And remember that you can see a free selection of video solutions to SAT questions at www.SATprepVideos.com.

Selection of Challenging Questions

We've just finished answering a whole test's worth of Improving Paragraphs questions. Now let's take a look through the College Board's Blue Book (the *Official SAT Study Guide*) and talk about some of the challenging Improving Paragraphs questions from the rest of the book.

We'll find that all of the other Improving Paragraphs questions rely on the same basic concepts from the Improving Sentences questions and the Passage-Based Reading questions that we've already discussed elsewhere in this book; our job as test-takers is really just to look for opportunities to apply those principles on each new question. Following along with these solutions in your copy of the Blue Book will help you continue to improve your performance on Improving Paragraphs questions.

As with all the other question explanations in this book, you'll need a copy of the second edition of the "Blue Book" to follow along. Let's get started!

Page 473, Question 30

This question is basically an Improving Sentences question. That means we should choose the answer that combines correct grammar with the most ideal stylistic patterns (all according to the College Board, of course).

The original version of the sentence isn't grammatically acceptable because it's a comma splice—in other words, it incorrectly uses a comma to join two sets of words that could each stand as complete sentences on their own. Choice (B) is grammatically okay. Choice (C) is grammatically unacceptable, since it would technically be making the "version" the thing that was doing the "expecting." Choice (D) is almost grammatically acceptable, but putting the word "these" in a new sentence introduces some ambiguity: "these" might refer to the plural word "reviews" or to the plural word "purists." (E) is grammatically acceptable because the comma after "purists" makes it clear that the phrase "those who expect" is referring to that word.

So that leaves us with (B) and (E) as grammatically acceptable options according to the SAT. Now we need to figure out which option has the best style according to the College Board. We can use the style patterns from the Improving Sentences questions for that. We see that (E) is shorter, has fewer words ending in "-ed," and has fewer words that are less than 5 letters long.

So (E) will be the choice that the College Board says is correct.

Page 473, Question 33

This question is essentially a Passage-Based Reading question, so we're just looking for the answer choice that describes the first paragraph of the essay.

(A) is the correct answer because the verb "elaborate" means to discuss something in detail, and the "view" being discussed in detail in the first paragraph is the view that these remakes are "disrespectful and a waste of time and money." The rest of the essay then "contrasts" with that view.

(B) is wrong because no personal experience is included in the first paragraph—the author never says, "I went to see movie X and this is what I thought . . ."

(C) is wrong because the first paragraph does *mention* what some modern critics have thought, but it doesn't *analyze* what they've thought. For this answer to be correct, the text would need to discuss the motivations and repercussions of modern criticism, which it doesn't do.

(D) is wrong because there is no introduction, and the passage isn't about any kind of approach to writing fiction.

(E) is wrong because the text never mentions playfulness.

Page 536, Question 30

This question is essentially an Improving Sentences question. To answer it, we'll find the version of the sentence with acceptable grammar and the most ideal stylistic choices.

The shortest answer choice for this question is (E), and it's grammatically acceptable. So it's going to be the right answer . . . as long as the word "it" at the beginning of the sentence is referring to a singular noun from the previous sentence. So we check the previous sentence, and confirm that the word "it" in sentence 2 is referring to the word "camp" from sentence 1. So (E) checks out as the correct answer.

Page 536, Question 32

This question probably looks pretty bizarre, but it's actually asking us to use the same kinds of paraphrasing skills we would use in a Passage-Based Reading question. The correct answer here is (D), because this sentence restates the ideas in sentence 5: "live together" in sentence 8 is the same thing as "eat and play together, share bunkhouses."

Page 536, Question 34

These types of questions are often confusing for untrained test-takers, but we should know by now that we're going to answer this by applying the rules and patterns from the Improving Sentences questions, particularly the patterns about making sentences as short as possible, avoiding words ending in "-ing" and "-ed," and avoiding short words.

Only (C) would bring the sentence more in line with those patterns, by swapping an "-ing" word ("being") and a short word ("that") for the word "since." (A) and (B) would only make the sentence longer, (D) would have no real effect, and (E) would create a grammatical mistake.

This question is just one more great example of how important it is to be aware of the subtle patterns on the SAT!

Page 603, Question 31

At first, this question looks like it's basically an Improving Sentences question. If we look carefully, though, we'll see that many of the answer choices seem grammatically and stylistically okay from the College Board's standpoint, but no two answer choices express exactly the same idea. That means we also need to bring in some Reading Comprehension skills to see which answer choice is restating the concepts in the original sentence.

One thing that's very important to realize here is that the second sentence is saying that the *worker* needs to "assume responsibility." We know this because the second sentence says "he or she" should assume it, and "he or she" can only refer to a singular noun. The only singular noun in the previous sentence is the word "worker," so the worker needs to do the assuming.

(D) might seem like a good answer choice, but (D) actually says that the only workers who need to assume responsibility are the ones "whose employers are familiar." The original text doesn't say that, though—it says that any worker should assume responsibility.

(B) is the only answer choice that gets that relationship exactly right, because it says that all workers need to assume responsibility, just like the original version of sentence 3.

Remember that it's absolutely critical to read things carefully and to think about the rules of the SAT! If you commit to doing that on each question, you'll be nearly unstoppable.

Page 604, Question 33

This question is essentially an Improving Sentences question. The shortest answer choice is (D), but it has a grammatical mistake: it results in a sentence fragment. So now let's think about other patterns.

(A) is a run-on sentence, so it can't be right.

(B) is pretty awkward, but let's try to quantify what's actually wrong with it (just calling something "awkward" is too subjective to be a reliable approach). It has 9 short words (which are words less than 5 letters long, as I mentioned in our discussion of the patterns to look out for on Improving Sentences questions).

(C) has 7 short words, along with 1 "-ing" word.

(E) has 5 short words and 1 "-ing" word.

So the answer choice with the fewest offensive words (according to the College Board's unwritten rules and patterns) is choice (E), which means (E) will be correct. It's grammatically acceptable and does the best job of conforming to the College Board's patterns of preferring the fewest short words and the fewest "-ed" or "-ing" words possible.

Just to be crystal clear, I'd like to reiterate that there's nothing actually wrong with short words or "-ing" words in real life. The reason we care about them on the SAT is that the College Board generally doesn't like to see those kinds of words in correct answers on Improving Sentences questions. Once more we see the extreme importance of knowing the unique rules that the test follows.

Page 661, Question 30

This question is basically a Passage-Based Reading question, so we'll answer it by reading carefully and avoiding any kind of subjective interpretation.

(A) works because the "possible response" might be that a person who reads sentence 1 wonders if "microphones" are involved, since sentence 1 mentions "listening in."

(B) might seem tempting, but the second sentence doesn't actually provide "historical background" *for sentence 1.* It does provide a historical fact, but it doesn't provide background for sentence 1 because sentence 1 isn't set in the historical time period mentioned in sentence 2. Sentence 2 is talking about how things were in the middle ages, but sentence 1 is talking about "this summer."

(C) is wrong because no idea is repeated.

(D) is wrong because no contrasting view is mentioned. The first sentence says the author "felt as if" something was happened, while the second sentence says that thing could not literally have happened. But the first sentence doesn't say that anything *did* happen—it just says the author *felt like* it happened. So there's no actual contrast here.

(E) is wrong for the same reason (D) is. It would have been inaccurate to say that the writer really was listening in on the middle age, but that's not what sentence 1 says—sentence 1 just says the writer "felt as if" that was happening, which isn't necessarily an inaccurate statement.

This question is one more example of the importance of reading every word carefully. (Now that this book is almost over, you've probably noticed that I've come back to the idea of reading everything carefully roughly a million times. There's a reason for that. Reading *everything* carefully is the single most important thing we can do as SAT-takers.)

Page 661, Question 35

This is basically a Passage-Based Reading question, so we'll answer it by looking carefully at the text.

(A) appears in the passage in places like sentence 6, when the author gives "background information" on the practical realities of traveling in the middle ages.

(B) would be kind of troubling to me: there's definitely description, but how can we know for sure if the College Board thinks the description is "imaginative?" I would put this answer aside and keep looking to see what the other choices are. If one of the other choices clearly isn't in the passage, then we'll know that must be right, and we'll know that the College Board apparently considers this kind of description to be "imaginative."

(C) is clearly not anywhere in the passage—not only are there no "rhetorical questions," but there aren't any questions at all, of any kind. There are no question marks. So we now know that (C) is the thing missing from the text, and (B) must be present in the text. This means (C) is correct, since the question asked us to find the one choice that wasn't present in the passage.

(D) is in the text because the entire passage is narrated in the first person.

(E) is in the text because sentences 10 and 11 contain quotations.

Page 778, Question 32

This question is essentially a Passage-Based Reading question.

(A) doesn't work because the topics in sentence 5 have already appeared in the essay.

(B) doesn't work for basically the same reason that (A) doesn't work. Even if Nancy Price is an example of something, she's already been mentioned, so sentence 5 doesn't provide an additional example of anything.

(C) works, and for a pretty subtle reason: the word "right" in the sentence emphasizes the word "there." I'll have more to say on this after we go through the other answer choices.

(D) doesn't work because there are no contrasting discussions in the essay.

(E) doesn't work because this is a statement of fact, not an opinion of the author.

This is a question that many test-takers will be inclined to guess on, or to skip, because none of the answer choices is likely to seem too appealing. We can only realize that (C) is correct if we notice that the phrase "right there" is a way to emphasize a particular location—in this context, the only way that the word "right" can make any sense is as a word emphasizing the word "there."

This is a pretty subtle thing to notice, but it's also as clear as day once we do notice it. And the ability to pay close attention and notice these kinds of things is exactly the kind of skill we need to have if we're going to get an elite score on the SAT.

Page 779, Question 35

This question is one that most untrained test-takers will struggle with, because they don't know the College Board's style patterns (which we talked about in the section on Improving Sentences questions).

But since we know those patterns, all we have to do is look for the answer choice that would violate those patterns the most (because the question asks us to find the worst answer choice in terms of those patterns, not the best one).

The two choices that would violate the patterns at all are (C) and (E). (C) adds an "-ed" word and makes the sentence a little longer, while (E) adds one extra short word and makes the sentence longer as well. So each choice adds in a new word that goes against the patterns, but if we look closely we can see that (E) makes the sentence slightly longer overall than (C) does. This means that (E) will be the revision that the College Board dislikes the most. Once more, the SAT's style patterns save the day.

I realize that it's a little ridiculous that the width of a couple of letters is enough to make one answer choice right and another wrong, but these are the principles the College Board has decided to follow, so these are the principles we have to use when answering questions on the SAT Writing section.

Page 840, Question 32

This question is basically an Improving Sentences question. Since the shortest answer choice, (C), has no grammatical mistakes, it's the right answer according to the College Board's rules and patterns. Some students like (A), but (A) is another example of a comma splice: both sets of words on either side of the comma could be a sentence by themselves, which makes a comma inappropriate.

Page 840, Question 34

This question asks us which sentence should be inserted into the paragraph. In these cases, we'll look for the answer choice that has the most in common with the concepts that are already in the passage, because that's what the College Board likes.

Choices (A) and (D) might both seem like pretty good options at first glance. In these cases, one of two things is basically possible: either there's some small distinction between the two choices that makes one of them right, or they're actually both wrong.

So let's see if we can identify any differences between them that are relevant to what the SAT likes when it comes to Improving Paragraphs questions.

One thing that jumps out at me is that (A) involves the idea of the mother teaching the speaker something, while (D) omits any mention of the mother.

Since the mother appears throughout the essay, and since we know that the College Board likes us to introduce sentences that include concepts that are already in the essay, we can tell that (A) must be the right answer here.

Remember that knowing the real rules and patterns of the test will always allow us to know which answers are correct with total certainty.

Page 840, Question 35

This question asks us where a new paragraph should begin, which is kind of an unusual thing for the College Board to ask. But we still answer this question by choosing the answer that will group similar concepts together into paragraphs.

(D) is correct because it allows us to group all the sentences about the speaker being an authority at school into one paragraph without other ideas being involved.

Page 897, Question 34

This question might look at first like an Improving Sentences question, but it actually has elements of Passage-Based Reading in it, as well. Many of the answer choices may seem grammatically or stylistically similar, but only one answer choice begins with a phrase that ties it back to the previous sentences in the essay. Choice (B) begins with "in addition," which shows that the idea in this sentence is meant as another example of the way that Hoover "triumphed over the limits of her position and the times in which she lived," as described in sentence 12.

This question is an excellent example of the way that an easily overlooked issue like the lead-in phrase on a sentence can clearly indicate which answer is correct once we notice it.

Page 958, Question 30

This question asks us how to handle sentence 4, so we'll rely mostly on the approach we would use for Improving Sentences questions. Since the question gives us the option to delete or move the sentence, we may also have to consider the College Board's patterns for ideal paragraphs. Let's see what happens.

(A) doesn't seem to make much sense because we should delete sentences if they only contain ideas that don't appear elsewhere in the paragraph, which isn't the case here.

(B) doesn't work because nothing would be improved from the standpoint of the College Board's patterns if those two sentences were switched.

(C) might look like a pretty bad answer at first, since it would make the sentence longer, which is generally not good on the SAT. But (C) actually fixes an SAT grammatical issue that we might not have noticed originally: the word "they" in sentence 4 technically can't refer to the word "elevator" in sentence 3, because "elevator" is singular and "they" is plural. So this answer choice actually fixes a grammatical issue that no other choice will fix, which is why it's correct.

(D) doesn't help any of the College Board's rules or patterns for the Writing section.

(E) just makes the sentence longer without fixing anything.

Once more we see the importance of reading carefully and knowing the test's rules!

Conclusion

Now you've covered everything you need to know in order to answer Improving Paragraphs questions on the Writing Section of the SAT. As long as you remember that these questions are mostly Improving Sentences and Passage-Based Reading questions in disguise, you'll have no problems.

The next page contains a one-page summary of the major ideas for the Improving Paragraphs questions. Make sure you don't stop reading after that, though—we still have a few important points to consider.

Video Demonstrations

If you'd like to see videos of some sample solutions like the ones in this book, please visit www.SATprepVideos.com. A selection of free videos is available for readers of this book.

Improving Paragraphs Quick Summary

This is a one-page summary of the major relevant concepts. Use it to evaluate your comprehension, jog your memory, whatever. For a more in-depth treatment of these ideas, see the rest of the section.

The Big Secret: These questions are basically <u>a combination of Improving Sentences questions and Passage-Based Reading questions</u>, with one more idea thrown in.

These questions can seem to vary widely on the surface but <u>they're all basically the same.</u>

<u>Questions that ask about fixing or combining sentences should be answered like Improving Sentences questions.</u> Find the choice that follows the SAT grammar rules and has the best SAT style according to the 3 Improving Sentences patterns.

<u>Questions that ask about the meaning of a word or phrase should be treated like Passage-Based Reading questions.</u>

The SAT likes paragraphs in which every concept appears more than once. So if you're asked to add or delete sentences, then:

- <u>add sentences that restate ideas in the paragraph and contribute the fewest new concepts</u>
- <u>delete sentences that mention ideas that aren't found   elsewhere in the paragraph</u>

Here's the Improving Paragraphs process:

1. Identify the type of question you're dealing with.
2. Use the modified Improving Sentences approach for questions about fixing or combining sentences.
3. Use the Passage-Based Reading approach for questions about the meanings of words or phrases.
4. If you're asked about adding or deleting sentences, add sentences that restate ideas in the paragraph, and/or delete sentences that mention ideas that aren't elsewhere in the paragraph.

For examples of these ideas in action, please see the sample Blue Book solutions in this Black Book.

Being An SAT Machine

"Trifles make perfection, and perfection is no trifle."
- Michelangelo

In this book, I talk a lot about how to answer individual questions. Obviously, that's an important part of beating the SAT.

But you may have noticed that the processes and sample solutions get pretty repetitive pretty quickly. My students often complain, "After a while, doing these questions is just the same thing over and over . . ."

Some teachers might be insulted by that, but when I hear those magic words I just smile and say, "Exactly!" On a standardized test, when answering questions begins to feel repetitive and automatic, you know you've made a huge improvement.

Standardized Tests Have Standardized Questions

It seems obvious, but a lot of people never realize that standardized tests must have standardized questions and standardized answers—otherwise, the results from one test day would have no relation to the results from another, and the test would be meaningless.

In writing the Black Book, my goal has been to teach you the standardization rules of the test, so that you can know how to attack every real SAT question you'll ever see.

Never forget that the SAT is a test with rules and patterns that it has to follow, and once you start to unlock them you almost can't go wrong—it's almost like you turn into an SAT machine.

An SAT Machine At Work

One of the things I often do for students is show them how I would take a section of the test. I don't just show them the processes and strategies I use, although the processes and strategies are definitely very important. I also show them the speed and the attitude I use to approach the test. What do I mean by that?

When I'm taking the SAT, I have an inner dialogue going on in my head. It's very simple and straightforward. I'm reading each question, thinking briefly about what kind of question it is, then walking myself through the various steps described in these pages. It's all second nature to me. And when I get to the answer choices, I'm ruthless about cutting them out—as soon as I see something wrong with an answer, it's gone. Bam. Bam. Bam. Question. Bam. First step. Bam. Second step. Bam. Answer choices—bam, bam, bam, bam, bam. Next question. Bam. I keep it going until I'm done with the section, then check my answers. Unless I get confused or lose my concentration, I usually finish each section in well under half the allotted time. And it's not because I'm rushing or anything. I just don't waste time thinking about any unnecessary aspects of the questions.

When I take a test, there's no dilly-dallying or second-guessing. I'm prepared, and I know what to expect, because I know the SAT is ALWAYS THE SAME in all the important ways.

Becoming An SAT Machine

When most students take the SAT, they let their minds wander. They don't realize that every question has one clear answer, so they waste their time trying to justify every answer choice to themselves. They don't have set processes to rely on. They don't know the recurring rules and patterns to look for in every question. In other words, they don't take advantage of any of the gaping holes in the SAT's armor. They're inefficient and unfocused, and their scores suffer for it.

So what do you do if you want to turn into a machine? The key thing is to remember that every question has one clear answer, and that you can find it. Stick to a game plan—know how to start in on any SAT question and keep going until you either arrive at the answer or decide to skip the question. Then just keep working your system all the way through the test. That's it. Don't get distracted. Rely on the test to give you the same sorts of questions you've seen before—because it definitely will. It has to.

In a way, taking the SAT is similar to taking a driving test. You know in advance which skills you'll be asked to demonstrate and what rules you'll have to follow during the test; what you don't know is the specific situation you'll be in when you demonstrate each skill. Keep this in mind—stay flexible about applying what you know, but never forget that the range of things you can be asked to do on the SAT is very limited.

Also, as weird as it might sound, you should strive for the SAT to be boring and repetitive. Some students look at the SAT as a way to be creative—what's the point of that? Find each answer, and practice finding it as efficiently as possible. You'll be attacking the test in a systematic, methodical way before you know it—and that's the secret to real SAT success.

What Are The College Board's Resources Good For?

"At the College Board, our mission is to connect students to college success."
- Gaston Caperton, former President of the College Board

I talk a lot about how you need to use College Board materials when you study, especially the Blue Book. The College Board is the company that writes the SAT, and they're the only source of real SAT questions, which are absolutely essential if you're going to prepare intelligently.

But that doesn't mean that you should take everything the College Board says about the SAT as the truth. Trusting them too much would be a huge mistake.

I keep telling you to practice with the Blue Book, which is the College Board publication *The Official SAT Study Guide*. But I don't want you to listen to the College Board's advice on test-taking, because it's usually pretty bad. So I've written this section of the Black Book to explain exactly how you should use the College Board's materials. You have to use them properly if you want to do your best.

The "Blue Book" (The Official SAT Study Guide)

The first thing we'll look at is the proper way to use the College Board publication *The Official SAT Study Guide*. I've gone through the book page-by-page to explain the best way to approach it.

Third unnumbered page

The third unnumbered page of *The Official SAT Study Guide* contains a letter from Gaston Caperton, the President of the College Board. It includes this sentence:

The best preparation for the SAT, and for college, is to take challenging courses.

This is laughable.

You should take challenging courses because they help you become a better person. They don't do anything at all to help you on the SAT, and it can be argued they don't do anything to help you in college either. I would love it if they did, but they don't.

Advanced courses will teach you to write well, for example, while the SAT will reward the sort of elementary, cookie-cutter writing that appears in our earlier discussion on the SAT Essay, and in the College Board's own sample essay. Advanced courses will teach you higher math principles that will never appear on the SAT. Advanced courses will teach you to read and analyze a text like a literary critic, but the SAT will ask you to forego all subtlety and nuance and answer questions like a third-grader writing a book report.

The best way to prepare for the SAT is to get a bunch of sample tests written by the College Board and pull them apart on a technical level to see what they keep doing, and then learn how to do those things—and only those things—well. And that's what the Black Book is all about.

Pages 3 – 6

These pages sketch out the format and background of the SAT and its development. You can read them if you want, but they're pretty useless as far as doing well on the test is concerned.

Pages 6 – 8

These pages explain the way the test is scored, and tell you how to interpret your score report. You'll definitely want to read them when you get your scores back, but if you haven't taken the test yet you can skip them for now.

Pages 9 – 10

This section explains the College Board's general theory about how you should prepare for the SAT.

Ignore it.

Pages 10 – 11

This lays out the online resources that are available to you through the College Board's web site.

Pages 12 – 13

You MUST read these pages before test day. They lay out the things you'll need to take with you to the testing site.

Pages 13 – 15

You can pretty much ignore this part. You should especially ignore the part on page 14 that talks about the difficulty level of questions going from easy to hard within a section. (See the section of this book called "8 Things You Thought You Knew About The SAT Are Wrong.")

Pages 15 – 17

These pages discuss the traditional guessing strategy. Skip them, and check out my section on SAT-guessing in the Black Book instead.

Pages 17 – 18

These pages give you the College Board's take on test anxiety. It might be useful to read this if you're looking for another perspective on the issue, but it isn't necessary.

Pages 20 – 26

These pages explain how to use the PSAT. They're useful as general information.

Pages 29 – 30

These pages give you the College Board's general advice on how to approach the Critical Reading Section. You should ignore it.

Pages 31 – 43

This section gives you some sample Sentence Completion questions and lets you see the College Board's approach to them. It's different from the approach I recommend, and it doesn't take you step-by-step through the process of completing any question.

Pages 44 – 48

These pages give you some sample Sentence Completion questions to practice on. Give them a shot if you want.

Pages 49 – 56

This section explains how the College Board suggests you approach Passage-Based Reading questions. You are STRONGLY cautioned to ignore these pages—they tell you to approach the questions subjectively, which is not only bad advice but would be an invalid basis for the design of a standardized multiple-choice test.

Pages 57 – 96

These pages give you some sample questions. The first questions also have sample responses. Give these a look if you want; you might find them useful for practice.

Pages 99 – 102

These pages introduce you to the Writing Section of the SAT. Ignore them.

Pages 103 – 108

These pages explain how the College Board thinks you should approach the essay part of the SAT. Ignore them. Make sure you especially ignore the scoring manual on page 105—instead, use the advice in this book.

Pages 105 – 119

These pages provide several useless writing exercises. Do them if you feel like it, but don't expect them to help you on the SAT at all.

Pages 130 – 136

This section provides several sample essay responses. Compare them—and the sample essay responses that appear elsewhere in the book—to the scoring guide on page 105 and decide for yourself if that guide is any real indication of what scores high on the SAT.

Pages 137 – 139

These pages introduce the Identifying Sentence Errors questions, and give you the College Board's advice for approaching them. Some of the advice is okay, like looking for the mistakes that commonly appear on the test. But other advice is probably not that helpful. For example, you're advised to practice by reading sentences out loud—even though acceptable spoken English and acceptable written English are pretty different, and you won't be able to read aloud on test day.

Pages 139 – 144

These pages give you a chance to practice rewriting sentences—something you'll NEVER do on the SAT. This is pretty much a waste of your time.

Pages 145 – 152

This section gives you some sample questions to practice on. Go for it if you want.

Pages 153 – 154

This section introduces you to the Improving Sentences questions and gives you the College Board's advice for these questions. As usual, you can ignore it.

Pages 154 – 160

These pages have more writing exercises on them, which are pretty much a waste of time as far as the SAT is concerned. Skip them, unless you feel like doing them for some non-SAT-related fun.

Pages 161 – 168

These pages have samples for the Improving Sentences questions. Do them if you feel like it; it can't hurt.

Pages 169 – 170

This section introduces you to the Improving Paragraphs questions. Again, it gives some pretty poor advice for these questions.

Pages 170 – 177

This section provides even more writing exercises that won't help you do multiple-choice questions at all.

Pages 178 – 188

These pages give you sample Improving Paragraphs questions to work on. It can't hurt to practice with them if you feel like it.

Pages 189 – 214

These pages let you practice all the question types in the SAT Writing Section. Give them a shot if you feel like it. Make sure to check out the sample essays on pages 197 – 212, and remember to compare them to the scoring guide on page 105. You'll see that high-scoring essays have several grammatical errors, and that the most reliable way to predict an essay's score is to see how long it is.

Pages 216 – 225

These pages introduce you to the Math Section of the SAT, and give you the College Board's ideas about the best way to approach it. You can skip this if you feel like it.

Pages 227 – 302

These pages take you through all the mathematical concepts you'll need for the SAT. This section is similar in content to the Math Toolbox in this book, but the Toolbox is more simplified. If you don't understand a concept after looking at the Toolbox list, or if you just want another explanation of something, then give this section a try. Just like the Toolbox, this part of *The Official SAT Study Guide* contains every single math concept you'll need on the SAT.

Pages 303 – 304

These pages explain how the College Board thinks you should approach multiple-choice questions on the SAT. Ignore this advice, especially the part on guessing (see my advice on guessing earlier in the Black Book instead).

Pages 305 – 342

This section provides sample multiple-choice questions, some with explanations. Give them a shot.

Pages 343 – 346

You MUST read these pages. They'll explain how to fill out the grids for the Student-Produced Response questions. They'll also remind you that it's okay to guess on these questions, because on these questions there's no penalty for wrong answers.

Pages 347 – 364

These pages give you sample problems for the Student-Produced Response questions on the SAT. Try them if you feel like it.

Pages 365 – 376

This section gives you general math questions to practice with. Try them out.

Pages 377 – 889

These pages are the meat of the College Board's book. They provide you with sample tests written by the test-maker, which you absolutely must use to get your score as high as possible.

The Official SAT Online Course

The College Board provides an online tool that you can use to get extra help on the test. It's called the Official SAT Online Course, and you can access it from www.collegeboard.com. It has a variety of tools that you might find useful as you apply to college—sample tests, lessons, study planners, and so on. Use these if you want.

The sample tests will be especially helpful as you search for more official SAT questions if you exhaust the ones from the Blue Book. The lessons and quizzes probably won't do you too much good, but I guess they can't hurt either apart from the time they take up.

Conclusion

You simply can't prepare for the SAT effectively if you don't use the sample tests and other resources provided by the College Board—the College Board is the only source of real SAT questions on the entire planet, and real SAT questions are essential to the preparation process.

But that doesn't mean you should take everything the College Board says at face value! Much of their advice reflects what they *wish* the SAT were like, not what it actually *is*.

8 Things You Thought You Knew About The SAT Are Wrong

"As a general rule the most successful man in life is the man who has the best information."
- Benjamin Disraeli

If you're taking the SAT, you're going to get a lot of advice from other people about the best way to approach the test. It might surprise you to know that the vast majority of SAT information that most people have access to is very, very incorrect. In my years of teaching people about the SAT, I've heard all sorts of myths, rumors, and lies about the test. Believe it or not, some of this misinformation comes from the College Board itself. Some of it comes from colleges, guidance counselors, and teachers. And still more comes from your friends and peers, and from popular web sites. Most—but not all—of the people who spread this misinformation are well-intentioned, but that doesn't change the fact that bad information leads to lower test scores for you, and that's bad.

With that in mind, I've set out a few common SAT myths, misconceptions, and lies about the SAT. But first, I'll tell you how to verify any SAT rumor you might hear in the future.

How To Find The Truth About The SAT

One of the strangest things about all the SAT myths and rumors that are out there is that it's so easy to disprove them with a little research, but nobody takes the time. This is a huge mistake.

Make a commitment to yourself that you won't accept a single new piece of SAT advice from anyone, no matter the source, without checking it out for yourself to see if it's true. (Yes, I'm including the Black Book in this statement—I'm sure it stands up to the test, unlike most of the other SAT advice you'll encounter.)

How do you check it out? If the advice is related to the SAT itself, you can usually check to see if it's true by looking at some sample tests WRITTEN BY THE COLLEGE BOARD. Of course, you can get these by consulting your copy of the Blue Book, *The Official SAT Study Guide*. Do NOT, under any circumstances, attempt to learn anything meaningful about the SAT by consulting a fake SAT test written by a test prep company or a web site. Many simply don't know how to write them correctly, and those fake tests are totally useless.

(Note that I'm not suggesting you take the College Board's advice about the SAT—I'm suggesting that you try out all SAT advice against the actual sample SATs written by the College Board. The College Board is often wrong about its own test, as strange as that might sound. You can prove this by comparing the essay-scoring chart on page 105 of the Blue Book to the actual high- and low-scoring essays that also appear in that book. What the College Board says it rewards is not what actually appears in those essays.)

If the advice is related to the way a particular college or university uses the SAT in its admissions process, one way to check it is to call up the school yourself and get the real answer, or visit the school's web site. The admissions people typically won't lie to you (notice I didn't say they'll NEVER lie to you). Unfortunately, admissions departments are not a perfect source of information. They may not always give you a straight answer about the role the SAT plays in their schools' selection processes. Fortunately, though, schools don't usually lie about their raw data—you can usually do an online search for a school's median SAT scores and grade point averages for the previous year's admissions pool, and that information is typically trustworthy.

So that's it—the only two places you should look to when you want to confirm something about the SAT are (1) the actual SAT, and (2) the schools you're interested in attending. That's it.

Notice who's not on that list: guidance counselors, friends, students and alumni of your target schools, even your parents. I'm not saying that all of these sources will be wrong all the time—I'm simply pointing out that these sources are never the final authority on the SAT. They might give you good information, but you'll never know for sure if it's good until you verify it with the actual test or with the schools you want to attend.

Now that we've established how to test all SAT-related advice, let's talk about some of the bad information that's out there.

Misinformation From The College Board

We've already talked about how to use the College Board's resources. As you'll see if you look at that section of the manual, much of the College Board's advice about taking the SAT is based on what can only be called a set of illusions about what the SAT really is and what it really does. (What's the rest of it based on? I can't tell, but most of it still isn't any good.) Let's take a look.

SAT Misconception 1: The SAT tests the skills that a good college student needs.

This is the major gimmick of the College Board. I explain what's wrong with this idea in almost every section of this manual: basically, there's no way that a standardized test can possibly measure a student's ability to perform in college, because college is a non-standardized environment.

This particular idea—the idea that the SAT actually measures something besides how well you do on the SAT—is very dangerous to SAT-takers. Since you're an SAT-taker, I want you to know the truth.

I can't tell you how many times a well-meaning student has told me that he wants to turn the SAT into a real intellectual challenge. He's going to take advanced calculus as a junior so he'll know enough math; he's going to read Cicero over the summer in the original Latin to learn how to craft a sentence; he's going to volunteer twenty hours a week tutoring young children to sharpen his mind and purify his soul.

Now, all of those things are great. They'll make you a more intelligent person and a more attractive candidate in the admissions process. But they absolutely will NOT help you on the SAT, because the SAT is NOT an indication of how intelligent or well-rounded you are. The SAT is basically an indication of how well you can read one sheet of paper and fill in the right bubbles on another sheet of paper that gets fed into a machine.

So, then, what's the best way to get ready for the SAT? By attacking it on a technical level. By pulling it apart and finding all the hidden rules and patterns that dictate how the questions are written. Establish processes that let you attack every single question like a machine. Master the small list of skills that are tested over and over again. In other words, do the stuff I teach you to do in this Black Book.

Give up the idea that the SAT tests college-related skills. We'd all like it to do that, but that isn't what it does. Read Cicero if you want to, but it won't help on the SAT much more than watching Sesame Street every morning.

Fact: The SAT is NOT a test of the skills you'll need in college. The best way to approach the SAT is to attack it on a technical level and turn yourself into an SAT machine.

SAT Misconception 2: "Educated" guessing is a good idea.

I've already covered this one in some depth. In case you missed it, though, check out the section on guessing.

Fact: Guessing on the SAT is NOT a good idea.

SAT Misconception 3: Hard questions appear at the end of each group of questions.

On page 14 of *The Official SAT Study Guide*, this sentence appears:

> Within a group of questions, . . . the easier ones come first and the questions
> become more difficult as you move along.

This is another one of those things everybody knows about the SAT that isn't actually true. The College Board tells you it's true. So do most major test-prep companies. But it isn't—at least, it's not always true, and it's not true for every test-taker.

There are two ways I can prove that you won't necessarily find the tenth question in a group more difficult than the first question. First, turn to any answer key page in the *Official SAT Study Guide* (the Blue Book) to see the difficulty levels that the College Board has assigned to all the questions for that sample test. You'll see that it's absolutely not true that every question is at least as difficult as the one before it. So that's one way to disprove this misconception.

But there's another, much better reason to ignore the idea of an order of difficulty on the SAT. The College Board assigns difficulty levels to questions based on how well other students do against the questions—for example, if most other people get a question right, the College Board decides it's an easy question. That means that the difficulty ranking assigned by the College Board has nothing to do with the specific concepts in the question, and assumes that you're exactly like the average test-taker, which you aren't. Most test-takers don't know how the test works, and don't know how important it is to read everything carefully. But you do know that. Most won't read this Black Book. But you will. So you're better prepared for the test than the people who are used to determine the difficulty ranking, which means you're likely to find that the difficulty ranking becomes increasingly meaningless to you.

So there are two major flaws with the idea of the difficulty ranking. First, the College Board doesn't present questions in a strict rank order. Second, and, more importantly, the ranking system it uses is meaningless to a well-trained test-taker anyway.

Fact: Any given SAT question might be easy or hard for you, regardless of whether it appears early or late in a group of questions.

Misinformation From Colleges

Believe it or not, colleges don't know that much about the SAT, even though they are the driving force that keeps it a popular test. After all, the latest changes to the SAT, which have made it more beatable than it ever was, were made largely at the request of the California University System—who thought they were turning the test into a better tool for measuring college-readiness, a tool that would be almost impossible to game. So be careful about what colleges say when it comes to the SAT.

SAT Misconception 4: Colleges don't care about the SAT.

I was actually taking a tour of Princeton years ago when someone asked the admissions rep giving the tour what Princeton thought of the SAT. He said that Princeton didn't care at all about a student's SAT score.

We asked him to repeat himself, and he said again that a student's SAT score didn't matter to Princeton at all.

Now, I'm not ready to say this guy was lying. He knows more about Princeton's admissions process than I do. But let's look at some facts from Princeton's own data.

Princeton's own fact sheet for a recent entering class shows that the middle 50% of those admitted for that year were in the top 1 percentile of all SAT-takers. That's awfully coincidental for a school that doesn't care about SAT scores, isn't it?

In addition, Princeton (like almost every other reputable school in America) takes the trouble of requiring students to submit SAT scores in the first place. Given that roughly 15,000 students apply to Princeton in a given year, let's assume that it takes an average of one minute for someone to receive a score report in an application, process it for review, and pass it along to a decision-maker for final consideration in conjunction with the rest of an application (probably a low estimate, but go with me here). That would mean that Princeton spends approximately 250 hours every admissions cycle—basically a month and a half of 40-hour work weeks for one employee—gathering data that it doesn't care about. Does that make any sense to you?

I'm only using Princeton as one example here. Lots of colleges tell their applicants they don't care about the SAT—but if that's true, why do the scores of their admitted applicants fall into such a narrow range every year? And why do they require you to submit scores from the SAT in the first place?

Fact: Colleges sure seem to spend a lot of time gathering SAT data from their students for it not to matter to them—and it's very coincidental that every college's pool of admitted students falls into a narrow SAT scoring band. The data suggest that most schools care about the SAT, even if they occasionally say otherwise.

Misinformation From Your Friends And Family

Now we're getting into a sore area. Most students are willing to accept that the information they get from the outside world might not be that reliable. But now I'm going to start talking about bad information you might be getting from the people closest to you, and that can hit home.

So let me repeat something one more time: I'm not suggesting that your friends and family are lying to you on purpose, or that they're out to make you score low on the SAT. I'm just saying that they might be misinformed, and when they try to pass their advice on to you it might not actually be any good. As always, take the time to verify any advice by going to the source—real sample tests from the College Board.

The advice you tend to get from friends and family is a hodge-podge of strategies, study tips, and who knows what else, so this section might seem a little scattered. Also, it's just about impossible to cover all the rumors floating around out there, so I'm only going to point out some of the major ones.

SAT Misconception 5: SAT Math stuff is for math people, and SAT Verbal stuff is for verbal people.

You hear people complain about this all the time. "I can't do well on the Math part of the SAT because I'm too creative," they'll say, or, "I'm too analytical to do well on subjective questions like Passage-Based Reading ones."

This isn't true at all. First of all, the human brain is too adaptable to be good at using only numbers or only words; if it weren't, we'd never survive. Except in the rarest of cases, people are not strictly good at either math or language.

But more importantly, the sections on the SAT don't really test Math and Reading skills, at least not in the way the people typically think of them. They just test general reasoning, using basic math and language concepts as the means to an end. In other words, the SAT Math Section isn't a traditional math test, the SAT Critical Reading Section isn't a traditional reading test, and the SAT Writing Section certainly isn't a traditional writing test. So even if your brain were designed to do well on only math or only language, it wouldn't matter on the SAT because the SAT doesn't test either of those things directly anyway.

Want proof? Have you ever met someone who thought she was a "math person" who scored hundreds of points lower on the math section than on the other parts of the SAT? I meet people like this all the time. You might even be one of them.

If you are one of them, do yourself two favors. First, stop pigeon-holing yourself. You can be good at anything you want to be good at. Second, realize that the SAT isn't really a math test or a language test, and just take it for what it is—a highly repetitive standardized test of basic skills and reasoning. Check out all the rules, patterns, and solutions in this Black Book. While they all involve paying careful attention to detail, not one of them rewards the kinds of skills that would be rewarded in the typical English, literature, or math class.

Fact: Anyone can do well on any part of the SAT—or on all of it—by attacking the test intelligently. That's what this Black Book is all about.

SAT Misconception 6: *Answer choices are distributed evenly throughout each section.*

A lot of students have told me they changed their answers on the SAT because the answer choices they originally liked didn't seem evenly distributed—it seemed like there were too many (A)s in a section, for example. When I ask them why they would worry about a thing like that, they say that somebody told them that the answer choices are always distributed evenly on the SAT.

This is partly true—over time, all the answer choices on the SAT are used equally. But within a particular section, the answer choices can be distributed quite unevenly. A particular section might clearly favor one, two, three, or four answer choices, or it might distribute its answer choices almost evenly. You never know.

Let's prove it. Turn to page 432 in *The Official SAT Study Guide*. You'll see an answer key from an actual SAT written by the College Board. Take a look at how often each answer choice appears in each section.

As you can see, there's absolutely no way to predict how many times a given answer choice should appear in a given section. So don't worry about the distribution of the answer choices you pick—just focus on trying to get every single question correct, and let the answer choices you select fall where they may.

Fact: Answer choices may or may not be distributed evenly on a given section. Don't worry about it.

SAT Misconception 7: *You can time the SAT to get a higher score.*

Some people will tell you that you should take the SAT at a particular time of year to get the highest possible score. The theory is based on the fact that the SAT is a norm-based test, which means that when you take it you're compared to other test-takers, not to some objective standard. So the idea is to try to take the test at the time of year when the people taking it with you are likely to do the worst.

This idea can't possibly work, for a variety of reasons. The simplest reason is that you can't predict when the weaker test-takers are more likely to take the test. Some people say they're more likely to take the test late in the academic year, because they're procrastinators. Some people think they take it early in their senior years so that they'll just barely make the admissions cutoffs. But even if one of these theories could be proven (they can't), you'd be ignoring the fact that the best test-takers are the ones who take the test often and early—and they're likely to be in the mix at any given point. So even if there were a time of year when the weakest test-takers took the test, the strongest test-takers are just as likely to be out in full force on any given date as they are on any other.

And there are other problems with this idea as well. For instance, if it were true that a particular month reliably attracted the weakest test-takers, then word would quickly spread to all the super-competitive, obsessive test-takers, who would start taking the test that month in order to gain a supposed advantage, and end up canceling out that supposed advantage.

(Of course, there are also other, more technical reasons why this idea is doomed to failure—the sample size is too large, for one thing, and statistical norming doesn't only take into account the people who take the test with you, for another. But don't worry about that for now—just remember that you can't time the test.)

Fact: It's impossible to time the SAT for a variety of reasons. Just take it when it fits your schedule.

Conclusion

We've just gone through several common SAT misconceptions. There are a lot more of them out there—you're certain to run across more of them as you continue to prepare. Just remember that you should always double-check everything you hear. You don't want to get a lower score than you deserve because you followed some bad advice.

The Nature of Elite Scores

"It is not because things are difficult that we do not dare. It is because we do not dare that they are difficult."
- Seneca the Younger

Imagine a hypothetical test with 100 questions of varying difficulty on various subjects. If you needed to answer any one question correctly, you could probably find one that seemed to be the easiest for you, and get it right.

Now imagine that you're working on the same imaginary test, and you've answered 90 questions correctly, and you want to get one more of the remaining ten. The odds are good that you've answered all of the questions that were easiest for you. All that are left are the ones you skipped, and now you're more likely to be stuck than you were when you just started out.

No imagine that you wanted to get nine of the ten remaining question, or even all ten. It would only get harder and harder, right?

My point is this: The more you improve on any test, the harder it is to keep improving. The more you succeed with the SAT, the rarer your opportunities for future success become. The more questions you master, the closer you come to having to deal with the questions you dislike most if you want to make any progress.

So making an elite score on the SAT (say, an overall score of 2250 or more) will require most people to prepare diligently and intelligently. Let's talk about how to do that.

Having The Right Attitude.

Your attitude is an important factor in preparing for the SAT.

Accountability

If you want a good score, *you* have to do it. That sentence is probably the most obvious one in this book, but it's also the most important. Every other strategy or attitude will fail you unless you take full accountability for your performance.

Many people feel that they have performance anxiety that makes them bad test-takers. Others think the test is biased against them. These people may be absolutely correct, but that will not help them improve their scores. The only thing that will help you improve is diligent, intelligent practice.

Thinking about nonspecific problems that you cannot fix will only distract you from other weaknesses that you *can* fix. When you conquer all the problems you can pinpoint, you may be surprised to find that there are no others left to deal with.

Persistence

You will fail in some way, however small or large, over the course of your SAT preparation. Everyone does. However, failure is as impermanent as you want it to be. If you are willing to work for it, every failure is literally another opportunity to succeed in the future

Remember to keep working until you achieve the score you want. As your progress becomes more and more difficult, remind yourself that it's only because you've already come so far, and that you can go even further.

Practicing For The SAT

Performing on the SAT, like any other skill, becomes easier if you practice it.

Choosing Your Pace

You will need some amount of some kind of practice; the kind and amount depend on how well you've done so far, in which areas, and how well you want to do in the future.

First, at the very least, everyone should become familiar with the question types by reading this Black Book and looking through a copy of the Blue Book (the College Board Publication *The Official SAT Study Guide*). Most people should take a timed practice SAT from the Blue Book in a reasonably simulated testing environment just to see how they do. However, if you have started early enough, and if you feel comfortable with it, you can just sign up for the test and take it once in order to get a realistic idea of your performance. In either case, the point is to find out where you stand, and which areas need work.

Once you grade your test or receive your score report, you can read it to find out how you performed in which areas. Obviously, you want to pick out the areas where you're not satisfied and work more on them. The way you work on them is up to you. You can do one problem at a time while reading through the steps in this Black Book, you can take one section of your trouble area at a time, or you can go ahead and take the full test.

However, you need to be sure to think about timing when you work up on a full section or a full test—you don't necessarily need to time every practice session, but you do need to remember that on test day you'll have a limited amount of time to answer questions.

You also have to be responsible in your practice. If you don't feel like you're practicing enough, or if you're not improving, then you need to put in more time, or go back to basics with the different sections of this book. Just keep working away at it. You get results depending on the quality of the work you put in, so if you want an elite score, remember: Work smarter *and* harder.

Assessing Weakness

As you practice you will notice certain areas of the test that seem to give you particular trouble. Take note, and work harder on those sections. There is no "I can't do it"—the information you need is there in every question, just learn to see it and use it. Don't be tempted to convince yourself that one question type is just too hard or flawed or has some other problem. You can do them all if you will only work on it.

When you do start to notice problem areas, see them as places where you have not yet succeeded, not places where you won't or can't succeed. Learn the difference between recognizing weakness and expecting failure.

Making it count

You can spend all the time in the world practicing, but if it's mindless practice, then you won't improve. Practice actively and intelligently. Don't try to look up every word in the verbal section and memorize its meaning, but if you feel like you keep seeing a word with which you are unfamiliar, go ahead and look it up and be sure you understand what it means; the odds aren't bad that you'll see it again somewhere.

However, if there is a word in the math section that you don't understand, look it up every time. This isn't as extreme, since there are far fewer of them in math than in verbal, but you cannot answer a math question without knowing the vocabulary.

Also, feel free to come up with your own tricks while practicing, but if your tricks don't work every time, then don't rely on them. When you've mastered all the techniques, you shouldn't just be right all the time; you should know that you're right, know why you're right, and know how you're right—every time. Remember: if you're not getting 800s (or whatever your goal is) in practice, you probably won't get them on the real test.

Parting advice

If you're putting in all this extra effort to reach an elite score, then you must have some larger goal in mind (improving your chances at a particular school, qualifying for a scholarship, or whatever). Keep that goal in mind. Let it motivate you to continue to work even when you don't want to. If you get your score report and you're not satisfied, think of it as a progress report and let your goal keep you working. Repeat this entire process thoroughly in order to optimize your improvement.

At the same time, treat each test as the real thing, because it is. Don't take a test thinking only that it will help you know what to do better later. It will, but always shoot for your goal or else you might not do as well as you can. Strive to do your best, *always.*

Advice For Non-Native Speakers Of American English

"Knowledge, then, is a system of transformations that become progressively adequate."
- Jean Piaget

The SAT involves a lot of reading, so it poses special challenges for students who aren't native speakers of American English. There are some things we can do to overcome these challenges to some extent.

First, Focus On Questions In Which Language Is Not A Problem

Before we start worrying about building up your vocabulary or grammar knowledge, the most important thing—and the easiest—is to focus on eliminating mistakes in the questions that you can understand well enough to answer with confidence. It doesn't make sense to try to learn a lot of big words if you haven't reached a point where knowing the words actually helps you to answer a question. So master the strategies in this book as much as you can before you start trying to memorize stuff.

Next, Focus On "Testing" Vocabulary

Most non-native speakers try to memorize the same lists of words that native speakers try to memorize—and it's just as big of a waste of time. Maybe even bigger.

Instead, focus on the kinds of words that come up often in the actual wording of the questions, rather than on words that seem exotic. For the Math section, learn words like "perimeter," "vertex," "quotient," "median," and so on. For Critical Reading, learn words like "undermine," "assert," "hypothesis," "argument," "preclude," and "contradict"—the kinds of words that actually frame the questions themselves, rather than the words that might show up as answer choices on Sentence Completion questions.

These are the kinds of words that native speakers would normally have no problems with, but that non-native speakers may never have studied specifically. They are absolutely critical if we want to understand what the test is actually asking us—and, most importantly, they are words that you will definitely encounter over and over again as you practice and take the real test, which sets them apart from those 1,000-word lists that people memorize in the vain hope of improving their Sentence Completion performance significantly.

The best way to discover which parts of "testing" vocabulary need your attention is to mark particular words and phrases that you encounter in real practice questions—again, pay particular attention to the stems of the question rather than the answer choices, although "testing" vocabulary words can also appear in the answer choices. In general, you can distinguish "testing" vocabulary words from relatively useless vocabulary words because the "testing" words will tend to be re-used much more frequently within a given section than the kinds of exotic words that appear on commercial vocab lists. If you run into a word like "undermine" in 3 or 4 different Critical Reading questions and don't feel like you know what it means, then it's probably a good idea to go online and look up the translation into your native language.

Then Focus On SAT Grammar And SAT Style

Notice that I'm specifically advising you to focus on learning *SAT grammar* and *SAT style*, which are guaranteed to differ from the kinds of grammar and style you learned when you studied English in school.

This is an area in which you can actually exceed a lot of native speakers if you put in a little effort, because most American students never study English grammar anymore—they often can't recognize parts of speech in a sentence. But if you're a non-native speaker who plans to take the SAT, there's a very good chance you've studied English extensively, so it will probably be easier for you to understand what the SAT rewards and punishes. You'll have to make small tweaks to your understanding of "textbook" English to answer every Writing question on the SAT, but, again, those should be easy enough to take care of if you've been studying English for a while.

(By the way, before you worry too much about SAT grammar and style, you should make sure that your target schools even care about the Writing score in the first place. Some schools don't think that the Writing part of the SAT is very valuable, and they may not consider it in their admissions decisions. You can often find out whether a school cares about that part of the test by looking at the school's web site, or by calling the office directly. Also be aware that the school may pay more attention to the Writing scores of non-native English speakers than they would to those of American students. But if you find out that your target schools don't care about the Writing section, then of course there's no real point in getting better at that part of the test.)

Next, Consider The Essay

If the schools that you're applying to are interested in the Writing score on the SAT, then you need to try to write the best essay you can. Remember that this is mostly a matter of length. But it's also important to try to avoid too much awkward phrasing—a little bit of awkwardness doesn't seem to hurt in most cases, but if you have a lot of it you increase the chance that an essay-grader will notice it and feel like he has to penalize your for it.

Also try to avoid using large words for their own sake. Remember that, in spite of the College Board's essay rubric, the graders don't care if your vocabulary is advanced. But if you use a lot of large words in a way that sounds forced and unnatural, you run the very real risk of making the grader think that your writing is awkward. So stick with the grammatical structures and the vocabulary that you're sure of, and focus on getting the length and the organization of the essay right.

Finally, Worry About "Vocabulary" Questions (If You Must)

After you've made sure that you never miss a question when there's no language barrier, and after you've beefed up your "testing" vocab, and after you've worked on the Writing section (assuming that your schools care about the Writing section) . . . only then would I *maybe* start trying to expand my vocabulary for Sentence Completion questions if I were you.

I know that it's frustrating to look at a question and feel like the only reason you're missing it is that it has words you don't know, but you have to remember that memorizing words from a list is very unlikely to have a significant positive impact on that situation, for all the reasons that I mentioned when we talked about Sentence Completion questions. If your goal is to get the most points you possibly can—and that really should be your goal, of course—then you have to realize that you'll probably have the easiest time picking up extra points by prioritizing things the way I've laid out here.

Conclusion

I hope you've found these tips useful. Remember that the SAT is a very unique test, but it's also a very repetitive test, and even a very basic one in a lot of ways. By focusing on the issues I've pointed out above, you should hopefully be able to maximize your score without wasting your time on things that won't really help you.

One Final Piece Of Advice
(Or: Every Question I've Ever Been Asked About The SAT Has Basically The Same Answer)

"The 'paradox' is only a conflict between reality and your feeling of what reality 'ought to be.'"
- Richard Feynman

I've helped a lot of people with a lot of standardized tests, and in a lot of formats. This means I've also gotten a lot of questions from a very wide variety of test-takers. Most of the time those questions are very polite and sincere, but sometimes they're downright accusatory—something along the lines of "You said I could use a certain strategy on this kind of question, but it didn't work and my score went down. What are you, some kind of idiot?"

So I wanted to close this book with some words of advice and encouragement for students who are still struggling with some area of the SAT.

First, the advice: In literally every single instance that I can recall in which a student has become frustrated with an idea in this Black Book, the underlying issue has always—ALWAYS—been that the student has overlooked or misunderstood at least one important detail.

Let me say that again.

When you try to apply the ideas in this book to real SAT questions from the College Board and get frustrated by your inability to determine the correct answer reliably, the reason is just about always that you've misread or misunderstood some important detail somewhere.

So when you're having a hard time with a question, whether during practice or on the actual day of the test, you must always, always, always assume that you've made a mistake somewhere, and then set out to find and correct that mistake. You need to develop an instinctive faith in the standardization of the test, and an assumption that, if something has gone wrong, it's gone wrong in your own head, and you can fix it.

Let me also say, very clearly, that all of us—myself included—will run into situations in which we are completely certain that the test has finally made a mistake. No matter how convinced we may be that this is the case, we must remember that we're actually the ones who've made the mistake, and we must go back and re-evaluate our decisions until we can figure out where we went wrong.

The most common type of mistake that I see students make is the general mistake of misreading something. Sometimes a question asks us to compare Passage 1 to Passage 2, but we choose the answer that compares Passage 2 to Passage 1 instead. Sometimes the question asks for the area and we find the perimeter. Sometimes we miss the word "not" in a Sentence Completion question and choose the antonym of the correct answer. Sometimes we overlook the word "positive" in a math question that describes a set of numbers. And so on.

At other times, we may think we know something that actually turns out to be wrong. Yesterday I was talking to a student who incorrectly thought that "taciturn" meant "peaceful" (this is the kind of misunderstanding that often comes from memorizing lists of vocabulary words, by the way). Until a couple of months ago, I though "pied" meant something like "famous" or "skillful," because of the story *The Pied Piper*. But it turns out that "pied" just refers to clothing that's made out of lots of different pieces of cloth stitched together, and I was completely wrong. Or a student might incorrectly think that zero is a prime number. These kinds of mistakes are harder to figure out during the actual moment of taking the test, because it's usually not possible to realize that something you believe isn't actually correct until after you've chosen the wrong answer and found out it's wrong.

No matter what the mistake, though, it ultimately comes down to some specific detail (or details) of the question that you have gotten wrong in some way. When you get stuck, your first instinct must always be to re-read the question (and the relevant part of the passage or diagram, if there is one), taking absolutely nothing for granted and expecting that you'll find out something is different from what you previously supposed. If you re-read a few times and still can't identify your mistake, you have to be ready for the possibility that some definition that you think you know (whether it's a word like "taciturn" or a word like "prime") might actually be wrong. And you have to consider skipping the question altogether.

Now that I've finished with the advice, let me offer some encouragement. I know how hard it is to stare at a question and feel defeated. I know the frustration you feel when you're sure you've answered a question correctly and you find out later that you were wrong. And I know that it's tempting, in those moments, to reject what you've learned here and assume that the SAT really is unbeatable, like everybody says.

But I'm here to tell you that those moments of frustration are also the moments that offer the most opportunity for progress. When you've wrestled with a question for a while and then you finally figure out how it works and where you went wrong, you learn a tremendous lesson about the test, and about how you've been approaching it. And your score improves.

When you truly figure out a challenging question, you learn something that you'll be able to apply on future questions, because the SAT is standardized. You also develop a stronger trust in the design of the test, which will help you in the future. More importantly, though, you can learn something about your own problem-solving process, because you can start to figure out what parts of the question kept you from understanding it correctly in the first place, and you can start to reflect on the process you used to uncover and correct that mistake, so that you can make that process much smoother in the future.

With the SAT, as with most areas of life, we make the most progress when we're confronted with a difficult situation that we eventually overcome. Good luck!

Thanks For Reading!

I've enjoyed sharing my SAT strategies with you, and I hope you've enjoyed learning how to beat the test, and that you're seeing good results with your practice sessions. It means a lot to me that so many students over the years have trusted me to help them at such an important time in their lives.

If this book has helped you understand the SAT better, I would really appreciate it if you could tell your friends about it, or even go on Amazon and leave an honest review. Here's the link to this book's Amazon page, if you'd like to do that: [INSERT LINK]

Appendix: Writing Toolbox

The multiple-choice questions on the SAT Writing section test a surprisingly limited number of concepts over and over again, and these concepts can be learned pretty quickly. Still, many SAT-takers are intimidated by these questions because very few of them have ever studied grammar, usage, or writing style in school.

Before we can talk about the hidden rules and patterns of the SAT Writing Section—before we can talk about real strategy, in other words—we have to lay down some basic ideas that will form the foundation for a successful approach to this part of the SAT.

Even if you think you have a good grasp of grammar and usage, you should probably read through this section at least twice. It will only take a few minutes, and you might find that you were misinformed about something.

The grammar principles we're about to discuss are NOT necessarily the same as what you might have learned in school! It's only enough information to get you through every real SAT Writing question. If something seems a little strange at first, just go with it—you'll see that this simplified approach allows you to prepare quickly and easily.

All The SAT Writing Concepts You Need to Know

The concepts you need to know for the SAT Writing section can be divided into two main groups: underlying grammatical ideas that do NOT appear on the test, and the higher-level concepts built on those ideas.

For this discussion, we'll start with the underlying ideas and move on to the higher-level concepts quickly. (I would much rather skip the underlying ideas altogether, since they don't actually appear on the SAT, but many of the higher-level concepts won't make sense without them.)

Underlying Grammatical Ideas

These basic ideas explain the essential foundation of written English as it appears on the SAT writing section. You'll probably find that you're familiar with most of this material, but there's a good chance you'll find some things you didn't know in here.

Parts Of Speech And Their Roles

Written English has nouns, verbs, adjectives, and conjunctions, among other things. Knowing how to identify these parts of speech, and knowing how they interact with each other, will make it possible to understand the concepts that are tested on the SAT writing section.

Nouns

Nouns are the first parts of speech that babies learn, because nouns are the things you can point to. A baby can point to its mother and say, "mommy," because the word *mommy* describes an actual, physical thing. The most basic nouns are things you can point at like a baby would.

Examples:

> *desk*, *computer*, *pillow*, *food*, and *airplane* are all
> nouns like this.

But there are other types of nouns as well. Some nouns represent ideas, like *happiness* or *fatalism*. These nouns are things that you can't point at. But don't worry—you can usually recognize them by their endings.

Examples:

> **If a word ends in *-ness, -ism, -hood, -ology,* or anything similar, it's probably a noun.**

Nouns can be either singular or plural. The plural form of a noun is usually formed with the suffix *-s* or the suffix *-es*, but there are some special nouns that form their plurals differently.

Examples:

> *shoe, box,* and *mouse* are all singular nouns, and *shoes, boxes,* and *mice* are the plural forms of those nouns.

Pronouns are a special sub-set of nouns. A pronoun is a word that shows us we're dealing with a noun we've already talked about. Usually, pronouns take the place of the nouns they refer to.

Examples:

> *I, you, he, she, it, we, they, me, you, him, her, us, them, one, which,* and *that* are all pronouns. When we have a sentence like *Thomas wants to know why he has to do the dishes,* the *he* lets us know that we're still talking about the same person. It would sound strange to say *Thomas wants to know why Thomas has to do the dishes,* so we use the pronoun *he* in place of the second *Thomas.*

On the SAT Writing Section, a pronoun must always be used in a way that clearly indicates which noun (or nouns) it replaces.

Example:

> This is a good sentence on the SAT:
>
> *Amy and Elizabeth were playing cards with Billy when Amy became angry with him.*
>
> - *him* is a pronoun that clearly refers to the noun *Billy,* which appears earlier in the sentence.
>
> This is a bad sentence on the SAT:
>
> **Amy and Elizabeth were playing cards with Billy when she became angry at him.*
>
> - *she* is a pronoun that could refer either to the noun *Amy* or to the noun *Elizabeth.*

On the SAT Writing Section, you can use either *one* or *you* as a pronoun that refers to an unspecified person, but the use must be consistent within a sentence.

Examples:

> **These are okay sentences on the SAT:**
>
> *One should take care to mind one's manners.*
>
> *You should take care to mind your manners.*
>
> - **One** and *you* **can both act as pronouns that refer generally to an unspecified person as long as they don't appear in the same sentence together.**
>
> **This is not an okay sentence on the SAT:**
>
> ***One should take care to mind your manners.***
>
> - **One** **cannot be used interchangeably with** *you*—**the usage must be consistent for each sentence.**

Subjects and objects

The common subject pronouns—pronoun forms which can appear as the subjects of verbs—are *I, you, he, she, it, we, they,* and *who*. These are the only pronoun forms that can be used as subjects, and, except for *you*, they can ONLY be used as subjects.

Examples:

> **This is a bad sentence on the SAT:**
>
> ***He gave the present to she.***
>
> - **He** **is a correctly-used subject pronoun, and its verb is** *gave*.
> - *she* **is a subject pronoun that is NOT being used as the subject of any verb.**
>
> **This is an acceptable sentence on the SAT:**
>
> *He gave the present to her.*
>
> - *her* **is not a subject pronoun and is not the subject of a verb.**

The SAT will often try to use subject pronouns where they don't belong!

Personal pronouns

When a pronoun takes the place of a noun that indicates a person, it has to be a personal pronoun.

Examples:

This is a bad sentence on the SAT:

*I gave the report to the supervisor which asked me for it.

- *supervisor* is a noun that indicates a person— supervisors are people.

- *that* is not a personal pronoun, even though it refers to the personal noun *supervisor*.

This is a good sentence on the SAT:

I gave the report to the supervisor who asked me for it.

- *who* is a personal pronoun that refers to the personal noun *supervisor*.

Verbs

Verbs are the second-most basic class of words. A verb is an action. Verbs are things you can do—the word *do* is a verb itself. Here's a test for identifying English verbs: if you can create a sentence that puts a word after word *cannot*, then that word can be a verb.

Examples:

jog, eat, initiate, and *go* can all be verbs in English; you can test this by creating sentences like *Judy cannot go to the movies*, where the word *go* is able to appear after the word *cannot*.

A verb takes different forms, called "conjugations," depending on the time period of the action the verb describes. For the purposes of the SAT, we only care about two aspects of a conjugation:

- whether a verb-form is singular or plural (the verb's "number"), and

- whether a verb's action takes place in the present, past, or future (the verb's "tense")

Singular versus plural verbs

Like nouns, verbs have singular and plural forms. Plural forms of verbs often end in *–s*.

Examples:

> In the sentence
>
> *Today we hike for the summit.*
>
> - *we* is a plural pronoun that requires a plural verb, and *hike* is a plural verb-form.
>
> In the sentence
>
> *Today Joe hikes for the summit.*
>
> - *Joe* is a singular noun that requires a singular verb, and *hikes* is a singular verb-form.

In many cases, the singular and plural forms of a verb are identical.

Examples:

> In the sentence
>
> *I like hiking.*
>
> - *Like* is a singular verb-form that correctly agrees with the singular pronoun *I*.
>
> In the sentence
>
> *We like hiking.*
>
> - *We* is a plural pronoun correctly modified by the plural verb-form *like*.

A verb must always agree in number with the noun or nouns that it modifies.

Examples:

> This is a correct sentence:
>
> *Monica and Alex enjoy the theater.*
>
> - *Monica* and *Alex* are each singular nouns.
> - *enjoy* is a plural verb-form that modifies two nouns.
>
> This sentence is incorrect:
>
> **Monica and Alex enjoys the theater.*
>
> - *enjoys* is a singular verb-form that might seem, at first, like it correctly modifies the noun *Alex*. But in this sentence it has to modify the phrase *Monica and Alex*, which consists of two singular nouns and requires a plural verb-form.

Mixing singular verbs with plural nouns, and plural nouns with singular verbs, is a common error on the SAT Writing Section. Always check to see which noun a verb is supposed to agree with!

Tenses of verbs

As we discussed before, verbs describe actions. These actions are either going on right now, already over, or about to happen later on. We have three basic tenses to describe when the action of a verb takes place: past, present, and future.

Examples:

In this sentence,

I love my grandmother.

- *love* is a present-tense verb-form, which indicates that the action of loving my grandmother is going on right now.

In this sentence,

I will love my children very much when I have them.

- *will love* is a future verb-form that indicates that the loving has not started yet.

In this sentence,

I loved my pet goldfish.

- *loved* is a past-tense verb-form, indicating that the act of loving has already finished.

There are other verb-forms that we have to be able to recognize on the SAT Writing Section, as well. It isn't necessary to know the names of these forms, but it is necessary to know whether they indicate action in the past or present. These verb-forms are the ones that use the "helping verbs" *to have* and *to be*.

For the purposes of the SAT Writing Section, all verb-forms that use any form of the helping verb *to have* indicate actions in the past.

Example:

In this sentence,

I had not improved my SAT score before I stopped guessing, but I have improved it since then.

- *had not improved* indicates an action in the past, because *had* is a form of the helping verb *to have*.

- *stopped* indicates an action in the past.

- *have improved* indicates an action in the past, because *have* is a form of the helping verb *to have*.

For the purpose of the SAT Writing Section, all verb-forms that use a past-tense form of the verb *to be* indicate actions in the past.

Example:

> In this sentence,
>
> *I was thinking about my homework last night.*
>
> - *was thinking* indicates an action in the past, because it includes the helping verb-form *was*, which is a past-tense form of the verb *to be*.

For the purpose of the SAT Writing Section, all verb-forms that use a present-tense form of the verb *to be* indicate actions in the present.

Example:

> In this sentence,
>
> *I am thinking about pie for dessert.*
>
> - *am thinking* indicates an action in the present, because it involves *am*, which is a present-tense form of the helping verb *to be*.

On the SAT Writing Section, all verbs in a sentence should indicate actions in the same time frame wherever possible.

Examples:

> This is an okay sentence on the SAT Writing Section:
>
> *The dinner you served us was delicious.*
>
> - *served* and *was* are both verb-forms that indicate action in the past.
>
> This sentence would not be acceptable on the SAT Writing Section:
>
> **The dinner you served us is delicious.*
>
> - *served* is a past-tense verb-form, indicating action in the past.
> - *is* is a present-tense verb-form, indicating action in the present.

The SAT Writing Section likes to test your ability to put verbs in the same tenses, so always be on the lookout when a sentence contains verbs that are in different tenses.

Conjugations of verbs

English verbs, like verbs in any other language, have specific conjugations that show their tenses. (Conjugations also show things like a verb's "mood" and "voice," but those aren't tested on the SAT Writing Section, so we won't worry about them.)

Example:

In this sentence,

Mrs. Smith has decided to buy a new car.

- *has decided* is the "past participle" conjugation of the verb *to decide.*

The SAT Writing Section will occasionally show you a verb-form that is conjugated incorrectly.

Examples:

This is a good sentence on the SAT:

The subject of money has arisen many times in our discussions.

- *has arisen* is a correct conjugation of the verb *to arise.*

This is a bad sentence on the SAT:

*The subject of money has arosen many times in our discussions.

- *has arosen* is not a verb-form in English; instead, it's a strange and incorrect combination of the proper past-tense form *arose* and the proper past participle *has arisen.*

Verb-forms as nouns

Two verb-forms can function as nouns. These are the *–ing* and *to* forms of verbs.

Examples:

In this sentence,

Singing is a lot of fun.

- *Singing* is a form of the verb *to sing* that acts like a noun—it's the subject of the verb-form *is.*

Special verbs: to be and to become

To be and *to become* are members of a special group of verbs called "copulars." Copular verbs are verbs that show us when two things are, or will be, the same thing. (You don't need to know the term "copular" for the SAT, by the way.)

To use a copular verb properly, you place a noun phrase before it, and either another noun phrase or an adjective phrase after it.

Examples:

In this sentence,

Muhammad Ali was a great boxer.

- *Muhammad Ali* is a noun phrase that is being equated to the noun phrase *a great fighter*.

- *was* is a singular, past-tense form of the copular verb *to be*, which is equating the noun phrase before it to the noun phrase after it.

- *a great boxer* is a noun phrase that is being equated to the noun phrase *Muhammad Ali*.

On the SAT Writing Section, the noun phrases on either side of a copular verb must have the same number.

Examples:

This is an acceptable sentence on the SAT Writing Section:

My cousins want to become astronauts.

- *My cousins* is a plural noun phrase that is being equated to the plural noun phrase *astronauts*.

- *to become* is a copular verb.

- *astronauts* is a plural noun that is being equated to the plural noun phrase *cousins*.

This is an unacceptable sentence on the SAT Writing Section:

*My cousins want to become an astronaut.

- *My cousins* is a plural noun phrase that is being equated to the singular noun phrase *an astronaut*, which is no good on the SAT.

- *to become* is a copular verb.

- *an astronaut* is a singular noun phrase that is being improperly equated to the plural noun phrase *my cousins*.

Adjectives and adverbs

Adjectives are single words that describe nouns. An adjective usually appears immediately before its noun, or before a list of other adjectives that appears before the noun.

Example:

In this sentence,

Sally ordered an Italian salad.

- *Italian* is an adjective that tells us something about the noun *salad*, and appears immediately before it.

When you want to use an adjective to modify something that is not a noun, you have to use the "adverb" form of the adjective. The adverb-form of an adjective almost always ends in *-ly*.

Example:

In this sentence,

That is a very cleverly written essay.

- *cleverly* is the adverb-form of the adjective *clever*, which modifies the word *written* (note that *written* not a noun, which is why it can only be modified by an adverb).

The SAT Writing Section will often try to fool you by incorrectly using an adjective form to modify a word that is not a noun.

Examples:

This is a bad sentence on the SAT:

*You have to move quick if you want a seat.

- *quick* is an adjective, but there is no noun after it, so it isn't modifying a noun and should appear as an adverb.

This is a correct sentence on the SAT:

You have to move quickly if you want a seat.

- *quickly* is an adverb that describes the verb *to move.*

Exception: adjectives with copular verbs

Remember our discussion of copular verbs like *to be* and *to become*, which equate the things on either side of them? For these special verbs, we can use adjective forms even when they don't appear immediately before nouns.

Example:

> This is an okay sentence on the SAT:
>
> *You have to be quick if you want a seat.*
>
> - *you* is a pronoun that is correctly modified by the adjective *quick*.
> - *to be* is a copular verb that equates the word *you* with the word *quick*.
> - *quick* is an adjective that does not appear before a verb but does appear after a correctly used copular verb.

Conjunctions

Conjunctions are words that link ideas to each other.

Examples:

> *and, either*, or, *neither, nor*, and *because* can all act like conjunctions on the SAT.

On the SAT, when two ideas are linked by a conjunction, the ideas must appear in the same form.

Examples:

> This is a good sentence on the SAT Writing Section:
>
> *Samantha likes singing, dancing, and acting.*
>
> - *singing, dancing*, and *acting* are all being linked together by the conjunction *and*, and they all appear in their –*ing* forms.
>
> This is a bad sentence on the SAT Writing Section:
>
> **Samantha likes singing, dancing, and to act.*
>
> - *singing, dancing*, and *to act* are all ideas linked together by the conjunction *and*, but they don't all appear in the same form— *singing* and *dancing* are in their –*ing* forms, but *to act* is in its *to* form.

Prepositions

Prepositions are words that describe the origins or relative positions of ideas in a sentence.

Example:

In the sentence

The letter from your mother is in the drawer under the table.

- *from your mother* is a prepositional phrase in which the preposition *from* shows that the origin of the letter is the noun phrase *your mother*

- *in the drawer* is a prepositional phrase in which the preposition *in* shows the position of the letter relative to the drawer

- *under the table* is a prepositional phrase in which the preposition *under* shows the position of the drawer relative to the table

Prepositions are also used in certain idioms in English, and the SAT likes to test your knowledge of these idioms occasionally.

Examples:

This is a bad sentence on the SAT:

*Joey's supervisor fell to love with the new idea.

- *fell to love* is an improper usage of an English idiom because the preposition *to* should be replaced with another preposition.

This is an acceptable sentence on the SAT:

Joey's supervisor fell in love with the new idea.

- *fell in love* is a proper usage of an English idiom.

Sometimes the SAT Writing Section places a prepositional phrase between a subject and its verb, and tries to trick you by making the verb agree with the noun in the prepositional phrase instead of with the actual subject.

Examples:

> This is an acceptable sentence on the SAT:
>
> *Andrea's list of chores is very complicated.*
>
> - *list* is the subject of the verb-form *is.*
> - *of chores* is a prepositional phrase that comes between the subject *list* and the verb *is*
> - *is* is a verb, so it has to be singular to match the singular noun *list*
>
> This is not an acceptable sentence on the SAT:
>
> **Andrea's list of chores are very complicated.*
>
> - *chores* is a plural noun, but it is NOT the subject in this sentence—the subject is *list*, and *chores* is part of a prepositional phrase that describes the subject.
> - *are* is a plural verb-form that has incorrectly been made to agree with the plural noun *chores*, which is not the subject of the sentence.

Comparatives

Comparatives are phrases that compare one idea to another.

They can be formed by pairing the *-er* form of an adjective with the word *than* in order to compare two or more things. (Where necessary, comparatives can also be formed with the words *more* or *less* before an adjective instead of with that adjective's *-er* form.)

Example:

> In this sentence, *nicer than* is a comparative:
>
> *I think your new car is nicer than your old one.*
>
> In this sentence, *more intelligent than* is a comparative:
>
> *This solution seems more intelligent than the old approach.*

Comparatives can also be formed with phrases that use the word *as* twice.

Example:

> In this sentence, the phrase *as interesting as* is a comparative phrase:
>
> *I don't think our calculus class is as interesting as our art class.*

When you see a comparative on the SAT, make sure that the phrase that comes right after the comparative phrase really belongs in the comparison.

Examples:

This is a good SAT sentence:

Your house is smaller than John's house.

- *smaller than* is the comparative phrase that compares the idea of *your house* to the idea of *John's house.*

This is a bad SAT sentence:

Your house is smaller than John.

- *John* is not what the phrase *Your house* should really be compared to; the way this sentence is written, it says that your house is smaller than a person named John.

Be on the lookout for comparatives in the SAT Writing Section! They're very often handled incorrectly

Clauses and phrases

A phrase is a group of words that serves a particular function in a sentence. Usually, this function is analogous to a part of speech.

A phrase can include one or more words.

Phrases are referred to by the functions they fulfill within their sentences. There are "noun phrases," "verb phrases," "prepositional phrases," "adverbial phrases," et cetera.

Examples:

In the sentence

The cat who lives next door likes my pineapple tree.

- *The cat* is a noun phrase.

- *lives next door* is a verb phrase.

- *The cat who lives next door* is a noun phrase that includes the noun phrase *The cat* and the verb phrase *lives next door*

- likes my pineapple tree is a verb phrase

- *my pineapple tree* is a noun phrase.

- (There are other phrases that could be said to exist in this sentence, but you get the idea.)

Don't worry if this doesn't make a lot of sense! The SAT doesn't actually test your knowledge of phrases, or your ability to pull phrases out of a sentence. We're only covering these ideas so that when we say, "the noun phrase such-and-such," you'll have some idea what we're talking about.

A clause is a group of words that includes a subject noun phrase, a verb phrase, and, if necessary, an object noun phrase.

Example:

> ## This is a complete clause:
>
> *This pizza recipe requires cheese.*
>
> - *This pizza recipe* is the subject noun phrase.
> - *requires* is the verb phrase.
> - *cheese* is the object noun phrase.

A clause can be either "independent" or "dependent."

A "dependent" clause begins with a conjunction.

An "independent" clause does not begin with a conjunction.

Example:

> ## In the sentence,
>
> *You have to sleep more because you study too much.*
>
> - **You have to sleep more is an independent clause because it has all the elements of a clause and does not start with a conjunction.**
> - *because you study too much* **is a dependent clause because it starts with the conjunction** *because.*

For the multiple-choice questions on the SAT Writing Section, every correctly written sentence must contain at least one independent clause.

Clauses and commas

Independent clauses cannot be separated from each other by a comma.

Examples:

> ## This is a bad sentence on the SAT:
>
> **I have not yet begun to fight, time is on my side.*
>
> - *I have not yet begun to fight* **is an independent clause including the subject pronoun** *I* **and the verb-form** *have begun.*
> - *time is on my side* **is an independent clause including the subject noun** *time* **and the copular verb-form** *is.*
>
> ## This is an acceptable sentence on the SAT:
>
> *I have not yet begun to fight; time is on my side.*

Conditionals

A "conditional" is a statement that uses the conjunction *if*. Properly written conditional sentences avoid using the word *would* in the clause that begins with *if*.

Examples:

> **This is a bad SAT sentence:**
>
> **I would have stopped by your house if I would have known you were home.*
>
> - *would have stopped* is acceptable because it appears in the clause *I would have stopped by*, which does not contain the word *if*.
> - *if* is the conditional conjunction.
> - *would have known* is incorrect here because it uses the word *would* in the same clause where the word *if* appears.
>
> **This sentence is acceptable on the SAT:**
>
> *I would have stopped by your house if I had known you were home.*
>
> - *would have stopped* is acceptable because it does not appear in the same clause as the conjunction *if*.
> - *if* is the conditional conjunction.

Dangling participles

A participle is a special verb-form that can end in *–ing, -en,* or *–ed.* They're often used at the beginning of a sentence.

Example:

> **In this sentence,**
>
> *Screaming for help, the mailman ran away from the angry dog.*
>
> - *Screaming* is a participle.

When these participles are used in standard written English, they are always understood to refer to the first noun phrase in the independent clause in the sentence.

Example:

> **In the sentence above,**
>
> - *Screaming for help* is the participial phrase, beginning with the participle *screaming* (an *–ing* word)
> - *the mailman ran away from the angry dog* is the independent clause (remember that an independent clause has a subject noun phrase and main verb phrase).

We know this participle was used correctly because the word *screaming* describes the word *mailman*, which is what we wanted to do.

Example:

> This sentence would be completely INCORRECT on the SAT:
>
> *Screaming for help, the dog chased the mailman down the street.*
>
> What's wrong with that? We still have a participial phrase (*screaming for help*) and an independent clause (*the dog chased the mailman down the street*), but the problem is that the participle in this sentence can't possibly describe the first noun phrase in the independent clause, which is *the dog.* This sentence is no good because the dog can't scream. Only the mailman can scream.

Participles show up often in the SAT Writing Section, and they're frequently used incorrectly, so look out for them!

Higher-Level Concepts: Ideal Sentences And Paragraphs On The SAT

Now that we've talked about the basic underlying grammatical rules you need for the SAT Writing Section, we need to discuss the sorts of things that the SAT considers to be "good" usage. To do this, we'll talk in terms of the "bad" and "good" patterns that appear on the SAT.

On the SAT Writing Section, ideal sentences are the ones that avoid certain "bad" patterns and make us of certain "good" patterns. The fewer "bad" patterns and the more "good" patterns a sentence has, the more "SAT-ideal" the sentence is.

"Bad" patterns that often appear in errors on the SAT Writing Section.	"Good" patterns that indicate correct usage on the SAT.
-ing words Errors on the SAT Writing Section often involve -ing words that don't correctly modify nouns they refer to, or that don't belong in a sentence at all.	Use of an -ing word so that it correctly modifies the first noun phrase after the comma in the sentence is acceptable on the SAT Writing Section; otherwise, avoid -ing words whenever possible.
-ed words Errors on the SAT Writing Section often involve -ed words that don't correctly modify the nouns they refer to.	Use of an -ed word so that it correctly modifies the first noun phrase after the comma in the sentence is also acceptable on the SAT Writing Section.
pronouns Errors on the SAT Writing Section often involve the use of pronouns when they aren't needed or when they don't refer to any particular noun.	Pronouns that agree with their main nouns in number are okay. It's also okay to use either *you* or *one*, as long the usage is consistent. Finally, pronouns must clearly indicate which nouns they're replacing.
non-parallelism Errors on the SAT often involve the use of conjunctions when the ideas joined by the conjunction are not in the same form.	Words and phrases joined by conjunctions should use parallel structures.
incorrect verb-forms Conjugating verbs incorrectly is an error on the SAT.	All verb use must be consistent with normal, standard usage.
non-agreement Using a pronoun that doesn't agree in number with its noun, or a verb that doesn't agree in number with its noun or pronoun, is an error on the SAT.	All pronouns in a correctly written sentence must agree in number with their main nouns, and all verbs with their nouns or pronouns.

"Bad" patterns that often appear in errors on the SAT Writing Section.	"Good" patterns that indicate correct usage on the SAT.
adjectives versus adverbs On the SAT, using an adjective to describe anything besides a noun is an error.	All adjectives in a correctly written sentence are used to describe nouns. Words that describe anything else appear as adverbs.
as **in general** On the SAT, the word *as* is likely to appear in poorly written sentences.	The word *as* can appear in a correctly written SAT sentence when it is used to compare two or more things, or when it's part of a phrase that correctly modifies the first noun that appears after a comma.
verb tense On the SAT, incorrect sentences often have verbs in multiple tenses.	Correctly written sentences on the SAT either place all verb phrases in the same tense or properly signify a tense shift with a time expression like *before* or *next year*.
commas separating complete clauses Incorrectly written sentences on the SAT often use EITHER a comma OR a conjunction to separate two complete clauses.	Correctly written sentences on the SAT either separate complete clauses with a semicolon or dash, or add a conjunction like *since, because,* or *and* between the comma and the beginning of the second clause.
to be, to become When the verb *to be* or *to become* is the only verb in a clause, incorrectly written SAT sentences often make the nouns on either side of the verb differ in number.	Correctly written SAT sentences make the noun phrases on either side of *to be* or *to become* appear in the same number.
removing *to be* **when possible** Incorrectly written SAT sentences often include the verb *to be* when they don't need to.	Correctly written SAT sentences use the verb *to be* either to equate two ideas or as a helping verb for other verbs-forms.
removing *the* **when possible** Incorrectly written SAT sentences sometimes use *a, an,* and *the* when they aren't necessary.	Correctly written SAT sentences use articles to modify noun phrases only when they're needed.

"Bad" patterns that often appear in errors on the SAT Writing Section.	"Good" patterns that indicate correct usage on the SAT.
parallelism with *than* Incorrectly written SAT sentences might use comparisons with *than* when the two things being compared don't have parallel structures.	Correctly written SAT sentences use comparisons with *than* only when the structures of the two things being compared are parallel, in order to assure that the proper things are being compared.
either/or* versus *either/and Incorrectly written SAT sentences occasionally use *and* with *either*.	When correctly written SAT sentences use the word *either*, it appears with the conjunction *or*, not *and*.
idioms—prepositions Incorrectly written SAT sentences sometimes misuse the prepositions in common idioms.	Correctly written SAT sentences use the normal prepositions in everyday idioms.
proper pronoun usage (he/him) Incorrectly written SAT sentences might use subject pronouns where object pronouns should appear.	Correctly written SAT sentences use object pronouns as the objects of verbs and prepositions.
conjunctions at beginning of sentence Incorrectly written SAT sentences often begin with conjunctions even though there are no independent clauses in the sentence.	Correctly written SAT sentences only begin with conjunctions when they include independent clauses later in the sentence. In other words, it's possible for a sentence to be grammatically acceptable on the SAT even if it begins with the word "because," as long as the sentence also contains an independent clause.
if* and *would have Incorrect SAT sentences use *would have* instead of *had* immediately after *if*.	Correctly written SAT sentences use *had* in *if* phrases, not *would have*.
removing *which* when possible Incorrectly written SAT sentences use *which* when they don't need to.	Correctly written SAT sentences avoid *which* whenever possible.
relative pronouns—personal with people Incorrect SAT sentences use impersonal pronouns to take the place of personal nouns.	Correctly written SAT sentences use personal pronouns to replace personal nouns.
comparatives Incorrectly written SAT sentences use both *more* and *–er* to form comparatives.	Correctly written SAT sentences use either *more* or the suffix *–er*—not both—to form comparatives.

avoiding conjunctions Incorrectly written SAT sentences might use conjunctions where they aren't necessary.	Correctly written SAT sentences only use conjunctions when necessary, and use them to link ideas appropriately.
phrases in place of "and" Incorrectly written SAT sentences might use phrases like "in addition to" or "as well as" instead of "and."	Correctly written SAT sentences only use the word "and" itself wherever "and" is appropriate. They don't just phrases like "in addition to" or "as well as" instead of "and."
"it" and "they" Incorrectly written SAT sentences might use the pronouns "it" and "they" without a clearly specified noun elsewhere in the sentence that matches the pronoun in number.	Correctly written SAT sentences only use the pronoun "it" when it refers to a singular noun elsewhere in the sentence, and they only use the word "they" when it refers to a plural noun elsewhere in the sentence.

About Paragraphs

Ideal paragraphs on the SAT are paragraphs that contain as few concepts as possible.

When adding a sentence to a paragraph in the Improving Paragraphs portion of the SAT Writing Section, add the sentence that contains the fewest concepts that are not already in the paragraph.

When removing sentences from paragraphs in the Improving Paragraphs portion of the SAT Writing Section, remove sentences that introduce concepts that do not appear elsewhere in the paragraph.